Walt Disney World & Orlando For Dummies, 2006

Cheat Sheet

Hidden Mickey Checklist

Started as an inside joke among Disney Imagineers, Hidden Mickeys (a.k.a. HMs) are now a Disney tradition. Today, dozens of subtle Mickey images — usually silhouettes of his world-famous ears, profile, or full figure — are hidden (more or less) in attractions and resorts throughout the Walt Disney empire. Many are strictly in the eye of the beholder, but discover a new one that's accepted into the pantheon by HM watchers and you're a made mouse. Here's a quick checklist to start you off on your HM treasure hunt through the World.

In the Magic Kingdom

- In the Haunted Mansion banquet scene, check out the arrangement of the plate and adjoining saucers on the table.
- In the Africa scene of It's a Small World, note the purple flowers on a vine on the elephant's left side.
- While riding Splash Mountain, look for Mickey lying on his back in the pink clouds to the right of the Zip-A-Dee Lady paddlewheeler.
- Take a good look at the French horn on the right side of the stage at Mickey's PhilHarMagic.

★ ★ ★ ★ ★ ★ ★ ★ ★ ★ ★ ★ ★ ★ ★ ★ ★

At Epcot

- In Journey Into Imagination, check out the little girl's dress in the lobby film of Honey, I Shrunk the Audience, one of five HMs in this pavilion.
- In The Land pavilion, don't miss the small stones in front of the Native American man on a horse and the baseball cap of the man driving a harvester in the Circle of Life film.
- As you cruise through the Mexico pavilion on El Rio del Tiempo, notice the arrangement of three clay pots in the marketplace scene.
- In Maelstrom in the Norway pavilion, a Viking wears Mickey ears in the wall mural facing the loading dock.
- There are four HMs inside Spaceship Earth, one of them in the Renaissance scene, on the page of a book behind the sleeping monk. It's up to you to spot the other three.

★ ★ ★ ★ ★ ★ ★ ★ ★ ★ ★ ★ ★ ★ ★ ★ ★

At Disney–MGM Studios

- At Jim Henson's Muppet*Vision 3D, take a good look at the top of the sign listing five reasons for turning in your 3-D glasses, and note the balloons in the film's final scene.
- In the Twilight Zone Tower of Terror, note the bell for the elevator behind Rod Serling in the film. There are more than 8 HMs in this attraction.
- By the way, the park's least Hidden Mickey is . . . itself. Yep. That's right. When viewed from the sky, the entire park is one giant Hidden Mickey.

★ ★ ★ ★ ★ ★ ★ ★ ★ ★ ★ ★ ★ ★ ★ ★ ★

In Animal Kingdom

- Look at The Boneyard in DinoLand U.S.A., where a fan and two hard hats form a HM.
- There are 25 Hidden Mickeys at Rafiki's Planet Watch, where Mickey lurks in the murals, tree trunks, and paintings of animals.

★ ★ ★ ★ ★ ★ ★ ★ ★ ★ ★ ★ ★ ★ ★ ★ ★

In the Resort Areas

- HMs are on the weather vane atop the Grand Floridian Resort & Spa's convention center and one forms a giant sand trap next to the green at the Magnolia Golf Course's 6th hole.

Found all of these HMs? Good for you. But these are just the tip of the mouse's tail. For more HMs — or to report your own brand-new sighting — check out www.hiddenmickeys.org.

Good For Grown-ups

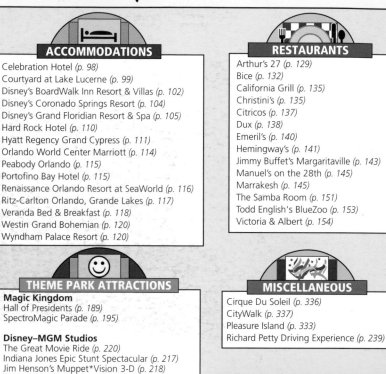

ACCOMMODATIONS

Celebration Hotel *(p. 98)*
Courtyard at Lake Lucerne *(p. 99)*
Disney's BoardWalk Inn Resort & Villas *(p. 102)*
Disney's Coronado Springs Resort *(p. 104)*
Disney's Grand Floridian Resort & Spa *(p. 105)*
Hard Rock Hotel *(p. 110)*
Hyatt Regency Grand Cypress *(p. 111)*
Orlando World Center Marriott *(p. 114)*
Peabody Orlando *(p. 115)*
Portofino Bay Hotel *(p. 115)*
Renaissance Orlando Resort at SeaWorld *(p. 116)*
Ritz-Carlton Orlando, Grande Lakes *(p. 117)*
Veranda Bed & Breakfast *(p. 118)*
Westin Grand Bohemian *(p. 120)*
Wyndham Palace Resort *(p. 120)*

RESTAURANTS

Arthur's 27 *(p. 129)*
Bice *(p. 132)*
California Grill *(p. 135)*
Christini's *(p. 135)*
Citricos *(p. 137)*
Dux *(p. 138)*
Emeril's *(p. 140)*
Hemingway's *(p. 141)*
Jimmy Buffet's Margaritaville *(p. 143)*
Manuel's on the 28th *(p. 145)*
Marrakesh *(p. 145)*
The Samba Room *(p. 151)*
Todd English's BlueZoo *(p. 153)*
Victoria & Albert *(p. 154)*

THEME PARK ATTRACTIONS

Magic Kingdom
Hall of Presidents *(p. 189)*
SpectroMagic Parade *(p. 195)*

Disney–MGM Studios
The Great Movie Ride *(p. 220)*
Indiana Jones Epic Stunt Spectacular *(p. 217)*
Jim Henson's Muppet*Vision 3-D *(p. 218)*
Rock 'n' Roller Coaster
    starring Aerosmith *(p. 221)*
Sounds Dangerous Starring Drew Carey *(p. 219)*
The Twilight Zone Tower of Terror *(p. 222)*

Animal Kingdom
Pangani Forest Exploration Trail *(p. 233)*
Maharajah Jungle Trek *(p. 234)*

Universal Studios Florida
Back to the Future The Ride *(p. 268)*
Men in Black: Alien Attack *(p. 269)*
Revenge of the Mummy *(p. 265)*
Terminator 2: 3/D Battle Across Time *(p. 263)*

SeaWorld
Clydesdale Hamlet *(p. 292)*
Journey to Atlantis *(p. 293)*
Kraken *(p. 293)*
Marine Mammal Keeper Experience *(p. 294)*

MISCELLANEOUS

Cirque Du Soleil *(p. 336)*
CityWalk *(p. 337)*
Pleasure Island *(p. 333)*
Richard Petty Driving Experience *(p. 239)*

Some may find it hard to believe, but Orlando is the top honeymoon destination in the country. The city is exceptionally receptive to small fries, so finding some calm inside the kiddie storm can be quite the challenge. You can't really avoid kids here as a rule, but here's a handy checklist of hotels, restaurants, and selected attractions that offer special appeal to adults.

Tip: Of all the theme parks in the city, Disney's Epcot (Chapter 13), Universal's Islands of Adventure (Chapter 19), and SeaWorld's Discovery Cove (Chapter 20) are the best for adults.

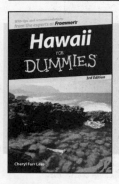

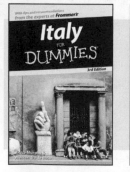
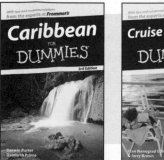

Walt Disney World® and Orlando

FOR

DUMMIES®

2006

by Laura Miller

WILEY

Wiley Publishing, Inc.

Walt Disney World® and Orlando For Dummies® 2006

Published by
Wiley Publishing, Inc.
111 River St.
Hoboken, NJ 07030-5774
www.wiley.com

Copyright © 2006 by Wiley Publishing, Inc., Indianapolis, Indiana

Published simultaneously in Canada

For general information on our other products and services, please contact our Customer Care Department within the U.S. at 800-762-2974, outside the U.S. at 317-572-3993, or fax 317-572-4002.

For technical support, please visit www.wiley.com/techsupport.

Wiley also publishes its books in a variety of electronic formats. Some content that appears in print may not be available in electronic books.

Library of Congress Control Number: 2005933995

ISBN-13: 978-0-7645-9660-5

ISBN-10: 0-7645-9660-8

Manufactured in the United States of America

10 9 8 7 6 5 4 3 2 1

1B/QY/RR/QV/IN

WILEY

About the Author

Laura Miller is a freelance writer based in Buffalo, New York, though she's spent countless hours scouring Central Florida's theme parks over the years — both with and without her husband and five kids. A family-travel expert who religiously makes an annual pilgrimage to the Land the Mouse Built, she's the author of *Frommer's Walt Disney World & Orlando 2005* and contributes to *Frommer's Florida* and *Frommer's Walt Disney World & Orlando with Kids*. She's currently researching and writing a guide to Florida for families.

Author's Acknowledgments

Thanks to Amy Voss at the Orlando/Orange County Convention & Visitors Bureau; Gary Buchanan at Walt Disney World; Susan Storey at Universal Orlando; and Jacquelyn Wilson at SeaWorld. Thanks also to all those who took the time out of their schedules to help me with this endeavor. A special thanks goes out to my family, most especially my five children; Ryan, Austin, Nicolas, Hailey, and Davis, for all of their assistance in helping to research and write this book.

Thanks as well to my agent, Julie Hill, whose constant encouragement, support, and enthusiasm keeps me going.

And, of course, a special thanks to my editor, Naomi Kraus, whose continued support and encouragement as well as her extensive knowledge of all things Disney have made this book more than just a Mickey Mouse affair.

Publisher's Acknowledgments

We're proud of this book; please send us your comments through our Dummies online registration form located at www.dummies.com/register/.

Some of the people who helped bring this book to market include the following:

Acquisitions, Editorial, and Media Development

Editors: M. Faunette Johnston, Production Editor; Naomi Kraus, Project Editor; and Jennifer Moore, Development Editor

Copy Editor: Jennifer Connolly

Cartographer: Andrew Murphy

Senior Photo Editor: Richard Fox

Cartoons: Rich Tennant (www.the5thwave.com)

Production

Project Coordinator: Ryan Steffen

Layout and Graphics: Lauren Goddard, Joyce Haughey, Stephanie D. Jumper, Heather Ryan, Julie Trippetti

Proofreaders: Leeann Harney, Jessica Kramer, Carl Pierce, TECHBOOKS Production Services

Indexer: TECHBOOKS Production Services

Publishing and Editorial for Consumer Dummies

Diane Graves Steele, Vice President and Publisher, Consumer Dummies

Joyce Pepple, Acquisitions Director, Consumer Dummies

Kristin A. Cocks, Product Development Director, Consumer Dummies

Michael Spring, Vice President and Publisher, Travel

Kelly Regan, Editorial Director, Travel

Publishing for Technology Dummies

Andy Cummings, Vice President and Publisher, Dummies Technology/General User

Composition Services

Gerry Fahey, Vice President of Production Services

Debbie Stailey, Director of Composition Services

Contents at a Glance

Maps at a Glance

Table of Contents

Introduction

● ●

*W*elcome to **Walt Disney World** and **Orlando, Florida,** a land ruled by a mouse who thinks nothing of sporting bright red shorts, gigantic white gloves, and big yellow shoes — a place that's for some, including the young and young-at-heart, absolutely magical. Walt Disney World has continued to evolve, bringing back its faithful followers, and enticing future fans. Though showing the wear and tear of a weakened economy, Walt Disney World has remained resilient; it continues to add attractions throughout its parks and regularly announces plans for future projects. Millions of people make the pilgrimage each year — a group that includes Olympic medal-winners, a prince or two, and of course us regular folks. To some, WDW is a national shrine, to others, a right of passage, albeit a crowded one.

For some folks, charting a successful course through the home of Mickey Mouse can seem like a lot of work. For you, it won't be. All you need to ensure an enjoyable trip to Orlando is patience, planning, and a little childlike wonder — now how hard is that?

About This Book

Pay full price? Read the fine print? Do it their way?

Excuse me. There's no need for any of that.

You picked this book because you know the *For Dummies* label, and you want to go to **Walt Disney World.** You also probably know how much you want to spend, the pace you want to keep, and the amount of planning you can handle. You may not want to tend to every little detail, yet you don't trust just anyone to make your plans for you.

In this book, I boil down what has become a world unto itself — **Walt Disney World** — and the surrounding Orlando area. Walt Disney's Florida legacy is still growing a full four decades after his death in 1966. At current count, **WDW** includes four theme parks and a dozen lesser attractions, two entertainment districts, tens of thousands of hotel rooms, scores of restaurants, and twin cruise ships.

Universal Orlando and **SeaWorld** add another four theme parks, three resorts, and an entertainment district to the mix. There are 80 or so additional smaller attractions nearby, as well as an avalanche of restaurants and more than 114,000 lodging rooms in Orlando.

How can anyone sort through all these choices, you ask? It takes experience.

Dummies Post-it® Flags

As you're reading this book, you'll find information that you'll want to reference as you plan or enjoy your trip — whether it be a new hotel, a must-see attraction, or a must-try walking tour. Mark these pages with the handy Post-it® Flags included in this book to help make your trip planning easier!

After decades of stomping through the House of the Mouse, I know where to find the best deals (deals that are not rip-offs). In this book, I guide you through **Walt Disney World** and **Orlando** in a clear, easy-to-understand way, so you can find the best hotels, restaurants, and attractions without having to read this book like a novel — cover to cover. Although you can read this book in that order if you choose, you can also flip to only those sections that interest you. I also promise not to overwhelm you with choices. I simply deliver the best, most essential ingredients for a great vacation.

Please be advised that travel information is subject to change at any time — and this disclaimer is especially true of prices (the theme parks like to raise theirs on a whim). I, therefore, suggest that you call ahead for confirmation or check the Internet when making your travel plans. Doing so is especially important when you have your heart set on visiting a particular attraction because theme parks are constantly making changes to their lineups, including shortening hours, closing shows on certain days, and boarding up restaurants in poor economic times.

The author, editors, and publisher cannot be held responsible for the experiences of readers while traveling. Your safety is important to us, however, so we encourage you to stay alert and be aware of your surroundings. Keep a close eye on cameras, purses, and wallets, all favorite targets of thieves and pickpockets.

Conventions Used in This Book

To make this book an easier reference guide for you, I use some handy abbreviations when I review hotels, restaurants, and attractions.

You'll probably notice first that I often substitute **WDW** or **Disney World** for **Walt Disney World** to spare you from having to read those three words again and again. Another common abbreviation that you'll find is the use of **Universal** in place of **Universal Orlando.** Also, because almost everything in Orlando revolves around its theme parks, you often find that I refer to the section of Central Florida that encompasses the theme parks as simply "the parks."

And because Orlando does its best to make you max them out, I use the following abbreviations for commonly accepted credit cards:

> AE: American Express
>
> DC: Diners Club
>
> DISC: Discover
>
> MC: MasterCard
>
> V: Visa

I also include general pricing information to help you decide where to unpack your bags or dine on the local cuisine. I use a system of dollar signs to show a range of costs for one night in a double-occupancy room or a meal at a restaurant.

Foolish Assumptions

As I wrote this book, I made some assumptions about you and what your needs might be as a traveler. Here's what I assumed about you:

- You may be an experienced traveler who hasn't had much time to explore Orlando and wants expert advice on how to maximize your time and enjoy a hassle-free trip.

- You may be an inexperienced traveler looking for guidance when determining whether to take a trip to **Walt Disney World** and Orlando and how to plan for it.

- You're not looking for a book that provides all the information available about Orlando or that lists every hotel, restaurant, or attraction available to you. Instead, you're looking for a book that focuses on the places that will give you the best experience in Orlando.

If you fit any of these criteria, then *Walt Disney World & Orlando For Dummies 2006* gives you the information you're looking for!

How This Book Is Organized

Walt Disney World & Orlando For Dummies 2006 is divided into seven parts. The chapters in each part lay out the specifics within each section's topic. Likewise, each chapter is written so that you don't have to read what came before or after, although I sometimes refer you to other areas for more information.

Here's a brief look at the parts.

Part I: Introducing Walt Disney World & Orlando

Think of this part as the hors d'oeuvres. In this part, I tempt you with the best experiences, hotels, eateries, and attractions at **Disney** and the rest of Orlando. I give you a little history lesson (but not to worry — no quiz will follow), suggest a few movies and books to get you in the Mickey mood, and then tip you to Orlando's best special events. Because the city has some pretty distinct seasons, I also delve into the pros and cons of visiting during different times of the year and even throw in a weather forecast.

Part II: Planning Your Trip to Walt Disney World & Orlando

This part covers the nitty-gritty of trip planning. Orlando has been known to take a chunk of change out of unsuspecting visitors' wallets, so I suggest some ways to save money so you don't feel like you have to take out a second mortgage to do this trip. I delve into the various ways to get here and give you the lowdown on vacation package options; they're a very popular method of traveling to Orlando — and there are a whole lot of them out there. And because I'd like everyone to have fun on their vacation, I also provide special tips for those who could use some more specialized trip information: families, seniors, travelers with disabilities, and gay and lesbian travelers.

Part III: Settling into Orlando

After I get you to Orlando, I introduce you to the neighborhoods and explore some of the *modus transporto* (local buses, trolleys, taxis, shuttles, and other vehicles to get from hither to yonder). I also give you the lowdown on Disney's special transportation system. From there, it's on to a discussion of the city's plethora of accommodation options and in-depth reviews of the best places to sleep. And because it takes lots of fuel to keep you going inside the theme parks, I discuss the city's best places to eat and tell you all about that most Orlando of dining experiences: the character meal. (Because what says Disney more than having dinner with Donald Duck and Goofy? Or Cinderella? Or Simba? Well, you get the idea.)

Part IV: Exploring Walt Disney World

You're now checked in and fueled up. Great. Welcome to **Walt Disney World,** the number one tourist destination in the country. You could easily spend months exploring this mammoth resort, but if you're like most visitors to the House of Mouse, you have only a week or less to get it all in. No worries. In this part, I explain Disney's ticket system and tell you about the best options in each of Disney's major parks. And if you don't think a visit to WDW would be complete without a set of Mickey ears or some other souvenir, I also fill you in on Disney's best shopping opportunities.

Part V: Exploring the Rest of Orlando

Can't face all Mickey, all the time? No problem. There is, in fact, a lot more to Orlando than Disney World. If theme parks are your thing, **Universal Orlando, SeaWorld,** and **Discovery Cove** all await you, and I fill you in on all their highlights. The city is also home to a plethora of smaller attractions and rides, and I provide in-depth information on the best of them. Should you prefer exercising your credit card to walking the parks, I let you know the best places for shopaholics to indulge. And if you need a break from the city itself, I give you two great day-trip options. One thing is for certain: You won't get bored.

Part VI: Living It Up after Dark: Orlando Nightlife

Kids may rule this town, but Disney and the rest of Orlando have discovered that many of you want to party into the night. In Part VI, I explore **Pleasure Island, CityWalk,** and other thriving Orlando hot spots. Then I give you details on Orlando's popular dinner shows and the city's performing arts. (Yes, Orlando does indeed have a respected cultural scene.)

Part VII: The Part of Tens

Every *For Dummies* book offers The Part of Tens. Finding this part in a *For Dummies* book is as certain as annual price hikes at Disney and Universal. In Part VII, I give you parting knowledge about cheap attractions and places to stay fit as a fiddle.

You also find two other elements near the back of this book. I have included an Appendix — your Quick Concierge — containing plenty of handy information you may need when traveling in Orlando, such as phone numbers and addresses of emergency personnel or area hospitals and pharmacies, contact information for baby sitters, lists of local newspapers and magazines, protocol for sending mail or finding taxis, and more. Check out this Appendix when searching for answers to the many little questions that may come up as you travel.

Should you desire even more detailed or specialized information, I also include a list of the best sources of Orlando and Disney information, from official tourist offices to Web sites to newspapers and magazines.

You can easily find the Quick Concierge because it's printed on yellow paper.

Icons Used in This Book

You find six icons throughout this guide:

 Keep an eye out for the Bargain Alert icon as you seek out money-saving tips or great deals.

Best of the Best highlights the best Orlando has to offer in all categories — hotels, restaurants, attractions, activities, shopping, and nightlife.

Watch for the Heads Up icon to identify annoying or potentially dangerous situations such as tourist traps, unsafe neighborhoods, budgetary rip-offs, and other things to beware.

Find out useful advice on things to do and ways to schedule your time when you see the Tip icon.

Because many of you will be toting kids when you visit Orlando, I decided to get some kids' input (namely, my five children, ages 4 to 12) on many of the popular rides and attractions in the city. This icon indicates a high approval rating.

This icon obviously indicates a low approval rating. Kids are kids and this rating may have been given for any number of unfathomable reasons. I'm just passing along my raw data.

Where to Go from Here

I've briefed you on what to expect from this book and told you how to use it to plan a magical vacation to **Walt Disney World** — no pixie dust necessary. So start reading; you have a lot to do before you arrive, from arranging a place where you'll rest your weary feet each night to exploring the best that Orlando's theme parks have to offer. Like the Boy Scouts' creed, the successful Orlando traveler needs to "be prepared;" follow the advice in this book, and you will be. So put on your Mouse ears and smile — you're going to **Disney World!**

Part I
Introducing Walt Disney World & Orlando

The 5th Wave   By Rich Tennant

"The hotel said they were giving us the
'Indiana Jones' suite."

In this part . . .

To get the most enjoyment out of a vacation — with the least amount of hassle — it helps to know what awaits you in your chosen paradise before the landing gear lowers. In this part, I highlight the joys of a trip to Orlando and give you the lowdown on the city's best bets, from rides and attractions to hotels and restaurants. I also tell you a bit about the city's history, teach you some of the local lingo, and fill you in on the best times of the year to visit Mickey.

Chapter 1

Discovering the Best of Walt Disney World & Orlando

In This Chapter

▶ Experiencing the best Orlando has to offer
▶ Finding the city's best hotels
▶ Getting a taste of the best dining in Orlando
▶ Boarding the coolest theme-park rides
▶ Discovering the greatest shows and attractions

*V*acationing in Orlando is like escaping to another time and place, a world of fantasy, a world filled with fun. The city attracts the young and the young at heart from all over the world who come for the theme parks, world-class resorts, and the area's spectacular natural beauty. It should come as no surprise to you that Orlando is the No. 1 family vacation destination in the United States, not to mention one of the top vacation destinations in the world. Yes, it gets crowded, and in the summer it's hot and sticky, but one thing you definitely won't be is bored.

Note: With the exception of the items listed in "The Best Orlando Experiences," I've highlighted all of the hotels, restaurants, and attractions in this chapter with a "Best of the Best" icon throughout the book.

Without further delay, here are the best of the best that Orlando and Walt Disney World have to offer.

The Best Orlando Experiences

If images of Cinderella Castle, its spires reaching high up to the sky, pop into your head the minute anyone mentions Orlando, you're not alone. The Magic Kingdom's iconic castle and the lovable Mouse who started it all are, by far, the most famous of all Disney icons and the reason most

Walt Disney World & Orlando

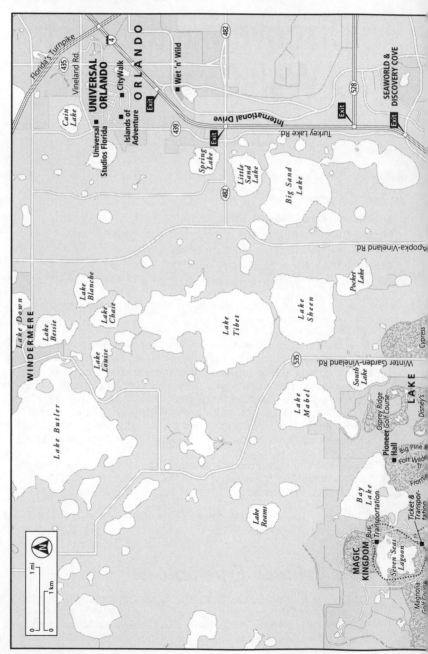

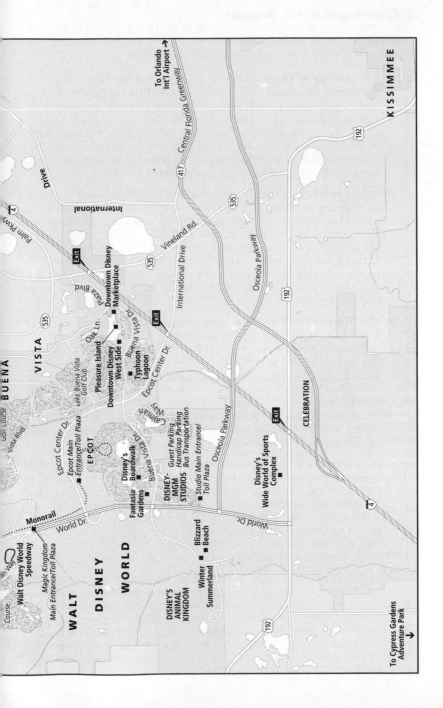

folks venture to the sunshine state in the first place. But keep in mind that while a visit to the Magic Kingdom is definitely one of the biggest highlights of an Orlando vacation, especially if you have kids, there are plenty more attractions and experiences that await:

✔ **Spend a day at Epcot.** At Epcot, you can find the high-speed thrills of *Mission: Space* and *Test Track,* the breathtaking experience of *Soarin'* over the California landscape, and the simple pleasure of splashing about in the dancing waters. Then it's off to tour some of the world's most unique countries along the World Showcase. Play on the Viking ship in *Norway,* dance with the oompah band in *Germany,* or try to belly dance with the natives in *Morocco.* For more on things to do at Epcot, see Chapter 13.

✔ **Spend another day at Disney's Animal Kingdom.** Head out on the *Kilimanjaro Safari* for an expedition through the African savanna, or make your way by foot through the rainforests and jungles of Asia for a glimpse of the exotic wildlife that inhabits the park. Travel back to the time when dinosaurs ruled the Earth. Be sure to catch *Mickey's Jammin' Jungle* parade, one of the most unique and lively parades in all of Disney. *Kali River Rapids* will leave you soaked, but that's half the fun. Check out Chapter 15 for details on other attractions in the park.

✔ **Visit Disney–MGM Studios.** You can find some of the most intense thrills in all of Walt Disney World here, with both the *Tower of Terror* and *Rock 'n Roller Coaster Starring Aerosmith* taking center stage. But be sure to take in some of the spectacular shows, too — this is a studio after all. Top billing goes to *Lights, Motors, Action! Extreme Stunt Show,* the parks newest addition, and the *Indiana Jones Stunt Spectacular.* Be sure to close out the night with the incredible *Fantasmic!,* an after-dark show that combines a love for all things Disney with the most amazing combination of water and fireworks. See Chapter 14 for the lowdown on all the park has to offer.

✔ **Experience Universal Studios Florida (USF).** Once just a diversion, Universal has worked hard to turn itself into a true destination. The rides here run the gamut from all ages to "what was I thinking?" Not-to-be-missed attractions include *Revenge of the Mummy, Terminator 2: 3-D Battle Across Time, Men in Black: Alien Attack,* and the most recent additions: *Fear Factor Live* and *Shrek 4-D.* Really feeling adventurous? Finish the day by getting slimed at *Nick Studios.* Chapter 18 offers information on other cool things to see and do at USF.

✔ **Test your physical limits at Islands of Adventure.** You can spin; you can fly upside down; you can get wet. And that's just in the first few hours in this park. Don't miss the *Amazing Adventures of Spider-Man; Dueling Dragons* twin roller coasters; *Jurassic Park: River Adventure;* and the big, green behemoth, the *Incredible Hulk* roller coaster. If it's really hot out, a good soak on *Popeye & Bluto's Bilge-Rat Barges* is just the thing to refresh you. For information on other adventures awaiting you in the park, see Chapter 19.

✔ **Find your own waterworld at SeaWorld and Discovery Cove.**
There are a few thrill rides at SeaWorld, namely *Journey To Atlantis,*
Kraken, and *Wild Arctic,* but the real reason to come to both of
these parks is the chance to interact with a variety of marine animals. Discovery Cove even gives you the chance to swim with a
dolphin. It's a bit pricy, but it's well worth it if you love animals.
For more information on both parks, see Chapter 20.

✔ **Watch an evening park performance.** Many of the parks love to
close out their day with a fireworks display or performance that's
guaranteed to impress. So check out the **Magic Kingdom**'s *Wishes*
or *SpectroMagic,* **Epcot**'s *Illuminations,* **Disney–MGM**'s *Fantasmic!,*
or **SeaWorld**'s *Oddyssea.* For a truly magical performance, see
Cirque du Soleil's *La Nouba;* it's expensive, but also unforgettable.
For information on all of these spectacles, see Chapters 12, 13, 14,
20, and 25.

✔ **Go to Gatorland.** An Orlando original, Gatorland has been astound-
ing visitors with its crocodiles and alligators since long before the
mouse moved in. Take in one of the amazing shows, such as *Gator
Wrestlin'* and *Gator Jumparoo,* or just take a leisurely stroll through
swamp and marsh on the boardwalks — no one's in a hurry here.
For more information on Gatorland, see Chapter 21.

The Best Hotels

One of the cool things about a trip to Orlando is the chance to stay at one
of its great resorts or themed hotels. Check out Chapter 9 for more in-
depth information about all the accommodations listed in this section:

✔ **Best for Families:** Both **Disney's Animal Kingdom Lodge** and
Wilderness Lodge offer rooms with bunk beds. Nearby Lake Buena
Vista is where you can find the **Nickelodeon Kids Suites Hotel,** a
first for the Nick brand, as well as the **Holiday Inn Sunspree,** which
features Kid Suites (which offer separate themed sleeping areas
with bunk beds for kids).

✔ **Best Inexpensive Hotels:** If your budget determines where you stay,
you have several good choices that offer basic amenities in convenient locations for a low price. On Disney property, choose the new
Pop Century Resort, which offers themed motel-style rooms for the
lowest prices in Mickeyville. The **Masters Inn Maingate** offers a good
location and moderate amenities for less than $50 a night, as does
the **Microtel Inn and Suites.**

✔ **Best Moderate Hotels: Disney's Coronado Springs Resort** edges
out the other two WDW moderate resorts with slightly larger rooms
and a cool Mayan temple pool.

✔ **Best for a Romantic Getaway:** The **Portofino Bay Resort** at
Universal is *molto* romantic with its quaint Italian village theme.

If money is no object, sweep your significant other off to a getaway at the lushly tropical **Ritz-Carlton, Grande Lakes** or the Mediterranean-inspired **Villas of Grand Cypress.**

✔ **Best Hotel for Business Travelers:** The **Orlando World Center Marriott** in Lake Buena Vista and the **Peabody Orlando** both offer an extensive array of business services and amenities.

✔ **Best Location:** All three Universal Orlando resorts are within walking distance of Universal's parks and CityWalk, and all offer boat transportation to the theme parks as well. But if I had to choose the best of the bunch for location and value, I like the **Royal Pacific Resort** best. At WDW, **Disney's Grand Floridian Resort and Spa** offers the best accommodations in the World and is right on the monorail. For those who must be in the thick of it all, **Disney's Yacht Club** and **Beach Club** (both close to Epcot) also get my vote.

✔ **Best Pools:** The **Hard Rock Hotel** boasts a sandy beach and an underwater sound-system that brings out the lounging rock star in you. Stormalong Bay is the name given to the 3-acre mini water park that calls itself a pool at **Disney's Yacht** and **Beach Club Resorts.** Away from the theme parks, the **Hyatt Regency Grand Cypress Resort** has an amazing lagoonlike pool that sports rock grottoes and 12 waterfalls.

The Best Restaurants

Fast food may rule in Orlando, but the city doesn't lack good places to dine. You can find more in-depth information about all of these restaurants in Chapter 10:

✔ **Best for Kids:** It's hard to go wrong with any of the **Walt Disney World** character breakfasts. Kids also seem to love the noisy jungle-themed **Rainforest Café** (locations at Downtown Disney and Animal Kingdom).

✔ **Best Seafood: Todd English's Blue Zoo** (inside the Dolphin) is a relative newcomer on the scene, but is already drawing raves. **Fulton's Crab House** at Pleasure Island is a longstanding favorite with a great wine list and a creative menu.

✔ **Best Steakhouse:** The highly regarded **Yachtsman Steakhouse** at Disney's Yacht Club offers wood-fire grilled steaks.

✔ **Best Dining with a View:** This one's a toss-up between **Manuel's on the 28th,** which offers a stunning after-dark view of the city and food to match, and **Arthur's 27,** which boasts spectacular views of Disney's fireworks and a winning wine list.

✔ **Best Buffet: Boma,** inside Disney's Animal Kingdom Lodge, offers the most eclectic buffet menu in Orlando, mingling traditional buffet items with exotic African fare.

✔ **Best Margarita:** Head to **Jimmy Buffet's Margaritaville,** of course. The mango margarita's the best of the bunch.

✔ **Best Spot for a Romantic Meal: Victoria & Albert's** is the runaway leader in this category.

✔ **Best Value: Kim Wu** has been a local favorite for over 20 years. **Café Tu Tu Tango** offers inexpensive tapas dishes, ranging from Cajun egg rolls with blackened chicken to alligator bites that are perfect for sharing.

The Best Thrill Rides

If you're a speed freak who lives for the ups and downs of a good ride, here are the top stomach churners and G-force generators in Orlando:

✔ *Mission: Space* (Epcot): Disney's latest contribution to the thrills category uses NASA technology to create an astronaut simulator so effective they've had to install "lunch bags" for all the motion sickness it causes. See Chapter 13.

✔ *Rock 'n Roller Coaster* (Disney–MGM Studios): You launch from 0 to 60 mph in 2.8 seconds and go right into the first inversion as 120 speakers in your "stretch limo" mainline Aerosmith at (yeeeow!) 32,000 watts right into your ears. See Chapter 14.

✔ *Twilight Zone Tower of Terror* (Disney–MGM Studios): The free-fall experiences (there are several possible scenarios) are more than thrilling — they're scary. After your legs stop shaking, *some of you* may want to ride again. See Chapter 14.

✔ *Summit Plummet* (Disney's Blizzard Beach): This one starts slow, with a lift ride (even in Florida's 100° dog days) to a 120-foot mountain summit. But it finishes with the world's fastest body slide, a test of your courage and swimsuit as it virtually goes straight down and has you moving sans vehicle at 60 mph by the end. See Chapter 16.

✔ *Revenge of the Mummy* (Universal Studios Florida): Universal's newest thrill ride combines a coaster run with magnetism and the best cinematic special-effects technology (flame ceilings, scarabs pouring out of the walls) for a ride that touches on your worst phobias. See Chapter 18.

✔ *The Amazing Adventures of Spider-Man* (Islands of Adventure): 3-D doesn't get any better than this chase-the-bad-guys ride where you twist, spin, and soar before a simulated 400-foot drop that feels an awful lot like the real thing. It's sure to get your Spidey senses tingling. See Chapter 19.

✔ *Dueling Dragons* (Islands of Adventure): Your legs dangle as you do five inversions at 55 to 60 mph and — get this! — three times come within 12 inches of the other roller coaster. See Chapter 19.

✔ *Incredible Hulk Coaster* (Islands of Adventure): You blast from 0 to 40 mph in two seconds, spin upside down more than 100 feet from the ground, and execute seven rollovers and two deep drops on this glow-in-the-dark roller coaster. You may find this hard to believe, but it's the smoothest ride around. See Chapter 19.

✔ *Jurassic Park River Adventure* (Islands of Adventure): Riders travel through a prehistoric land inhabited by fierce, unbelievably real-looking dinosaurs. Creatures five stories tall growl and bare their teeth, some within inches of your face. As if that weren't enough, after being threatened by a Tyrannosaurus rex, you plunge 85 feet almost straight down into the water below. See Chapter 19.

✔ *Kraken* (SeaWorld): This floorless, open-sided coaster uses speed (up to 65 mph), steep climbs, deep drops, and seven loops to create a stomach-churning ride that lasts far too long for some folks. See Chapter 20.

The Best of the Rest

For those who can't stomach the thought of boarding anything that pulls the same G-forces as a fighter jet or induces adrenaline rushes of any sort of magnitude, the theme parks have several exceptional (and tamer) rides and shows that nobody should overlook:

✔ *Haunted Mansion* (Magic Kingdom): Forget the unfortunate Eddie Murphy film and be sure to visit this cult favorite, which shows off Disney's knack for details as 999 ghosts offer up more delights than frights. See Chapter 12.

✔ *Pirates of the Caribbean* (Magic Kingdom): This one's another oldie but goodie, made even more popular by the Oscar-nominated film of the same name. You've got randy, rum-filled pirates and lots of yo-ho-ho music. See Chapter 12.

✔ *Test Track* (Epcot): Fasten your seatbelts. This collaboration with GM allows riders to take a "car" through a series of standard motor vehicle test sequences that include a near crash, a speed run, and some rather interesting weather. It's not adrenaline pumping enough to be considered a thriller, but it's definitely a cool ride. See Chapter 13.

✔ *Soarin'* (Epcot): *Soarin'* is the latest ride to debut at Epcot. After boarding the multiseat gliders, you'll find yourself flying high over some of California's most spectacular landscapes with realistic multisensory effects. See Chapter 13.

✔ *Indiana Jones Epic Stunt Spectacular* (Disney–MGM Studios): Special effects, razzle-dazzle stunts, and pyrotechnics make this stunt show worth the (incredibly long) wait. Wear a bright-colored shirt, wave your arms spastically, and you may be called up on stage as an extra. See Chapter 14.

✔ *Lights, Motors, Action! Stunt Spectacular* (Disney–MGM Studios): The thrill of a high-speed car chase, pyrotechnics, special effects, and some amazing stunt driving add up to an action-packed show for the whole family. See Chapter 14.

✔ *Jim Henson's Muppet*Vision 3-D* (Disney–MGM Studios): The action takes place in a perfect recreation of the Muppets' theater (complete with the blessedly crotchety Statler and Waldorf critiquing the action from the balcony) and is a zany mix of 3-D film, animatronics, and live-action and special effects. See Chapter 14.

✔ *Festival of the Lion King* (Animal Kingdom): One of the best shows in town, this is a don't-miss Broadway-esque version of the famous Circle of Life. See Chapter 15.

✔ *Kilimanjaro Safaris* (Animal Kingdom): At this must-see attraction, the special safari trucks bump you about as you head out into Disney's version of the African wilderness. You'll enjoy the thrill of seeing giraffes and zebras up close. See Chapter 15.

✔ *Men in Black Alien Attack* (Universal Studios Florida): Zap icky aliens with ray guns as you ride through the streets of New York. At the conclusion, you tackle the Big Roach himself and then get rated by Will Smith for your shooting prowess. See Chapter 18.

✔ *Shrek 4-D* (Universal Studios Florida): This attraction uses 3-D movie effects married with seats that move and bounce to continue the story of Shrek and Fiona. It's fun for all ages and *very* popular! See Chapter 18.

✔ *Terminator 2: 3-D Battle Across Time* (Universal Studios Florida): This production features the creepy-steely T-1,000,000 and live-action doubles of Arnold Schwarzenegger and Edward Furlong, who roar onto the stage on Harleys and then into a giant movie screen, a very cool trick you absolutely must see. This show's an absolute winner. See Chapter 18.

✔ *Popeye & Bluto's Bilge-Rat Barges* (Islands of Adventure): A bit too tame to be considered a thrill ride, this white-water raft experience can have you soaked in no time at all. If the waves don't get you, the kids firing water soakers at you from the sidelines won't miss. See Chapter 19.

✔ *Shamu Adventure* (SeaWorld): Even if you've seen the show before — and they change it regularly, to keep things interesting — you still "ooh" and "ahh" as the sleek, black-and-white killer whale shoots out of the water. See Chapter 20.

✔ *Shark Encounter* (SeaWorld): At this aquatic exhibit, you find a walk-through tunnel populated with the scarier denizens of the deep, such as moray eels, barracudas, rays, scorpion fish, and (of course) sharks. It's the coolest aquarium in town. See Chapter 20.

Chapter 2

Digging Deeper into Orlando

*T*his chapter offers a bit of perspective into how Orlando evolved from a sleepy little southern town to the theme park capital of the world. After our quick trip back in time, I give you an overview of Florida's cuisine scene and then offer a tutorial on the local lingo. For those of you who want even more background on Orlando and WDW, I wrap up this chapter by recommending some books and films.

History 101: The Main Events

Believe it or not, there was life in Orlando before Mickey. The city's transformation into theme-park mecca didn't happen overnight. And it may never have happened if Walt Disney hadn't run out of real estate in California.

Orlando B.D. (Before Disney)

Before there was Disney, Universal, SeaWorld and the wealth of other tourist attractions that exist today, Central Florida was ruled by the economics of the three "C" industries: cotton, cattle, and citrus.

Originally named Jernigan, the town now known as Orlando had its genesis in the remnants of an Army post that was abandoned in 1849. The name was officially changed to Orlando in 1857, though the origin of the moniker is somewhat opaque. (Depending on whom you ask, the city was named for a plantation owner, the friend of a city commissioner, or a character from Shakespeare's *As You Like It.*) The cattle and cotton industries thrived here until the Civil War, when area homesteaders realized that citrus trees were far easier to grow than cotton and just about every field was taken over by lush orange groves. At its peak, in the 1950s, more than 80,000 acres of citrus trees were thriving throughout Central Florida. The '50s also saw two major developments that would bring even more people and industry to the area: the building of the space center at nearby Cape Canaveral and (most important of all) the invention of air-conditioning.

Around this time, Walt Disney began making waves by opening Disneyland in Anaheim, California. The doors officially opened July 17, 1955, and it was an instant hit. Soon, the overwhelming demand made it obvious to Walt that he needed to expand. However, his 27 acres in the middle of the city didn't exactly give him the room for his next endeavor. So he turned his eyes eastward to Florida.

Orlando A.D. (After Disney)

In a top-secret operation that would have impressed even the CIA, Walt Disney began a search for the site of his next theme park, and, having decided on his new location, began secretly buying up land through dummy corporations. On November 11, 1965 (the city's version of "D" Day) — after Disney had acquired more than 28,000 acres for a mere $5.5 million — he came clean and announced that a new Disney theme park would be built in Orlando, Florida. Unfortunately Walt never got to see his dream become a reality. He passed away the morning of December 15, 1966, a mere year after his plans were unveiled. His brother, Roy O. Disney, decided the right thing to do was to carry on in Walt's name.

Construction began on the **Magic Kingdom** (see Chapter 12) and its first two resorts in 1969. On a fine fall day, October 1, 1971, Roy O. Disney led the dedication ceremony that officially opened the **Walt Disney World Resort** to the public.

SeaWorld (see Chapter 20) splashed onto the scene soon after, when it opened to the public in December 15, 1973. And it seemed, for a while, that its opening would be it on Orlando's expansion front. But Disney continued to break attendance records each year and, not content to rest on its laurels — or its acres of empty land — the Walt Disney World Resort continued expanding. In 1982, 11 years after Magic Kingdom opened, **Epcot** (see Chapter 13) was christened the second WDW theme park. In 1989, the **Disney–MGM Studios** (see Chapter 14), a behind-the-scenes look at Tinseltown, became the third jewel in the WDW park crown. At the same time, WDW added **Typhoon Lagoon** (a 56-acre water theme park; see Chapter 16), and **Pleasure Island** (a nightclub district for adults; see Chapter 25).

A year later, **Universal Studios Florida** (see Chapter 18) brought the world of movies to life in Orlando, opening its doors in 1990. Direct competition spurred Disney to create its fourth, and currently, last, theme park in Orlando. A cross between conservation park and theme park, **Animal Kingdom** (see Chapter 15) opened its doors on Earth Day, April 22, 1998. Universal immediately countered with **CityWalk,** a vast nighttime entertainment district (see Chapter 25). Not to be outdone, Disney stormed back by consolidating its three major after-park-hours entertainment, dining, and shopping venues — Disney's West Side, Pleasure Island, and the Disney Village Marketplace — into an all-encompassing zone called **Downtown Disney.** The Disney folks also started their own cruise line for good measure.

Universal didn't follow out to sea, but it upped the ante when it opened its second park in 1999. **Islands of Adventure** (see Chapter 19) was all about the thrills of the theme-park experience. Islands, when combined with CityWalk, USF, and several on-property resorts, helped Universal complete its transformation into the resort destination of **Universal Orlando,** as it's now known. Not just a day trip, anymore, Universal now offers the total vacation experience, just as Disney does.

The most recent theme-park addition to the Orlando roster came unexpectedly from SeaWorld. They decided to keep doing what they do best and opened **Discovery Cove** (see Chapter 20) in 2000. More than just a theme park, this is an all-inclusive interactive marine experience, offering snorkeling and dolphin swims. Even more surprising, SeaWorld added its first roller coaster, the unquestionably thrilling *Kraken.*

Things have died down a bit in the expansion department, but the theme parks are hardly sitting still, constantly revising and building new attractions. Orlando currently offers more than 95 attractions, 114,000 hotel rooms, and 5,100 restaurants, as well as the second largest convention center in the nation. The city is showing signs of an improved economy, and the travel landscape has recently begun to see the numbers reflected in visitor turnout as it once again is reaching sky-high levels. Tourism, of course, has become the leading industry for Central Florida with more than 43 million visitors annually and an economic impact of $24.9 billion. And it all started because of a mouse named Mickey.

Taste of Orlando: Local Cuisine

Offerings have improved in recent years as the city has opened a fair share of good restaurants, but the Orlando dining scene can't compete with the likes of foodie cities like San Francisco or New York. And if there's a predominant cuisine, it's one of the fast-food variety, with the many casual eateries, a few steps higher on the food chain, coming in a very close second. The biggest decision most theme-park goers have to make is whether to opt for a burger, a taco, or a hot dog along with the ubiquitous french fries. And don't worry about finding a branch of your favorite chain, should the urge strike you; the odds are that you can find not just one, but several outlets of it within reach of your hotel.

Though the city caters to a rich and diverse clientele, don't expect to find an equitable number of ethnic eateries. The most famous spots in town for ethnic cuisine are **Epcot's World Showcase** restaurants. Although theme-park food is not exactly first-class, some of it can be surprisingly good. On the healthy front, you will find plenty of fresh fruit — Orlando is still a major citrus town. And even the theme parks now offer a few healthier and vegetarian options beyond the usual fast food.

The biggest news on the city's dining front over the last five years has been the increasing number of gourmet spots for finicky foodies. Famous culinary magicians, such as Wolfgang Puck, Emeril Lagasse, and Todd English, have all opened restaurants here. A few first-class steakhouses will please carnivores. And Universal has stepped up theme-park dining a few notches with the addition of their Islands of Adventure eateries. Something you can't find, however, is a bevy of high-class seafood restaurants; landlocked Orlando isn't nearly as stuck on seafood as most other cities, especially the way those along the coastlines are. If you must have that lobster, however, a list of a few noteworthy spots, along with all my other best picks for dining, can be found in Chapter 10.

Given the importance the city places on entertainment value, it probably shouldn't surprise you that Orlando's most famous dining experience — **the Character Meal** — doesn't really revolve around the cuisine. The name says it all: You and the kids get to chow down on buffet food with Mickey or Goofy, SpongeBob Squarepants, or even Shamu. The fare at these ubiquitous events, staged at most of the theme parks in some form or another, and even at select hotels, won't often tickle your taste buds, but the food's not really the point. Who cares what pancakes taste like when Cinderella's smiling beatifically at your enthralled three-year-old or Mickey's posing with you for that all-important Kodak moment? Disney's turned their character meals into something of an art form, and Universal and SeaWorld have recently followed suit. For a rundown of the best character meals in town, see Chapter 10.

Words to the Wise: The Local Lingo

Though good old-fashioned English is all you need to know in order to have a blast in Orlando, the theme parks do have a language all their own. Knowing the right word or phrase may help ease your way as you navigate the maze of the city's rides and attractions. Here's a rundown of common terms you'll likely come across while in Orlando:

- ✔ **FASTPASS.** This is Disney's legal line-jumping pass, and it's available at most of **WDW**'s primo park rides. You insert your park ticket into a machine, which spits out a pass with a time window (usually of about an hour) stamped on it. You come back within the window indicated, and you can get in a special line with little to no wait. For more on FASTPASS, see Chapter 11.

- ✔ **Universal EXPRESS.** This is Universal's answer to Disney's FASTPASS, and it works in pretty much the same way. For more information, see Chapter 18.

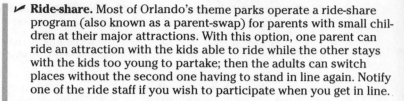

- ✔ **Ride-share.** Most of Orlando's theme parks operate a ride-share program (also known as a parent-swap) for parents with small children at their major attractions. With this option, one parent can ride an attraction with the kids able to ride while the other stays with the kids too young to partake; then the adults can switch places without the second one having to stand in line again. Notify one of the ride staff if you wish to participate when you get in line.

- ✔ **Cast member.** In its ever-present attempt to keep up the illusion that **WDW** is some kind of giant on-going production, Disney refers to its staff as cast members. Whatever you call them, they are almost always knowledgeable and well trained.

- ✔ **Advanced Dining Reservations.** This is the Disney version of a restaurant reservation (and the concept is being used increasingly at other Orlando restaurants as well). Instead of reserving an exact time at a restaurant, you reserve the right to arrive at a specific time and get the next available table (which can sometimes — though not often — take up to 30 minutes). For more on this system, see Chapter 10.

In addition, many locals commonly shorten or abbreviate the major theme-park names, as do a number of the highway signs you'll see on the road. **Universal Orlando** is often just referred to as **Universal** and **Universal Studios Florida** is shortened to **Universal Studios** or abbreviated **USF**, while **Islands of Adventure** is either **Islands** or **IOA**. **Walt Disney World** is usually known merely as **Disney World, Disney,** or **WDW.**

Background Check: Recommended Books and Movies

The best Walt Disney World & Orlando guidebook on the planet (yes, this one) covers almost everything most travelers need and want to know. But, to be fair, here are a few others that can get you into Mickey mode before you arrive:

- ✔ *The Walt Disney World Trivia Book* (2004; Intrepid Traveler Publishing) is loaded with fun facts and minutiae about Disney World. Hundreds of multiple-choice questions keep you and your kids entertained even as they enlighten.

- ✔ *Married to the Mouse: Walt Disney World and Orlando* (2003; Yale University Press) is a serious and not always flattering look at the relationship between the Disney corporation and the city of Orlando. It's a trifle didactic in tone, but its in-depth details make it fascinating reading nonetheless.

- ✔ *Since the World Began* (1996; Hyperion) was published to coincide with Disney World's 25th anniversary and is a history of

WDW's first 25 years. It offers a lot of interesting information and insight into the creation of all Disney's parks and resorts.

✔ *Orlando: City of Dreams* (2003, Arcadia) is a meticulously researched history of Orlando before it became the city of the Mouse.

✔ *How It Feels to Be Colored Me* (1928), *Mules and Men* (1935), *Their Eyes Were Watching God* (1937), *The Florida Negro* (1938), and other books and essays by Zora Neale Hurston, chronicle life and racism in Florida, including Eatonville, the town just north of Orlando where she grew up. If you're a Hurston fan, don't miss the listing for the January festival in her honor in the Calendar of Events in Chapter 3.

If your tastes run more toward the visual medium, there's no shortage of films that can get you in the mood for your Orlando vacation. Here are a few viewing suggestions before you set out on your trip:

✔ Disney's plethora of animated films will introduce kids to the characters and ride themes they'll be running into inside WDW. A few recent goodies include *Finding Nemo, The Lion King, Toy Story* (and *Toy Story 2*), *Aladdin, Lilo & Stitch, 101 Dalmatians, The Little Mermaid,* and *Beauty and the Beast.* For an introduction to Disney's classic characters (who are alive and well in the theme parks), I suggest *Cinderella, Alice in Wonderland, Peter Pan, Sleeping Beauty, Dumbo, Pinocchio,* and *Fantasia* (though it may be a tad too sophisticated for very young kids).

✔ If you prefer live action to animation, break out the popcorn and put on any of these pictures, all of which are represented in some form or another inside the Disney parks: *Mary Poppins; Honey, I Shrunk the Kids; Swiss Family Robinson;* and, more recently, *The Haunted Mansion* and the Oscar-nominated *Pirates of the Caribbean.*

✔ They do say it's the place to "Ride the Movies" so it should come as no surprise that **Universal Studios Florida** is filled with rides and attractions that seemingly put you smack in the middle of some of their most famous films. Some of the best previews include *The Mummy, Back to the Future, Twister, Jaws, Men in Black, Shrek, E.T.,* and *Terminator 2: Judgment Day.* If you're heading to **Islands of Adventure,** then *Jurassic Park, X-Men,* and *Spider-Man* should be on to your movie list. Pick up a copy of *Cat in the Hat* (or any one of Dr. Seuss's classic books for that matter) for the younger kids.

Universal caters more to teens and adults than Disney does, and these films (like the rides they inspired) are definitely aimed more at that audience; so take your child's age into consideration before popping that movie in.

✔ Before heading off to **SeaWorld,** you may want to watch a few marine-related National Geographic specials to get some background on some of the animals you can see in that park.

Chapter 3

Deciding When to Go

• •

In This Chapter

▶ Considering the pros and cons of traveling in each season
▶ Checking out Orlando's weather patterns
▶ Consulting a calendar of special occasions

• •

*A*lthough Orlando is bustling with activity throughout the year, some seasons are definitely busier than others. When you go may very well affect what you see, how much you pay, and how long you stand in line. In this chapter, I explain the advantages and disadvantages of visiting during the spring, summer, fall and winter months so you can decide the best time for your big vacation.

The Secrets of the Seasons

Although Orlando has something for all ages, the city is primarily a destination for families. So anytime children are out of school, whether for break or a three-day holiday, the theme parks are a tangle of pushy, sweaty little bodies. By far the busiest times to visit are during spring break (Feb to mid-Apr), the summer (Memorial Day weekend to Labor Day weekend), and the winter holidays (mid-Dec to early Jan). Keep in mind that any holidays that fall during those peak-season weeks bring with them exponential increases in crowd levels, and a vacation experience that may very well border on the insane.

Obviously, your vacation experience would be the best when crowds are thinnest and the weather is mild. In most destinations, such times would normally describe the off season; however, there really is no off season in Orlando. As the tourists begin their homeward journey, business clients and the convention trade start pouring in, and they come in droves. International visitors also keep things busy year-round. This year-round popularity means that many hotels don't offer a traditional high- and low-season rate scale, and it also means that you need to book your trip as early as possible.

 My favorite time of year to head to Orlando is between September and October. The crowds tend to be thinnest following the Labor Day weekend and through the first two weeks of October as school is once again back in session. Florida residents often scoot to the parks during this time for a day trip or a long weekend. But most out-of-state guests don't have that luxury. If you have younger children, consider pulling them out of school for a few days during the slower months to avoid the horrendous lines. Ask their teachers for schoolwork to take with you. You can also suggest that your kids write a report on an educational element of the vacation. (And yes, they'll actually learn something while they're traipsing around places like **Innoventions** and the **World Showcase** at Epcot).

Even if you come during the off season, the parks run close to full tilt, although operating hours are generally markedly shorter. No matter what time of year you find yourself heading to Orlando, you'll want to be aware of that season's perks and pitfalls.

Spring: Excitement blooms in Orlando
Spring is sensational in Orlando because

- ✔ The weather is mild. Sunny days are followed by cool breezy nights. By early spring the flowers are beginning to bloom, and they are bursting with color later in the season. If your hometown is still blanketed by feet of snow, you'll be in heaven.

- ✔ Accommodations often offer spring discounts (with the exception of the weeks surrounding the Easter holiday, when rates can be at their highest).

- ✔ The lines inside the theme parks are relatively short. Visit on a weekday, and your wait for a ride is likely to be less than 30 minutes (again the exception being the two, sometimes three, weeks on either side of the Easter holiday, which can bring with it some of the longest lines of the year).

But keep in mind that

- ✔ Without a winter, spring is fleeting. The daytime hours can already be hot and humid by late April, although the really sticky weather doesn't usually arrive until mid- to late May.

- ✔ The high pollen count can drive allergy sufferers crazy.

- ✔ April is, by far, one of the busiest months to visit, especially around Easter. College students are headed down for their share of fun in the sun while families take advantage of the time off for travel. Hotels are booked well in advance, the lines are, at times, unbearable, and the crowds border on being intolerable. Everything, including the roadways, restaurants, hotels, and the parks, is jam-packed with people.

Summer: Have fun in the Orlando sun
Summer is superb in Orlando because

- ✔ Daylight is plentiful, and most parks take full advantage by remaining open until 9 p.m. or often later (10, 11, or even midnight closings are not out of the question), and long days are many times capped off by spectacular nighttime fireworks displays.

✔ Crowds are manageable. Even though it's one of the most popular seasons, it pales in comparison to spring break and the winter holidays. The weekends are busier than at almost any other time of the year, but the weekdays bring a bit of relief.

✔ August brings with it back-to-school sales at Orlando's many malls and outlets.

✔ All hotels, major restaurants, and indoor tourist attractions in Central Florida have air conditioning.

✔ Orlando has some of the coolest pools and unique water parks. Splashing around in any one of them makes for a fun way to beat the heat.

However, keep in mind that

✔ Outside, the heat and humidity can be downright oppressive. The phrase "I'm mellllllllting" takes on new meaning. Those with respiratory problems would do best to avoid Orlando in summer, when it may feel like you're trying to breath in a steam room.

✔ Crowds and sweat create a sometimes unpleasant perfume in the air. And with the UV index at its extreme, you'll burn in less than 20 minutes without a good sunscreen.

✔ There's not much of a chance of getting discounts. Why should anyone cut prices when everything is running at capacity?

Fall: Harvest good times in Orlando

Fall is fabulous in Orlando because

✔ With schools back in session, crowds are at their thinnest.

✔ Accommodations that do give discounts often offer them in the fall.

✔ With smaller crowds, wait times for lines can be 30 minutes or less. In fact, I've sometimes gotten off a ride, only to turn around and walk right back on.

But keep in mind that

✔ Although the weather is cooler, the temperature doesn't get as mild as spring until Thanksgiving or later.

✔ Shorter crowds mean shorter park hours. Closing times of 6 or 7 p.m. (sometimes even earlier) are not uncommon.

✔ Once mid-December arrives, so do the higher prices.

Winter: You'll be warm and welcome in Orlando

Winter is wonderful in Orlando because

- ✔ Orlando doesn't have a true winter — although some nights approach freezing temperatures, the days are still relatively mild and sunny. January and February have the biggest temperature swings. One day it can reach 80°, the next it may only get into the 40's.

- ✔ With the exception of the holiday period from mid- December to just after New Year's — the busiest season of all — lines at the parks don't get much shorter than they do during this time of year.

However, remember that

- ✔ The many conventions held in Orlando throughout the year keep room rates from plunging completely, and conventioneers can take over entire hotels, sometimes making rooms hard to find.

- ✔ During the Thanksgiving and mid-December to early January holidays, the parks are just as crowded (if not more so) as summer weekends.

Weather Warnings

You don't need to worry too much, but knowing a little about Florida's weather-related temper tantrums is a good idea. Here's a list of weather events that you may experience during your stay:

- ✔ **Hurricanes:** The Gulf and Atlantic hurricane seasons run from June 1 to November 30. In an average year, the Atlantic churns out ten of these storms, and one or two touch Florida. The Gulf adds three to five. The good news: Orlando's inland location generally means the worst a hurricane can do is ruin a couple days of vacation with heavy rains and the occasional tornado. (That said, in Aug and Sept of 2004, hurricanes Charley, Frances, and Jeanne swept through Orlando causing massive shutdowns and evacuations. While this was an extremely rare occurrence, it's something to keep in mind.)

- ✔ **Lightning:** This scary but beautiful show, courtesy of Mother Nature, makes regular appearances during Orlando's frequent summer thunderstorms.

  Don't let lightning ruin your trip, however. Unless you go out of your way to attract it, lightning's wrath likely won't bother you. Use common sense and you should be fine.

- ✔ **Sun:** Florida isn't called the Sunshine State without good reason. Make sure that you use plenty of sunscreen (an SPF of 30 or higher is recommended) during your trip. Florida tourism thrives on the sun, but you won't enjoy your vacation much if you're laid up with a painful sunburn or, even worse, sun poisoning.

Sunburns can really ruin a fun day at the parks. Preventing your skin from turning a magnificent, and painful, shade of red is simple: Slather yourself and your kids (even the ones in covered strollers) with a sun block that has a SPF of at least 30 (50 is even better for the kids) and that, preferably, contains zinc or titanium oxide. Pick a formula that's both waterproof and sweatproof. And don't forget to keep re-applying it, especially after you hit the swimming pool. Every two hours is best. Likewise, remember to bring a wide-brimmed hat and don't forget a Florida native's favorite fashion statement — sunglasses.

To avoid dehydration, another vacation killer, drink more fluids than you think you need. By the time you're thirsty and cranky from walking around in the heat, you're already dehydrated. Ignoring these signs could lead to heat exhaustion or worse. Avoid caffeinated or carbonated beverages, as well as alcoholic drinks and those high in sugar — these actually cause you to lose more body fluids. Sports drinks can supplement fluids in your body, but water should be your first choice.

 Freeze a couple water bottles to bring along — they stay cold far longer and save you a few dollars in the end (especially as you can refill them at a fountain for free throughout the day).

Take frequent breaks under the shade of a tree or in the comfort of air-conditioning, especially if you have kids in tow. Wearing lightweight light colored clothing will all help alleviate the affects of the searing sunshine.

For those looking for exact forecasts, log onto www.weather.com the week of your trip and use zip code 32830 to get a ten-day forecast for the area.

Table 3-1 lists, by month, average high and low temperatures recorded in Central Florida.

Table 3-1	Central Florida Average Temperatures											
	Jan	Feb	Mar	Apr	May	June	July	Aug	Sep	Oct	Nov	Dec
High (°F/°C)	72/22	73/23	78/26	84/29	88/31	91/33	92/33	92/33	90/32	84/29	78/26	73/23
Low (°F/°C)	49/10	50/10	55/13	60/16	66/19	71/22	73/23	73/23	73/23	65/19	57/14	51/11

Orlando's Calendar: Attractions in Review

In this section, I list (by month) just a few of Orlando's many exciting festivals and special events. Please double-check with the festivals' respective governing organizations before planning your vacation around any of them. Event dates, as with everything else, are subject to change.

You can access the Orlando/Orange County Convention & Visitors Bureau Web site at www.orlandoinfo.com for information about other upcoming events.

January

The second-ranked teams from the Southeastern and Big Ten college football conferences square off against each other at the annual **Capital One Florida Citrus Bowl.** Tickets are $55 before November 1 and $65 up until the day of the game. Call ☎ **800-297-2695** or 407-423-2476 for information or **Ticketmaster** at ☎ **877-803-7073** or 407-839-3900 (on the Internet, go to www.fcsports.com). January 2.

Why walk through the WDW parks, when you can run the **Walt Disney World Marathon** (☎ **407-939-7810;** www.disneysports.com)? The 26.2-mile course starts and ends at Epcot, winding through each of the other Disney parks, as well as along the Boardwalk. Spots fill up fast, so if this sounds like something you want to do, you had better sign up as soon as you finish reading this sentence. The entrance fee will run you $95. A half-marathon ($85), beginning at Epcot, making its way through the Magic Kingdom, and ending back at Epcot, is an option for those not quite ready for all 26 miles. Those with children won't be left behind as the **5K Family Fun Run** ($25–$30) winds around Epcot's World Showcase with shorter races especially designed for the kids, including a 100, 200, 400, and infant diaper dash (each costs $5). January 7 and 8.

The four-day **Zora Neale Hurston Festival** (☎ **407-647-3307;** www.zora nealehurstonfestival.com) is celebrated in Eatonville, the first incorporated African-American town in America. It highlights the life and works of author Zora Neale Hurston. Eatonville is 25 miles north of the parks. Admission is $5 to $10 adults, $3 kids ages 4 to 17. Lectures or seminars are extra. Last weekend in January.

February

Authentic parade floats from New Orleans, stilt walkers, and traditional doubloons and beads add to all the fun at **Mardi Gras at Universal Studios Florida** (☎ **800-837-2273** or 407-363-8000; www.universal orlando.com). Not unlike the original celebration, this party is flowing with plenty of alcohol, making it more of an adult-oriented event — though, thankfully, you don't have to show any skin to get beads thrown at you. On Saturday nights, nationally known bands and artists ranging from K.C. and the Sunshine Band to Donna Summer play the stage inside the park. All Mardi Gras events are included in the regular price of admission to the park. Daily from mid-February to mid-March.

The **Atlanta Braves** head south for spring training to **Disney's Wide World of Sports Complex.** They play a 16-game spring season that begins in early March. Tickets are $13 to $21. For general information, call ☎ **407-939-GAME** or check online at www.disneysports.com. To purchase tickets, call Ticketmaster at ☎ **877-803-7073** or 407-839-3900. You can also get online information at www.atlantabraves.com or www.majorleaguebaseball.com. Beginning in late February.

March

The ten-day **Florida Film Festival** (call ☎ **407-644-6579** or 407-629-1088; www.floridafilmfestival.com or www.enzian.org), showcasing the year's best independent and foreign films, has become one of the most respected regional film events in the country. Single tickets are $10 or less, with special ticket packages also available. Mid-March.

Spanning two weekends in March, **SeaWorld's BBQ Fest** (☎ **800-423-8368**; www.seaworldorlando.com) offers a great barbecue buffet while listening to the sounds of popular country artists. The concerts are included with regular park admission, but the buffet is an additional $14.95 adults and $8.95 for children ages 9 or younger. Mid-March.

Also in mid-March, you can enjoy the wonderful **Winter Park Sidewalk Arts Festival** (☎ **407-672-6390**; www.wpsaf.org), which is rated as one of the nation's most prestigious fine arts festivals and draws artists from all over North America. Each year, more than 350,000 people enjoy this free three-day event filled with art, food, children's activities, and performances by nationally recognized jazz artists. Third weekend in March.

April

From garden beds color-coordinated to form those famous Mickey ears to whimsical topiaries specially grown and groomed to take the shape of Disney's classic characters, the six-week **Epcot International Flower and Garden Festival** (☎ **407-934-7639**; www.disneyworld.com) is geared towards those with an appreciation of what Disney can do to Mother Nature's finest foliage. Nightly classic-rock and pop concerts are featured at the America Gardens Theater near the American Pavilion. Included with regular Epcot admission. Late-April to early June.

May

More than 100 acts from around the world participate in the eclectic ten-day **Orlando International Fringe Festival** (☎ **407-648-0077**; www.orlandofringe.com), which takes place at various locations in downtown Orlando. Entertainers perform everything from drama to political satire, experimental theater, and *Hamlet*. Ticket prices vary, but most performances are less than $10. Usually starts third week of May.

Whether you're a Jedi-in-training or Darth Vader–wannabe, the Force will be with you during the four **Star Wars Weekends at Disney–MGM Studios** (☎ **407-934-7639**; www.disneyworld.com). In addition to various *Star Wars*–themed shows and parades, each weekend features meet-and-greets with actual actors from the movies such as Anthony Daniels (C3PO) and Peter Mayhew (Chewbacca). Included with regular Disney–MGM admission. Begins in mid-May.

June

Gay Days (www.gayday.com or www.gaydays.com) draws tens of thousands of gay and lesbian travelers to Central Florida. This event began in 1991 as an unofficial event at **Disney World** that ended up attracting 50,000 people. It has expanded to a week-long celebration, during which, **Universal Orlando** and **SeaWorld** also host events. Keep in mind, red is the color of choice for event-goers during this week, and Saturday is when they descend en masse on the **Magic Kingdom.** First weekend in June.

July

Orlando heats up as **Independence Day** is celebrated with bands, singers, dancers, and unbelievable fireworks displays at **Disney's Star-Spangled Spectacular** (☎ 407-824-4321; www.disneyworld.com). The parks stay open late for the occasion. **SeaWorld** (☎ 407-351-3600; www.seaworld.com) exhibits a dazzling laser/fireworks spectacular, and Orlando's **Lake Eola Park** (☎ 407-246-2827; cityoforlando.net) features activities and entertainment throughout the late afternoon as well as a free nighttime fireworks display. Local radio station WXXL hosts an annual **Fourth of July concert** (☎ 407-916-7800; www.wxxl.com) in Altamonte Springs that brings in Top-40 radio acts, such as Jessica Simpson, to play for thousands of people outdoors. July 4.

September

One weekend each September, the **Magic Kingdom** plays host to a contemporary Christian and Gospel music festival, **Night of Joy,** featuring top artists. This event is very popular, so get tickets early. Admission to the concert is separately ticketed from regular admission; Magic Kingdom attractions are included. Ticket prices are $36.95 (one night), $59.95 (two nights), and $79.95 (all three nights). Call ☎ 407-824-4321 or visit www.nightofjoy.com for concert details. Universal goes head-to-head with Disney, scheduling its **Rock the Universe** Christian music concert the very same weekend (☎ 800-837-2273; www.rocktheuniverse.com). Tickets are $35.95 for one night or $58.95 for both nights; admission includes entrance to **Universal Studios** after 4 p.m., the concerts, and full use of the park's rides and attractions until 1 a.m. Second weekend in September.

Later in the month, **SeaWorld** offers a weekend of sensational music, concerts, dance, food sampling, and crafts to celebrate Hispanic culture in Florida at its **Viva La Musica** (☎ 800-423-8368; www.seaworld orlando.com). Admission is included with regular park admission. Last weekend in September.

October

At the six-week **Epcot International Food & Wine Festival** (☎ 407-824-4321; www.disneyworld.com), you have the chance to sip and savor the food and beverages of 30 countries for the measly sum of $3 to $5 per sample. Events include wine-tastings, seminars, concerts, and celebrity-chef cooking demonstrations. Some specially ticketed dinners or wine-tastings are available at prices ranging from $85 to $175. You must be 21 or over to enjoy the libations, but all ages can enjoy the culinary treats. October 1 to mid-November.

Orlando is frightfully fun in October as **Islands of Adventure** transforms its grounds with haunted attractions for about 20 or so nights in honor of Universal Orlando's **Halloween Horror Nights** (☎ **800-837-2273** or 407-363-8000; www.universalorlando.com). Complete with live bands, special shows, a psychopath's maze, and hundreds of ghouls and goblins roaming the streets, the studio closes at dusk and then reopens in a new, chilling form at 7 p.m. The park charges full adult admission ($54.75) for this event (children under 10 aren't permitted), which lasts until about midnight. Guests aren't allowed to wear costumes so that Universal employees can spot their peers. This event tends to sell out, especially nearer to Halloween, so get your tickets early. Runs on select nights in October.

If your young ones are more into treats than tricks for Halloween, Mickey hosts the annual **Mickey's Not-So-Scary Halloween Party** (☎ **407-824-4321**; www.disneyworld.com) at the **Magic Kingdom,** complete with special parades and a complimentary family photo. Each guest is also given a Halloween bag, and, throughout the park, cast members hand out treats. This is a separately ticketed event held after regular park closing, but most attractions are open. Tickets are $32 for adults and $26 for children 9 or younger. This event tends to sell out, especially nearer to Halloween, so get your tickets early (they go on sale in May!). Runs on select nights in October.

November

Soap opera–fanatics from all over the world descend upon **Disney–MGM Studios** during the **ABC Super Soap Weekend** (☎ **407-824-4321**; www.disneyworld.com) to get up-close-and-personal with their favorite stars from ABC's long-running soaps — *All My Children, One Life to Live,* and *General Hospital.* The event is included with regular park admission. First weekend of November.

Downtown Disney Marketplace is home to **The Walt Disney World Festival of the Masters** (☎ **407-824-4321**; www.disneyworld.com), one of the largest art shows in the South. The exhibition features top artists, photographers, and craftspeople — all winners of juried shows throughout the United States. Admission to the festival is free to all. The second weekend in November.

December

During the **Disney Christmas festivities,** Main Street in the **Magic Kingdom** is lavishly decked out with lights and holly, and carolers welcome visitors. Thousands of colored lights illuminate an 80-foot tree.

Epcot and **Animal Kingdom** also offer special embellishments and entertainment throughout the holiday season, as do all Disney resorts. **Disney–MGM Studios** offers the world-famous **Osbourne Family Spectacle of Lights.** One holiday highlight includes **Mickey's Very Merry Christmas Party,** an after-dark ticketed event, which takes place on weekends at the **Magic Kingdom** and offers a traditional Christmas parade and fireworks display. Admission ($33.95 adults, $23.95 kids 3 to 9) includes cookies, cocoa, and a souvenir photo. The best part? Shorter lines for rides.

Another holiday highlight is the **Candlelight Procession** at **Epcot,** which features hundreds of candle-holding carolers, a celebrity narrator telling the Christmas story, and a 450-voice choir that's very moving. Regular park admission is required, but special dinner packages include special seating for the event ($29–$42 for adults, depending on the Epcot restaurant chosen; $11 for ages 3–11, regardless of restaurant). Call ☎ **407-824-4321** for details on these events or visit www.disneyworld.com. Dates vary, but most events are staged at various times in December.

Part II

Planning Your Trip to Walt Disney World & Orlando

The 5th Wave   By Rich Tennant

"Good news! I got us a great theme park inspired flight to Orlando. The 'Bumpity Flubbity Flight to Adventure'."

In this part . . .

Okay, it's nitty-gritty time. In this part, I suggest some ways you can save money on your vacation and lay out the different ways you can get to Disney World and Orlando. I also sort out the various travel packages available to the city and offer suggestions on buying travel insurance, staying healthy, and staying in contact with those who didn't get to make the trip. And so everyone has a good time, I also offer dedicated advice to those people who have special travel needs or interests, be it families, seniors, or gays and lesbians.

Chapter 4
Managing Your Money

· ·

In This Chapter

▶ Managing your dollars and cents
▶ Cutting your vacation costs
▶ Paying for it all

· ·

Developing a realistic budget is an important key to enjoying your vacation — the last thing you want to experience when you get to Orlando is sticker shock, as Central Florida is famous for its ability to exact a pound of flesh from even the most cost-conscious traveler. From hotel rooms to meal tabs to admission fees, you can easily break the bank if you don't do some homework and set some limits in advance. The good news is that there are ways to avoid blowing your bankroll, and I show them to you in this chapter.

Planning Your Budget

When it comes to your Orlando vacation, working out a budget may be the single most important thing you do. The hard part is sticking to it after you've been swept up in all the excitement. Mickey and his pals are masters when it comes to separating you from your money. But by using the tips I give you, you can come up with a pretty accurate estimate of what a trip to Mickey's place may cost you.

 When making your budget, be sure to include every possible expense, especially hidden charges that are almost never quoted when you inquire about hotel or rental-car rates, attraction admissions, and restaurant prices unless you specifically ask. Florida sales taxes, which run from 6.5 percent on merchandise to almost 25 percent on rental cars, are chief on the list of these hidden charges. For more information, see "Taxes" in the Appendix.

Another hidden expense many travelers fail to budget for is tips. Orlando is a tip-happy place. A 15-percent tip is the general rule for restaurant service and cab rides. The hotel housekeeper deserves $1 to $2 a day for cleaning your mess, making your beds, and keeping you stocked with towels and toilet paper. Baggage handlers usually receive at least $1 per bag. And don't forget about a $1 to $2 tip for valet parking.

Most of your Orlando vacation expenses fall into six categories:

- ✔ **Lodging.** The average rack rate for a three-star hotel in Orlando is about $85 per night (see Chapter 9). In most cases, those rates include any children younger than 12, and usually younger than 18, staying in your room. The lowest rates at **WDW** are those at the **All-Star resorts,** which, depending on the season, run from $77 to $131. They're pricier than comparable rooms in the outside world; they're tiny, basic, and heavily themed, but they're on Disney soil.

- ✔ **Transportation.** Some hotels offer free shuttles to the parks; others take you for a fee (see Chapter 8 for more information). If you stay at **Disney,** you can access its free transportation system (though it's plodding). Rental-car rates start at about $35 a day after you've tossed in Florida's various taxes and surcharges (which can total up to 20–25 percent above the quoted rate). And don't forget to add the $8 ($9 for some) daily charge to park your car at the theme parks — though you won't have to pay this at the Disney parks if you're a guest at one of Mickey's resorts. If you're a fan of valet parking, add at least $12 to $15 per day (and possibly a whole lot more) for fees and tips. If you're flying into Orlando, don't forget to add the cost of getting to the airport, airport parking (if you're driving yourself), airline tickets (you can find tips for getting the best airfare in Chapter 5), and transportation from the Orlando airport to your room. If you're driving to Orlando, be sure to include your fuel costs and tolls.

- ✔ **Dining.** Satisfying your stomach in Orlando is the biggest variable in your budget, and outside of admissions and tickets, it can easily end up being your biggest expense. If you're happy with a diet of nothing but fast food, expect an average of $30 to $40 per person, per day. Adding one or two restaurant meals jumps the average up to $40 to $60 per person, per day, including tax and tip; and expect to spend $60 or more per person if you dine mostly in the theme parks or at **Disney**'s and **Universal**'s resorts, where prices are almost 25 percent higher than those in the outside world. (See Chapter 10 for more information on dining.) Keep in mind that food in the parks and resorts is overpriced and is, for the most, part average at best (though there are exceptions). Outside the parks, you can find delis and pizzerias for takeout as well as assorted budget minded eateries.

- ✔ **Attractions.** Your expenses for attractions depend on which parks you plan to visit and how many days you spend at each. When you throw in sales tax, **Disney, Universal,** and **SeaWorld** charge just over $60 per adult and around $50 per child age 3 to 9, per day. (See Chapters 12–16 and 18–20 for information about the individual parks.) If you're planning to visit any of these parks more than once, buying a multiday and, in some cases, multipark pass is the by far the best way to go. Chapter 21 also includes some less expensive and even free attractions that you can visit if you want to cut your costs and broaden your experiences.

✔ **Shopping.** Orlando is a shopper's paradise, with several large malls and outlets (see Chapter 22) and an array of souvenir shops to choose from. The amusement park gift shops are notorious for inflating prices on souvenirs, and although I don't recommend picking up more than a couple of souvenirs at the parks, be prepared for their ability to lure you in. Budget accordingly.

✔ **Nightlife.** If you stick to the theme park options, plan on dropping about $30 to $40 for admission to the various nightspots and a few $5 beers. (See Chapter 25 for information about the various park nightlife options.) If you have a car (rental or your own), downtown options can come in slightly less, at around $20 to $30 for cover charges and a few beers.

After estimating your expenses, be sure to tack on another 15 to 20 percent to your budget as a safety net — there's bound to be a pair of fuzzy light-up Mickey ears calling the name of someone in your group.

Table 4-1 outlines various vacationing costs in Orlando.

Table 4-1	What Things Cost in Orlando	
	U.S.$	*U.K.£ (As of this writing, $1.84 = 1£)*
Taxi from airport to WDW (4–5 people)	52	28
Shuttle (round-trip) from airport to WDW (adult fare)	29	16
Double room at Masters Inn Maingate, Kissimmee	39–95	21–52
Double room at Disney's All-Star Resorts	77–131	42–71
Double room at Disney's Coronado Springs Resort	134–209	73–114
Double room at Hard Rock Hotel Universal Orlando	229–409	125–223
Double room at Disney's Grand Floridian	349–870	190–473
Coca-Cola (restaurant)	1.50	0.80
Bottle of beer (restaurant)	2.95	1.60
All-you-can-eat buffet dinner at Akershus in Epcot, not including tip or wine	19	10
Six-course fixed-price dinner for one at Victoria & Albert's, not including tip or wine	95–125	52–68
Child 1-day, 1-park admission to Walt Disney World	48	26
Adult 1-day, 1-park admission to Walt Disney World	60	33

(continued)

Table 4-1 *(continued)*

	U.S.$	U.K.£ *(As of this writing, $1.84 = 1£)*
Child 2-day Universal Orlando Pass	95	52
Adult 2-day Universal Orlando Pass	105	57
Child 4-day Magic Your Way ticket with Park Hopper Option to Walt Disney World	183	99
Adult 4-day Magic Your Way ticket with Park Hopper Option to Walt Disney World	220	120

Cutting Costs — but Not the Fun

You can conserve your cash in more than just a couple of ways when you vacation in Orlando. Using these tips can keep your costs manageable:

✔ **Visit off season.** Hotel prices in the off-season (Sept–Nov or Apr to early June) can be substantially lower, depending on the property.

✔ **Travel midweek.** If you can travel on a Tuesday, Wednesday, or Thursday, you may find cheaper flights to your destination. When you ask about airfares, see if you can get a cheaper rate by flying on a different day. For more tips on getting a good fare, see Chapter 5.

✔ **Try a package tour.** For many Orlando destinations, you can book airfare, hotel, ground transportation, and even some additional perks just by making one call to a travel agent or packager, for a price much less than if you put the trip together yourself. (See Chapter 5 for more on package tours.)

✔ **Ask whether your kids can stay in the room with you.** A room with two double beds usually doesn't cost any more than one with a queen-size bed. And many hotels don't charge you the additional person rate if the additional person is pint-size and related to you. Many Orlando hotels offer "suites" with bunk beds or separate sleeping areas for kids. They may cost more than a regular room, but even if you have to pay extra for the extra space or a rollaway bed, you can save hundreds by not taking two rooms.

✔ **Reserve a room with a refrigerator and coffeemaker.** You don't have to slave over a hot stove to cut costs; several motels have minifridges, coffeemakers, and even a microwave. Buying supplies for breakfast saves you money — and probably calories.

✔ **Don't bunk with Mickey.** This one may be hard to swallow for those who want to immerse themselves in all things Disney. And if your vacation can't be complete without a stay on Walt Disney

World property, then by all means go for it. But if you're on a tight budget, you can stay in some wonderful, themed (albeit, non-Mickey) properties for considerably less than you would pay for the cheapest Disney hotels.

✔ **Take advantage of your in-and-out privileges if you have a multi-day pass to a theme park.** Go back to your hotel for a picnic lunch and a swim or nap. You can eat economically, miss the midday sun, and refuel for an afternoon or, in some cases, an evening at the park without having to pay admission fees again.

✔ **Avoid splurging — pace yourself.** Your money goes fastest when you overexert yourself exploring the parks, and you end up too hungry, thirsty, or tired to care about how much you spend. Be sure to schedule rest breaks throughout the day and begin each day with a big breakfast (several hotels offer spreads that are included in their room rates). You can find several buffets outside the parks for around $4 to $6 (see Chapter 10).

✔ **Brown-bag it.** Bringing your own food is extremely cost-effective. The parks are wise to this scheme and many don't allow coolers, but they generally ignore it when you aren't obvious about it, so make your operation covert — hide food in a fanny pack or back-pack. If you don't want to schlepp food, do bring drinks or stop often at drinking fountains — the bottled water and soda prices in the parks can have you wondering if the theme parks are selling liquid gold instead of Coke.

✔ **Try expensive restaurants at lunch instead of dinner.** Lunch tabs are usually a fraction of what dinner costs at a top restaurant, and the menu often boasts many of the same specialties.

✔ **Don't rent a gas guzzler.** Renting a smaller car is cheaper, and you save on gas to boot. For more on car rentals, see Chapter 5.

✔ **Don't spend every day at a theme park.** Discover your hotel's pool, playground, workout room, and other freebies, or head out of town to a state park, beach, or one of the lower-priced attractions away from theme park central.

✔ **Skip the souvenirs.** Your photographs and your memories could be the best mementos of your trip. If you're concerned about money, you can do without the T-shirts and other trinkets.

✔ **Hit the Web.** The Web site www.mousesavers.com keeps track of almost all available discounts for Disney-related vacations (from room discount codes to special packages and promotions). If you want to stay at a Disney resort, Mousesavers will likely help you save money doing it.

✔ **Receive instant discounts with an Orlando Magicard.** The Orlando Magicard is good for up to $500 in discounts on accommodations, car rentals, attractions, and more. Better yet, the card is free. You can get a Magicard from the Orlando/Orange County Convention &

Visitors Bureau, 8723 International Dr., Suite 101, Orlando, FL
32819 (☎ **800-643-9492** or 407-363-5872; www.orlandoinfo.com/
magicard/index.cfm). You may also be eligible for other discounts
if you're a member of AARP, AAA, the military, or service clubs, so
don't be bashful — just ask.

Handling Money

You're the best judge of how much cash you feel comfortable carrying or
what alternative form of currency is your favorite. That's not going to
change much on your vacation. True, you'll probably be moving around
more and incurring more expenses than you generally do (unless you
happen to eat out every meal when you're at home), and you may let
your mind slip into vacation gear and not be as vigilant about your
safety as when you're in work mode. But, those factors aside, the only
type of payment that won't be quite as available to you away from home
is your personal checkbook.

Using ATMs and carrying cash

The easiest and best way to get cash away from home is from an ATM
(automated teller machine). The **Cirrus** (☎ **800-424-7787;** www.master
card.com) and **PLUS** (☎ **800-843-7587;** www.visa.com) ATM networks
span the globe; look at the back of your bank card to see which network
you're on, then call or check online for ATM locations at your destination. You can find ATMs at all of Orlando's major theme parks; check the
guide map you get upon entering each park for locations.

Keep in mind that many banks impose a fee every time your card is used
at a different bank's ATM. In Florida, you're assessed an average charge
of $2.75 when you use an ATM that isn't affiliated with your bank. (That's
on top of any fees your bank may charge.)

Be extremely careful when using ATMs, especially at night and in areas
that are heavily traveled but not well lighted. Don't let the land of
Mickey lull you into a false sense of security. Minnie and Goofy won't
mug you — but thieves working the theme park zones may.

Charging ahead with credit cards

Credit cards are a safe way to carry money: They also provide a convenient record of all your expenses and generally offer relatively good
exchange rates. You can also withdraw cash advances from your credit
cards at banks or ATMs, provided you know your PIN. If you've forgotten
yours, or didn't even know you had one, call the number on the back of
your credit card and ask the bank to send it to you. It usually takes five
to seven business days, though some banks provide the number over
the phone if you tell them your mother's maiden name or some other
personal information.

Dollars — Disney style

Walt Disney World theme parks and some resorts offer their own way of paying. You can use your electronic room key as a debit card in Disney's shops and restaurants — items are charged directly to your room.

Although I don't recommend doing so, you can buy Disney Dollars (currency with cute little pictures of Mickey, Goofy, or Minnie on it) at the resorts or the guest services desk in each of the parks. The bills come in $1, $5, and $10 denominations, and they're good at shops, restaurants, and resorts throughout **Walt Disney World** and in Disney stores elsewhere on the planet. This currency provides no real benefit other than its negligible souvenir value. If you want to trade Disney Dollars for real currency upon leaving, you end up facing — you guessed it! — one more line in the theme parks.

Be advised that refunds for deposits on wheelchairs, strollers, and such in the theme parks are often paid in Disney Dollars. But if you're persistent, you can get your refunds in Uncle Sam's currency, instead of Mickey's.

Keep in mind that you start paying interest on credit card cash advances the minute you get them and it's generally much higher than the rate for charging your purchases.

Toting traveler's checks

These days, traveler's checks are less necessary because most cities have 24-hour ATMs that allow you to withdraw small amounts of cash as needed. However, keep in mind that you will likely be charged an ATM withdrawal fee if the bank is not your own. So if you're withdrawing money every day, you may be better off with traveler's checks — provided that you don't mind showing identification every time you want to cash one. All of the major theme parks and resorts accept traveler's checks from major banks.

If you choose to carry traveler's checks, be sure to keep a record of their serial numbers separate from your checks in the event that they are stolen or lost. You'll get a refund faster if you know the numbers.

Dealing with a lost or stolen wallet

Be sure to contact all of your credit-card companies the minute you discover your wallet has been lost or stolen and file a report at the nearest police precinct. Your credit-card company or insurer may require a police report number or record of the loss. Most credit-card companies have an emergency toll-free number to call if your card is lost or stolen; they may be able to wire you a cash advance immediately or deliver an emergency credit card in a day or two. Call the following emergency numbers in the United States:

- **American Express** ☎ **800-221-7282** (for cardholders and traveler's check holders)
- **MasterCard** ☎ **800-307-7309** or 636-722-7111
- **Visa** ☎ **800-847-2911** or 410-581-9994

For other credit cards, call the toll-free number directory at ☎ **800-555-1212.**

If you need emergency cash over the weekend when all banks and American Express offices are closed, you can have money wired to you via **Western Union** (☎ **800-325-6000;** www.westernunion.com).

Identity theft or fraud is a potential complication of losing your wallet, especially if you've lost your driver's license along with your cash and credit cards. Notify the major credit-reporting bureaus immediately; placing a fraud alert on your records may protect you against liability for criminal activity. The three major U.S. credit-reporting agencies are **Equifax** (☎ **800-766-0008;** www.equifax.com), **Experian** (☎ **888-397-3742;** www.experian.com), and **TransUnion** (☎ **800-680-7289;** www.transunion.com). Finally, if you lose all forms of photo ID, call your airline and explain the situation; they may allow you to board the plane if you have a copy of your passport or birth certificate and a copy of the police report you've filed.

Chapter 5

Getting to Orlando

● ●

In This Chapter

▶ Getting a good airline fare
▶ Arriving in Orlando by car
▶ Taking the train to Orlando
▶ Checking out package tours

● ●

*G*etting to your destination isn't always half the fun of your trip, but you can choose ways to get from point A to point B without too much hassle or expense. In this chapter, I eliminate the travel double talk, shed the useless options, and make sure that you have a fun and easy time planning your getaway.

Flying to Orlando

Getting to Orlando by plane is a breeze. Almost every major domestic airline offers direct service to Mickeyville from most major cities in the U.S. and Canada. A number of international carriers also fly direct from several major European and South American cities.

Finding out which airlines fly there

If you're flying to Orlando, the best place to land is **Orlando International Airport** (☎ 407-825-2001; www.orlandoairports.net). The airport, also known as OIA, offers direct or nonstop service from approximately 60 U.S. and 25 international cities. About 40 scheduled airlines and several charters feed more than 31 million people through its gates annually. For a list of all the major airlines that fly into the city, see "Toll-free Numbers and Web Sites" in the Appendix. **Delta** (☎ 800-221-1212; www.delta.com) provides nearly 20 percent of the flights to and from Orlando International Airport, offering service from roughly 150 cities.

The sheer number of flights in and out of its gates makes OIA the top dog as far as local airports go, and its location reinforces that even more. The airport connects to highways, Interstate 4, and toll roads that get you (whether you're driving or being driven) into the heart of it all within 30 or 40 minutes (fewer if you're headed into downtown Orlando). If a proposed train running from the airport to the theme park zones ever gets built, OIA will become that much more convenient.

Orlando Sanford International Airport (☎ 407-585-4500; www.orlando sanfordairport.com) is much smaller than the main airport, but it has grown a bit in recent years, thanks mainly to a small fleet of international carriers including **Air 2000, Britannia,** and **Jetsgo,** as well as several regional airlines such as **Southeast, TransMeridian,** and **Vacation Express.** While you may save money flying into Sanford International, it has some drawbacks. The flight schedules aren't always convenient; the airlines using the airport don't serve all that many cities; and you definitely need a rental car — the airport is on the northern side of Orlando, well over 45 minutes away from Walt Disney World.

Getting the best deal on your airfare

Competition among the major U.S. airlines is unlike that of any other industry. Every airline offers virtually the same product (basically, a coach seat is a coach seat is a . . .), yet prices can vary by hundreds of dollars.

Business travelers who need the flexibility to buy their tickets at the last minute and change their itineraries at a moment's notice — and who want to get home before the weekend — pay (or at least their companies pay) the premium rate, otherwise known as the _full fare._ But if you can book your ticket far in advance, stay over Saturday night, and are willing to travel midweek (Tues, Wed, or Thurs), you can take advantage of far less expensive ticket prices — usually only a fraction of the full fare. On most flights, even the shortest hops within the United States, can cost upwards of $1,000 or more, but a 7- or 14-day advance purchase ticket may cost half that amount, possibly even less. Obviously, planning ahead pays.

The airlines also periodically hold sales, in which they lower the prices on their most popular routes. These fares have advance purchase requirements and date-of-travel restrictions, but you can't beat the prices. As you plan your vacation, keep your eyes open for these sales, which tend to take place in seasons of low travel volume — September to November and April to early June. You almost never see a sale around the peak summer vacation months of July and August, or around Thanksgiving or Christmas, when many people fly, regardless of the fare they have to pay.

Another option is to fly on one of several no-frills airlines — low fares but no amenities — that service Orlando. The biggest is **Southwest Airlines** (☎ 800-435-9792; www.southwest.com), which has flights from many U.S. cities to Orlando. **Spirit Air** (☎ 800-772-7117; www. spiritair.com) offers a good selection of flights (several of them cross-country) to Orlando out of several U.S. cities. **JetBlue Airways** (☎ 800-538-2583; www.jetblue.com) is a low-cost carrier that operates mostly on the Eastern Seaboard but offers a number of routes from the West Coast. **AirTran Airways** (☎ 800-247-8726; www.airtran.com) regularly has sales on routes to Orlando from around the country and offers the option to upgrade to business class on most flights at the gate for only $35 for each segment of your flight. Most of these so called no-frills airlines actually offer more in the way of extras than many of the larger carriers do, given all of the cutbacks and reductions in service of late, making them an all-around good buy.

Booking your flight online

The "big three" online travel agencies, **Expedia** (www.expedia.com), **Travelocity** (www.travelocity.com), and **Orbitz** (www.orbitz.com) sell most of the air tickets bought on the Internet. (Canadian travelers should try www.expedia.ca and www.travelocity.ca; U.K. residents can go for expedia.co.uk and opodo.co.uk.) Each has different business deals with the airlines and may offer different fares on the same flights, so shopping around is wise. Expedia and Travelocity will also send you an **e-mail notification** when a cheap fare becomes available to your favorite destination. Of the smaller travel agency Web sites, **SideStep** (www.sidestep.com) receives good reviews from users. It's a browser add-on that purports to "search 140 sites at once," but in reality only beats competitors' fares as often as other sites do.

Great **last-minute deals** are available through free weekly e-mail services provided directly by the airlines. Most of these deals are announced on Tuesday or Wednesday and must be purchased online. Most are only valid for travel that weekend, but some (such as Southwest's) can be booked weeks or months in advance. Sign up for weekly e-mail alerts at airline Web sites or check mega-sites that compile comprehensive lists of last-minute specials, such as **Smarter Living** (smarterliving.com). For last-minute trips, **www.site59.com** in the U.S. and **www.lastminute.com** in Europe often have better deals than the major-label sites.

If you're willing to give up some control over your flight details, use an *opaque fare service* like **Priceline** (www.priceline.com) or **Hotwire** (www.hotwire.com). Both offer rock-bottom prices in exchange for travel on a "mystery airline" at a mysterious time of day, often with a mysterious change of planes en route. The mystery airlines are all major, well-known carriers — and the possibility of being sent from Philadelphia to Orlando via Omaha is remote. But your chances of getting a 6 a.m. or 11 p.m. flight are pretty high. Hotwire tells you flight prices before you buy; Priceline usually has better deals than Hotwire, but you have to play their "name our price" game. *Note:* In 2004, Priceline added non-opaque service to its roster. You now have the option to pick exact flights, times, and airlines from a list of offers — or to bid on opaque fares as before.

Great last-minute deals are also available directly from the airlines themselves through a free e-mail service called *E-savers.* Each week, the airline sends you a list of discounted flights, usually leaving the upcoming Friday or Saturday and returning the following Monday or Tuesday. You can sign up for all the major airlines at one time by logging on to **Smarter Living** (www.smarterliving.com), or you can go to each individual airline's Web site. Airline sites also offer schedules, flight booking, and information on late-breaking bargains.

Driving to Orlando

Driving to Orlando is sometimes a less expensive and potentially more scenic option, unless the distance is so great that making the road trip eats up too much of your vacation (and, thanks to rising gas prices, your budget as well).

Table 5-1 lists how far several cities are from Orlando.

Table 5-1	Driving to Orlando
City	*Distance from Orlando*
Atlanta	436 miles
Boston	1,312 miles
Chicago	1,120 miles
Cleveland	1,009 miles
Dallas	1,170 miles
Detroit	1,114 miles
New York	1,088 miles
Toronto	1,282 miles

Need directions? No problem.

- From Atlanta, take I-75 South to the Florida Turnpike to I-4 West.

- From Boston and New York, take I-95 South to I-4 West.

- From Chicago, take I-65 South to Nashville, and then I-24 South to I-75 South to the Florida Turnpike to I-4 West.

- From Cleveland, take I-77 South to Columbia, South Carolina, and then I-26 East to I-95 South to I-4 West.

- From Dallas, take I-20 East to I-49 South, to I-10 East, to I-75 South, to the Florida Turnpike, to I-4 West.

- From Detroit, take I-75 South to the Florida Turnpike to I-4 West.

- From Toronto, take Canadian Route 401 South to Queen Elizabeth Way South to I-90 (New York State Thruway) East to I-87 (New York State Thruway) South to I-95 over the George Washington Bridge, and continue south on I-95 to I-4 West.

AAA (☎ **800-222-1134;** www.aaa.com) and some other automobile clubs offer free maps and optimum driving directions to their members (among several other worthwhile travel perks). In addition, several comprehensive Web sites offer door-to-door driving directions with personalized map routing, including **MapQuest,** www.mapquest.com; **MapBlast!,** www.map blast.com; and **Yahoo! Maps,** http://maps.yahoo.com.

Arriving by Train

Amtrak (☎ **800-872-7245;** www.amtrak.com) trains pull into two central stations: 1400 Sligh Blvd. in downtown Orlando (about 23 miles from Walt Disney World) and 111 Dakin Ave. in Kissimmee (about 15 miles from Walt Disney World).

Amtrak's Auto Train allows you to bring your car to Florida without having to drive it all the way. The service begins in Lorton, Virginia — about a four-hour drive from New York, two hours from Philadelphia — and ends at Sanford, Florida, about 23 miles northeast of Orlando. Reserve early for the lowest prices. Fares begin at $530 ($1,100 with a berth) for two passengers and one auto. Call Amtrak for more details.

As with airfares, you can sometimes get discounts if you book train rides far in advance. But you may find some restrictions on travel dates for discounted train fares, mostly around the very busy holiday periods. If you're willing to travel off season, however, and spend four or more of your vacation days in transit, you can score rare deals like an offer listed a while back for a Los Angeles–Orlando round-trip for $50. Amtrak also offers money-saving packages, including accommodations (some at **WDW** resorts), car rentals, tours, and so on. For vacation package information, call ☎ **877-YES-RAIL.**

Choosing a Package Tour

For popular destinations, such as **Walt Disney World,** package tours can be a smart way to go. In many cases, a package tour that includes airfare, hotel, and transportation to and from the airport costs less than the hotel alone on a tour you book yourself. That's because packages are sold in bulk to tour operators, who then resell them to the public. It's kind of like buying your vacation at a buy-in-bulk store — except the tour operator is the one who buys the 1,000-count box of candy bars and resells them 10 at a time at a cost that undercuts the local supermarket.

Package tours can vary as much as those candy bars, too. Some offer a better class of hotels than others; others provide the same hotels for lower prices. Some book flights on scheduled airlines; others sell charters. Some packages limit your choice of accommodations and travel days.

If you choose to buy a package, think strongly about purchasing travel insurance, especially when the tour operator asks you to pay up front. But don't buy insurance from the tour operator! If they don't fulfill their obligation to provide you with the vacation you've paid for, you have no reason to think they'll fulfill their insurance obligations either. Obtain travel insurance through an independent agency. See Chapter 7 for more information about buying travel insurance.

Where can I find travel packages?

To find package tours, check out the travel section of your local Sunday newspaper or the ads in the back of national travel magazines such as *Travel & Leisure, National Geographic Traveler,* and *Condé Nast Traveler.* **Liberty Travel** (call ☎ **888-271-1584** to find the store nearest you; www.libertytravel.com) is one of the biggest packagers in the Northeast and usually boasts a full-page ad in Sunday papers.

Another good source of package deals is the airlines themselves. Most major airlines offer air/land packages, including **American Airlines Vacations** (☎ **800-321-2121**; www.aavacations.com), **Delta Vacations** (☎ **800-221-6666**; www.deltavacations.com), **Continental Airlines Vacations** (☎ **800-301-3800**; www.covacations.com), and **United Vacations** (☎ **888-854-3899**; www.unitedvacations.com). Several big **online travel agencies** — Expedia, Travelocity, Orbitz, Site59, and Lastminute.com — also do a brisk business in packages. If you're unsure about the pedigree of a smaller packager, check with the Better Business Bureau in the city where the company is based, or go online at www.bbb.org. If a packager won't tell you where it's based, don't fly with them.

Theme-park offerings

Disney offers a dizzying array of packages that can include airfare, accommodations on or off Disney property, theme-park passes, a rental car, meals, and a Disney cruise. Disney offers seasonal packages, as well as special themed vacations, including, but not limited to, golf, honeymoons, spa makeovers, and so on.

Here are some of the plusses of booking a Disney package tour:

✔ Using **Disney** as your source for an all-Disney vacation is hard to beat. The company's Web site (www.disneyworld.com) offers special planning tools that help visitors design and price their own Disney vacation packages. There's even a "Magical Gatherings" option for families and large groups traveling together that offers special planning tips and features.

✔ Nobody knows the Diz better than its own staffers.

✔ Disney reps can offer rooms in all price ranges ($77 and up).

✔ New ticketing options allow far more flexibility than ever before, so you don't end up with all that extra stuff you really don't want.

However, be aware of the following drawbacks to Disney package deals:

✔ Resort guests receive the same perks, whether you buy your Disney package from Disney or someone else (and sometimes other places, such as AAA, offer additional perks to those booking with them instead of directly with Disney).

✔ You have to prod Disney reservation agents for details. If you don't ask about them to begin with, the agents frequently don't volunteer suggestions, such as the possibility that you can save money if you start your Disney vacation a day earlier or later.

✔ Some WDW package perks aren't always worth the extra money you pay in the package price. For example, if they say you get your picture taken with Mickey as part of the deal, expect that you can find a better deal elsewhere and pay for your own photo. What you're really paying for is the convenience of having Disney plan the details.

✔ If you want to see more of Orlando than **WDW** (and most people do), you need to compare the offerings of a Disney agent with those of a regular travel agent. A motivated travel agent can put together a package of Disney and non-Disney accommodations and attractions for less than the amount WDW charges.

For detailed information on Disney packages, write to **Walt Disney World,** Box 10000, Lake Buena Vista, FL 32830-1000; call ☎ **407-828-8101;** or go online to www.disneyworld.com to order a *Walt Disney World Vacations* brochure or DVD. You'll find a dizzying menu of options from which to choose.

Although not on the same scale as Disney, the packages at **Universal Orlando** have improved greatly since the addition of the **Islands of Adventure** theme park (see Chapter 19), the **CityWalk** entertainment district (see Chapters 10 and 25), and the **Portofino Bay, Hard Rock,** and **Royal Pacific hotels** (see Chapter 9). Your package choices include resort stays, VIP access to the parks, rides, and often restaurants and discounts to other non-Disney attractions. **Universal** also offers packages that include travel and transportation. Contact **Universal Studios Vacations** at ☎ **800-711-0080** or 800-447-0672 for TTY users, or surf online to www.universalstudiosvacations.com.

SeaWorld also offers packages that include rooms at a handful of Orlando hotels including the **Renaissance Orlando Resort at SeaWorld** (see Chapter 9), car rental, tickets to SeaWorld (see Chapter 20) and, in some cases, tickets to other theme parks. You can get information at ☎ **800-557-4268** or online at www.seaworldvacations.com.

Area hotels often join forces with the parks by offering special ticket deals or stay-and-play packages, so be sure to ask when making your hotel reservations. The **World Center Marriott** often offers SeaWorld packages, and **JW Marriott Orlando, Ritz-Carlton Orlando, and**

Grande Lakes (see Chapter 9) often offer holiday packages featuring special meals, park tickets, and discounted rates.

Other places to find packages

Beside airline and theme-park packages, you can also find packages elsewhere. If you have Internet access, the **United States Tour Operators Association**'s Web site (www.ustoa.com) has a search engine that enables you to look for operators that offer packages to specific destinations.

Other package specialists include:

- ✔ **Touraine Travel** (☎ **800-967-5583;** www.tourainetravel.com) offers a wide variety of tour packages to **Disney** and Disney properties, **Universal Orlando,** and **SeaWorld.**

- ✔ If you're a linkster, try **Golfpac Vacations** (☎ **800-327-0878;** www.golfpacinc.com), which offers a slate of play-and-stay packages — from basic to comprehensive. Another option providing similar services is **Golf Getaways** (☎ **800-800-4028;** www. golfgetaways.com).

Chapter 6

Catering to Special Travel Needs or Interests

In This Chapter

▶ Finding family travel tips
▶ Sending seniors on their way with travel advice
▶ Discovering travel tips for people with disabilities
▶ Getting advice for gay and lesbian interests

*W*orried that your kids are too young or that you're too old to enjoy **Disney** and beyond? Afraid you may experience barriers blocking your access or lifestyle? In this chapter, I dispense a little advice for travelers with specific needs.

Traveling with the Brood: Advice for Families

If you have enough trouble getting your kids out of the house in the morning, dragging them thousands of miles away may seem like an insurmountable challenge. But family travel can be immensely rewarding, letting you see the world through smaller pairs of wondrous and curious eyes. Orlando loves kids and welcomes them like no other city in the world. In addition to its theme parks, Orlando has plenty of smaller kid-friendly attractions. All but a few restaurants offer lower-priced children's menus (see Chapter 10 for more info on kids and dining), and most hotels love their younger guests, providing pint-size pools and, in some cases, special gifts and programs. (See Chapter 9 for kid-friendly hotels.)

Despite Orlando's reputation as one of the kid-friendliest places around, you may find some of its attractions a bit too edgy, sophisticated, or intense for kids, including many of **Epcot**'s exhibits (see Chapter 13) and many of the primo thrill rides at **Islands of Adventure** (see Chapter 19). Likewise, you may find other attractions, such as **Discovery Cove** (see Chapter 20), somewhat cost-prohibitive, even for adults.

Traveling with tots

Traveling with young children can often bring you more stress than relaxation on your vacation. Consider that younger children have special needs. They require frequent bathroom breaks and have very short attention spans. (Does the phrase, "Are we there yet?" ring a bell?) Here are a few general suggestions for making travel plans for you and your youngsters:

- ✔ **Consider age — are your kids old enough?** Do you really want to bring an infant or a toddler to an overcrowded, usually overheated world that he or she may not appreciate because of his or her age? The large number of stroller-pushing, toddler-toting parents in the parks suggests that many people think the experience isn't too terrible, but I'm warning you anyway. If your child or grandchild is 4 years old or younger, he or she may be able to appreciate only some of the parks' offerings, though a good deal of **Disney's Magic Kingdom** is geared to youngsters (see Chapter 12). However, some of the costume-wearing characters may intimidate very young kids. And no matter how organized you are, little ones are going to slow you down. Ask yourself whether your kids are the right age to make the most out of a trip that costs the equivalent of a developing nation's GNP.

- ✔ **Accommodations for the little ones.** Kids younger than 12 (and at times up to 17) can usually stay for free in their parents' room at most hotels. Look for places that have pools and other recreational facilities so you have the option to spend a day or two away from the parks without incurring too many additional expenses. If you want to skip a rental car and aren't staying at Disney, **International Drive** is the next-best place for centralized rooms, restaurants, and attractions. The I-Drive trolley makes frequent runs up and down the thoroughfare, hotels often offer family discounts (see Chapter 9), and many provide free or moderate-cost shuttles to **Walt Disney World, SeaWorld,** and **Universal Orlando.**

- ✔ **Sitter services.** Most Orlando hotels, including all of Disney's, offer some form of baby-sitting services (usually from an outside service) and several feature counselor-supervised activity programs for children who've been toilet-trained. Baby-sitting rates usually run $10 to $15 per hour for the first child, and often offer a discounted rate for additional children.

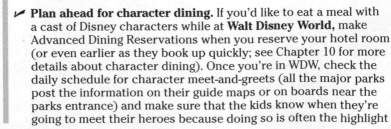

- ✔ **Plan ahead for character dining.** If you'd like to eat a meal with a cast of Disney characters while at **Walt Disney World,** make Advanced Dining Reservations when you reserve your hotel room (or even earlier as they book up quickly; see Chapter 10 for more details about character dining). Once you're in WDW, check the daily schedule for character meet-and-greets (all the major parks post the information on their guide maps or on boards near the parks entrance) and make sure that the kids know when they're going to meet their heroes because doing so is often the highlight of their day. A little planning can help you avoid running after every character you see, which only tires your little ones and gives you sore feet. And remember — the "in" thing is getting character autographs, so take my advice: If price is no object, buy an autograph book at the parks (it doubles as a good souvenir) or buy one at home and bring it along.

✔ **Keep tabs on the little ones in the land of Mickey.** Getting lost inside a theme park is easy no matter what your age. For adults and older kids, make sure that you arrange a lost-and-found meeting place as soon as you arrive in the park. Attach a name tag to younger kids (on the inside of their clothes) and find a park employee as soon as you've been separated from your party. I list lost-and-found locations in my descriptions of the major theme parks in Chapters 12 to 16 and 18 to 20. Consider carrying along a pair of two-way walkie-talkies to help keep in touch with everyone.

✔ **Pack to toddler-proof your hotel room.** Although your home may be toddler-proof, hotel rooms aren't. Bring outlet covers and whatever else is necessary to prevent an accident from occurring in your room.

✔ **Stay safe in the sun.** Don't forget to bring sunscreen for the entire family. If you forget, buy sunscreen with a 30 SPF or higher rating before you go out in the sun. Slather your young children — even if they're in a stroller — and make sure that you pack a hat for infants and toddlers. Likewise, make sure that everyone traveling with you drinks plenty of water to avoid dehydration.

✔ **Remember ride restrictions.** Most parks explain their height restrictions for certain attractions or identify those that may unsettle young children. (I also list these restrictions in my discussions of the major theme parks in Chapters 12–16 and 18–20.) Save yourself and your kids some grief before you get in line and experience disappointment. Remember that a bad trip down a darkened tunnel or a scary loop-de-loop can make your youngster cranky for the rest of the day.

✔ **Take time out for a show.** Catching an inside, air-conditioned show two or three times a day provides a nice break for everyone, especially on hot and steamy summer afternoons. You may even get your littlest tikes to nap in the darkened theater. Be sure to arrive at least 20 minutes early if you want good seats, but not so early that the kids go berserk waiting. (Most of the waiting areas are outside, even if the show is inside.)

✔ **Pack a snack.** When dreaming of your vacation, you probably don't envision hours spent waiting in lines. Unfortunately, doing so is inevitable. Store some lightweight snacks in an easy-to-carry backpack, especially when traveling with small kids. You'll save yourself headaches and money.

✔ **Bring your own stroller.** Although you have to haul it to and from the car and on and off trams, trains, and monorails at Disney, having your own stroller can be a tremendous help. It's with you when you need it — say, back in the hotel room as a high chair, or for an infant in a restaurant when a highchair is inappropriate. And it's an absolute lifesaver at **Universal Studios Florida** and **Islands of Adventure,** where you face long walks from the parking lot to the ticket booths. Your stroller should be lightweight, easy to fold and unfold with one hand, have a canopy, be able to recline for naps, and have plenty of storage space. The parks offer stroller rentals for between $7 and $15, however, these are hard and uncomfortable. They don't recline and have little or no storage space for kid gear. And they are absolutely inappropriate for infants and toddlers. They are good, however, if you have older kids who just need an occasional break from all the walking. For infants and small toddlers, you may want to bring a snugly sling or backpack-type carrier for use in traveling to and from parking lots and while you're standing in line for attractions.

✔ **Take a break.** The **Disney, Universal,** and **SeaWorld** parks all feature some rather unique play areas that offer parents a rest and the kids a place to continue to have fun. Schedule two or three visits to these spots a day, depending on your stamina. Many of these zones include water toys, and some parks have major water-related rides, so packing a change of clothes for the whole family is a good idea. Rent a locker ($5–$7) and store your spare duds until you need them. During summer months, the Florida humidity can keep you feeling soggy all day, so you'll appreciate the fresh clothing, especially if you're headed out for dinner afterwards.

✔ **Plan playtime for parents. Walt Disney World** and **Universal Orlando** offer a ride-share program for parents traveling with small children. On many "big kid" rides, one parent can ride the attraction while the other stays with the kids, and then the adults can switch places and the second parent can ride without having to stand in line again. Notify a staff member that you want to take advantage of this program when you get in line.

Finding kid-friendly tours

Many theme parks design tours for the younger set that include great sources of age-appropriate entertainment.

SeaWorld has justifiably earned its reputation as a park that makes education fun with a variety of tours. One of the most interesting is the *Polar Expedition Guided Tour.* This hour-long journey gives kids a chance to come face to face with a penguin and get a behind-the-scenes look at polar bears and beluga whales. *Saving a Species,* another hour-long tour, allows you to see some of the park's rescue and rehabilitation work with several species, including manatees and rare sea turtles. And shark fans will enjoy the *Predators* tour. All tours are kid-friendly, although the latter two may appeal more to older children. SeaWorld tours are offered on

More fun options for kids

Many of Disney's resorts offer special options for the young set. Here's just a sampling of the best programs for kids:

- **Disney's Grand Floridian Resort** offers a *Pirate Cruise Adventure,* where children ages 4 to 10 depart from the Grand Floridian Marina to visit exotic "ports of call" to follow clues and collect "buried treasure." Most kids will have a jolly good time. It's offered Monday, Wednesday, and Thursday from 9:30 to 11:30 a.m. and the $28 price tag includes lunch. *Grand Adventures in Cooking* invites up to 12 youngsters, 3 to 10 years old, to make dessert in a two-hour decorating class ($20 per child, usually Tues and Fri). The *Wonderland Tea Party* gives kids the same age a one-hour primer in cupcake decorating — with their fingers! They also feast on heart-shaped PBJs and sip apple juice "tea" while they play with Alice and the Mad Hatter ($23 per child, weekdays).

- **Disney's Animal Kingdom Lodge** features daily *Junior Researcher* (animal familiarization) and *Junior Chef* (cookie decorating) enrichment programs that are free for children staying at the lodge, as is the nightly African storytelling. Both programs are geared to potty-trained children ages 3 to 9; if you're interested, ask about them at check-in.

- At **Disney's Wilderness Lodge,** you can take advantage of a special family option that both kids and adults enjoy: *The Flag Family program.* If you're selected, the entire family can traipse up to the Wilderness Lodge's roof in the morning (times seem to vary, so ask) and raise the American flag that flies over the resort. You get a picture, a certificate, and a fabulous view. If you're interested, ask at the front desk upon check-in.

For information on all of the above programs, call ☎ **407-827-4321** or surf the Net to www.disneyworld.com for more information on all of Disney's family offerings.

a first-come, first-served basis, so reserve a place at the Guided Tour Information desk when you enter the park. They cost $15 per adult, $12 ages 3 to 9, in addition to park admission ($60 adults, $48 kids). Call ☎ **800-406-2244** or go to www.seaworld.com for more information.

At **Walt Disney World,** the *Family Magic Tour* features an interactive scavenger hunt and costs $25 per person, plus park admission ($60 for adults, $48 for children 3–9). Call ☎ **407-939-8687** or go to www.disneyworld.com.

Making Age Work for You: Tips for Seniors

Although Orlando is kid and family oriented, many of its hotels, restaurants, and attractions also roll out the red carpet for older travelers, especially those coming with grandkids. The theme parks don't offer discounted admission to seniors, but several attractions do, as does the city's public transport system. You can find other discounts from several sources listed in this section.

Members of **AARP** (formerly known as the American Association of Retired Persons), 601 E St. NW, Washington, DC 20049 (☎ 888-687-2277 or 202-434-2277; www.aarp.org), get discounts on hotels, airfares, and car rentals. AARP offers members a wide range of benefits, including *AARP: The Magazine* and a monthly newsletter. Anyone over 50 can join.

Many reliable agencies and organizations target the 50-plus market. **Elderhostel** (☎ 877-426-8056; www.elderhostel.org) arranges study programs for those aged 55 and over (as well as for a spouse or companion of any age) in the United States and in more than 80 countries around the world. Most courses last five to seven days in the United States (two to four weeks abroad), and many include airfare, accommodations in university dormitories or modest inns, meals, and tuition.

Recommended publications offering travel resources and discounts for seniors include: the quarterly magazine *Travel 50 & Beyond* (www.travel50andbeyond.com); *Travel Unlimited: Uncommon Adventures for the Mature Traveler* (Avalon); *101 Tips for Mature Travelers,* available from Grand Circle Travel (☎ 800-221-2610 or 617-350-7500; www.gct.com); *The 50+ Traveler's Guidebook* (St. Martin's Press); and *Unbelievably Good Deals and Great Adventures That You Absolutely Can't Get Unless You're Over 50* (McGraw-Hill), by Joann Rattner Heilman.

Accessing Orlando: Advice for Travelers with Disabilities

A disability need not prevent you from savoring the magic of Orlando and **Walt Disney World.** Many of the city's attractions and hotels are designed to accommodate the needs of individuals with disabilities, from specially equipped guest rooms to audio aids for the sight impaired. A little advance research and planning, however, is a smart idea.

Finding accommodating lodgings

Every hotel and motel in Florida is required by law to maintain a special room (or rooms) equipped for wheelchairs, but keep in mind that the law is being phased-in over time, so some hotels may not yet have rooms for those with disabilities. A few have wheel-in showers. **Walt Disney World's Coronado Springs Resort** (☎ 407-934-1000), which opened in 1997, maintains 99 rooms that are designed to accommodate guests with disabilities, so make your special needs known when making reservations. For other information about special Disney rooms, call ☎ 407-939-7807.

If you don't mind staying 15 minutes from Disney, **Yvonne's Property Management** (☎ 877-714-1144 or 863-424-0795; www.villasinorlando. com) is a rental agency for, among other things, some handicapped-accessible homes that have multiple-bedrooms, multiple-baths including accessible showers, full kitchens, and pools outfitted with lifts. Most cost less than $200 a night and are located in Davenport.

Getting around

Public buses in Orlando have hydraulic lifts and restraining belts for wheelchairs, and they serve **Universal Orlando, SeaWorld,** shopping areas, and downtown Orlando. When staying on **Disney** property, you can use shuttle buses that accommodate wheelchairs.

If you need to rent a wheelchair or an electric scooter for your visit, **Walker Medical & Mobility Products** will deliver one to your room; it offers a model that accommodates guests weighing up to 375 pounds that fits into Disney's transports and monorails and into rental cars. For more information, call ☎ 888-726-6837 or 407-518-6000; or visit Walker's Web site at www.walkermobility.com. You can also rent conventional and electric chairs daily at the theme parks (see Chapters 12–16 and 18–20).

Many of the major car-rental companies now offer hand-controlled cars for drivers with disabilities. See the Appendix in the back of the book for the major rental companies' toll-free numbers and Web sites. **Avis Rent-a-Car** has an **Avis Access** program that offers such services as a dedicated 24-hour toll-free number (☎ 888-879-4273) for customers with special travel needs; special car features such as swivel seats, spinner knobs, and hand controls; and accessible bus service.

Amtrak (☎ 800-872-7245; www.amtrak.com) can provide you with redcap service, wheelchair assistance, and special seats if you give 72-hour notice. Travelers with disabilities also are entitled to a 15 percent discount off the lowest available adult coach fare. Documentation from a doctor or an ID card proving your disability is required, however. Amtrak also provides wheelchair-accessible sleeping accommodations on its long-distance trains. Amtrak permits service dogs aboard, and they travel free. TTY service also is available at ☎ 800-523-6590 or by writing to P.O. Box 7717, Itasca, IL 60143.

Greyhound (☎ 800-752-4841; www.greyhound.com) allows a physically challenged passenger to travel with a companion for a single fare. When you call 48 hours in advance, the bus line also arranges assistance along the route of your trip. It also permits service dogs aboard.

Maneuvering through theme parks

All the parks offer parking as close as possible to the entrance for people with disabilities. Tell the parking booth attendant about your special needs, and he or she can direct you to the appropriate spot.

Each park's guide map tells you what to expect when you arrive. Most theme-park rides and shows, especially the newer ones, are designed to be accessible to a wide variety of guests. Likewise, theme parks often give people in wheelchairs (and their parties) preferential treatment so that they can avoid long lines. If you need crutches or suffer from some other medical problem that may restrict your mobility in any way, you're probably better off renting a wheelchair; the amount of walking you need to do in the parks may wear you down quickly. You can rent wheelchairs at most major Orlando attractions, but you'll probably be more comfortable in your chair from home (and will save some money, too).

Keep in mind, however, that wheelchairs wider than 24½ inches may make navigating through some attractions difficult. And crowds can make getting around tough for any guest.

Walt Disney World

The Magic Mickster offers a *Guidebook for Guests with Disabilities* that details many services. Disney no longer mails them prior to visits, but you can pick one up at *Guest Relations* near the entrances of the four parks. They're also available at some resorts. You can also call ☎ 407-824-4321 or ☎ 407-824-2222 for answers to questions about special needs. For accessibility issues relating to the WDW resorts, call ☎ 407-939-7807. A special link at the bottom of Disney's Web site at www.disneyworld.com leads to a host of information for those with disabilities. Examples of Disney services include the following:

✔ Almost all **Disney** resort hotels have rooms for people with disabilities.

✔ You can find Braille directories inside the **Magic Kingdom** in front of *City Hall,* and at *Guest Relations* in the other parks (a $25 refundable deposit is required). You can pick up complimentary guided-tour audiocassette tapes and recorders (a $25 refundable deposit is required) at *Guest Relations* to assist visually impaired guests.

✔ Assisted-listening devices are available to amplify the audio at selected attractions at WDW parks. At some attractions, guests also can get handheld wireless receivers that display captions about those attractions. (Both services are free but require a $25 refundable deposit). Inquire at *Guest Relations* inside each park.

✔ Sign translation is available for most of Disney's live shows on a rotating schedule: Mondays and Thursdays at the Magic Kingdom, Tuesdays and Fridays at Epcot, Sundays and Wednesdays at Disney–MGM Studios, and Saturdays at Disney's Animal Kingdom. Guests desiring sign translation should call Disney at ☎ 407-824-4321 (voice) or 407-827-5141 (TTY) at least two weeks in advance.

✔ Several attractions inside the major parks offer special closed-captioned LED screens for the hearing-impaired. Inquire at *Guest*

Relations inside each park for the list of attractions currently offering this option.

✔ Service animals are allowed in all parks and on some rides.

Universal Orlando

If you're physically challenged, go to *Guest Services,* located just inside the main entrances of **Universal Studios Florida** and **Islands of Adventure,** to get a *Riders Guide,* a Telecommunications Relay System (TTY), or other special assistance. You can rent wheelchairs from the concourse area of the parking garage. Wheelchairs can navigate the entry lines at all attractions with the exception of *Back to the Future,* which has a special access entrance. **Universal** also provides audio descriptions on cassette for visually impaired guests and has sign-language guides and scripts for its shows. (Advance notice is required; call ☎ **800-837-2273** or 407-363-8000 for details, or check each park's Web site at www.universalorlando.com for details.) Sign language–interpreting services are available at Universal Studios Florida or Islands of Adventure, at no charge. Arrangements for an appointment with an interpreter should be made one to two weeks in advance by contacting the **Sign Language Services Department** at ☎ **888-519-4899** (toll-free TTY), 407-224-4414 (local TTY), or 407-224-5929 (voice).

SeaWorld

SeaWorld provides a guide booklet for guests with disabilities, although most of its attractions are accessible to people in wheelchairs. You can pick one up at *Guest Services* inside the park or download it at www.seaworldorlando.com. **SeaWorld** also provides a Braille guide for the visually impaired and a very brief synopsis of its shows for the hearing impaired. Sign language–interpreting services are available at no charge, but must be reserved by calling ☎ **407-363-2414** at least a week in advance of your visit. Assisted-listening devices are available at select attractions for a $20 refundable deposit. For a complete rundown on all of your options, head to *Guest Services* when you enter the park; you can also call ☎ **407-351-3600** for more information.

Advice for Gay and Lesbian Travelers

The popularity of Orlando as a destination for gay and lesbian travelers is apparent in the development of the Gay Day Celebration at **Disney World** into **Gay Days** weekend festivities. Gay- and lesbian-related events also take place at **Universal** and **SeaWorld.** These festivals are scheduled the first weekend in June and draw tens of thousands of gay and lesbian travelers to Central Florida. Find information at www.gayday.com or www.gaydays.com.

You also can get information about events for **Gay Days** and for events that occur throughout the year from **Gay, Lesbian & Bisexual Community Services of Central Florida,** 934 N. Mills Ave., Orlando, FL

32803 (☎ **407-228-8272;** www.glbcc.org). Welcome packets usually include the latest issue of *Triangle,* dedicated to gay and lesbian issues, a calendar of events pertaining to Florida's gay and lesbian community, and information and ads for the area's clubs. **Gay Orlando Network** (www.gayorlando.com) is another good resource.

Both the entertainment industry and theme parks have helped build a strong gay and lesbian community in Orlando. Same-sex dancing is acceptable at most clubs at **WDW's Pleasure Island,** especially the large and very popular *Mannequins Dance Club.* Many of **Universal's CityWalk** establishments are similarly gender blind. The tenor of crowds can change, however, depending on what tour is in town, so respect your own intuition.

If you're interested in sampling some of the other local gay and lesbian hot spots, check out the following places:

- ✔ **The Club at Firestone,** 578 N. Orange Ave. at Concord Street, in a converted garage that still bears the Firestone sign (☎ **407-426-0005;** www.clubatfirestone.com). Go-go boys dance on lifts converted into raised platforms, and a diverse group boogies on the large concrete floor. This is a serious dance club, with dark lighting, cavernous rooms, and a high-energy atmosphere, which also sometimes features well-known DJs. Saturdays are the best day to visit for a heavy gay-centric crowd. It's open daily from 9 p.m. to 2 a.m. The cover charge varies from $5 to $10. Limited lot parking is available for $3 to $5.

- ✔ **Parliament House,** 410 N. Orange Blossom Trail just west of downtown (☎ **407-425-7571;** www.parliamenthouse.com). This resort is one of Orlando's wilder, and most popular, gay spots, although it's not particularly fancy and not in the best neighborhood in town. It is, however, a popular place to drink, dance, and watch shows that include female impersonators and male revues. The Parliament House has six bars and clubs. Its disco opens daily at 9 p.m., except on Sunday when things start up at 3 p.m.; show times vary. Cover charges vary but usually don't rise above $10.

- ✔ **Southern Nights,** 375 S. Bumby Ave. between Anderson Street and Colonial Drive (☎ **407-898-0424;** www.southern-nights.com). Voted "Best Gay Bar" by readers of a local alternative weekly paper, Southern Nights offers theme nights for women on Saturday and for men on Friday. Female-impersonator shows are featured during the week. At press time, it was closed for major renovations, but it's due to reopen in 2006. In the past it was open nightly, hours varying according to event. Cover charges vary but usually don't rise above $10. Self-parking is free, while valet parking costs $5.

The International Gay and Lesbian Travel Association (IGLTA) (☎ **800-448-8550** or 954-776-2626; www.iglta.org) is the trade association for the gay and lesbian travel industry and offers an online directory of gay- and lesbian-friendly travel businesses; go to their Web site and click on "Members."

Many agencies offer tours and travel itineraries specifically for gay and lesbian travelers. **Above and Beyond Tours** (☎ 800-397-2681; www. abovebeyondtours.com) is the exclusive gay and lesbian tour operator for United Airlines. **Now, Voyager** (☎ 800-255-6951; www.nowvoyager. com) is a well-known San Francisco–based gay-owned and operated travel service. **Olivia Cruises & Resorts** (☎ 800-631-6277 or 510-655-0364; www.olivia.com) charters entire resorts and ships for exclusive lesbian vacations and offers smaller group experiences for both gay and lesbian travelers.

The following travel guides are available at most travel bookstores and gay and lesbian bookstores, or you can order them from **Giovanni's Room** bookstore, 1145 Pine St., Philadelphia, PA 19107 (☎ 215-923-2960; www.giovannisroom.com); *Out and About* (☎ 800-929-2268 or 415-644-8044; www.outandabout.com), which offers guidebooks and a newsletter ($20/year; 10 issues) packed with solid information on the global gay and lesbian scene; *Spartacus International Gay Guide* (Bruno Gmünder Verlag; www.spartacusworld.com/gayguide) and *Odysseus,* both good, annual English-language guidebooks focused on gay men; the *Damron* guides (www.damron.com), with separate, annual books for gay men and lesbians; and *Gay Travel A to Z: The World of Gay & Lesbian Travel Options at Your Fingertips* by Marianne Ferrari (Ferrari International; Box 35575, Phoenix, AZ 85069), a very good gay and lesbian guidebook series.

Chapter 7

Taking Care of the Remaining Details

· ·

In This Chapter

▶ Sorting out your rental-car options
▶ Buying travel and medical insurance
▶ Dealing with illness away from home
▶ Staying in touch using the Web and cellphones
▶ Getting through airport security

· ·

*Y*ou're almost ready to leave for Orlando. All you need to do is take care of a few last-minute details, plan an itinerary, put the dog in the kennel, stuff your bags with everything that's clean, water the geraniums, pay the mortgage, and finish 50 other 11th-hour musts.

The information in this chapter gives you planning tips and saves you from wasting precious vacation hours after you're in Magic Mickeyville. You can discover whether it's worth your while to rent a car, get advice about buying travel insurance, check out your options should you get sick on your trip, find out how to keep in touch with your relatives back home, and figure out how to navigate your way through today's airline security procedures.

Renting a Car — Or Not

First off, you have to decide whether you need a rental car for your Orlando vacation. If you're going to spend most of your time at a resort, especially **Walt Disney World,** you may not need a car. Disney has its own free transportation system; buses, ferries, trams, and monorails run throughout the property, connecting all its resorts, parks, and entertainment venues. (See Chapter 8 for more information about the Disney transportation system.)

The Disney system does have some notable drawbacks: You're a prisoner of **WDW**'s often slow and indirect schedule. Depending on your starting point and your destination, it can take up to an hour to get where you're going. During peak hours in the busiest seasons, you may have trouble getting a seat on the bus, so keep that in mind if you're traveling with kids, seniors, or with companions with disabilities. Also, if you're bringing along children and strollers, consider the frustration factor of loading and unloading strollers and all their paraphernalia on and off buses, ferries, and trams.

If you plan to spend most of your time at **Universal Orlando** and stay at one of its resorts, a rental car may also be unnecessary. All of Universal's resorts offer boat transportation to its theme parks and **CityWalk** (See Chapters 18 and 19 for more on Universal's theme parks).

If you won't be spending all your time solely at either WDW or Universal, and you want to visit **SeaWorld** and other attractions or areas of Central Florida, you need to either rent a car or choose an alternate form of transportation, such as one of a number of hotel shuttles. (Some are free; others charge an average of $7–$12 per person.) **Mears Transportation,** which is a shuttle service, and taxis (though horridly expensive) are other options. (See Chapter 8 for more information on transportation options in Orlando, including the I-Ride Trolley.) Getting several people to the parks on a daily basis can be expensive if you choose these routes, but you can save on car-rental fees, gas, and the $8 or $9-per-day parking fee at the major attractions if you take advantage of Orlando's transit system. You need to decide whether the added convenience and mobility of a rental car is worth the extra expense; if you plan to be in Orlando only for a short while or are traveling with kids, I definitely recommend you shell out for the car in order to maximize your vacation mobility.

WDW has an **Alamo** car-rental desk (☎ **800-327-2996**) right on property, so if you're interested in renting only for a day or two instead of your entire vacation, this may be a good option for you.

Getting a good rate

Car rental rates vary even more than airline fares. The price depends on the size of the car, the length of time you keep it, where and when you pick it up and drop it off, where you take it, and a host of other factors. Doing a little research may save you hundreds of dollars.

- ✔ Weekend rates may be lower than weekday rates. If you're keeping the car five or more days, a weekly rate may be cheaper than the daily rate. Ask whether the rate is the same for pickup Friday morning as it is for Thursday night.

- ✔ Some companies may assess a drop-off charge if you don't return the car to the same rental location; others, notably National, don't.

- ✔ Check whether the rate is cheaper if you pick up the car at a location in town rather than at the airport.

- ✔ Find out whether age is an issue. For drivers under 25, many car-rental companies add on a fee, while some don't rent to them at all.

Under-age rental fees are common in Orlando and can add as much as $15 a day to your total rate.

✔ If you see an advertised price in your local newspaper, be sure to ask for that specific rate; otherwise you may be charged the standard (higher) rate. Don't forget to mention membership in AAA, AARP, and trade unions. These memberships usually entitle you to discounts ranging from 5 to 30 percent.

✔ Check your frequent-flier accounts. Not only are your favorite (or at least most-used) airlines likely to have sent you discount coupons, but most car rentals add at least 500 miles to your account.

✔ As with other aspects of planning your trip, using the Internet can make comparison shopping for a car rental much easier. You can check rates at most of the major agencies' Web sites. Plus, all the major travel sites — **Travelocity** (www.travelocity.com), **Expedia** (www.expedia.com), **Orbitz** (www.orbitz.com), and **Smarter Living** (www.smarterliving.com), for example — have search engines that can dig up discounted car-rental rates.

Most car-rental companies charge on a 24-hour basis. That means if you pick up the car at 3 p.m., you need to return it by 3 p.m. on the specified end date of your rental. Often, if your flight arrival and departure times in Orlando are far apart (say you arrive at 10 a.m. and don't fly out until 8 p.m.), you need to rent the car for a day longer than your stay. However, if the inbound and outbound flight times are within an hour or two of each other, inquire about hourly rates — they may be less than the cost of another full day. If you want information about specific rental-car companies serving Orlando, see the Appendix in the back of this book.

Adding up extra rental costs

In addition to the standard rental prices, other optional charges apply to most car rentals (and some not-so-optional charges, such as taxes). The **Collision Damage Waiver (CDW),** which requires you to pay for damage to the car in a collision, is covered by many credit-card companies. Check with your credit-card company before you go so you can avoid paying this hefty fee (as much as $20 a day).

The car-rental companies also offer additional **liability insurance** (if you harm others in an accident), **personal accident insurance** (if you harm yourself or your passengers), and **personal-effects insurance** (if your luggage is stolen from your car). Your insurance policy on your car at home probably covers most of these unlikely occurrences. However, if your own insurance doesn't cover you for rentals or if you don't have auto insurance, definitely consider the additional coverage (ask your car-rental agent for more information). Unless you're toting around the Hope diamond, and you don't want to leave that in your car trunk anyway, you can probably skip the personal-effects insurance, but driving around without liability or personal accident coverage is never a good idea. Even if you're a good driver, other people may not be, and liability claims can be complicated.

Some companies also offer **refueling packages,** in which you pay for your initial full tank of gas up front and can return the car with an empty gas tank. The prices can be competitive with local gas prices, but you don't get credit for any gas remaining in the tank. If you reject this option, you pay only for the gas you use, but you have to return the car with a full tank or face charges of $3 to $4 a gallon for any shortfall. If you usually run late and a fueling stop may make you miss your plane, you're a perfect candidate for the fuel-purchase option.

Playing It Safe with Travel and Medical Insurance

Three kinds of travel insurance are available: trip-cancellation insurance, medical insurance, and lost luggage insurance. The cost of travel insurance varies widely, depending on the cost and length of your trip, your age and health, and the type of trip you're taking, but expect to pay between 5 and 8 percent of the vacation itself. Here is my advice on all three:

✔ **Trip-cancellation insurance** helps you get your money back if you have to back out of a trip, if you have to go home early, or if your travel supplier goes bankrupt. Allowed reasons for cancellation can range from sickness to natural disasters to the State Department declaring your destination unsafe for travel. (Insurers usually won't cover vague fears, though, as many travelers discovered who tried to cancel their trips in Oct 2001 because they were wary of flying.)

A good resource is **Travel Guard Alerts,** a list of companies considered high-risk by Travel Guard International (www.travelinsured.com). Protect yourself further by paying for the insurance with a credit card — by law, consumers can get their money back on goods and services not received if they report the loss within 60 days after the charge is listed on their credit card statement.

Note: Many tour operators, particularly those offering trips to remote or high-risk areas, include insurance in the cost of the trip or can arrange insurance policies through a partnering provider, a convenient and often cost-effective way for the traveler to obtain insurance. Make sure the tour company is a reputable one, however, and avoid buying insurance from the tour or cruise company you're traveling with so you don't put all your money in one place.

✔ For domestic travel, buying **medical insurance** for your trip doesn't make sense for most travelers. Most existing health policies cover you if you get sick away from home — but check before you go, particularly if you're insured by an HMO.

✔ **Lost-luggage insurance** isn't necessary for most travelers. On domestic flights, checked baggage is covered up to $2,500 per ticketed passenger. On international flights (including U.S. portions of international trips), baggage coverage is limited to approximately $9 per pound, up to $635 per checked bag. If you plan to check items more valuable than the standard liability, see whether your valuables are covered by your homeowner's policy, get baggage insurance as part of your comprehensive travel-insurance package, or buy **Travel Guard's "BagTrak"** product. Don't buy the over-priced insurance at the airport. Be sure to take any valuables or irreplaceable items with you in your carry-on luggage because many valuables (including books, money and electronics) aren't covered by airline policies.

If your luggage is lost, immediately file a lost-luggage claim at the airport, detailing the luggage contents. For most airlines, you must report delayed, damaged, or lost baggage within four hours of arrival. The airlines are required to deliver luggage, once found, directly to your house or destination free of charge.

For more information, contact one of the following recommended insurers: **Access America** (☎ 866-807-3982; www.accessamerica.com); **Travel Guard International** (☎ 800-826-4919; www.travelguard.com); **Travel Insured International** (☎ 800-243-3174; www.travelinsured.com); and **Travelex Insurance Services** (☎ 888-457-4602; www.travelex-insurance.com).

Staying Healthy When You Travel

Getting sick can ruin your vacation, so I *strongly* advise against it. (Of course, last time I checked, the bugs weren't listening to me any more than they probably listen to you.)

If you have a serious or chronic illness, talk to your doctor before leaving on a trip. For conditions such as epilepsy, diabetes, or heart problems, wear a **MedicAlert identification tag** (☎ 888-633-4298; www.medicalert.org), which immediately alerts doctors to your condition and gives them access to your records through Medic Alert's 24-hour hot line.

Preventing the easily preventable

The biggest health obstacle you'll encounter in Orlando will be the strong Florida sun. Limit your exposure, especially during the first few days of your trip and, thereafter, during the hours of 10 a.m. to 2 p.m., when the sun is at its strongest. Use a sunscreen with at least a sun protection factor (SPF) of 25 (especially for children) and apply it liberally and often. If you have children under a year old, check with your pediatrician before applying a sunscreen — some ingredients may not be appropriate for infants. A hat and sunglasses are de rigueur fashion in Florida for a reason and keep you from suffering sun glare or a painful sunburn.

Dehydration is another potential issue when touring Orlando. Be sure to drink plenty of fluids and see that any children traveling with you do so as well. Note that soft drinks loaded with caffeine, a diuretic, can cause or make dehydration worse, so stick to water or decaffeinated drinks.

Finally, the bane of many a theme park walker who hasn't hoofed it anywhere lately are blisters. If you have problematic feet, bring comfortable walking shoes, lots of socks, and buy some protective moleskin. A change of socks mid-day may keep you from hobbling by nightfall.

Knowing what to do should you get sick

All the major theme parks have first-aid stations; ask a park employee or consult your park map for its location. **Doctors on Call Service** (☎ **407-399-3627**) is a group that makes house and room calls in most of the Orlando area 24 hours a day.

To find a dentist, call **Dental Referral Service** (☎ **800-235-4111;** www. dentalreferral.com). They can refer you to the nearest dentist who meets your needs. Phones are staffed weekdays from 10 a.m. to 7 p.m.

If your ailment isn't a life-threatening emergency, use a walk-in clinic in Orlando. You may not get immediate attention, but you'll probably pay around $75 rather than the $300 minimum for just signing in at an emergency-room counter. **Centra-Care** (www.centracare.org) has several walk-in clinics listed in the Yellow Pages, including ones on Vineland Road near Universal (☎ **407-351-6682**) and at Lake Buena Vista near Disney (☎ **407-934-2273**) among others.

You can fill your prescriptions at dozens of pharmacies listed in the Yellow Pages. **Walgreen**'s operates a 24-hour pharmacy at 7650 W. Sand Lake Rd. (☎ **407-345-9497;** www.walgreens.com); for other locations in the area, check the company's Web site.

Staying Connected by Cellphone or E-mail

Want to tell the folks back home that you arrived safe and sound? Or e-mail them that digital snapshot of your meeting with Mickey? It's easier than ever to stay in touch with your friends, family, even the office (unlucky for you), while you're on the road.

Using a cellphone across the U.S.

Just because your cellphone works at home doesn't mean it'll work elsewhere in the country (thanks to our nation's fragmented cellphone system). It's a good bet that your phone will work in Orlando, however. But take a look at your wireless company's coverage map on its Web site before heading out — T-Mobile, Sprint, and Nextel are particularly weak in rural areas. If your wireless company doesn't have good coverage in the Orlando area, **rent** a phone that does from **InTouch USA** (☎ **800-872-7626;** www.intouchglobal.com) or a rental-car location, but beware that you'll pay $1 a minute or more for airtime.

If you're not from the U.S., you'll be appalled at the poor reach of our **GSM (Global System for Mobiles) wireless network,** which is used by much of the rest of the world. Your phone will probably work in most major U.S. cities; it definitely won't work in many rural areas. (To see where GSM phones work in the U.S., check out www.t-mobile.com/coverage/national_popup.asp). And you may or may not be able to send SMS (text messaging) home. Assume nothing — call your wireless provider and get the full scoop. In a worst-case scenario, you can always rent a phone; InTouch USA delivers to hotels.

Accessing the Internet away from home

Travelers have any number of ways to check their e-mail and access the Internet on the road. Of course, using your own laptop — or even a PDA (personal digital assistant) or electronic organizer with a modem — gives you the most flexibility.

But even if you don't have a computer, you can still access your e-mail and even your office computer from cybercafes. It's hard nowadays to find a city that *doesn't* have a few cybercafes. Although there's no definitive directory for cybercafes — these are independent businesses, after all — two places to start looking are at **www.cybercaptive.com** and **www.cybercafe.com**.

Inside **Walt Disney World,** you can find an Internet cafe inside *DisneyQuest,* and you can also send e-mail at *Innoventions* in **Epcot,** though you have to pay the park admission fees to use the Web terminals. Payphones with touch-screen displays offering Internet access have been installed at locations throughout Walt Disney World; you can access your e-mail for 25¢ a minute with a 4-minute minimum.

Aside from formal cybercafes, most **public libraries** offer Internet access free or for a small charge. Avoid **hotel business centers** unless you're willing to pay exorbitant rates.

Most major airports now have **Internet kiosks** scattered throughout their gates. These kiosks, which you'll also see in shopping malls, hotel lobbies, and tourist information offices, give you basic Web access for a per-minute fee that's usually higher than cybercafe prices. The kiosks' clunkiness and high price mean they should be avoided whenever possible.

To retrieve your e-mail, ask your **Internet Service Provider (ISP)** whether it has a Web-based interface tied to your existing e-mail account. If your ISP doesn't have such an interface, you can use the free **mail2web** service (www.mail2web.com) to view and reply to your home e-mail. For more flexibility, you may want to open a free, Web-based e-mail account with **Yahoo! Mail** (http://mail.yahoo.com). (Microsoft's Hotmail is another popular option, but Hotmail has severe spam problems.) Your home ISP may be able to forward your e-mail to the Web-based account automatically.

If you are bringing your own computer, the buzzword in computer access is **Wi-Fi** (wireless fidelity), where you can get high-speed connection without cable wires, networking hardware, or a phone line, and more and more hotels, cafes, and retailers are signing on as wireless "hotspots." You sign up for wireless-access service much as you do cellphone service, through a plan offered by one of several commercial companies that have made wireless service available in airports, hotel lobbies, and coffee shops. **T-Mobile Hotspot** (www.t-mobile.com/hotspot) serves up wireless connections at more than 1,000 Starbucks coffee shops nationwide. **Boingo** (www.boingo.com) and **Wayport** (www.wayport.com) have set up networks in airports and high-class hotel lobbies. Best of all, you don't need to be staying at the Four Seasons to use the hotel's network; just set yourself up on a nice couch in the lobby. The companies' pricing policies can be Byzantine, with a variety of monthly, per-connection, and per-minute plans, but, in general, you pay around $30 a month for limited access — and as more and more companies jump on the wireless bandwagon, prices are likely to get even more competitive.

You can also find a few **free wireless networks.** To locate these free hotspots, go to www.personaltelco.net/index.cgi/Wireless Communities.

WDW offers Wi-Fi access and high-speed Internet connections to guests at several of its resorts, and all **Universal Orlando**'s resorts offer high-speed Internet access. Most business and higher-end hotels in Orlando offer at least an in-room dataport and several offer Internet connections. You can bring your own cables, but most hotels rent them for around $10. Call your hotel in advance to see what your options are.

In addition, major Internet Service Providers (ISP) have **local access numbers** in Orlando, allowing you to go online by simply placing a local call. Check your ISP's Web site or call its toll-free number and ask how you can use your current account away from home and how much it will cost.

Keeping Up with Airline Security

With the federalization of airport security, security procedures at U.S. airports are more stable and consistent than ever. Generally, you'll be fine if you arrive at the airport one hour before a domestic flight and two hours before an international flight; if you show up late, tell an airline employee and he or she will probably whisk you to the front of the line.

Bring a **current, government-issued photo ID** such as a driver's license or passport. Keep your ID at the ready to show at check-in, the security checkpoint, and sometimes even the gate. (Children under 18 don't need government-issued photo IDs for domestic flights, but they do for international flights to most countries.)

In 2003, the Transportation Security Administration (TSA) phased out gate check-in at all U.S. airports. And **E-tickets** have made paper tickets nearly obsolete. Passengers with E-tickets can beat the ticket-counter lines by using airport **electronic kiosks** or even **online check-in** from your home computer. To check-in online, log on to your airlines' Web site, access your reservation, and print out your boarding pass — the airline may even offer you bonus miles to do so! If you're using a kiosk at the airport, bring the credit card you used to book the ticket or your frequent-flier card. Print out your boarding pass from the kiosk and simply proceed to the security checkpoint with your pass and a photo ID. If you're checking bags or looking to snag an exit-row seat, you can do so using most airline kiosks. Even the smaller airlines are employing the kiosk system, but always call your airline to make sure these alternatives are available. **Curbside check-in** is also a good way to avoid lines, although a few airlines still ban curbside check-in; call before you go.

Security checkpoint lines are getting shorter than they were during 2001 and 2002, but some doozies remain. If you have trouble standing for long periods of time, tell an airline employee; the airline will provide a wheelchair. Speed up security by not wearing metal objects such as big belt buckles. If you've got metallic body parts, a note from your doctor can prevent a long chat with the security screeners. Keep in mind that only ticketed passengers are allowed past security, except for folks escorting disabled passengers or unaccompanied children.

Federalization has stabilized **what you can carry on** and **what you can't**. The general rule is that sharp things are out, nail clippers are okay, and food and beverages must be passed through the X-ray machine — but security screeners can't make you drink from your coffee cup. Bring food in your carryon rather than checking it, as explosive-detection machines used on checked luggage have been known to mistake food (especially chocolate, for some reason) for bombs. Travelers in the U.S. are allowed one carry-on bag, plus a personal item such as a purse, briefcase, or laptop bag. You can stuff all sorts of things into a laptop bag; as long as it has a laptop in it, it's still considered a personal item. The TSA has issued a list of restricted items; check its Web site (www.tsa.gov/public/index.jsp) for details.

Airport screeners may decide that your checked luggage needs to be searched by hand. You can now purchase luggage locks that allow screeners to open and re-lock a checked bag if hand-searching is necessary. Look for **Travel Sentry certified locks** at luggage or travel shops and Brookstone stores (you can buy them online at www.brookstone.com). These locks, approved by the TSA, can be opened by luggage inspectors with a special code or key. For more information on the locks, visit www.travelsentry.org. If you use something other than TSA-approved locks, your lock will be cut off your suitcase if a TSA agent needs to hand-search your luggage.

Part III
Settling into Orlando

The 5th Wave
By Rich Tennant

"Oh, that? That's part of our character dining experience. Haven't you ever seen 'A Bug's Life'?"

In this part . . .

*O*rlando isn't New York or London, but it can seem overwhelming at first. Getting around the tourist areas and
downtown Orlando can be a little intimidating. Don't worry,
though — it isn't as complicated as it looks. In this part, I
walk you through the city's neighborhoods, tell you where
to catch local transportation, and erase any confusion you
may have.

Once you've got your bearings, I review the city's best hotels
so you can zero in on a room that's right for you. Then I detail
Orlando's A-List eateries and give you lists of the city's best
restaurants by price, location, and cuisine. And for dessert,
you get a thorough rundown of that most quintessential of
Orlando experiences — character meals.

Chapter 8

Arriving and Getting Oriented

. . . .

In This Chapter

▶ Landing at the airport

▶ Exploring Orlando's neighborhoods

▶ Getting information when you arrive

▶ Exploring Orlando's transportation options

. . . .

*A*ll roads in Orlando *don't* lead to **Disney,** although the reverse may seem true to first-time visitors. Yes, you'd be hard-pressed to drive along a street or highway without coming across a sign directing you to **Walt Disney World,** but this abundance of directions doesn't mean that you won't find other signs pointing you to the rest of the city's highlights. In this chapter, you take the first step, getting from the airport to the parks, and you gain some insight about Orlando's "other" major neighborhoods.

Arriving in Orlando

Unlike many tourist-oriented cities, Orlando's airports do not lie in the heart of the city's action. But fear not — both of the cities airports are relatively user-friendly, and getting to the any one of the theme parks is a generally hassle-free experience.

Navigating the airport

While some of your fellow travelers (in particular, those unfortunate souls who didn't read this book) are aimlessly meandering through the hallways of the **Orlando International Airport** (☎ **407-825-2001;** www. orlandoairports.net), you'll zippity-do-dah to baggage claim and into your chariot of choice. Though the airport itself is generally easy to navigate, it's usually quite busy, there are plenty of distractions, and it can take you a while to get from point A to point B.

Follow the signs carefully to get from the terminal you land in to baggage claim. (You may need to take the tram to the main terminal and then go to Level 2 for your bags.) *Note:* If you're arriving from a foreign country, you have to go through Immigration before baggage claim and then through Customs after picking up your luggage.

If you need cash, ATMs are located in the arrival and departure terminals near the three pods of gates (1–29, 30–59, and 60–99). ATMs also are located where shuttles deposit you in the main terminal. If you need to convert your pounds, euros, and so on to U.S. dollars, you can find currency exchanges (open 9:30 a.m.–8 p.m.) opposite the ATMs at the locations described above.

Most major car-rental companies are located at the airport (on Level 1) with others located a mile or so down the road. Keep in mind that if the company you choose is at a nearby location instead of right on-site, you'll need to take the shuttle to pick up your car. (See the Appendix in the back of this book for the toll-free numbers of the major rental companies.) You can catch hotel shuttles or taxis on the ground level of the main terminal.

If you're arriving on one of the newer regional or international budget airlines that serves **Orlando Sanford Airport** (☎ 407-585-4000; www.orlandosanfordairport.com), you'll appreciate the smaller airport layout. Baggage claim is downstairs, ATMs are found in the gate areas, and most of the car-rental companies have locations right at the airport.

Finding your way to your hotel

The **Orlando International Airport** is a 25- to 40-minute hop, skip, and long jump from Walt Disney World, depending on traffic, and 15 to 25 minutes from Universal Orlando and downtown. **Mears Transportation Group** (☎ 407-423-5566; www.mearstransportation.com) is the major shuttle player. It runs vans between the airport (you board at ground level) and all Disney resorts and official hotels, and most other area properties, every 15 to 25 minutes. Round-trip to downtown Orlando or International Drive is $25 for adults ($18 for kids 4–11); it's $29 for adults ($21 for kids) to **Walt Disney World/Lake Buena Vista** or Kissimmee/U.S. 192.

Quick Silver Tours &Transportation (☎ 407-299-1434; www.quicksilver-tours.com) is more personal. You're greeted at baggage claim with a sign bearing your name. The cost is more than Mears, but it's coming for you, not other travelers, too. And it's going only to your resort. Included is an array of services, including a quick stop for groceries. Rates run $70 (up to four, round-trip) to I-Drive/Universal Orlando and $90 to $100 to Disney. If you have a larger group (five or more, round-trip) and require a van, the rates run $85 to Universal and I-Drive and $105 to $115 to Disney. **A Selective Transportation** (☎ 888-784-2522 or 407-354-2456; www.selectivelimo.com) is another company that offers a very high level of service. For $180, you get round-trip stretch limo service from the airport to your hotel for up to eight people; the price includes a free stop at a supermarket for food supplies, safety seats for any children in your party, and a complimentary stuffed Mickey Mouse for the kids. Cheaper shuttle rates are also available; check their Web site for specials.

Taxis are another option when your party has enough people. The standard rates for **Ace Metro** (☎ 407-855-0564) and **Yellow Cab** (☎ 407-699-9999) run as high as $3.25 for the first mile and $1.75 per mile thereafter, although you can sometimes get a flat rate. A one-way trip to the I-Drive area could cost upwards of $30 or more, to Disney closer to $60, and to the U.S. 192 area, expect to pay around $50. Vans and taxis load on the ground level of the airport.

A few hotels offer free shuttle service to and from the airport, so be sure to ask when booking your room. Hotel shuttles load on the ground level.

If you're driving from the airport with a rental car, you have two options. You can take the north exit out of the airport to 528 West (a toll road, also known as the BeeLine Expressway). Follow the signs to I-4, then go west to exits marked for Disney (you'll find three), and follow the signs to the appropriate area. Your drive should take about 30 to 40 minutes if traffic isn't too heavy. Disney exits are clearly marked on big green signs. This route is also best if heading to Universal Orlando, SeaWorld, or the International Drive area. If your destination is solely Disney, you can also take the south exit from the airport, which leads you down Boggy Creek Road to SR 417 West (another toll road known as the Greeneway). Exit onto 536 and follow the signs straight into Disney. This route has less traffic but costs about an extra dollar in tolls.

When you're traveling from **Orlando Sanford Airport,** a rental car is really your best bet — even if you only rent it for the days you arrive and depart Orlando (if this is the case, choose a company with locations in or near your hotel for pick-ups and drop-offs). Taxi or shuttle service from the airport is expensive; expect a minimum fare of $60 to the Universal Orlando/International Drive areas and a minimum fare of $100 to the Disney and Kissimmee areas.

Upon leaving Sanford airport, exit onto Lake Mary Boulevard. From here, you can take the 417/Greeneway exit and follow that to Disney. Or you can go past that exit and take the one for I-4 West, which leads you past downtown to all the major theme-park attractions. Again, the Greeneway is the less traveled, faster route, but it's a toll road. For either route, expect about 45 minutes to the Universal Orlando/International Drive areas and about 60 minutes to Disney (even longer if driving I-4 between 3 and 6 p.m.).

Figuring Out the Neighborhoods

Though the area encompassing the various theme parks and their accompanying paraphernalia (hotels, restaurants, and so on) is almost always referred to as Orlando, the region is actually made up of some very distinct sections, several of which are not actually in Orlando proper at all.

Walt Disney World

The empire, its big and little parks, resorts, restaurants, shops, and assorted trimmings, are scattered across 30,500 acres, or a total area of about 41 square miles. What you may find most surprising is that **WDW** isn't really located in Orlando at all — it's just southwest of the city proper, off I-4 between West U.S. 192 and S.R. 535. If you choose to stay with Mickey you'll find that convenience has its price. Accommodations at the mouse's house can run as much as double the price of nearby Kissimmee hotels and resorts. On the plus side, you get access to the free Disney Transportation System (though at times that may not be that big of plus) and a handful of perks and privileges (such as early park entry and extra evening hours) that are extended only to Disney resort guests.

Also on Disney property is **Downtown Disney,** an area off to itself encompassing three very distinctive zones: **Downtown Disney West Side** and **Pleasure Island,** Disney's two nighttime entertainment districts, and **Downtown Disney Marketplace,** the nearby shopping district. Combined, they're filled with restaurants, shops, entertainment venues, and clubs; each quite unique in its offerings, atmosphere, and price. Downtown Disney is closest to the Lake Buena Vista zone described later.

 Even if you're not staying or driving in Mickeyville, getting a map of the Walt Disney World Transportation System is a good idea, so you can see where everything is. It's currently included in *Disney's Planning Guide to Recreation, Dining, and Shopping,* which is free and available at the *Guest Relations* desks inside all the Disney hotels and theme parks.

Lake Buena Vista

Lake Buena Vista is Disney's next-door neighborhood. It's where you find "official" (yet not Disney-owned) hotels, and it's close to **Downtown Disney** and all of its offerings. This charming area has manicured lawns, tree-lined thoroughfares, and free transportation throughout the realm, but it may take a while to get from Point A to Point B because of a combination of slow shuttle service and heavy traffic. There is a plethora of shops, services, and restaurants practically at your doorstep, and all within minutes from the Mouse. Although this area is not nearly as costly as Walt Disney World itself, it's generally more expensive than International Drive and Kissimmee.

Orlando Neighborhoods

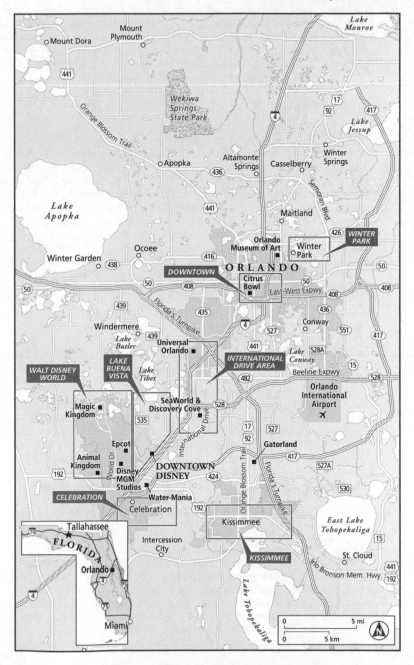

Celebration

Imagine an entire town designed by Disney, with perfect white picket fences, tree lined walkways, and gingerbread trimmed houses. In **Celebration,** Disney redesigned reality to reflect an idealized version of Small Town, U.S.A. The 4,900-acre town has thousands of residents living in beautiful colonial-and Victorian-inspired homes. Celebration's downtown area is, however, designed for tourists, though it does have charming appeal. It's filled with upscale shops, boutiques, restaurants, and coffee shops, and it even has its own small, yet elegant, hotel.

Kissimmee

Way back before Mickey moved to town, **Kissimmee** was the hotspot. Overlooked, in recent years, with the expansion of the International Drive and Lake Buena Vista tourist districts, Kissimmee is being revived and made more tourist-friendly with the addition of wide walkways, landscaping, and improved roadways. Although still filled with some of the tackier T-shirt shops and tourist traps in the area, some moderately priced hotels and even a few luxury resorts have begun to spring up just to the south. Kissimmee is only a short drive (roughly 10–15 miles) southeast from the House of Mouse and, with plenty of modest motels and resorts, it's a great choice for travelers on a budget. The town centers on U.S. 192/Irlo Bronson Memorial Highway, which, alas, is perennially under construction.

International Drive

Known locally as I-Drive, the tourist mecca of **International Drive** extends 7 to 10 miles north of the Disney kingdom between Highway 535 and the Florida Turnpike. From bungee jumping and skate boarding, surfing to shopping, themed restaurants, more than a hundred hotels, and a slew of shops, this stretch of road is *the* tourist strip in Central Florida. It's home to the **Orange County Official Visitors Center** and offers easy access to **SeaWorld** and **Universal Orlando.** The northern half of I-Drive beyond Sand Lake Road is already packed, and developers continue to eat up space in the southern half, especially near the Orange County Convention Center; south of the Bee Line Expressway (528) the resorts become far more spread out than in the north. Traffic along this route is perennially problematic, so be sure to allot plenty of extra time if you're traveling on it during the morning and evening rush hours.

Dr. Phillips

Once a non-descript residential area dotted with a few odd shops and doctors offices, the **Sand Lake strip** of **Dr. Phillips,** just west of I-4, has been developed into an upscale shopping and dining mecca. The new mall complexes at the intersection of West Sand Lake Road and Dr. Phillips Boulevard now host no fewer than a dozen fine dining restaurants. For a quiet and sophisticated dining experience, outside the commotion of the theme parks, this is by far your best bet.

Downtown Orlando

Right off I-4 East, **Downtown Orlando** is actually north of the theme-park areas and is home to loads of clubs, shops, cultural attractions, and restaurants. Dozens of antiques shops line **Antique Row** on Orange Avenue near Lake Ivanhoe. Hotels in this area are mostly aimed at business travelers, as this is also the commercial center of the city and isn't a convenient place to stay if visiting the theme parks is the major point of your trip to Orlando. A few B&Bs draw couples seeking more sophisticated surroundings, and it is a great place for a night out on the town.

Winter Park

Just north of downtown Orlando, the quiet town of **Winter Park** is where many of Central Florida's old-money families call home (and where new-money ones come to shop and dine). It's noteworthy for **Park Avenue,** a collection of upscale shops and restaurants along a tree lined, cobblestone street. Winter Park's appeal comes from its sophisticated, yet charming, upscale offerings and has little, if any, kid appeal. It's definitely too far north to use as a home base if you plan on spending much of your time at the Disney parks. If you want some quiet time away from the theme-park madness, though, it's a nice place to spend an afternoon.

Finding Information after You Arrive

 After you've landed, your best and most immediate source for up-to-date information is the concierge or the front desk at your hotel (especially if you're staying at Disney or Universal, as they're more knowledgeable than most).

If you're in the International Drive area, stop for information at the official **Orlando Visitors Center,** 8723 International Dr. (☎ **407-363-5872;** www.orlandoinfo.com), just four blocks south of Sand Lake Road.

Both the *Orlando Weekly* (distributed every Thurs) and Friday's calendar section in the *Orlando Sentinel* include plenty of tourist-friendly information about dining and entertainment.

At Orlando International Airport, arriving passengers can find assistance at **The Magic of Disney** (third level, right behind the Northwest Airlines ticket counter) and **Disney Earport** (across from the Hyatt Regency), two shops located in the main terminal. They sell Disney multiday park tickets, make dinner, show, and hotel reservations, and provide brochures and information. Facilities are open daily from 7 a.m. to 8 p.m.

Also in the main terminal at the airport, you'll find two locations each of the **Universal Studios Store** and the **SeaWorld Store,** as well as a **Kennedy Space Center Store.** All provide similar services with ticketing and are open daily from 7 a.m. to 8 p.m.

Getting Around Orlando

Your major decision regarding Orlando transportation will be whether to use **Walt Disney World**'s transportation system (which is truly useful only to those staying at a **WDW** resort), use your own car (yours or a rental), or stick to other means. The system that works best for you depends on what you want to see, where you're staying, and how much time (and money) you want to spend getting around the city.

By Disney's transportation system

If you plan to stay at a Disney resort or an official hotel (see Chapter 9 for more information about Disney hotels) and spend the majority of your time visiting Disney parks, you can probably skip a rental car — at least for most of your stay. A free transportation network runs through **Disney World.** Buses, ferries, water taxis, and monorails operate from two hours prior to the parks' opening until two hours after closing. Likewise, Disney offers service to **Downtown Disney, Typhoon Lagoon, Blizzard Beach, Pleasure Island, Fort Wilderness Resort & Campground,** and all the Disney resorts.

The advantages of using Disney's transportation system include

- ✔ It's free.
- ✔ You save on car-rental and gasoline charges.
- ✔ You don't have to pay $8 a day to park in the theme-park lots. (*Note:* Disney resort guests are exempt from parking fees at the theme parks.)
- ✔ If your party wants to split up, you can easily head elsewhere while others remain behind without being stranded.
- ✔ During busy periods when Disney's parking lots may close (and this does happen), those riding the transportation system will still get to the parks.

Disadvantages include

- ✔ You're at the mercy of Disney's schedule.
- ✔ The shortest distance between two points is not always a straight line. You may very well have to take a ferry to catch a bus to get on the monorail to reach your hotel. The system makes a complete circuit, but doesn't necessarily travel the most direct route for *you.* It can take an hour or more to get somewhere that's right across a lagoon from you.
- ✔ You must endure multiple stops, particularly on buses and at peak periods, with crowds that may well force you to wait for the next bus.
- ✔ Parents may find herding young children and their accompanying paraphernalia off and on buses exhausting.

If you plan to travel on the Disney network, first verify with the driver, the bell staff, or someone at your hotel's guest-relations desk that you're taking the most direct route. Keep asking questions along the way. Unlike missing a highway exit, missing a stop on the bus route means you have to take another ride on the Mickey-go-round.

By car

Most visitors to Orlando — especially those staying a week or more — choose to rent a car for at least a day or two in order to venture beyond the parks. (Yes, there *is* far more to Florida than its thrills and theme parks.) See Chapter 7 for more information on renting a car in Orlando; check out the Appendix at the back of this book for toll-free numbers of various car-rental agencies.

Orlando's major artery is ***Interstate 4.*** Locals call it I-4 or that #@$*%^#!! road, because it's often horridly congested, especially during weekday rush hours (7–9 a.m. and 4–6 p.m.), when it more likely resembles a parking lot. I-4 runs diagonally across the state from Tampa to Daytona Beach. Exits from I-4 lead to all WDW properties, Universal Orlando, SeaWorld, International Drive, U.S. 192, Kissimmee, Lake Buena Vista, downtown Orlando, and Winter Park. Most of the exits are well marked, but construction is common, and exit numbers occasionally change. If you get directions by exit number, always for ask the name of the road as well to avoid getting lost. (Cellphone users can call ☎ 511 to get a report of I-4 delays.)

Despite the fact that when you look at any map of the area it will seem that I-4 runs north to south, on road signs, it's always listed as east and west. To avoid getting lost, remember that I-4 west takes you towards Disney World (and Tampa) from Universal Orlando, I-Drive and downtown Orlando; I-4 east heads from Disney and Kissimmee towards Universal Orlando (and Daytona).

The **Florida Turnpike** crosses I-4, near Universal Orlando, and links with I-75 to the north. U.S. 192, a major east-west artery that's also called the Irlo Bronson Memorial Highway, reaches from Kissimmee to U.S. 27, crossing I-4 near the **WDW** entrance road. Farther north, the BeeLine Expressway toll road (or Hwy. 528) goes east from I-4 past **Orlando International Airport** to Cape Canaveral and the **Kennedy Space Center.** The East-West Expressway (also known as Hwy. 408) is another toll road that runs from I-4 near downtown east to SR 50 by the University of Central Florida. The final major toll road, SR 417 (also known as the Greeneway), partially encircles the eastern edge of Orlando starting at I-4 just south of Disney and winds past the southern edge of Orlando International Airport before ending up near the northern edge of Orlando by the Orlando Sanford Airport.

One of the area's lesser known roads, **Turkey Lake Road** runs parallel to I-4 and is often used by locals to avoid the heavy traffic of I-4 from **WDW** to **Universal Orlando.** It starts as the Palm Parkway near Disney and turns into Turkey Lake Road just past the hotel area, eventually running right up to Universal. It intersects with both Central Florida Parkway, which takes you right to **SeaWorld,** and Sand Lake Road, which takes you to both Dr. Phillips and the I-Drive areas.

Here are a few (in some cases, redundant) tips for driving in Orlando.

- ✔ Remember to allow for rush-hour traffic from 7 to 9 a.m. and 4 to 6 p.m. daily.

- ✔ In Florida, you can turn right on red after coming to a full stop and making sure that the coast is clear (unless signs say otherwise). Consider yourself warned: If you're sitting at a red light with your blinker on and not turning right, you'll probably hear horns blaring. Make sure that your path is clear and then *move it.*

- ✔ Don't try to drive and read the road map at the same time (it just needed to be said).

- ✔ Posted speed limits are enforced vigorously. Fines for speeding begin at more than $150. Pay particular attention to road construction and school zones, where speed limits are reduced and speeding fines are doubled — they're not kidding.

- ✔ Remember the Name Game: International Drive is called I-Drive. Irlo Bronson Memorial Highway is U.S. 192 or just 192. Highway 528 is the BeeLine Expressway. State Route 535 is also known as Apopka Vineland. State Road 50 is more commonly called Colonial Drive, and Highway 417 is also known as the Greeneway.

- ✔ You must have a handicap permit to park in handicap parking places. Handicap permits from other states are honored, but a disabled license plate alone won't do.

- ✔ Buckle up: Florida law says front- and rear-seat passengers alike must wear a seat belt. This includes children, who, if younger than age 5, must be restrained in an approved safety seat (seat belt or booster seat) and, if younger than age 3, in an approved car seat. If you don't want to bring your own from home, most car-rental agencies can provide one for about $10 a day.

- ✔ In an emergency, dial ☎ **911,** or you can reach the Florida Highway Patrol on a cellphone by dialing ☎ ***FHP.**

By taxi

Yellow Cab (☎ 407-699-9999) and **Ace Metro** (☎ 407-855-0564) are among the taxicab companies serving the Orlando area. But for day-to-day travel to and from the attractions or restaurants, cabs are expensive unless your group has five or more people. Rates can run as high as $3.25 for the first mile and $1.75 per mile thereafter, though sometimes you can get a flat rate.

By shuttle

Mears Transportation Group (☎ **407-423-5566;** www.mears transportation.com) operates shuttle buses to all major attractions, including **Universal Orlando, SeaWorld,** and **Disney.** Shuttles also run to **Kennedy Space Center** at Cape Canaveral and **Busch Gardens** in Tampa and it is also one of the most cost effective of all the shuttle services available. (For more about great attractions just outside of Orlando, see Chapter 23.) Rates vary by destination.

By trolley

The **I-Ride Trolley** on International Drive (☎ **407-248-9590;** www.iride trolley.com) runs every 20 to 30 minutes, from 8 a.m. to 10:30 p.m. (75¢ for adults, 25¢ for seniors, kids younger than 12 ride free; exact change is required). An unlimited one-day pass also is available for $2 per person. The main route runs from the Belz Factory Outlet Malls to SeaWorld with an additional route that runs along Universal Boulevard from Sea World Road to Kirkman Road. Because of I-Drive's heavy traffic, the trolley is usually the best way to get around whenever you're staying or spending a good portion of the day in this area.

By motorcycle

If you have a valid motorcycle license, you can rent bikes at **Orlando Harley Davidson,** 3770 37th St. (☎ **877-740-3770** or 407-423-0346; www. orlandoharley.com), and **American V Twin,** 5101 International Drive (☎ **800-268-8946** or 407-903-0058; www.amvtwin.com/orlando_ harley_rentals.html). Their inventories can be in short supply, so call in advance. You must be at least 21 (and sometimes 25) years of age, have a motorcycle license, and have a major credit card. Rentals start at about $750 per week (or around $150 per day) and include helmets, locks, and a brief orientation.

 Reserve months in advance when you're visiting during **Bike Week** — in late February and early March — or **Biketober Fest** in mid-October. (Both events are held in Daytona Beach, but many bikers still stay in Orlando.)

By bus

Lynx (☎ **407-841-5969;** www.golynx.com) public bus stops are marked with a paw print. Some bus routes serve **Disney, Universal Orlando, International Drive,** and the downtown area ($1.25 for adults, 50¢ for kids ages 8–18), but they are slow going and not very visitor-friendly.

On foot

I don't recommend traveling on foot anywhere in Orlando, but it is occasionally necessary to walk across a parking lot or street. Be extremely careful. With rare exception, this city isn't conducive to strolling. Within the safe confines of the theme parks, you'll have no problems hoofing it (in fact, you'll be on your feet quite a bit), but walking anywhere outside the theme parks is a thrills-and-chills experience most people would prefer to avoid. Orlando is among the most dangerous cities in the country for pedestrians, according to a Washington, D.C.–based research group. Wide roads designed to move traffic quickly and a shortage of sidewalks, streetlights, and crosswalks are to blame.

Chapter 9

Checking In at Orlando's Best Hotels

. . . .

In This Chapter

▶ Finding a hotel room that meets your needs

▶ Getting a good room rate

▶ Clicking your way to a reservation

▶ Knowing what to do if you don't have a reservation

▶ Checking out the best hotels

. . . .

*W*here you plant yourself during your Orlando vacation determines many things about your trip, including your itineraries, the amount of money you spend, and your need, if any, for a car rental. Deciding where to stay in the city isn't easy because its 114,000 rooms come in many different flavors: hotels, motels, bed and breakfasts (B&Bs), and so on. Luckily, I show you how to narrow down your choices.

Getting to Know Your Options

Something you can take to the bank: Unlike the less competitive areas of Florida, almost all hotels in Orlando — at least the ones listed in this guide — have been either built or renovated in the past 10 or 12 years (though it's likely renovations have been closer to within the last 1–3 years), so you can expect reasonably modern trimmings. The city sometimes seems like Chain Central, and you will find branches of pretty much every major hotel and motel chain in the major tourist zones, especially on International Drive and in Kissimmee. Note that even the high-end properties tend to have a more relaxed feel than counterparts in other cities thanks to the theme parks; you're more likely to see Goofy hats than Gucci ones here. (See the Appendix at the back of this guide for a list of the major hotel chains' toll-free numbers.)

Every hotel that I list in this chapter has air-conditioning and at least one pool (or I tell you otherwise). Most have cable TV, and some offer in-room movies, Internet connections, and Nintendo for a fee. Likewise, many have hair dryers, coffeemakers, and in-room safes. Almost all hotels in the city (with a few exceptions that I alert you to) offer free parking, but few these days throw in breakfast with your room rate (most that do tend to fall on the lower end of the price scale). Most places in Orlando try to make kids feel as if they're Mickey's favorite relatives and offer lots of little extras and amenities for families. While that's great for parents, Orlando (believe it or not) is the top honeymoon destination in the United States, so there are plenty of places that cater to the adults, too.

Avoiding children for almost any length of time during your visit is next to impossible, but if you're childfree and don't relish the thought of screaming kids in the room next door, there are ways to improve the odds to your favor. The bad news is that the quiet definitely costs you. As a general rule — Disney and Universal Orlando properties not included — the more expensive a hotel is, the less likely you are to run into children (but keep in mind that even the business hotels here still cater to the family market in some form or another). Some of Orlando's B&Bs don't allow children younger than 16 to stay as guests, and these often feature luxurious rooms that rival those of the big resorts. If you don't want to spend the extra money, remember that few people spend much time in their rooms anyway.

Price and location, when all is said and done, are the factors that really decide where you rest your head for the night. Although you pay more for the best locations, you may find these hotels well worth the conveniences they offer. The closer your hotel is to the things you want to do and see, the less time and money you waste getting to your destination. And that's why the two major players in town are deserving of a closer look.

Walt Disney World

Disney has the corner on the Orlando hotel market, boasting high occupancy rates even during slow times. There are 22 Disney-owned-and-operated resorts and nine "official" hotels — those that are privately owned but have earned Disney's seal of approval — located on WDW property.

Disney's accommodations run the gamut from motel-style rooms to grand villas with full kitchens. The decision to bunk (or not to bunk) with the Mouse is probably the most important one you make regarding your accommodations. To decide whether an on-property stay is right for you, consider these facts: The benefits of lodging in Mickey's back-yard include:

- ✔ Unlimited free transportation via the **Walt Disney World Transportation System**'s buses, monorails, ferries, and water taxis to and from the four theme parks, resorts, and smaller attractions. This also means you're guaranteed admission to all the parks, even during peak times when parking lots fill to capacity and many folks not staying with Mickey are left in the cold.

✔ Free parking inside theme-park lots if you choose to chauffeur yourself. (Other visitors pay $8 a day.)

✔ Kids younger than 17 stay free in their parent's room, and reduced-price children's menus are available in most restaurants.

✔ Access to some of the best hotel pools in all of Orlando.

✔ Resort guests can charge most purchases (including meals) made anywhere inside **WDW** to their room. You can also usually have them delivered to your room at no extra charge.

✔ You can purchase **WDW** park and attraction tickets right at your hotel's guest-relations or concierge desk, avoiding the often long lines at the parks themselves. (See Chapter 11 for more on WDW admission options.) You can also make reservations for dining and preferred tee times at Disney's golf courses through guest relations or the concierge.

✔ No resorts are more convenient to the Disney parks and attractions.

✔ The **Extra Magic Hour** allows resort guests before- and after-hours admission to one of the four theme parks. Disney distributes a schedule that lists which parks are open extra hours on what days and at what time (for information, see Chapter 11).

✔ Disney's **Magical Express** transports you and your luggage from the airport to your resort if you fly via participating airlines (currently American, Continental, Delta, Song, United, Ted, and Northwest) to Orlando International Airport. Your luggage will appear in your resort room without you ever having to retrieve it from baggage claim in Orlando. You will be transported (round-trip) to your resort at no additional charge in a special Disney shuttle. Other great perks include the ability to print your boarding pass prior to departing from your resort, therefore avoiding at least one line at the airport. This service is available throughout the *Happiest Celebration on Earth,* which kicked off in May 2005 and will run through late 2006.

The drawbacks of staying with the Mouse include:

✔ The **Walt Disney World Transportation System** can be excruciatingly time-consuming and difficult to maneuver with young children and all their paraphernalia.

✔ Resort rates are about 20 to 30 percent higher than prices at comparable hotels and motels located beyond the parks' boundaries.

✔ You may wind up a prisoner of **Disney,** unable to avoid the stiff pricing for meals, trinkets, and so on.

✔ Without your own vehicle, it's difficult and expensive to leave Disney property to experience the rest of what Orlando has to offer (which is quite a bit).

Universal Orlando

Universal Orlando is actually a relatively new player on the Orlando hotel scene and only boasts three properties (though plans to tack on at least two more in the future have been drawn up). The Universal resorts are all operated by the luxury **Loews Hotel group** and the standard of accommodations is actually a bit better than the majority of those at Disney. If your itinerary favors Universal Orlando, staying at one of its three properties affords you some rather meaningful perks at the Universal parks.

The benefits of staying at one of Universal's three resorts:

- ✔ Unlimited free transportation via water taxi from the resorts to **CityWalk** and both Universal parks.

- ✔ Unlike Disney, Universal Orlando's smaller number of resorts means everything really is within walking distance of the parks.

- ✔ Resort guests enjoy special privileges at the Universal Orlando theme parks, including *front-of-the-line access to rides* and preferred seating at shows and many restaurants from the day of check-in to the day of check-out. This is a huge benefit, especially during the more crowded months when lines can be excruciatingly long. All you have to do is show your room key and you can bypass the regular lines. Additionally, guests are allowed early entry to the parks on scheduled days.

- ✔ Universal's resorts all accept pets, so Fido or Fluffy can live the luxurious lifestyle right along with you instead of having to be relegated to a kennel.

The drawbacks of staying at the Universal resorts are as follows:

- ✔ While there is shuttle service to **SeaWorld** and **Wet 'n Wild** from the resorts, you'll have to arrange your own transportation if you want to set foot on Disney property.

- ✔ Resort rates are at least 30 percent higher than at comparable hotels and motels (though, honestly, few are really comparable) located even a block from the parks. You won't find anything for under $100 a night.

- ✔ As when staying at a Disney resort, you're subjected to higher prices for dining and other vacation necessities.

- ✔ Universal resorts don't offer free parking (it costs $6 a day), which is a universal perk everywhere else in the theme-park zones!

Finding the Best Room at the Best Rate

The **rack rate** is the published (and usually the maximum) rate a hotel charges for a room. It's the rate you get if you walk in off the street and ask for a room for the night. You sometimes see these rates printed on the fire/emergency exit diagrams posted on the back of your door. Hotels are happy to charge you the rack rate, but you can almost always do better. Perhaps the best way to avoid paying the rack rate is surprisingly simple: Just ask for a cheaper or discounted rate and it's likely you'll get one.

Reserving a room through the hotel's toll-free number may also result in a lower rate than calling the hotel directly. On the other hand, the central reservations number may not know about discount rates at specific locations. Your best bet is to call both the local number *and* the toll-free number and see which one gives you a better deal. Whatever you do, don't ever come to town without a reservation. Orlando is a year-round destination, it has a heavy convention and business trade, and school lets out during varying times of the year in other nations. If you come without a reservation, you may find yourself extremely disappointed — or even completely out of luck.

If you're a student, senior, military or government employee (or retiree), or a member of AAA or AARP, ask about discounts. The Orlando/Orange County Convention and Visitors Bureau's free **Magicard** (☎ 800-643-9492; www.orlandoinfo.com) is good for a family of six and offers hundreds of dollars in discounts on accommodations, car rentals, attractions, and restaurants. The **Entertainment Book** (www.entertainment book.com) is another good source for discounts on hotels, car rentals, restaurants, and attractions. It costs $25 for the Orlando version, but you will recoup your investment after using just a few coupons.

As a rule, Disney resorts, villas, and official hotels don't offer regular discounts other than for slight seasonal variations. **WDW's** 2005 value seasons or lowest rates were available from January 1 to February 16, August 28 to October 4 (except Labor Day weekend), and November 27 to December 19. Regular season rates were available from April 17 to August 27 and October 5 to November 26. Peak rates applied from February 17 to April 16, and December 20 to December 31. While the actual dates will shift a little (and those listed are for the value and moderate resorts and vary slightly for the deluxe and vacation-club level resorts), the same periods should apply in 2006.

One of the best ways to catch a break from Mickey's prices is through a travel package (see Chapter 5). **Disney** offers vacation plans that can include meals, tickets, recreation, airfare, rentals, dinner shows, and other features. Call the **Central Reservations Office** (☎ 407-934-7639) or go to www.disneyworld.com to book both rooms and packages or to get the lowdown on WDW, including vacation brochures and DVDs.

Before calling Disney to make reservations, take a moment to visit **MouseSavers** (www.mousesavers.com). This unofficial Disney discount site is extremely diligent about keeping up-to-date listings on all discounts offered by Disney, whether it be room discount codes or details on special package deals. Spending a few minutes looking over the listings can save you hundreds of dollars when booking direct with Disney.

When booking your room, don't forget to allow for the area's combined sales and resort taxes. In Orange County (Orlando, Lake Buena Vista, Winter Park, and Maitland), the tax equals 11 percent. In Osceola County (Kissimmee/St. Cloud), the taxes add 12 percent to your bill.

When making your reservation, ask some pointed questions to make sure that you have the best room in the house. For example, always ask for a corner room. They're usually larger and quieter, include more windows and light than standard rooms, and don't always cost more. Likewise, ask which floor and side has the best view, if there is one, as well as whether the hotel is renovating. (If so, request a room away from the renovation work.) You can also ask about the location of the restaurants, bars, and clubs in the hotel — these may be a source of irritating noise. If you aren't happy with your room when you arrive, talk to the front desk. If they have another room, they will likely accommodate you — within reason, of course.

Surfing the Web for Hotel Deals

Shopping online for hotels is generally done one of two ways: by booking through the hotel's own Web site or through an independent booking agency (or a fare-service agency like Priceline). These Internet hotel agencies have multiplied in mind-boggling numbers of late, competing for the business of millions of consumers surfing for accommodations around the world. This competitiveness can be a boon to consumers who have the patience and time to shop and compare the online sites for good deals — but shop they must, for prices can vary considerably from site to site. And keep in mind that hotels at the top of a site's listing may be there for no other reason than that they paid money to get the placement.

You almost never find a **WDW** resort on any discounter's Web site. If you want to book a Disney hotel online, you have to go through a packager or Disney's own Web site at www.disneyworld.com. Each individual resort is listed on the site and information is available on rooms, rates, floor plans, restaurants, recreation, and so on. The only hotels on Disney property that you can book through a discounter are the "official" hotels.

Of the "big three" sites, **Expedia** offers a long list of special deals and "virtual tours" or photos of available rooms so you can see what you're paying for (a feature that helps counter the claims that the best rooms are often held back from bargain-booking Web sites). **Travelocity** posts unvarnished customer reviews and ranks its properties according to the AAA rating system. Also reliable are **Hotels.com** and **Quikbook.com**. An excellent free program, **TravelAxe** (www.travelaxe.net), can help you search multiple hotel sites at once, even ones you may never have heard of — and conveniently lists the total price of the room, including the taxes and service charges. It covers a large number of Orlando's best hotels, and I heartily recommend giving it a try.

Another booking site, **Travelweb** (`www.travelweb`), is partly owned by the hotels it represents (including the Hilton, Hyatt, and Starwood chains) and is therefore plugged directly into the hotels' reservations systems — unlike independent online agencies, which have to fax or e-mail reservation requests to the hotel, a good portion of which get misplaced in the shuffle. More than once, travelers have arrived at the hotel, only to be told that they have no reservation. To be fair, many of the major sites are undergoing improvements in service and ease of use, and Expedia will soon be able to plug directly into the reservations systems of many hotel chains — none of which can be bad news for consumers. In the meantime, it's a good idea to **get a confirmation number** and **make a printout** of any online booking transaction.

In the opaque Web site category, **Priceline** and **Hotwire** are even better for hotels than for airfares; with both, you're allowed to pick the neighborhood and quality level of your hotel before offering up your money. Priceline's hotel product even covers Europe and Asia, though it's much better at getting five-star lodging for three-star prices than at finding anything at the bottom of the scale. On the down side, many hotels stick Priceline guests in their least desirable rooms. Be sure to go to the **BiddingforTravel** Web site (`www.biddingfortravel.com`) before bidding on a hotel room on Priceline; it features a fairly up-to-date list of hotels that Priceline uses in major cities. For both Priceline and Hotwire, you pay up front, and the fee is nonrefundable. *Note:* Some hotels do not provide loyalty program credits or points or other frequent-stay amenities when you book a room through opaque online services.

Arriving Without a Reservation

My first bit of advice: Don't come to Orlando without a reservation. If you do, you're more likely to end up feeling like Grumpy than Happy. This advice is especially true when it's high-travel season and rooms are both pricey and scarce. If you do, however, decide to head for Orlando on a spur-of-the-moment inspiration, there are a few options to pursue before setting up camp in your car.

 The **Orlando Visitors Center** is related to the Orlando/Orange County Convention and Visitors Bureau. These folks find last-minute rooms for nonplanners. Room rates, depending on the seasons, can be a bargain. However, you can get a room only for the night you visit the center, and you have to come in person to find out what is available. The **Visitors Center** is located in Orlando at 8723 International Drive, a mile west of Sand Lake Road (☎ **407-363-5872** for information only).

Your only other option is to try the reservation service listed in the "Surfing the Web for Hotel Deals" section earlier in this chapter.

Orlando's Best Hotels

All the rates in this section are per night double, but many accommodations, including all **Disney** resorts, allow kids younger than 17 to stay free with their parents or grandparents (as long as the number of guests doesn't exceed the maximum occupancy). However, always ask about rates for kids when booking your room. Also, unless otherwise noted, all the hotels in this section offer free self-parking.

 To make it easy for you to recognize expensive versus moderately priced hotels, each of the following entries includes one or more $ symbols. See Table 9-1 "Key to Hotel Dollar Signs" for the meaning behind the symbols. In general, expect higher hotel prices on the more upscale digs as well as those in or near the attractions. Almost every hotel in Orlando caters to families with children, but I list hotels, resorts, and inns that are especially good fits for adults on the "Good for Grown-ups" list found on this book's tear-out cheat sheet.

 Several of the properties in this chapter add resort fees that can range from $5 to upwards of $15 to their daily room rates. That's part of an unfortunate but growing hotel trend of charging for services that used to be included in the rates, such as use of the pool, admission to the health club, or in-room coffee, safe, or phones (each hotel varies greatly). If it's a concern, ask if your hotel charges such a fee (and just what it's for) when booking so you don't get blindsided at checkout. At some hotels the fee is optional, and you don't need to pay it if you don't use the amenities or recreational facilities it covers.

Table 9-1	Key to Hotel Dollar Signs	
Dollar Sign	*Price Range*	*What to Expect*
$	Less than $100	Accommodations at this level generally include basic trimmings and limited space. They also lean toward the no-frills side. Those at the higher end may offer amenities such as hair dryers, coffeemakers, cable TV, a midsize pool, a kid's play area, and continental breakfast. If they're multistory, they also usually have an elevator.

Dollar Sign	Price Range	What to Expect
$$	$101–$200	Lodgings in this price range probably offer a choice of king-size or double beds, possibly suites if they fall in the higher end, a full range of amenities (hair dryer, coffeemakers, two TVs in the two-room models, multiline phones and, possibly, a modem line, VCRs, free daily newspaper, and designer shampoos), and room service. Rooms are slightly larger, and a Jacuzzi and fitness center may accompany the pool. The continental breakfast probably includes fresh fruit, granola, and muffins rather than day-old doughnuts and little boxes of cereal. The hotel may also have at least one palatable on-site restaurant. Some may have a guest-services desk for purchasing attraction tickets and making dinner arrangements.
$$$	$201–$300	Hotels at this level are sure to have a guest-services desk, possibly a concierge. They also usually include a large, resort-style pool, possibly a second smaller or toddler pool, and multiple Jacuzzi tubs (some of the higher-end rooms have their own), a fitness center, and occasionally a small spa. Rooms generally have multiple phones, minibars, a bath *and* separate shower. Many rooms are larger, some with small sitting areas, a pull-out sofa, and large work desks. Some hotels in this category offer supervised children's programs and activities.
$$$$	$301 and up	Nothing in this price range is impossible. In addition to the amenities in the previous categories, many of these hotels offer concierge levels, extra-large rooms, spacious suites, 24-hour room service, gorgeous pool bars, and live entertainment in their lounges. Some also include full-service spas, gourmet restaurants, shopping arcades, and tight security. Recreational facilities are usually extensive and lavish. Many offer supervised children's programs and activities.

Walt Disney World & Lake Buena Vista Accommodations

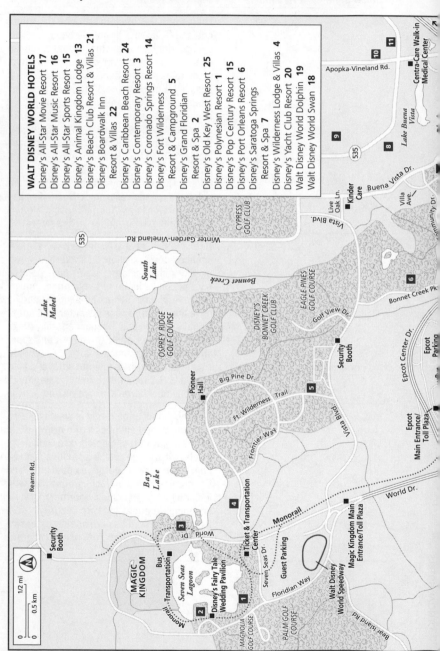

WALT DISNEY WORLD HOTELS

Disney's All-Star Movie Resort **17**
Disney's All-Star Music Resort **16**
Disney's All-Star Sports Resort **15**
Disney's Animal Kingdom Lodge **13**
Disney's Beach Club Resort & Villas **21**
Disney's Boardwalk Inn
Resort & Villas **22**
Disney's Caribbean Beach Resort **24**
Disney's Contemporary Resort **3**
Disney's Coronado Springs Resort **14**
Disney's Fort Wilderness
Resort & Campground **5**
Disney's Grand Floridian
Resort & Spa **2**
Disney's Old Key West Resort **25**
Disney's Polynesian Resort **1**
Disney's Pop Century Resort **15**
Disney's Port Orleans Resort **6**
Disney's Saratoga Springs
Resort & Spa **7**
Disney's Wilderness Lodge & Villas **4**
Disney's Yacht Club Resort **20**
Walt Disney World Dolphin **19**
Walt Disney World Swan **18**

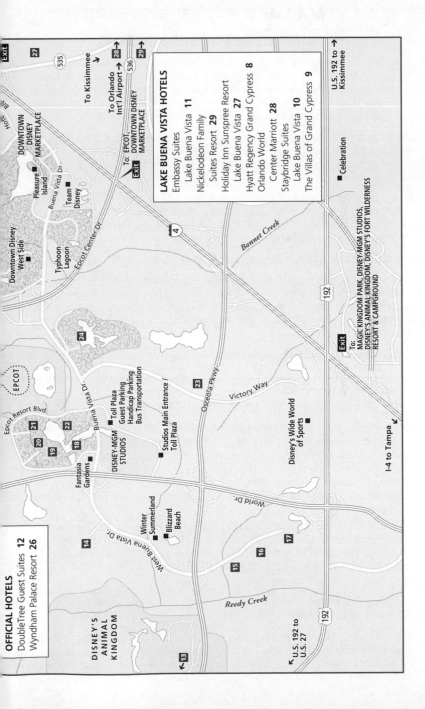

LAKE BUENA VISTA HOTELS

Embassy Suites
Lake Buena Vista **11**
Nickelodeon Family
Suites Resort **29**
Holiday Inn Sunspree Resort
Lake Buena Vista **27**
Hyatt Regency Grand Cypress **8**
Orlando World
Center Marriott **28**
Staybridge Suites
Lake Buena Vista **10**
The Villas of Grand Cypress **9**

OFFICIAL HOTELS
DoubleTree Guest Suites **12**
Wyndham Palace Resort **26**

DOWNTOWN DISNEY MARKETPLACE

Pleasure Island

Team Disney

Buena Vista Dr.

Downtown Disney West Side

Typhoon Lagoon

Epcot Center Dr.

To Kissimmee

To Orlando Int'l Airport

To: EPCOT, DOWNTOWN DISNEY MARKETPLACE

Exit

535

536

27

28

29

4

Bonnet Creek

192

Celebration

U.S. 192 to Kissimmee

Exit

To:
MAGIC KINGDOM PARK, DISNEY-MGM STUDIOS,
DISNEY'S ANIMAL KINGDOM, DISNEY'S FORT WILDERNESS
RESORT & CAMPGROUND

EPCOT

Epcot Resort Blvd.

Buena Vista Dr.

Toll Plaza
Guest Parking
Handicap Parking
Bus Transportation

DISNEY-MGM STUDIOS

Studios Main Entrance /
Toll Plaza

Fantasia Gardens

24

21

22

20

18

19

23

Victory Way

Osceola Pkwy.

Disney's Wide World of Sports

I-4 to Tampa

West Buena Vista Dr.

Winter Summerland

Blizzard Beach

World Dr.

14

15

16

17

DISNEY'S ANIMAL KINGDOM

Reedy Creek

U.S. 192 to
U.S. 27

192

13

A home away from home

If you want all the comforts of home or are traveling in a group of five or more, you might consider bypassing hotels or motels in favor of a rental condo or home. Rates vary widely depending on quality and location, and some may require a 2- or 3-night minimum stay. A lot of these properties are 5 to 15 miles from the theme parks and offer no transportation, so having a car is a necessity.

On the plus side, most have two to six bedrooms and a convertible couch, two or more bathrooms, a full kitchen, multiple TVs and phones, and irons. Some have washers and dryers. Homes often have their own private, screen-enclosed pool, while condos have a common one.

On the minus side, they can be lacking in services. Most don't have daily maid service, and restaurants can be as far away as the parks. (There's another reason you'll need a car.) Be sure to check and see if they offer dinnerware, utensils, or salt-and-pepper shakers — it generally depends on the level of the home chosen.

Rates range from about $75 to $450 per night ($300–$3,200 per week).

All Star Vacation Homes offers an array of homes and condos, all of which are within only 4 miles of Disney and close to all the areas restaurants and attractions. Homes fall into a wide range of luxury and size. Many have private, screened-in pools. Call ☎ **888-249-1779** or 407-997-0733 or see their offerings online at www.allstar vacationhomes.com.

AmeriSuites Universal
$–$$ International Drive Area/Universal Orlando

It's tough to beat the value and roominess of these kitchenette-equipped suites, especially if your goal is to be very close to the Universal theme parks without having to pay the heftier rates that come with staying on park property. The modern, spacious rooms allow you to stretch out more than in standard hotel/motel accommodations, and the location is especially convenient if Universal Orlando is your target. The free buffet breakfast is a bonus.

See map p. 113. 895 Caravan Crt. (Take I-4 to Exit 75B/Kirkman Rd., then turn right at the first light, Major Boulevard, and the next right, Caravan Court. The hotel is on the right.) ☎ *800-833-1516 or 407-351-0627. Fax: 407-331-3317.* www.amerisuites. com. *151 units. Rack rates: $89–$139. AE, DC, DISC, MC, V.*

Celebration Hotel
$$–$$$$ Kissimmee

Located in the Disney-esque town of Celebration, this upscale and charmingly sophisticated hotel has a three-story, wood-frame design straight out of 1920s Florida. A bit off the beaten path, it offers a romantic atmosphere for couples, although children are welcome. All rooms offer dataports, safes, hair dryers, and TVs with Nintendo. Suites and studios have refrigerators and wet bars. Other amenities include a pool, Jacuzzi, and fitness center. Shops, an 18-hole golf course, a movie theater, and several restaurants are within walking distance. A free shuttle to **WDW** parks, and transportation for a fee to other parks are available.

See map p. 109. 700 Bloom St. (Take I-4 to the U.S. 192 exit, go east to second light, then right on Celebration Ave.) ☎ ***888-499-3800*** *or 407-566-6000. Fax: 407-566-6001.* www.celebrationhotel.com. *115 units. Rack rates: $139–$219; $289–$470 suites. Daily resort fee: $5. Valet parking: $13. AE, DC, DISC, MC, V.*

Comfort Suites Maingate East
$–$$ **Kissimmee**

Set back from the main drag, this fairly new and welcoming hotel is one of the nicest in the area. The lobby and accommodations — consisting of studio and one-bedroom suites — are bright and inviting. The main pool and the children's pool, with an umbrella fountain to keep everyone cool, are open around the clock. For entertainment, Old Town (a small-scale shopping, dining, and entertainment complex) is next door, and a great miniature golf course is located just in front of the property.

See map p. 109. 2775 Florida Plaza Blvd. (Take I-4 to the US 192 exit, go east 1¾ miles, then right on Florida Plaza Boulevard.) ☎ ***888-782-9772*** *or 407-397-7848. Fax: 407-396-7045.* www.comfortsuitesfl.com. *198 units. Rack rates: $65–$150. AE, DC, DISC, MC, V.*

Comfort Suites Maingate at Formosa Gardens
$–$$ **Kissimmee**

Just across the street from the La Quinta Inn Lakeside (see below) and up the road from WDW, this clean, comfortable, place to stay has kept itself modern and in good shape. The "suites" have a small dividing wall slightly separating the living area from the sleeping quarters, but the illusion of privacy is there. Accommodations are a bit bigger than most and can squeeze in up to six. A bit of tropical landscaping gives it an inviting atmosphere and shelters guests from busy U.S. 192. At least 10 restaurants and a small shopping plaza are within walking distance, and there's a miniature golf course right across the street. A buffet breakfast is included in the cost.

See map p. 109. 7888 W. Irlo Bronson Memorial Hwy/U.S. 192 (Take I-4 to Exit 64B/West Hwy. 192; hotel is 3 miles on left). ☎ ***888-390-9888*** *or 407-390-9888. Fax: 407-390-09811607.* www.kisscomfortsuite.com. *150 units. Rack rates: $50–$150. AE, DC, DISC, MC, V.*

Courtyard at Lake Lucerne
$–$$$ **Downtown Orlando**

This charming B&B hideaway is located within walking distance to several of downtown's cultural attractions, upscale eateries, and shops. It is made up of several historic buildings: The Norment-Parry Inn is an 1883

Victorian-style home with six rooms decorated with English and American antiques; four have sitting rooms, and all have private baths. A honeymoon suite has a walnut bed, fireplace, and a small, glass-enclosed porch. The I. W. Phillips House, built in 1919, is a Southern jewel with three upstairs suites, one with a whirlpool, and all with verandas overlooking the gardens and fountain. The Dr. Phillip Phillips House (1893) and the Wellborn (1946) round out the offerings. Rates include a continental breakfast.

211 N. Lucerne Circle E. (Take Orange Avenue south; immediately following City Hall, turn left onto Anderson. After 2 lights, at Delaney Avenue, turn right. Take first right onto Lucerne Circle. Follow the brown "historic inn" signs.) ☎ ***800-444-5289*** *or 407-648-5188. Fax: 407-246-1368.* www.orlandohistoricinn.com. *30 units. Rack rates: $89–$225 double. AE, DC, MC, V.*

Crowne Plaza Orlando-Universal
$$$–$$$$ International Drive Area/Universal Orlando

Sleek, modern, and upscale, this 15-story hotel is close to **Universal Orlando** and **SeaWorld** (about midway between them), although getting to Disney is no problem because the hotel offers free shuttles to all the major parks. It's also close to the I-Ride Trolley, making it easy to get to the many attractions and eateries lining I-Drive. Subdued, but well appointed, rooms offer floor-to-ceiling windows. Some of the pricier rooms are in the Atrium Tower, where glass elevators climb to the top. Other perks include a fitness center and heated pool. This place is geared to business travelers and adults without kids in tow.

See map p. 113. 7800 Universal Blvd. (From I-4, take Sand Lake Road/Highway 482 east to Universal, then left.) ☎ ***866-864-8627*** *or 407-355-0550. Fax: 407-355-0504.* www. crowneplazauniversal.com. *400 rooms. Rack rates: $219–$279 double; $450–$600 suites. Valet parking: $8.50. AE, DISC, MC, V.*

Disney's All-Star Movie Resort
$–$$ Walt Disney World

Kids aren't the only ones amazed by the, uh, aesthetics of this resort. When did you last see architecture as inspiring as Goliath-size Dalmatians leaping from balconies? If you're not saying, "Oh, brother!" by now you may enjoy all the larger-than-life versions of a host of other characters from famous Disney movies (*Toy Story, 101 Dalmatians,* and *Fantasia* among others) that decorate the buildings here, and the low (by Mickey standards) rates will thrill some travelers. The All-Star Resorts that follows this listing are pretty much the same, save the theme — expect tiny (260 sq. ft.) rooms and postage-stamp size bathrooms with few frills but plenty of families. Either way you're "on property," and you're enjoying the lowest prices your Mouse money can buy. This All-Star resort has a family-friendly food court that serves pizza, pasta, sandwiches, salads, burgers, chicken, and family-dinner platters. Room service is very limited. Each of the All-Star resorts features a main pool, smaller second pool, toddler pool, and a very small playground as well as an arcade.

See map p. 96. 1991 W. Buena Vista Dr. ☎ **407-934-7639** *or 407-939-7000. Fax: 407-939-7111.* www.disneyworld.com. *1,920 units. Rack rates: $77–$131 double. AE, DC, DISC, MC, V.*

Disney's All-Star Music Resort
$–$$ **Walt Disney World**

If you insist on staying on Disney property and are on a tight budget, the rates at the All-Star's are difficult to beat. But you'd better be prepared for full-time family togetherness, as the mouse-size rooms mean you'll be up close and personal. (They're about the size of what you get on a cruise ship if you choose a midprice cabin). And if the idea of residing in buildings decorated with immense musical notes and other music-related motifs doesn't appeal, head elsewhere.

See map p. 96. 1801 W. Buena Vista Dr. (at World Drive and Osceola Parkway). ☎ **407-934-7639** *or 407-939-6000. Fax: 407-939-7222.* www.disneyworld.com. *1,920 units. Rack rates: $77–$131 double. AE, DC, DISC, MC, V.*

Disney's All-Star Sports Resort
$–$$ **Walt Disney World**

Adjacent to the **All-Star Music Resort,** this 82-acre property is an instant replay of its sister All-Stars. It draws sports fans looking for a vacation and visual overload. The buildings feature football (huge helmets protect stairwells from rain), baseball, basketball, tennis, and surfing motifs. Amenities include a brightly decorated food court, very limited room service, babysitting (from an outside service), a guest-services desk (a standard at Disney resorts), pools, and a video arcade. Like its two siblings (listed previously), the All-Star Sports Resort is fairly isolated in WDW's southwest corner. Renting a car is a far better choice than relying on the Disney Transportation System if you want to get anywhere quickly.

See map p. 96. 1701 W. Buena Vista Dr. (at World Drive and Osceola Parkway). ☎ **407-934-7639** *or 407-939-5000. Fax: 407-939-7333.* www.disneyworld.com. *1,920 units. Rack rates: $77–$131 double. AE, DC, DISC, MC, V.*

Disney's Animal Kingdom Lodge
$$$–$$$$ **Walt Disney World**

Disney's newest arrival offers the exotic atmosphere of an African game preserve. The rooms follow a *kraal* (semicircular) design, giving guests a hit-or-miss view of 130 species of birds and 75 giraffes, gazelles, and other grazing animals on the 30-acre savanna. The huge picture windows in the lobby offer similar views, while the interior public areas are adorned with authentic African artwork and artifacts. The rooms are quite comfortable, although bathrooms are a bit cramped (a problem with many of Disney's properties). Two of the best and most unique restaurants (Jiko and Boma) are located here. Not surprisingly, this resort is the closest you can stay to **Animal Kingdom,** but almost everything else on **WDW** property is quite a distance away. And although families appreciate the animals and wide array of activities for kids (not to mention the bunk beds available in some rooms and the supervised kids' club), the more relaxed and sedate nature of the resort also makes it a good spot for couples. A concierge level is available.

See map p. 96. 2901 Osceola Pkwy. (west of Buena Vista Drive.) ☎ *407-934-7639 or 407-938-3000. Fax: 407-939-4799.* www.disneyworld.com. *1,293 units. Rack rates: $199–$620 double; $435–$620 concierge; $640–$2,300 suites. AE, DC, DISC, MC, V.*

Disney's Beach Club Resort
$$$$ Walt Disney World

It's only a brisk walk to **Epcot** from the Beach Club, which resembles the grand seaside resorts that once dotted the eastern seaboard around the turn of the 20th century. The Beach Club's atmosphere is a bit more casual than its sister resort (the Yacht Club, listed below) that shares its many restaurants and recreational facilities. Though still upscale, brightly colored beach umbrellas, seashells, and a casual Cape Cod feel permeate the resort. Kids love the 3-acre, free-form, sand-bottom swimming pool of Stormalong Bay, winding its way along the beachfront. Rooms can sleep up to five, and views range from the pool to the parking lot. The villas, added in 2002, sleep up to eight. Studios have kitchenettes, while the one and two bedroom villas have full kitchens, washer/dryers, and whirlpool baths. All units come with balconies. The BoardWalk, Swan, and Dolphin resorts are just a short walk across the bridge, adding their own entertainment and dining options to the mix. The proximity to the parks (MGM and Epcot especially), as well as other resorts, makes it one of the best upscale destinations at Disney, especially for families.

See map p. 96. 1800 Epcot Resorts Blvd. (Off Buena Vista Dr.) ☎ *407-934-7639 or 407-934-8000. Fax: 407-934-3850.* www.disneyworld.com. *583 units, 205 villas. Rack rates: $294–$680 double; $495–$675 concierge; $495–$2,165 suites; $400–$1,040 villas. AE, DC, DISC, MC, V.*

Disney's BoardWalk Inn
$$$$ Walt Disney World

More than any other Disney property, the BoardWalk Inn appeals to those looking for a sliver of yesterday. The 1940s "seaside" resort overlooks a village green and lake. Some of the Cape Cod–style rooms have balconies (rooms sleep up to five), and the corner units offer a bit more space. Center rooms on the upper floors facing the lake have the best view of the nightly fireworks at Epcot. Recreational facilities are extensive and include two pools set in a lavish Coney Island atmosphere, tennis, fishing, boating, bike rental, and even a moonlight cruise. The villas sleep up to 12, and the 1-, 2-, and 3-bedroom villas have full kitchens, washer/dryers, and whirlpool baths. The resort has a quarter-mile boardwalk reminiscent of those once made popular along the mid-Atlantic seaboard, featuring shops, restaurants, and street performers, which means you'll find plenty to do after the sun goes down. *Note:* Rooms overlooking the boardwalk have the best views, but they tend to be noisy thanks to the action below.

See map p. 96. 2101 N. Epcot Resorts Blvd. (north of Buena Vista Drive). ☎ *407-934-7639 or 407-939-5100. Fax: 407-934-5150.* www.disneyworld.com. *378 units, 520 villas. Rack rates: $294–$690 double; $435–$690 concierge; $560–$2,095 suites; $400–$1,970 villas. AE, DC, DISC, MC, V.*

Disney's Caribbean Beach Resort
$$ Walt Disney World

This moderately priced hotel's amenities may not be quite as extensive as those at some of Disney's higher-end properties (or those in the same class outside the World), but the hotel still offers great value for families. Grouped into five Caribbean island–themed villages, many of the rooms offer views out over the beaches and the water. Standard rooms feature two double beds, small bathrooms, and privacy curtains for a vanity area with a double sink. The main swimming pool resembles a Spanish-style fort, and most of the villages have their own basic pool as well. Other pluses are a nature trail, small aviary, and a picnic area. The hotel also has a restaurant, as well as a lively market-style food court. The closest park is the **Disney MGM–Studios,** though it can take up to 45 minutes to get there using Disney transportation — it's probably best to rent a car if you stay here. *Note:* When booking, ask for a recently refurbished room.

See map p. 96. 900 Cayman Way (off Buena Vista Drive toward Epcot on Sea Breeze Drive and Cayman Way). ☎ *407-934-7639 or 407-934-3400. Fax: 407-934-3288.* www. disneyworld.com. *2,112 units. Rack rates: $134–$209 double. AE, DC, DISC, MC, V.*

Disney's Contemporary Resort
$$$–$$$$ Walt Disney World

If location is a priority, the Contemporary has one of the best in the World because the monorail literally runs through the hotel, allowing you a fast track to **Epcot** or the **Magic Kingdom.** The 15-story, A-frame resort — Disney's first in Florida — overlooks the manmade Seven Seas Lagoon and Bay Lake. The original rooms in this tower were built separately and then slid into the framework, an unusual process befitting the futuristic architecture. The separate two-story **Garden Wing** buildings were added several years later. Standard rooms are among Disney's biggest, a plus for families. The more expensive **Tower** rooms (which will undergo renovation from 2005–2006) have the best views, and the higher floors tend to be quieter. The pool area is virtually a mini water park, and many of Disney's watersports options are headquartered here. The hotel offers three restaurants, including one of the more-popular character meals (see Chapter 10), and a health club.

 This is the least themed of the expensive Disney resorts, and the décor scheme could be described as business bland, so if you want an all-Mickey atmosphere, stay elsewhere.

See map p. 96. 4600 N. World Dr. ☎ **407-934-7639** *or 407-824-1000. Fax: 407-824-3539.* www.disneyworld.com. *1,053 units. Rack rates: $244–$490 double; $405–$2465 concierge; $800–$1,190 suites. AE, DC, DISC, MC, V.*

Disney's Coronado Springs Resort
$$ Walt Disney World

The spirit of the American Southwest can be felt throughout this moderately priced resort, which has a slightly more upscale feel than others of its class. Rooms are housed in four- and five-story hacienda-style buildings with terra-cotta tile roofs and palm-shaded courtyards. Some overlook the 15-acre Golden Lake; the better your view, the higher the price. Rooms feature two double beds (the décor differs in each section, but the layout is the same), with a small bathroom and dual vanities set inside a separate niche. Ninety-nine rooms are specially designed to accommodate travelers with disabilities, and nearly three-quarters of the rooms are nonsmoking. If you like to swim, you'll delight in the Mayan temple–inspired main pool. Dining options include a restaurant and a food court. The nearest park is **Animal Kingdom,** but the Coronado is at the southwest corner of **WDW** and a good distance from most other areas in the park.

See map p. 96. 1000 Buena Vista Drive. ☎ **407-934-7639** *or 407-939-1000. Fax: 407-939-1001.* www.disneyworld.com. *1,967 units. Rack rates: $134–$209 double; $290–$1,190 suites. AE, DC, DISC, MC, V.*

Disney's Fort Wilderness Resort & Campground
$–$$$ Walt Disney World

This woodsy, 780-acre resort delights campers, but it's quite a hike from most of the Disney parks, except the **Magic Kingdom** (and even it might feel far away if you use Disney transportation to get there). Even so, you'll have more than enough to keep you busy right here. Guests enjoy extensive recreational facilities, ranging from a riding stable to a nightly campfire with fishing, biking, and swimming among the offerings. Secluded campsites offer 110/220-volt outlets, barbecue grills, picnic tables, and kids' play areas. Wilderness cabins (actually, they're cleverly disguised trailers) can sleep up to six people; they also have living rooms, fully equipped eat-in kitchens, coffeemakers, hair dryers, and barbecue grills. Nearby Pioneer Hall plays host to the rambunctious *Hoop-Dee-Doo Musical Revue* (see Chapter 24) nightly. The nightly campfire and marshmallow roast, followed by a Disney movie, shown right in the great outdoors, is a big hit with families.

Some sites are open to pets (the ones with full hook-ups), at an additional cost of $3 per site — not per pet — which is less expensive than using the WDW resort kennel, where you pay $9 per pet.

See map p. 96. 3520 N. Fort Wilderness Trail (located off Vista Boulevard). ☎ **407-934-7639** *or 407-824-2900. Fax: 407-824-3508.* www.disneyworld.com. *784 campsites, 408 wilderness cabins. Rack rates: $38–$89 campsites; $234–$339 cabins. AE, DC, DISC, MC, V.*

Disney's Grand Floridian Resort & Spa
$$$$ Walt Disney World

You won't find a more luxurious address — in a Victorian sense anyway — than this 40-acre *Great Gatsby*–era resort on the shores of the Seven Seas Lagoon. It's a great choice for couples seeking a bit of romance, especially honeymooners who aren't on a tight budget. The Grand Floridian is Walt Disney World's upper-crust flagship, and it's as pricey as it is plush. The opulent, five-story, domed lobby hosts afternoon teas accompanied by piano music. In the evenings, an orchestra plays big-band tunes. Virtually all of the inviting Victorian-style rooms overlook a garden, pool, courtyard, or the Seven Seas Lagoon; many have balconies and the "dormer rooms" have vaulted ceilings. The hotel is one of three on the Disney monorail line. The resort also has a first-rate health club and spa, as well as five restaurants, including the incomparable **Victoria & Albert** (see Chapter 10).

See map p. 96. 4401 Floridian Way (northwest corner of the WDW property, just north of the Polynesian Resort). ☎ *407-934-7639 or 407-824-3000. Fax: 407-824-3186.* www.disneyworld.com. *900 units. Rack rates: $349–$645 double; $460–$870 concierge; $615–$2,535 suites. AE, DC, DISC, MC, V.*

Disney's Old Key West Resort
$$$–$$$$ Walt Disney World

The peace and quiet of a remote locale away from the dizzying Disney theme-park pace is just part of your reward when you stay here. This **Disney Vacation Club** timeshare property mirrors turn-of-the-20th-century Key West, though the theme is tastefully understated. Pastel colors and gingerbread trim adorn the charming buildings while palm trees are scattered about providing a bit of shade along the beaches. Tourists can rent rooms here when their owners are not using them, and they're a great choice for large families or long stays. The accommodations include studios, along with one, two, and three-bedroom villas that have full kitchens, washer/dryers, Jacuzzis, and balconies. Recreational facilities are extensive and include beaches, pools, an array of watersports, a playground, video arcade, and more. There's a restaurant as well as a large grocery store.

See map p. 96. 1510 N. Cove Rd. (off Community Drive). ☎ *407-934-7639 or 407-827-7700. Fax: 407-827-7710.* www.disneyworld.com. *761 units. Rack rates: $259–$379 studios; $350–$1,505 villas. AE, DC, DISC, MC, V.*

Disney's Polynesian Resort
$$$$ Walt Disney World

The 25-acre Polynesian Resort was built when Disney first opened its doors and sort of resembles the South Pacific. Though it has aged, it still offers one of the best locations — just across from the **Magic Kingdom** and right on the monorail line. The guest rooms are reasonably large, and most have balconies or patios, with bamboo and rattan furnishings. The Tahiti and Rapa Nui buildings have rooms that are slightly larger, but they are also the furthest from the main building, dining, and volcano pool area.

Numerous recreational activities are available, including fishing and boat rentals. The *Spirit of Aloha Dinner Show* (see Chapter 24) is the big nighttime activity here, and **Ohana** is a favorite restaurant for families as it features kid-friendly activities during the dinner hour.

Though the South Pacific theme may bring on visions of romance, many a honeymooner who stays here is dismayed to discover the resort is over-flowing with kids. Adults looking for privacy beware.

See map p. 96. 1600 Seven Seas Dr. (off Floridian Way, across from Magnolia Palm Drive). ☎ *407-934-7639 or 407-824-2000. Fax: 407-824-3174. www.disneyworld. com. 853 units. Rack rates: $304–$580 double; $410–$2,550 concierge level and suites. AE, DC, DISC, MC, V.*

Disney's Pop Century Resort
$–$$ Walt Disney World

Flower power, the Rubik's Cube, and Play-Doh still rule supreme at the Pop Century Resort. Nestled behind the Caribbean Resort, near Disney's Wide World of Sports, this newest Disney value property is still a work in progress, as only one section of the resort was open at press time. The remainder will open in phases over the next few years. This value (Disney's word for budget) resort is perhaps the most fun for adults, who will enjoy the many reminders of their past, including a bowling alley–shaped pool and a three-story tall Big Wheel. The all-too-small rooms are in buildings decorated with pop culture references from the last four decades and mirror those at the All-Star Resorts in most every way. Forget frills — there aren't any; though, because it's new, there's been no wear and tear yet. Amenities include a brightly decorated food court, baby-sitting, three pools, and video arcade.

See map p. 96. 1050 Century Dr. (midway between Buena Vista Drive and Osceola Parkway). ☎ *407-934-7639 or 407-938-4000. Fax: 407-938-4040. www.disneyworld. com. 2,880 units. Rack rates: $77–$131 double. AE, DC, DISC, MC, V.*

Disney's Port Orleans Resort
$$ Walt Disney World

Port Orleans has the best location, landscaping, and the coziest atmos-phere of the resorts in this class. This Southern-style property is really a combination of two distinct resorts: the French Quarter and Riverside. Overall, this resort offers some romantic spots and is relatively quiet, making it popular with couples; but the pools, playgrounds, and array of activities make it a favorite for families as well. The Doubloon Lagoon pool in the French Quarter is a family favorite, with a water slide that curves out of a Sea Serpent's mouth before entering the recently refurbished pool. The rooms and bathrooms (equivalent to all rooms at Disney's moderate resorts) are somewhat of a tight fit for four (the Alligator Bayou rooms have a trundle bed, allowing for an extra person), but the vanity areas now have privacy curtains. **Boatwright's Dining Hall** (see Chapter 10) serves New Orleans–style cuisine; there's also a lively food court. Port Orleans is just east of Epcot and Disney–MGM Studios. *Note:* All 1,080 rooms in the French Quarter side reopened in March 2004 after closing for a top-to-bottom refurbishment. The 2,048 rooms in Riverside will be renovated in phases.

See map p. 96. 2201 Orleans Dr. (off Bonnet Creek Parkway). ☎ *407-934-7639 or 407-934-5000 (French Quarter) or 407-934-6000 (Riverside). Fax: 407-934-5353 (French Quarter) or 407-934-5777 (Riverside).* www.disneyworld.com. *3,056 units. Rack rates: $134–$209 double. AE, DC, DISC, MC, V.*

Disney's Saratoga Springs Resort & Spa
$$$–$$$$ Walt Disney World

This new **Disney Vacation Club** timeshare property opened its first section in spring 2004, and rooms are rented out to tourists when owners aren't using them. It's a good choice for large families or long stays. It's modeled after the luxurious upstate–New York country retreats of the late 1800s. The small, resort town of Saratoga Springs is evoked through lavish gardens, Victorian architecture, a pool designed to look like natural springs, and a country setting. The renowned spa offers a chance for relaxation and rejuvenation — both necessary after a day or two at the parks. The accommodations include studios, and one, two, and three-bedroom villas that have full kitchens or kitchenettes, coffeemakers, hair dryers, and all the comforts of home. The property has a restaurant, playground, video arcade, and four pools. The water taxi can transport you to Downtown Disney for more evening entertainment options.

See map p. 96. 1960 Broadway. (off Buena Vista Drive, next to Downtown Disney Marketplace). ☎ *407-934-7639 or 407-827-7700. Fax: 407-827-7710.* www.disneyworld.com. *552 units (upon completion). Rack rates: $259–$379 studios; $350–$1,505 villas. AE, DC, DISC, MC, V.*

Disney's Wilderness Lodge
$$$–$$$$ Walt Disney World

Here's an option for those who like the great outdoors but prefer the comfort of an indoor resort. The geyser out back, the mammoth stone hearth in the lobby, and bunk beds for the kids are just a few reasons this resort is a favorite of families, though couples will find the surroundings to their liking as well. The theme of the Great American Northwest is felt throughout the lodge; its rustic architecture is patterned after a lodge at Yellowstone National Park. The immense and winding swimming area cuts through the rocky landscaping. The nearest park is the Magic Kingdom, but because the resort is in a remote area, it can take some time to get there. The main drawback is the difficulty in accessing other areas via the WDW Transportation System.

The 181 units at the adjacent **Villas at Disney's Wilderness Lodge** were added in November 2000. This is another Disney Vacation Club timeshare property that rents vacant rooms. It offers a more upscale mountain retreat experience, and more room than accommodations at the Wilderness Lodge, though the properties share a grand lobby, amenities, and array of activities. Two restaurants are on site.

See map p. 96. 901 W. Timberline Dr. (on Seven Seas Drive, south of the Contemporary Resort on the southwest shore of Bay Lake). ☎ **407-934-7639** *or 407-938-4300. Fax: 407-824-3232.* www.disneyworld.com. *909 units. Rack rates: $199–$395 double; $360–$1,220 concierge level and suites; $284–$1,015 villas. AE, DC, DISC, MC, V.*

Disney's Yacht Club Resort
$$$$ Walt Disney World

The posh resort resembles a turn-of-the-20th-century New England yacht club and is located on the 25-acre lake it shares with the Beach Club (also listed in this chapter), which is a notch below in sophistication and atmosphere. This property is geared more toward adults and families with older children, although young kids are still catered to (you're in Disney World, after all). The relatively large rooms sleep up to five, and most rooms have patios or balconies, although some views are of the asphalt parking lots. The resort has two restaurants, an extensive swimming area that it shares with the Beach Club, a marina, and two tennis courts. **Epcot** is a mere 10- to 15-minute walk from the front door, and the BoardWalk, Swan, and Dolphin are just across the bridge.

See map p. 96. 1700 Epcot Resorts Blvd. (off Buena Vista Drive). ☎ **407-934-7639** *or 407-934-7000. Fax: 407-924-3450.* www.disneyworld.com. *630 units. Rack rates: $294–$525 double; $435–$2,345 concierge level and suites. AE, DC, DISC, MC, V.*

Doubletree Guest Suites Resort
$$–$$$ Lake Buena Vista/ Official WDW Hotel

This seven-story, all-suite hotel is the best of the "official" hotels for large families. Young patrons get their own check-in desk and theater. All accommodations are two-room suites that offer 643 square feet, and there's plenty of space for up to six to catch some zzzzs. You'll also find an array of recreational facilities, including a pool and two lighted tennis courts. Bus service to WDW parks is free and is available, for a fee, to other parks. Downtown Disney is only minutes away.

See map p. 96. 2305 Hotel Plaza Blvd. (just west of Apopka–Vineland Road/Highway 535; turn into the entrance to Downtown Disney Marketplace). ☎ **800-222-8733** *or 407-934-1000. Fax: 407-934-1015.* www.doubletreeguestsuites.com. *229 units. Rack rates: $119–$279 double. AE, DC, DISC, MC, V.*

Embassy Suites Lake Buena Vista
$$–$$$ Lake Buena Vista

Set near the end of Palm Parkway, just off Apopka-Vineland, this fun and welcoming all-suite resort is close to all the action of Downtown Disney and the surrounding area, yet still remains a quiet retreat. Each suite sleeps five and includes separate living area (with a pullout sofa) and sleeping quarters. The roomy accommodations make it a great choice for

U.S. 192/Kissimmee Accommodations

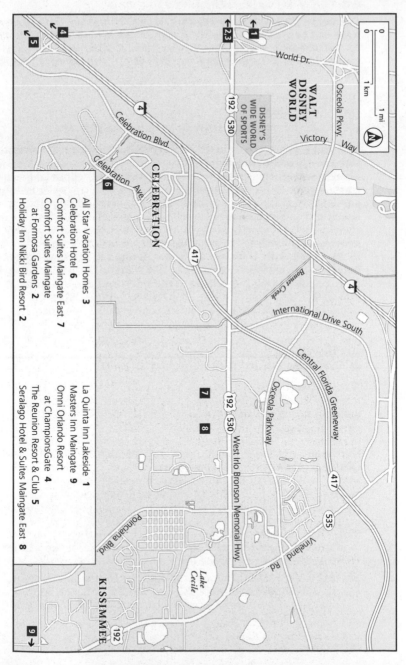

All Star Vacation Homes **3**
Celebration Hotel **6**
Comfort Suites Maingate East **7**
Comfort Suites Maingate
at Formosa Gardens **2**
Holiday Inn Nikki Bird Resort **2**

La Quinta Inn Lakeside **1**
Masters Inn Maingate **9**
Omni Orlando Resort
at ChampionsGate **4**
The Reunion Resort & Club **5**
Seralago Hotel & Suites Maingate East **8**

families. Some of the other perks here include a complimentary cooked-to-order breakfast and a daily manager's reception.

See map p. 96. 8100 Lake Avenue. (From I-4 take the Highway 535/Apopka-Vineland Road exit east to Palm Parkway. Follow ½ mile to Lake Avenue on the right.) ☎ *800-257-8483 or 407-239-1144. Fax: 407-238-0230.* www.embassysuites orlando.com. *333 units. Rack Rates: $129–$229. Valet parking: $7. AE, DC, DISC, MC, V.*

Hard Rock Hotel
$$$–$$$$ International Drive area/Universal Orlando

You can't get rooms closer to **CityWalk, Islands of Adventure,** or **Universal Studios Florida** than those at this California mission–style hotel. This Loews resort is on par with WDW's **Animal Kingdom Lodge,** although its rooms are 15 percent larger. Rooms come with two queens or one king and feature all the standard amenities. The giant outdoor pool with sand beach and underwater sound system is capable of bringing out the lounging rocker in you. Unfortunately, although the rooms are relatively sound-proof, a few notes seep through the walls, so ask for a room away from the lobby area if quiet is important to you. **Camp Li'l Rock** will keep the kids entertained while also offering Mom and Dad the chance for some time off. Free transportation is available to the **Universal** and **SeaWorld** parks. As for **Disney,** you're on your own. The biggest perk: Guests get no-line access to almost all rides and restaurants at Universal's theme parks.

See map p. 113. 5000 Universal Blvd. (Take I-4 to the Kirkman Road/Highway 435 exit and follow signs to Universal Orlando.) ☎ *888-232-7827 or 407-363-8000. Fax: 407-224-7118.* www.loewshotels.com/hotels/orlando. *654 units. Parking: self-parking $6; valet $12. Rack rates: $229–$409 double; $409–$1,770 suites. AE, DC, DISC, MC, V.*

Holiday Inn Nikki Bird Resort
$$ Kissimmee

Here's another great family base and the closest Holiday Inn to **Walt Disney World's** main gate. The resident mascot, Nikki, wanders the 26-acre resort, which offers extensive recreational facilities and Camp Nikki, a supervised kids' club. Kids 12 and younger eat free with a paying adult (two kids per adult) and are also treated to nightly entertainment, including puppet shows, songs, and games. Standard rooms sleep four, while **Kid Suites** have a separate area for youngsters. Suite themes vary. All accommodations feature refrigerators and microwaves. Transportation to the WDW parks is free; it's available for a fee to the other parks.

See map p. 109. 7300 Irlo Bronson Memorial Hwy. (located on U.S. 192 just west of I-4). ☎ *800-206-2747 or 407-396-7300. Fax: 407-396-7555.* www.holidayinnsof centralflorida.com. *530 units. Rack rates: $99–$149 double; $119–$179 Kid Suites. AE, DC, DISC, MC, V.*

Holiday Inn Sunspree Resort Lake Buena Vista
$$ Lake Buena Vista

Also close to the **Disney** parks, this Holiday Inn caters to kids in a big way. They get their own check-in desk, can watch a movie at the theater in the lobby area, or have fun at Camp Holiday, the supervised activity center (one of the best around). The hotel's spacious **Kid Suites** accommodate up to six and have themes such as a space capsule, igloo, jail, and more. Standard rooms are somewhat smaller and sleep four. All accommodations feature refrigerators and microwaves. If you like sleeping in, ask for a room that doesn't face the pool area. Kids younger than 12 eat free in their own restaurant, though fine dining it isn't (kids wouldn't appreciate that anyway).

See map p. 96. 13351 Lake Buena Vista (located off Highway 535 near the Crossroads Shopping Center). ☎ *800-366-6299 or 407-239-4500. Fax: 407-239-7713.* www.kid suites.com. *507 units. Rack rates: $99–$149 for up to 4 people; $119–$179 Kid Suites. AE, DISC, MC, V.*

Hyatt Regency Grand Cypress
$$$–$$$$ Lake Buena Vista

A resort destination in and of itself, this hotel is a great place to get away from the Disney-crowd frenzy while still remaining close to the action. You need deep pockets to stay here, but the reward is a palatial resort with lush foliage. The hotel's 18-story atrium has inner and outer glass elevators, which provide a unique thrill. The beautifully decorated rooms offer the usual amenities. Recreational facilities are extensive and include golf (45 holes), 12 tennis courts (5 lighted), 2 racquetball courts, a spa, an adjoining equestrian center, and more. The property's half-acre, 800,000-gallon pool is one of the best in town, with caves, grottoes, and waterfalls. There's free transportation to **WDW,** however you'll have to pay to go elsewhere. If you're in need of a break, the kids can play at the supervised childcare facility, one of the better ones around.

See map p. 96. 1 N. Jacaranda (Highway 535 north of Disney's Lake Buena Vista entrance or Hotel Plaza Boulevard). ☎ *800-233-1234 or 407-239-1234. Fax: 407-239-3837.* www.hyattgrandcypress.com. *750 units. Rack rates: $239–$585 double; $695–$5,750 suites. Optional resort fee: $13. Valet parking: $12. AE, DC, DISC, MC, V.*

JW Marriott Orlando, Grande Lakes
$$–$$$$ International Drive Area/Universal Orlando

Opened in 2004, this Moorish-themed resort is situated on 500 acres of lush, tropical landscaping at the new Grande Lakes development, just east of **SeaWorld.** The guest rooms are on par with those in Disney's moderate class. Ask for a west-facing room for the best views. The smoke-free resort is home to six restaurants and lounges and shares its recreational facilities with the neighboring Ritz-Carlton (see later this chapter), including a Greg Norman–designed 72-par golf course and a 40,000-square-foot spa. The best feature is the fabulous landscaped 24,000-square-foot Lazy River pool, which winds through rock formations and small waterfalls. I could do without is the $11 per day parking fee, however.

See map p. 113. 4040 Central Florida Pkwy. (at the intersection of John Young Parkway, 2 miles east of SeaWorld). ☎ *800-576-5750 or 407-206-2300. Fax: 407-206-2301.* www.grandelakes.com. *1,000 units. Parking: $11 self-parking; $15 valet. Rack rates: $89–$369 double; $299–$4,000 suites. AE, DC, DISC, MC, V.*

La Quinta Inn Lakeside
$–$$ **Kissimmee**

The hand-painted exteriors, lobby, and common areas of this recently renovated hotel give it a unique charm not found in its hotel brethren. Just up the road from the Disney entrance, this 24-acre resort looks deceptively small when you first pull up (most of the accommodations are hidden behind the lobby area), but amenities include numerous recreational options (pools, playgrounds, and so on), a food court, good-sized convenience store, and a bountiful, free breakfast. Rooms are standard in size and offerings, but are nicely decorated and will comfortably sleep four. Other pluses include a childcare facility and free transportation to *all* the major theme parks. A continental breakfast is included.

See map p. 109. 7769 Irlo Bronson Memorial Hwy./U.S. 192. (Take I-4 to Exit 64B/U.S. 192 West); the hotel is approximately 3 miles on the right). ☎ *800-531-5900 or 407-396-2222. Fax: 407-396-7087.* www.laquintainnlakeside.com. *651 units. Rack Rates: $59–$139. Rates include continental breakfast. AE, DC, DISC, MC, V.*

Masters Inn Maingate
$ **Kissimmee**

Clean rooms, a heated outdoor pool, free continental breakfast, and free shuttles to the **Disney** parks, all for under $50 a night, have made this property a budget favorite. Some two-room suites are available at terrific prices as well. There are two other Masters Inn properties in the Orlando theme-park areas, but this one, nearest the **Magic Kingdom,** has received the ultimate approval for a property trying to get in good with Mickey — an official stamp of approval as a Disney "Good Neighbor" hotel.

See map p. 109. 2945 Entry Point Blvd. (on U.S. 192, 2 miles west of the Walt Disney World main gate entrance and I-4). ☎ *800-337-2076 or 407-396-7743. Fax: 407-396-6307.* www.mastersinnorlando.com. *106 units. Rack rates: $39–$69 double; $84–$104 suites. Rates include continental breakfast. AE, DISC, MC, V.*

Microtel Inn and Suites
$ **International Drive Area/Universal Orlando**

This newer budget chain property, centrally located near the intersection of Sand Lake Road and International Drive, offers clean basic rooms and minisuites with microwaves and refrigerators. The hotel even throws in a free breakfast and local calls. *Business Travel News* (the hotel is near the

International Drive Area Accommodations

Amerisuites Universal **3**
Crowne-Plaza
  Orlando Universal **6**
Hard Rock Hotel **2**
JW Marriott Orlando,
  Grande Lakes **9**
Microtel Inn and Suites **5**
Peabody Orlando **7**
Portofino Bay Hotel **1**
Renaissance Orlando
  Resort at SeaWorld **8**
Ritz-Carlton Orlando,
  Grande Lakes **9**
Royal Pacific Resort **4**

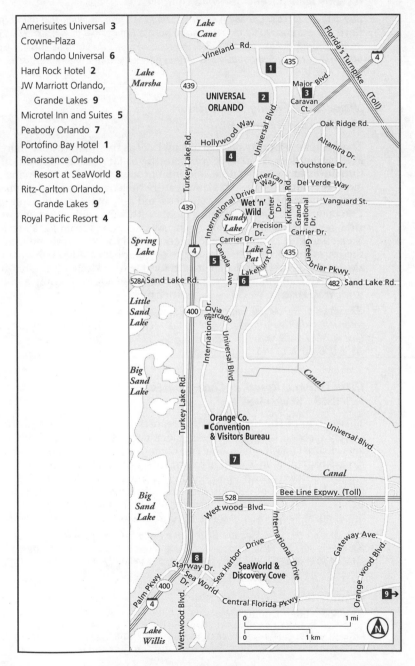

Orlando Convention Center and is popular with convention-goers) recently named it the best value in the city.

See map p. 113. 7531 Canada Ave. (Take Sand Lake Road a block east of International Drive; the entrance to Canada Avenue is next to Popeye's Chicken). ☎ **800-248-7890** *or 407-828-2828. Fax: 407-827-6338.* www.microtelsuitesorlando.com. *128 units. Rack rates: $60 double; $70 suites. Rates include continental breakfast. AE, DISC, MC, V.*

Nickelodeon Family Suites Resort
$$–$$$ Lake Buena Vista

This all-suite property opened in July 1999 as the Holiday Inn Family Suites Resort and does a fantastic job catering to families. A $20-million transformation into an official Nickelodeon property, in 2004, has made it even more kid friendly. The suites now feature Nick-decorated bedrooms for the kids, complete with bunk or twin beds and a TV and video-console system. The resort offers two sprawling pools with waterslides and flumes; poolside game areas and a game room; wake-up calls from Nick stars; daily Nick-character breakfasts; a food court; and live entertainment featuring the only Orlando appearance of the popular Nickelodeon characters outside of Universal Orlando. Most suites come with kitchenettes, but the new three-bedroom units have full kitchens. The location — only a mile away from **Walt Disney World** — is another plus.

See map p. 96. 14500 Continental Gateway (From I-4, take the Highway 536/ International Drive exit east 1 mile to the resort.) ☎ **877-387-5437** *or 407-387-5437. Fax: 407-387-1489.* www.nickhotel.com. *800 units. Rack rates: $169–$275 suites. AE, DC, DISC, MC, V.*

Omni Orlando Resort at ChampionsGate
$$$–$$$$ Kissimmee

This is one of the newest luxury resorts to spring up just south of the Disney district. Extensive meeting facilities are coupled with comprehensive leisure facilities, including two championship golf courses designed by Greg Norman, a vast pool area with its very own lazy "river," a 10,000-square-foot European spa, and much more. The beautifully-appointed rooms feature 9-foot ceilings and a complete roster of amenities, including plush robes. The service is as impressive as the facility itself, with a lengthy list of guest services, including a program especially geared to youngsters.

See map p. 109. 1500 Masters Blvd. (Take I-4 to Exit 58 and bear right.) ☎ 407-390-6664. *Fax: 407-390-6660.* www.omnihotels.com. *730 units. Rack rates: $199–$350 double; $450–$2,500 suites. Daily resort fee: $10. Valet parking: $12. AE, DC, DISC, MC, V.*

Orlando World Center Marriott
$$–$$$$ Lake Buena Vista

One of the top places to stay in Orlando, this 230-acre resort is popular with the business crowd, couples, and families alike. The resort's sports facilities are first class, and its grotto swimming pool features waterfalls and hidden spas. A recent $6 million renovation enhanced the 200-acre golf course, as well as the dining and lobby areas. The large, comfortable, and beautifully decorated rooms sleep four with options for larger parties available. The upper floors facing **Disney** have great views of nightly fireworks. The location, only minutes to Disney via a less-congested road, can't be beat.

See map p. 96. 8701 World Center Dr. (on Highway 536 between I-4 and Highway 535). ☎ *800-621-0638 or 407-939-4200. Fax: 407-238-8777.* www.marriottworld center.com. *2,111 units. Parking: $6 self-parking; $16 valet. Rack rates: $159–$410 double; $750–$1,600 suites. AE, DC, DISC, MC, V.*

Peabody Orlando
$$$$ International Drive Area/Universal Orlando

Welcome to the home of the famous — drum roll, maestro, *s'il vous plaît* — **Marching Mallards.** These real ducks march through the lobby into their luxury pool each morning at 11 a.m. (no kidding!), accompanied by — what else? — John Philip Sousa's marching music and a red-coated duck master, and then back out at 5 p.m.

The Peabody Hotel is located across from the Convention Center, in the thick of all the action I-Drive has to offer, including attractions, restaurants, and shopping. Guest rooms, even standard ones, are lavishly furnished and come with numerous amenities. The Peabody offers not only the best service in town but also some of the best hotel dining — look for its signature restaurant, **Dux,** in Chapter 10. You'll have to pay for transportation to all the theme parks, so a rental car is a good idea if you want to stay here.

The Peabody is scheduled to begin a major expansion, which will double its room capacity and add more family-friendly elements (which are lacking), sometime during 2005.

See map p. 113. 9801 International Drive (between the BeeLine Expressway and Sand Lake Road). ☎ *800-732-2639 or 407-352-4000. Fax: 407-354-1424.* www.peabody orlando.com. *891 units. Rack rates: $400–$490 double; $750–$1,700 suites. Valet parking: $10. AE, DC, DISC, MC, V.*

Portofino Bay Hotel
$$$–$$$$ International Drive Area/Universal Orlando

Another Loews property, this one really delivers for those with deep pockets. Inspired by a comment from director Steven Speilberg, who at the time was working on a ride at Islands of Adventure, it offers six restaurants/lounges, a spa, a beach pool with a fort and water slide, and a fitness center in a package that's convincingly designed to look like the Mediterranean seaside village of Portofino, Italy. The accommodations offer four-poster beds with cloud-soft pillows, and bathrooms outfitted with marble tubs and tiled foyers. Rooms are state-of-the-art "smart rooms" that provide security, adjust room temperature, and report malfunctions as they occur. The hotel offers free transportation to **Universal's** and **SeaWorld**'s parks, but (they're not stupid!) forget the free ride to the **Disney** ones. Best feature: Guests get no-line access to almost all rides at Universal's theme parks. *Note:* Getting around the resort involves ascending and descending numerous stairs.

See map p. 113. 5601 Universal Blvd. (From I-4, take Kirkman Road/Highway 435 and follow the signs to Universal.) ☎ *888-322-5541 or 407-503-1000. Fax: 407-224-7118.* www.loewshotels.com/hotels/orlando. *750 rooms. Parking: $6 self-parking; $12 valet. Rack rates: $259–$429 double; $459–$2,200 suites and villas. AE, DC, DISC, MC, V.*

Renaissance Orlando Resort at SeaWorld
$$–$$$ International Drive Area/Universal Orlando

Large rooms, good service, and a luxurious interior (a 10-story atrium houses lush gardens, cascading waterfalls, a koi pond, and an elegant free-flight aviary) are this hotel's calling cards. Its most valuable feature, however, is a location that's perfect if you're going to **Universal, SeaWorld** (it's right across the street), and, to a lesser degree, the second-tier I-Drive attractions. The beautifully decorated rooms are oversized, allowing for plenty of space to spread out and relax. The Renaissance has four lighted tennis courts, a health club, spa and sauna, and a completely renovated pool area, as well as two restaurants, and arguably the best Sunday brunch in Orlando. Transportation to the parks is available for a fee, though most guests can easily walk to SeaWorld.

See map p. 113. 6677 Sea Harbour Dr. (From I-4, follow signs to SeaWorld; the hotel is across from the attraction.) ☎ *800-327-6677 or 407-351-5555. Fax: 407-351-1991.* www.renaissancehotels.com. *778 units. Rack rates: $149–$309 double. AE, DC, DISC, MC, V.*

The Reunion Resort & Club
$$$–$$$$ Kissimmee

One of the newest luxury resorts to open its gates, the Reunion is a resort community still in its early phases of development (with a completion date some 10 years into the future). Currently operational are a handful of the villas and vacation homes as well as an extensive onsite water park (in addition to other resort pools located throughout the property), a tennis complex, stables, retailers, restaurants, and a spa. Two championship golf courses are currently operational with a third underway. A **kids' program** offering a variety of supervised activities is set to begin soon as well. Future plans include two luxury hotels, additional villas, resort homes, condominiums, town homes, and more. Just down the way (at ChampionsGate) there's a small shopping plaza with a grocery store, pharmacy, and a handful of shops, businesses, and very casual eateries.

See map p. 109. 1000 Reunion Way. (Take I-4 to Exit 58; turn left onto Highway 532, go approximately ¾ mile; the hotel entrance is on the left.) ☎ *888-418-9611 or 407-662-1000. Fax: 407-662-1111.* www.reunionresort.com. *To eventually include 8,000 units. Rack rates: $255–$495 villas; $305–$835 homes. Greens fees and cart fees vary. AE, DC, DISC, MC, V.*

Ritz-Carlton Orlando, Grande Lakes
$$$–$$$$ International Drive Area/Universal Orlando

Part of the lush 500-acre Grande Lakes Resort complex, this luxury resort — styled like an Italian palazzo — opened in 2004. All the spacious guest rooms feature dual private balconies, flat-screen TVs, and oversized marble bathrooms with separate bathtub and shower. For the ultimate experience, upgrade to the Club Level to receive butler service, Bulgari bath amenities, an in-room DVD/VCR/CD player, and free snacks. There are seven on-site restaurants and lounges and the Ritz shares some recreational amenities with the neighboring JW Marriott (see the review earlier in this chapter), including a Greg Norman–designed golf course and a 40,000-square-foot spa. The resort's **Ritz Kids program** includes a children's pool and playground, separate check-in area, and on-site nanny service (for a fee). Kids' suites offer equally lavish accommodations especially designed for younger guests. You will need your own transportation if you want to visit the parks and attractions.

See map p. 113. 4012 Central Florida Pkwy. (at the intersection of John Young Parkway, 2 miles east of SeaWorld). ☎ 800-576-5760 or 407-206-2400. Fax: 407-206-2401. www.grandelakes.com. 584 units. Valet parking: $15. Rack rates: $229–$399 double; $599–$5,000 club level and suites. AE, DC, DISC, MC, V.

Royal Pacific Resort
$$$ International Drive Area/Universal Orlando

The newest **Universal** resort sports an attractive Polynesian theme that's the best of the bunch. Highlights of the property include an exquisite orchid garden, five restaurants and lounges (one run by famed chef Emeril Lagasse), and a lagoon-style pool — the largest in Orlando. The guest rooms are smaller than those at Universal's other hotels, but are comfortable and are far better than those at comparable Disney resorts. The Royal Pacific isn't cheap, but it offers good value for the money, especially when you factor in the hotel's free transport to Universal's theme parks, where guests get no-line access to almost all rides. One thing I could do without: The outrageous $6 self-parking charge, especially when the parking lot is quite a hike from the hotel.

See map p. 113. 4500 Universal Blvd. (Take I-4 to the Kirkman Road/Highway 435 exit and follow signs to Universal Orlando.) ☎ 800-232-7827 or 407-503-3000. Fax: 407-503-3202. www.loewshotels.com/hotels/orlando. 1,000 units. Parking: $6 self-parking; $12 valet. Rack rates: $199–$369 double; $299–$1,670 suites. AE, DC, DISC, MC, V.

Seralago Hotel & Suites Maingate East
$–$$ Kissimmee

Location (it's just down the road from Disney) and price are just some of the perks here. This newly revamped hotel (formerly the Holiday Inn & Suites Maingate East) sports all new colors and a bright new look, but it still features the themed **Kid Suites** with separate sleeping areas for your children, as well as standard rooms and regular two-room suites. The rooms provide a reasonable amount of space for a family of five, with the two-room unit sleeping up to eight. There are plenty of family recreational activities, from swimming to tennis, and the hotel's movie theater shows free family films nightly. There's also a family-friendly food court, and kids 12 and younger eat free (two kids per paying adult) in the hotel's cafe.

See map p. 109. 5678 Irlo Bronson Memorial Hwy./U.S. 192. (Take I-4 to Exit 64A to U.S. 192; the hotel is 2 miles on the right.) ☎ *800-366-5437 or 407-396-4488. Fax: 407-396-8915.* www.orlandofamilyfunhotel.com. *614 units. Rack rates: $59–$119. AE, DC, DISC, MC, V.*

Staybridge Suites Lake Buena Vista
$$–$$$ Lake Buena Vista

A Summerfield Suites in a previous life, this recent addition to the Staybridge Suites chain is located just off Apopka–Vineland, close to the action of Downtown Disney and the theme parks, as well as many restaurants. An excellent choice for families, this hotel's room sizes, price, and friendly staff are three more good reasons to stay here. Featured are one- and two-bedroom suites (can sleep up to eight), all with full kitchens (some two-bedroom suites have two bathrooms). The suites have large, comfortable, separate living areas when compared to other all-suite hotels. A continental breakfast is included.

See map p. 96. 8751 Suiteside Dr. (From I-4, take the exit for 535, turn right; follow to Vinings Way Road, turn right; the hotel is located on the left.) ☎ *800-866-4549 or 407-238-0777. Fax: 407/238-2640.* www.ichotelsgroup.com. *150 units. Rack rates: $159–$299. Rates include continental breakfast. AE, DC, DISC, MC, V.*

Veranda Bed & Breakfast
$$ Downtown Orlando

Located in Thornton Park, this inn near scenic Lake Eola is an option if you want to stay near the downtown museums but not in a motel or hotel. Its four buildings date to the early 1900s. All units (studios to suites) include private baths and entrances; some have garden tubs, balconies, kitchenettes, and four-poster beds. The two-bedroom, two-bath Key Lime Cottage ($209) sleeps four and has a full kitchen. Rates include a continental breakfast. The B&B doesn't offer transportation to the parks, meaning a rental car is a necessity for most guests. *Note:* Children are not permitted.

115 N. Summerlin Ave. ☎ *800-420-6822 or 407-849-0321. Fax: 407-849-0321, ext. 24.* www.theverandabandb.com. *12 units. Rack rates: $109–$139 double; $209 cottage. Rates include continental breakfast. AE, DC, DISC, MC, V.*

The Villas of Grand Cypress
$$$–$$$$ Lake Buena Vista

Meet the sister of the Hyatt Regency Grand Cypress (listed earlier in this chapter). The one- to four-bedroom villas, a short drive from the larger hotel, offer privacy not found in most resorts. You can play 45 holes of golf on Jack Nicklaus–designed courses or take lessons at the golf academy. The horse crowd loves the top-of-the-line equestrian center; riding lessons and packages are available. (See Chapter 27 for more information on riding.) The Mediterranean-style villas, which range from junior suites to four-bedroom affairs, have patios or balconies, and Roman tubs. Larger villas have full kitchens. There's free shuttle service to the resort's recreational facilities and to the **WDW** parks. Unlike its sister Hyatt property, this resort caters primarily to adults, but Villa guests with kids can use the Hyatt's childcare as well as recreational facilities.

See map p. 96. 1 N. Jacaranda (off Highway 535, past the Disney entrance on Hotel Plaza Boulevard, about a mile on the right). ☎ *800-835-7377 or 407-239-4700. Fax: 407-239-7219.* www.grandcypress.com. *146 villas. Rack rates: $215–$2,000 villas. Daily resort fee: $12. AE, DC, DISC, MC, V.*

Walt Disney World Dolphin
$$$–$$$$ Walt Disney World/Official WDW Hotel

What a wonderful place for folks a) not on a budget, b) wanting to be close to **Epcot** and **Disney–MGM Studios,** and c) desperate to stay in a place that answers the question: What kind of gingerbread would Dali have created if he were an architect? It's hard not to notice the massive, 56-foot twin dolphin caricatures on the roof of this resort. Once inside the lobby, you'll encounter prints from the likes of Matisse and Picasso.

Rooms offer views of the grounds and parts of **WDW** and were upgraded throughout 2004. The resort shares its extensive recreational facilities, including a grotto pool with waterfalls, water slide, and whirlpools, as well as a Body by Jake health club, and soon a new luxury Mandara Spa, with its sister hotel the **Walt Disney World Swan** (listed later in this chapter). The hotel offers free transportation to the **WDW** parks, but you have to pay for a ride to the others.

Though it's essentially treated as a Disney hotel, and guests get the same privileges as a Disney resort guest, this one is actually owned and operated by Starwood hotels as a Westin Resort. As a result you may find discounts for this one that wouldn't otherwise be available at Disney-owned hotels. On the downside, it also means you get socked with a daily resort fee.

See map p. 96. 1500 Epcot Resorts Blvd. (off Buena Vista Drive, next to Walt Disney World Swan). ☎ *800-227-1500 or 407-934-4000. Fax: 407-934-4884.* www.swan dolphin.com. *1,509 units. Rack rates: $259–$409 double; $625–$3,255 suites. Daily resort fee: $10. AE, DC, DISC, MC, V.*

Walt Disney World Swan
$$$–$$$$ Walt Disney World/Official WDW Hotel

Located on the same property as the Dolphin, the Swan offers another chance to stay on Magic Mickey's property without being bombarded by Mouse décor. This 12-story Westin hotel is topped with dual 45-foot swan statues and seashell fountains. The Swan and Dolphin hotels are connected by a canopied walkway and both share recreational facilities, including four pools and four lighted tennis courts. The luxurious rooms are a shade smaller than those in the Dolphin but have Nintendo games (for a fee), and Westin's signature "Heavenly Bed" (firm mattress, down blanket, comforter, and five pillows). The resort underwent a major renovation in 2003 by original architect Michael Graves, who redid the resort in tones of silver-blue and white. You can get a free ride to the **Disney** parks and transportation, for a fee, to the other theme parks.

See map p. 96. 1200 Epcot Resorts Blvd. (off Buena Vista Dr., next door to the Walt Disney World Dolphin). ☎ *800-248-7926, 800-228-3000, or 407-934-3000. Fax: 407-934-4499.* www.swandolphin.com. *758 units. Rack rates: $259–$495 double; $865–$2,835 suites. Daily resort fee: $10. Valet Parking $14. AE, DC, DISC, MC, V.*

Westin Grand Bohemian
$$–$$$$ **Downtown Orlando**

The Grand Bohemian has an early-20th–century Euro-Bohemian look. It caters almost exclusively to the business and romance crowds, which means you'll find few children on the premises. Its rooms feature an Art Deco motif, with plenty of chrome, reds, purples, and mirrors. The "Heavenly Beds" (firm mattresses, down comforters, blankets , and five pillows) are among the best in Orlando. The upper floors on the east side overlook the pool; the north side faces downtown. The hotel, which is smoke free, has more than 100 pieces of 19th- and 20th-century American fine art. This isn't the most convenient hotel if your vacation is solely centered on the parks, but it is far enough away if you need a break from all the manic energy of screaming kids and adults in costume. Not to mention the wonderful downtown nightlife right outside the front door.

325 S. Orlando Ave. (It's across from City Hall.) ☎ *866-663-0024 or 407-313-9000. Fax: 407-313-6001.* www.grandbohemianhotel.com. *250 units. Rack rates: $169–$389 for up to 4; $379–$579 and up suites. Valet parking: $18. AE, DC, DISC, MC, V.*

Wyndham Palace Resort
$$–$$$ **Lake Buena Vista/Official WDW Hotel**

The hotel's spacious accommodations — most with lake-view balconies or patios — are literally across the road from **Downtown Disney.** It's an ideal spot for honeymooners or those looking for a romantic weekend getaway. Many of the appealing business-standard rooms have balconies or patios; ask for one above the fifth floor with a "recreation view." Because business people make up 75 percent of its guests, the hotel offers some of its best rates in July and August, contrary to the other Orlando mainstream tourist resorts. Amenities include three pools, a fully equipped spa, a sauna, a video arcade, and two restaurants, including the 27th-floor Arthur's 27 (see Chapter 10). Rates include free transportation to **Disney;** you pay a fee for transportation to the other theme parks.

See map p. 96. 1900 Buena Vista Drive (off Highway 535, turn in the entrance to Downtown Disney Marketplace; the hotel is on Hotel Plaza Boulevard). ☎ *800-996-3426 or 407-827-2727. Fax: 407-827-6034.* www.wyndhamorlando

hotels.com. *1,014 units. Rack rates: $149–$269 double; $209–$618 suites. Daily resort fee: $10. AE, DC, DISC, MC, V.*

Index of Accommodations by Neighborhood

Downtown Orlando

Courtyard at Lake Lucerne ($–$$$)
Veranda Bed & Breakfast ($$)
Westin Grand Bohemian ($$–$$$$)

International Drive Area/Universal Orlando

AmeriSuites Universal ($–$$)
Crowne Plaza Orlando-Universal ($$$–$$$$)
Hard Rock Hotel ($$$–$$$$)
JW Marriott Orlando, Grande Lakes ($$–$$$$)
Microtel Inn and Suites ($)
Peabody Orlando ($$$$)
Portofino Bay Hotel ($$$–$$$$)
Renaissance Orlando Resort at SeaWorld ($$–$$$)
Ritz-Carlton Orlando, Grande Lakes ($$$–$$$$)
Royal Pacific Resort ($$$)

Lake Buena Vista (including Official WDW Hotels)

Doubletree Guest Suites Resort ($$–$$$)
Embassy Suites Lake Buena Vista ($$–$$$)
Holiday Inn Sunspree Resort Lake Buena Vista ($$)
Hyatt Regency Grand Cypress ($$$–$$$$)
Nickelodeon Family Suites Resort ($$–$$$)
Orlando World Center Marriott ($$–$$$$)
Staybridge Suites Lake Buena Vista ($$–$$$)
The Villas of Grand Cypress ($$$–$$$$)

Walt Disney World Dolphin ($$$–$$$$)
Walt Disney World Swan ($$$–$$$$)
Wyndham Palace Resort ($$–$$$)

Kissimmee

All Star Vacation Homes ($–$$$$)
Celebration Hotel ($$–$$$$)
Comfort Suites Maingate East ($–$$)
Comfort Suites Maingate at Formosa Gardens ($–$$)
Holiday Inn Nikki Bird Resort ($$)
La Quinta Inn Lakeside ($–$$)
Masters Inn Maingate ($)
Omni Orlando Resort at ChampionsGate ($$$–$$$$)
The Reunion Resort & Club ($$$–$$$$)
Seralago Hotel & Suites Maingate East ($–$$)

Walt Disney World

Disney's All-Star Movie Resort ($–$$)
Disney's All-Star Music Resort ($–$$)
Disney's All-Star Sports Resort ($–$$)
Disney's Animal Kingdom Lodge ($$$–$$$$)
Disney's Beach Club Resort ($$$$)
Disney's BoardWalk Inn ($$$$)
Disney's Caribbean Beach Resort ($$)
Disney's Contemporary Resort ($$$–$$$$)
Disney's Coronado Springs Resort ($$)
Disney's Fort Wilderness Resort & Campground ($–$$$)
Disney's Grand Floridian Resort & Spa ($$$$)
Disney's Old Key West Resort ($$$–$$$$)
Disney's Polynesian Resort ($$$$)
Disney's Pop Century Resort ($–$$)

Disney's Port Orleans Resort ($$)
Disney's Saratoga Springs Resort &
Spa ($$$–$$$$)

Disney's Wilderness Lodge
($$$–$$$$)
Disney's Yacht Club Resort ($$$$)

Index of Accommodations by Price

$$$$ ($301 and up)

All Star Vacation Homes (Kissimmee)
Celebration Hotel (Kissimmee)
Crowne Plaza Orlando-Universal
(International Drive Area)
Disney's Animal Kingdom Lodge (Walt
Disney World)
Disney's Beach Club Resort (Walt
Disney World)
Disney's BoardWalk Inn (Walt Disney
World)
Disney's Contemporary Resort (Walt
Disney World)
Disney's Grand Floridian Resort & Spa
(Walt Disney World)
Disney's Old Key West Resort (Walt
Disney World)
Disney's Polynesian Resort (Walt
Disney World)
Disney's Saratoga Springs Resort &
Spa (Walt Disney World)
Disney's Wilderness Lodge & Villas
(Walt Disney World)
Disney's Yacht Club Resort (Walt
Disney World)
Hard Rock Hotel (International Drive
Area/Universal Orlando)
Hyatt Regency Grand Cypress (Lake
Buena Vista)
JW Marriott Orlando, Grande Lakes
(International Drive Area)
Omni Orlando Resort at
ChampionsGate (Kissimmee)
Orlando World Center Marriott (Lake
Buena Vista)
Peabody Orlando (International Drive
Area)
Portofino Bay Hotel (International
Drive Area/Universal Orlando)
The Reunion Resort & Club
(Kissimmee)

Ritz-Carlton Orlando, Grande Lakes
(International Drive Area)
The Villas of Grand Cypress (Lake
Buena Vista)
Walt Disney World Dolphin (Lake
Buena Vista/Official WDW Hotel)
Walt Disney World Swan (Lake Buena
Vista/Official WDW Hotel)
Westin Grand Bohemian (Downtown
Orlando)

$$$ ($201–$300)

Doubletree Guest Suites Resort (Lake
Buena Vista/Official WDW Hotel)
Embassy Suites Lake Buena Vista
(Lake Buena Vista)
Nickelodeon Family Suites Resort
(Lake Buena Vista)
Renaissance Orlando Resort at
SeaWorld (International Drive Area)
Royal Pacific Resort (International
Drive/Universal Orlando)
Staybridge Suites (Lake Buena Vista)
Wyndham Palace Resort (Lake Buena
Vista)

$$ ($101–$200)

Disney's Caribbean Beach Resort
(Walt Disney World)
Disney's Coronado Springs Resort
(Walt Disney World)
Disney's Port Orleans Resort (Walt
Disney World)
Holiday Inn Nikki Bird Resort
(Kissimmee)
Holiday Inn Sunspree Resort Lake
Buena Vista (Lake Buena Vista)
Veranda Bed & Breakfast (Downtown
Orlando)

$ *(Less than $100)*

AmeriSuites Universal (International Drive)

Comfort Suites Maingate East (Kissimmee)

Comfort Suites Maingate at Formosa Gardens (Kissimmee)

Courtyard at Lake Lucerne (Downtown Orlando)

Disney's All-Star Movie Resort (Walt Disney World)

Disney's All-Star Music Resort (Walt Disney World)

Disney's All-Star Sports Resort (Walt Disney World)

Disney's Fort Wilderness Resort & Campground (Walt Disney World)

Disney's Pop Century Resort (Walt Disney World)

La Quinta Inn Lakeside (Kissimmee)

Masters Inn Maingate (Kissimmee)

Microtel Inn and Suites (International Drive Area)

Seralago Hotel & Suites Maingate East (Kissimmee)

Chapter 10

Dining and Snacking in Orlando

* *

In This Chapter

▶ Sampling Orlando's eateries
▶ Dining options for the budget-conscious
▶ Exploring the best dining in Orlando
▶ Sharing a meal with the Mouse and other characters

* *

*W*ith more than 5,000 restaurants in the Orlando area, there's certainly no lack of dining choices. New restaurants are opening all the time with just as many stale ones closing. Most are surprisingly decent (Orlando is, after all, a city where food tends to be viewed merely as fuel); though some of the more recent entries on the dining scene are definitely making their mark. In this chapter, I offer general pointers about dining in the land of Diz, explain the ins and outs of making reservations, provide detailed reviews of the city's best restaurants, and give you the lowdown on Orlando's most famous meal experience: character dining.

Getting the Dish on the Local Scene

Few people come to Orlando with fine dining on the mind, though it's a lot easier to find nowadays than it used to be. The city has its fair share of fancier spots that can compete with the best in the country (**Disney's Victoria & Albert, Emeril Lagasse**'s two Universal Orlando restaurants, **Manuel's on the 28th**), but most visitors tend to dine at the chains, which are seemingly everywhere you turn, or inside the theme parks, where the food doesn't often astound, but the atmosphere is right. In this city, the emphasis tends to be more on the experience and the theme than it is on the food (which, most restaurant execs appear to reason, is used to generate enough kick to get through the attractions without your tank getting empty).

With only a very few exceptions, if you want truly first-class cuisine without having to take out a second mortgage, you have to get out of the theme-park zones. Restaurants catering to locals (especially in the Dr.

Philips area and Winter Park, but also in Downtown Orlando) usually offer excellent food and a sophisticated atmosphere at prices far less daunting than inside the major tourist zones, with a small handful of others located in downtown Orlando as well. I review a number of excellent local restaurants in this chapter.

Most Orlando restaurants go out of their way to cater to kids, offering children's menus, diversions such as crayons at the table, high chairs, and so on. The high kid-quotient generally means a higher volume level and a more jovial atmosphere. Adults seeking a quiet, sophisticated, or romantic night out do have options, however, and I note restaurants that offer some respite from the kids on the "Good for Grown-ups" list found on this book's tear-out cheat sheet.

Orlando's own tend to dine early (as do most visitors with kids). For a more leisurely and relaxed meal, try to eat dinner after 8:30 p.m., but don't wait too late — except for a few fast-food joints, many restaurants close between 10 and 11 p.m.

For more information on the types of Orlando cuisine, see Chapter 2.

Dressing down

Didn't pack the tux this time around, or just not a fan of dressing for dinner? The good news is the city's casual attitude generally extends to most of its restaurants, so you can leave the penguin suits and long gowns at home. At the theme parks, nobody will look at you twice if you walk in to an otherwise formal atmosphere in shorts and a T-shirt. That said, there are a few high-end restaurants that do require formal or semi-formal attire; if a coat and tie is called for at a restaurant, I note it in the restaurant reviews in this chapter.

Lighting up

If you're a smoker, don't plan on lighting up over dinner. Effective July 1, 2003, a state constitutional amendment banned smoking in Florida's public workplaces, including all restaurants and bars that serve food. Stand-alone bars that serve virtually no food are exempt, and so are designated smoking rooms in hotels and motels, but they are becoming fewer and farther between.

Making reservations

Reserving a table is a wise idea for most of Orlando's finest restaurants, but in most cases, you can wait to make same-day reservations. You will find, of course, some exceptions to this rule, and I note them in the appropriate restaurant reviews.

Advanced Dining Reservations (previously known as Priority Seating) is the only option available at most **Disney** properties. This practice is Mickey's way of saying that you get the next available table after you arrive (at your pre-arranged arrival time). Understand however, you'll probably still have to wait 10 to 15 minutes after you get to the restaurant before actually being seated. I recommend that you always call as far ahead as possible to make an Advanced Dining Reservation. If you try walking in off the street to find a table, you may not get one before your stomach starts growling at you (if you get one at all). Call ☎ 407-939-3463 to stake a claim to a table at Mickey's place. If you're staying at a **WDW** resort, you can make Advanced Dining Reservations at the hotel's *Guest Relations* desk, with the concierge, or dial ☎ 55 from your room phone and arrange it yourself.

Don't even think of showing up for a **Disney character meal** (see "Dining with Disney Characters" at the end of this chapter) without an Advanced Dining Reservation made far in advance if you want to ensure you get a table. Some of the meals take Advanced Dining Reservations up to two years ahead of time — and some of them book up within minutes.

You can also make Advanced Dining Reservations after you're inside the Disney parks — best done immediately upon your arrival. At **Epcot,** make reservations at the **Worldkey** interactive terminals at *Guest Relations* in **Innoventions East,** at **Worldkey Information Service** satellites located on the main concourse to World Showcase, and at **Germany** in World Showcase, or at the restaurants themselves. In the **Magic Kingdom,** you can sign up at *Guest Relations* inside City Hall or at the restaurants. For **Disney–MGM Studios,** reserve a table via *Guest Relations* just inside the entrance or at the restaurants. At **Animal Kingdom,** reserve at *Guest Relations* near the entrance.

Worried **WDW** can't entertain your vegetarian taste buds? Looking for kosher food? Disney can usually handle those diets and other special ones (for people who need fat-free or sugar-free meals, or for folks who have allergies or a lactose intolerance, for example), as long as guests give Disney advance notice — usually no more than 24 hours. It's a good idea to discuss these requirements when you make your Advanced Dining Reservation arrangements. Select counter-service eateries now offer specialty food items on their menu (check your park map for details on which ones and what they offer). If you're not staying at WDW, call ☎ 407-939-3463.

Tipping and taxes in Orlando

Sales tax on restaurant meals and drinks ranges from 6.5 to 7 percent throughout the Orlando area. (These taxes don't apply to groceries.) In addition, the standard tip in full-service restaurants is 15 percent, and a 12 percent tip is usually warranted at a buffet where a server brings your drinks, fetches condiments, and cleans the table. If you have a pre-dinner drink, leave a small tip to reward the server.

Make sure that you carefully look over your check before coughing up a tip because some restaurants have started automatically tacking a gratuity onto your bill, especially for larger groups. There's no sense doubling a tip for routine service.

Trimming the Fat from Your Dining Budget

If you're staying in the parks until closing, you may find it more convenient to eat there, but you'll probably pay an average of 25 percent more than in the outside world. (Dinner for two at a sit-down restaurant in **WDW,** including tax and tip, can cost $50 or more — sometimes, a lot more especially if you add in appetizers, dessert, and drinks.) If you don't mind ditching Mickey every now and again, you can substantially decrease your eating expenses.

Here are a few suggestions to get the most out of your dining dollars:

- ✓ I won't list all of them, but if you spend any time on International Drive or U.S. 192/Irlo Bronson Memorial Highway between Kissimmee and Disney, you'll see all sorts of billboards peddling all-you-can-eat breakfast buffets at chain restaurants for $4 to $7. A buffet is a great way to fuel up for the day early and skip or, at least, lighten up on lunch. The drawback: You loose valuable time when the parks are less crowded.

- ✓ Make sure you pick up all the free magazines and ad books that you see everywhere in Orlando hotels, tourist information centers, most convenience stores, newspaper racks, highway rest areas, and so on. These publications include coupons good for a second meal free, discount prices on entrees, or a free dessert, beverage, or appetizer with a meal. Also, watch for ads from restaurants that offer kids-eat-free specials or discounts for early birds.

- ✓ Inexpensive (by now you know that's a relative term) kids' menus (usually $7 and under) are common at most of Orlando's moderately priced and family-style restaurants. Many also offer place mats with mazes or pictures to color.

- ✓ If you enjoy a cocktail before dinner, don't ignore places with happy-hour specials, including two-for-one drinks — some at bargain rates — usually from 4 to 7 p.m. Again, you can find listings in the free area guides in hotel lobbies and other places throughout Orlando.

- ✓ If your vacation won't be complete without trying at least one of the sit-down theme park restaurants, consider scheduling your meal at lunch instead of dinner, when prices are almost always significantly cheaper.

- ✓ If you're on a tight budget and your room has a kitchen, or at least a spot to sit and grab a bite, consider dining in a night or two and saving a few bucks. Area grocers, many with delis that turn out ready-to-eat treats, include **Albertson's,** 7524 Dr. Phillips Blvd., (☎ **407-352-1552;** www.albertsons.com) and **Gooding's** at the Crossroads Shopping Plaza in Lake Buena Vista, 12521 Hwy. 535/ Apopka–Vineland Ave., (☎ **407-827-1200;** www.goodings.com), with another location at 8255 International Drive (☎ 407-352-4215).

> ## Cutting food costs inside WDW
>
> Eating at Disney parks can set you back more than a few bucks. For example, a 20-ounce bottle of cola or spring water is $2.50 or more. To save money, buy a bottle (or six-pack) of water from a local grocery costing far less, (freeze it the night before to keep it really cold) and take it with you to the park, refilling it at water fountains throughout the day. Also, in **Animal Kingdom,** you can belly up to the bar at the Rainforest Cafe, order a soda for $2.50, and get a free glass of water. If you're eating lunch, the average price per person is barely under $10 if you eat at the counter service–style fast-food areas, but it's much less expensive than at the full-service eateries. One of the cheapest entrees at the parks is a smoked turkey drumstick for $4.75 (and they're huge!). You also can get a pineapple float for around $2.75.
>
> Most of the resorts at Disney offer a refillable mug, which is good for refills there for the duration of your WDW visit (the mugs must be used at the resort in which they were purchased). The cost for the glass in most of the resorts is $12. At most resorts, the refills are free (with a list of select beverages), although a few of them charge $1. The price may seem steep, but if you consider that most sodas cost around $2 or more individually and you take into account how much you'd drink during your stay, it's actually a good deal. Some of Disney's water parks have refillable glasses, but refills are limited to the day you're in the park. For more information, call Disney at ☎ 407-934-7639.

Gooding's also offers a delivery service — visit the Web site or call for details. You can find even more options in the Orlando Yellow Pages under "Grocers."

✔ Purchase discounted gift certificates to many Universal Orlando/International Drive area restaurants from **Clear Channel of Orlando's Dining Deals** Web site (http://halfprice.ccorlando.com). The selection varies per radio station per week, but the average deal is a $50 certificate for $25. You can also bid to win dining certificates to a variety of Orlando area restaurants via **IBidUSA** (www.ibidusa.com) and **Restaurant.com** (www.restaurant.com). Bids of $3 to $5 have been known to win $25 gift certificates at some of the city's best restaurants.

Orlando's Best Restaurants

In this section, I review, in alphabetical order, what I think are some of Orlando's best restaurants. I also throw in some handy indexes at the end of the chapter to help you narrow down your choices by category.

Because you may spend a lot of time in the **Walt Disney World** area, I've given special attention to choices there. Don't worry, though. I haven't forgotten to toss in plenty of worthwhile restaurants outside of Disney's domain — including a handful of **Universal Orlando**'s latest entries (you can find in-park dining options for the Universal theme parks in Chapters 18 and 19) and some of the favorites elsewhere around town.

 Sit-down restaurants in the WDW _theme parks_ (not their resorts) require admission, with one exception: the **Rainforest Café** at Animal Kingdom. Unless you are a Disney resort guest, all of the Disney theme-park restaurants will also set you back $8 in parking fees (the same goes for **Universal Orlando**'s restaurants, unless you arrive after 6 p.m., when parking becomes free). And keep in mind, too, alcohol isn't served in Magic Kingdom restaurants, but liquor is served at Animal Kingdom, Epcot, and Disney–MGM Studios restaurants, and elsewhere in the Disney domain, as well as at the other major theme parks.

 Dining in Orlando constitutes your biggest vacation expenditure. To make it easy for you to recognize expensive versus moderately priced restaurants, each of the following entries includes one or more $ symbols, based upon the average price of an adult dinner entree and one non-alcoholic drink. For the meaning behind the dollar symbols, see Table 10-1.

Table 10-1	Key to Restaurant Dollar Signs
Dollar Sign	_Price Range_
$	Less than $10
$$	$11–$25
$$$	$26–$50
$$$$	$51 and up

 Arthur's 27

$$$–$$$$ **Lake Buena Vista   INTERNATIONAL**

Come first for the 27th-floor sunsets and spectacular view of Disney's sparkling fireworks display. (You can get a much cheaper look from the Top of the Palace Lounge, next door.) Beyond the long distance visuals, the atmosphere is romantic and mellow. It has the elegant feel of a 1930s supper club, filled with intimate alcoves, but minus the clouds of cigarette smoke. You can choose from selections such as herb-crusted rack of lamb or pineapple and soy glazed duck, though the entrees aren't always as impressive as the price may indicate. Overall, portions lean toward the small size. Select four- and five-course meals are also available. The wine list is commendable but priced well above retail.

See map p. 130. 1900 Lake Buena Vista Drive, in the Wyndham Palace Resort & Spa. ☎ _**407-827-3450.** Reservations recommended. Main courses: $31–$51; fixed-price menu $68–$74. No kids' menu. AE, DC, DISC, MC, V. Open: Daily 6–10 p.m. Jacket suggested for men._

Walt Disney World & Lake Buena Vista Restaurants

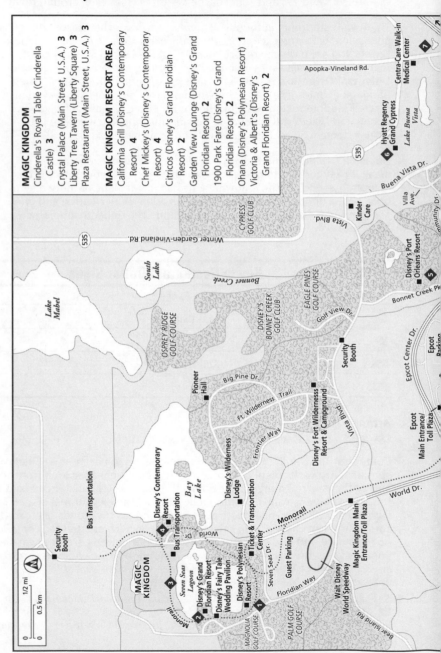

MAGIC KINGDOM
Cinderella's Royal Table (Cinderella Castle) **3**
Crystal Palace (Main Street, U.S.A.) **3**
Liberty Tree Tavern (Liberty Square) **3**
Plaza Restaurant (Main Street, U.S.A.) **3**

MAGIC KINGDOM RESORT AREA
California Grill (Disney's Contemporary Resort) **4**
Chef Mickey's (Disney's Contemporary Resort) **4**
Citricos (Disney's Grand Floridian Resort) **2**
Garden View Lounge (Disney's Grand Floridian Resort) **2**
1900 Park Fare (Disney's Grand Floridian Resort) **2**
Ohana (Disney's Polynesian Resort) **1**
Victoria & Albert's (Disney's Grand Floridian Resort) **2**

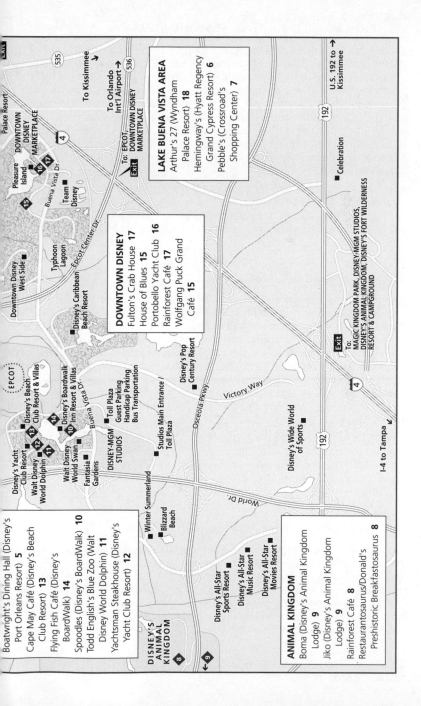

To Kissimmee →

535

536

To Orlando
Int'l Airport →

LAKE BUENA VISTA AREA
Arthur's 27 (Wyndham
Palace Resort) **18**
Hemingway's (Hyatt Regency
Grand Cypress Resort) **6**
Pebble's (Crossroad's
Shopping Center) **7**

Palace Resort

DOWNTOWN
DISNEY
MARKETPLACE

Pleasure
Island

Buena Vista Dr.

Team
Disney

To: EPCOT,
DOWNTOWN DISNEY
MARKETPLACE

Exit

Epcot Center Dr.

Typhoon
Lagoon

Downtown Disney
West Side

DOWNTOWN DISNEY
Fulton's Crab House **17**
House of Blues **15**
Portobello Yacht Club **16**
Rainforest Café **17**
Wolfgang Puck Grand
Café **15**

Disney's Caribbean
Beach Resort

Disney's Pop
Century Resort

EPCOT

Disney's Beach
Club Resort & Villas

Disney's Boardwalk
Inn Resort & Villas

Buena Vista Dr.

Toll Plaza
Guest Parking
Handicap Parking
Bus Transportation

Disney's Yacht
Club Resort

Walt Disney
World Dolphin

Walt Disney
World Swan

Fantasia
Gardens

DISNEY-MGM
STUDIOS

Studios Main Entrance /
Toll Plaza

Victory Way

Osceola Pkwy.

Disney's Wide World
of Sports

192

Celebration

U.S. 192 to →
Kissimmee

192

Exit
To:
MAGIC KINGDOM PARK, DISNEY-MGM STUDIOS,
DISNEY'S ANIMAL-KINGDOM, DISNEY'S FORT WILDERNESS
RESORT & CAMPGROUND

4

I-4 to Tampa ↓

Winter Summerland

Blizzard
Beach

World Dr.

Disney's All-Star
Sports Resort

Disney's All-Star
Music Resort

Disney's All-Star
Movies Resort

ANIMAL KINGDOM
Boma (Disney's Animal Kingdom
Lodge) **9**
Jiko (Disney's Animal Kingdom
Lodge) **9**
Rainforest Café **8**
Restaurantosaurus/Donald's
Preshistoric Breakfastosaurus **8**

DISNEY'S
ANIMAL
KINGDOM

Boatwright's Dining Hall (Disney's
Port Orleans Resort) **5**
Cape May Café (Disney's Beach
Club Resort) **13**
Flying Fish Café (Disney's
BoardWalk) **14**
Spoodles (Disney's BoardWalk) **10**
Todd English's Blue Zoo (Walt
Disney World Dolphin) **11**
Yachtsman Steakhouse (Disney's
Yacht Club Resort) **12**

Atlantis
$$$ International Drive Area   SEAFOOD/STEAKS

Although a tad pricey, this small and elegant restaurant offers some of the better seafood in Orlando. The atmosphere is intimate with dark woods, chandeliers, and booths separated by etched glass. The periodically changing menu offers treats such as a Mediterranean seafood medley (Florida lobster, black grouper, shrimp, and scallops), and grilled sea bass. But the champagne **Sunday brunch** served in the Renaissance Orlando Resort's huge atrium is the real crowd-pleaser. Themes change, but the 100-item menu includes quail, duck, lamb chops, Cornish hen, clams, mussels, snapper, sea bass, and sushi. A reservation for brunch is recommended, given the crowds.

See map p. 139. 6677 Sea Harbour Dr., in the Renaissance Orlando Resort at SeaWorld. ☎ **407-351-5555.** www.renaissancehotels.com. *Reservations recommended. Main courses: $24–$36; Sunday brunch $32 adults, $16 kids. AE, DISC, DC, MC, V. Open: Daily 6–10 p.m.; Sunday brunch 10:30 a.m.–2 p.m.*

Bice
$$–$$$ Universal Orlando   ITALIAN

The newest restaurant on the scene at Universal Orlando is located in the romantic Italian setting of the Portofino Bay Hotel. Replacing the Delfino Riviera, the restaurant serves Italian fare in an upscale atmosphere, though it's a bit more down-to-earth than its predecessor. Bice is a family-owned-and-operated restaurant with several other locations throughout North America, Latin America, Asia, and the Middle East. The menu includes items such as a Belgian endive salad in a light Dijon mustard dressing with gorgonzola cheese and toasted walnuts; spaghetti with Maine lobster, cherry tomatoes, and braised green onions; and veal chops in a porcini sauce. You can choose to dine inside with views that overlook the waterways along the piazza of the hotel, or at a table on the piazza itself.

See map p. 139. 5601 Universal Studios Blvd., in the Portofino Bay Hotel. ☎ **407-503-3463** *or 407-503-1415.* www.universalorlando.com. *Reservations recommended. Main courses: $18–$49. AE, MC, V. Open: Daily 5:30–10:30 p.m.*

B-Line Diner
$–$$ International Drive Area   AMERICAN

Sink into an upholstered booth or belly up to a stool at the counter of this restaurant, whose décor is straight out of the '50s. Gleaming chrome, black-and-white tile, and red leather create a vision of yesterday's roadside diners in this informal and friendly gathering place. Dig into hearty portions of comfort foods, such as chicken pot pie, roast pork with apples, or a ham-and-cheese sandwich on a baguette. Health foods and vegetarian specials also are available.

Although this is a diner-style restaurant and there is a kids' menu, it's not a good spot to take young children as it's located at The Peabody, a very upscale hotel.

See map p. 139. 9801 International Drive, across from Orlando Convention Center. In Peabody Orlando Hotel. ☎ ***407-345-4460.*** www.peabody-orlando.com. *Reservations not accepted. Main courses: breakfast $4–$16; lunch $7–$18; dinner $9–$26. AE, DC, DISC, MC, V. Open: Daily 24 hours.*

Boatwright's Dining Hall
$–$$ Walt Disney World Resorts   NEW ORLEANS

A family atmosphere (lively and noisy), good food (by Disney standards), and reasonable prices (ditto) make Boatwright's a hit with Port Orleans Resort guests. Most entrees have a Cajun/Creole spin. The jambalaya is sans seafood, but it's filled with veggies, rice, chicken and sausage, and it's got a kick. Vegetarians will appreciate the vegetable medley or four cheese ravioli; other entrees include bayou seafood stew, bourbon glazed chicken, glazed pork ribs, and a hearty pot roast. Boatwright's is modeled after a 19th-century boat factory, complete with the wooden hull of a Louisiana fishing boat suspended from its lofty, beamed ceiling. Most kids like the wooden toolboxes on every table; each contains a saltshaker that doubles as a level, a wood-clamp sugar dispenser, a pepper-grinder-cum-ruler, shop rags (to be used as napkins), and a little metal pail of crayons.

See map p. 130. 2201 Orleans Dr., in Disney's Port Orleans Resort. ☎ ***407-939-3463.*** www.disneyworld.com. *Advanced Dining Reservations recommended. Main courses: breakfast $7–$11; dinner $14–$20. AE, DC, DISC, MC, V. Open: Daily 7–11:30 a.m. and 5–10 p.m.*

Bob Marley — A Tribute to Freedom
$ Universal Orlando   CARIBBEAN

This combination club and restaurant is housed in a replica of the late singer's home in Kingston, Jamaica, complete with red-tile roof and green shutters. Live reggae plays nightly, but the decibel level doesn't get as high as at Jimmy Buffett's Margaritaville (reviewed later in this chapter). The small menu has modestly priced light fare, including a jerk snapper sandwich served on coca bread with yucca fries or a tomato-based fish chowder. Of course, most folks don't leave without sipping a Red Stripe — Jamaica's beer of champions.

1000 Universal Studios Plaza. In CityWalk. ☎ ***407-224-2262.*** www.universal orlando.com. *Reservations not accepted. Main courses: $6–$10. AE, DISC, MC, V. Open: Daily 4 p.m.–2 a.m.*

Boma
$$ Walt Disney World Resorts   AFRICAN

Follow your nose to the wood-burning grill and open kitchen at this African-influenced eatery inside **Disney's Animal Kingdom Lodge.** The large wood tables remain in the shape of the tree trunks and colorful banners hang from the thatched roof. The selection and variety here are vast and often unique. Adventurous diners can expect such treats as Moroccan seafood salad (mussels, scallops, shrimp, and couscous) and curried-coconut, seafood stew, alongside more familiar favorites at the restaurant's breakfast and dinner buffets. Kids have their own station serving up chicken, pasta, and mac 'n' cheese. Chefs are on hand behind the open buffet to answer questions about the cuisine. The wine list features an array of South African offerings.

See map p. 130. 2901 Osceola Pkwy., in Disney's Animal Kingdom Lodge. ☎ *407-939-3463.* www.disneyworld.com. *Advanced Dining Reservations recommended. Breakfast buffet: $15 adults, $8 ages 3–11; Dinner buffet: $25 adults; $11 ages 3–11. AE, DC, DISC, MC, V. Open: Daily 7–11 a.m. and 5–10 p.m.*

Bubbalou's Bodacious BBQ
$–$$ International Drive Area   AMERICAN

You can smell the hickory smoke emerging from the chimney of this restaurant for blocks. This is, hands down, some of the best barbecue you'll find anywhere. And, if nothing else, you have to love the name. The atmosphere is extremely informal, but watch the sauces. Even the mild may be too hot for tender palates; the killer sauce comes with a three-alarm warning — you may not be able to taste anything else for days. If you can eat the night or day away, go for "The Big-Big Pig" platter (beef, sliced pork, and turkey with fixins). And it wouldn't be a barbecue without plenty of brew on hand.

See map p. 139. 5818 Conroy Rd. (a few blocks north of Universal Orlando at the intersection of Kirkman and Conroy). ☎ *407-423-1212.* www.bubbalous.com. *Reservations — you're kidding! Main courses: $4–$13. AE, MC, V. Open: Mon–Thurs 10 a.m.–9 p.m.; Fri–Sat 10 a.m.–10 p.m.*

Café Tu Tu Tango
$$–$$$ International Drive Area   INTERNATIONAL

This colorful eatery with the flair of an artists loft features treats from Latin America, Asia, the Caribbean, the Middle East, and the United States. It's an ideal spot for sampling different dishes; every order comes in a miniature size. The roasted pears on pecan crisps — topped with Spanish bleu cheese and a balsamic reduction — are a must. Chocolate fiends will not want to pass up the dessert of handmade truffles — truly to die for. Guests frequently see an artist bringing a canvas to life. You can also buy wine by the glass or bottle. *Note:* Although, individual tapas are relatively inexpensive, ordering several tapas and drinks can easily turn this meal into a $$$ restaurant.

See map p. 139. 8625 International Drive (just west of the Mercado Shopping Center). ☎ *407-248-2222.* www.cafetututango.com. *Reservations not required. Main courses: Tapas (small plates) $4–$11 (even those with small appetites will want two or three). AE, DC, DISC, MC, V. Open: Sun–Thurs 11:30 a.m.–11 p.m.; Fri–Sat 11:30 a.m. to midnight.*

California Grill
$$–$$$ **Walt Disney World Resorts   AMERICAN**

The 15th-floor views of the **Magic Kingdom** and environs are stunning, and the food is pretty good, too. The Art Deco dining room features an exhibition kitchen with a wood-burning oven and rotisserie. The constantly changing menu features fresh market fare, as well as pizzas and pastas. Highlights may include seared yellowfin tuna that arrives rare, soft-shell crabs with corn salad, or black grouper with mushroom risotto. The Grill also has a nice sushi and sashimi menu (Dungeness crab, eel, tuna, and more), ranging from appetizers to large platters. The restaurant sports a grand wine list and some excellent vegetarian options.

See map p. 130. 4600 World Dr., at Disney's Contemporary Resort. ☎ *407-939-3463 or 407-824-1576.* www.disneyworld.com. *Advanced Dining Reservations recommended. Main courses: $20–$35; sushi $10–$22. AE, DC, DISC, MC, V. Open: Daily 5:30–10 p.m.*

Les Chefs de France
$$–$$$ **Epcot   FRENCH**

Three famous French chefs — Paul Bocuse, Roger Vergé, and Gaston LeNotre — concocted the menu at this restaurant, which serves respectable fare that's far better than the usual theme park offerings. The Art Nouveau interior is agleam with mirrors and candelabras, and etched-glass and brass dividers create intimate dining areas. Dinner entrees include Mediterranean seafood casserole (grouper, scallops, and shrimp dusted with saffron and then allowed to swim in a mild garlic sauce) and grilled tenderloin of beef with a Bordeaux wine sauce. The sauces tend to be on the lighter side than at most traditional French restaurants. The restaurant also offers a substantial wine list.

See map p. 136. In France Pavilion, World Showcase. ☎ *407-939-3463 or 407-827-8709.* www.disneyworld.com. *Advanced Dining Reservations suggested. Main courses: lunch $10–$18; dinner $14–$30. AE, DC, DISC, MC, V. Open: Daily noon to 3:30 p.m. and 5 p.m. until 1 hour before park closing.*

Christini's
$$–$$$ **Dr. Phillips Area   ITALIAN**

The numerous awards and trophies on the walls attest to restaurateur Chris Christini's high standard of service. The fact that he's been around since 1984 shows he's a survivor. Count on his restaurant for a possible peek at show-biz celebrities from down the road at Disney–MGM and Universal. A tender broiled veal chop seasoned with sage and served with applesauce is one of the headliners. Another good choice is the pan-seared Chilean sea bass over shrimp-and-lobster risotto. The food is quite good, and the wine list is definitely a winner. The atmosphere is somewhat formal, making it a good spot for a romantic night out.

Epcot Restaurants

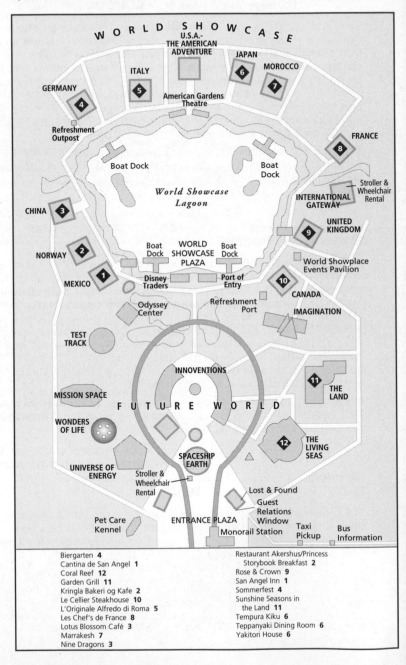

Biergarten **4**
Cantina de San Angel **1**
Coral Reef **12**
Garden Grill **11**
Kringla Bakeri og Kafe **2**
Le Cellier Steakhouse **10**
L'Originale Alfredo di Roma **5**
Les Chef's de France **8**
Lotus Blossom Café **3**
Marrakesh **7**
Nine Dragons **3**

Restaurant Akershus/Princess
  Storybook Breakfast **2**
Rose & Crown **9**
San Angel Inn **1**
Sommerfest **4**
Sunshine Seasons in
  the Land **11**
Tempura Kiku **6**
Teppanyaki Dining Room **6**
Yakitori House **6**

See map p. 139. 7600 Dr. Phillips Blvd. ☎ 407-345-8770. www.christinis.com. *Reservations recommended. Main courses: $18–$45 (many under $27). AE, DC, DISC, MC, V. Open: Daily 6–11 p.m. Jackets suggested for men and dresses for women.*

Cinderella's Royal Table
$$–$$$ Magic Kingdom   AMERICAN

Ornate murals of colored tile line the castle walls leading to the restaurant's entrance where the Gothic interior, which includes leaded-glass windows and a spiral staircase, transport you to a time of knights and kings. Your meal is delivered by servers who address you as "M'Lord" or "M'Lady." You can order from a menu with fancy names (the Grand Duke, for example), but it boils down to roasted chicken, crusted salmon, and a New York strip. The location and ambience are what makes this restaurant so popular, but the food is reasonably good, too. (For information on the character breakfast held here, see "Dining with Disney Characters" later in this chapter.)

See map p. 130. Inside Cinderella Castle on Main Street. ☎ 407-939-3463. www. disneyworld.com. *Advanced Dining Reservations highly recommended. Main courses: lunch $13–$16; dinner $21–$26. AE, DC, DISC, MC, V. Open: Daily 11:30 a.m.–2:45 p.m. and 4 p.m. until 1 hour before park closing.*

Citricos
$$–$$$ Walt Disney World Resorts   FRENCH

The chef of this bright and airy restaurant makes a statement with French, Alsatian, and Provençal cuisine with California and Florida touches. (Whew!) Depending on when you visit, the menu may include basil-crusted rack of lamb, pan-seared sea bass with shellfish bouillabaisse, or grilled salmon with fennel ravioli and Swiss chard. The Old World–style dining room filled with wrought-iron railings, mosaic-tile floors, and flickering lights, features a show kitchen and spectacular views of the **Seven Seas Lagoon** and **Magic Kingdom** fireworks. The wine cellar is well stocked; you can add a three-course wine pairing for $25.

See map p. 130. 4401 Floridian Way, Disney's Grand Floridian Resort & Spa. ☎ 407-939-3463. www.disneyworld.com. *Advanced Dining Reservations recommended. Main courses: $21–$45. AE, DC, DISC, MC, V. Open: Wed–Sun 5:30–10 p.m.*

Coral Reef
$$–$$$ Epcot   SEAFOOD

Seafood rules at this very popular restaurant, which offers fabulous views of the **Living Seas aquarium** and a dash of classical music to help set a romantic tone. The menu, unfortunately, is less imaginative than the ambience. Entrees include grilled mahimahi with wasabi-mashed potatoes and collard greens, and Florida snapper, with a decent selection of landlubber fare as well. The Reef serves wine by the glass. *Note:* Diners get fish-identifier sheets with labeled pictures so they can put names on the faces swimming by their tables.

See map p. 136. In the Living Seas Pavilion. ☎ **407-939-3463.** www.disneyworld. com. *Advanced Dining Reservations recommended. Main courses: lunch $13–$24; dinner $16–$32. AE, DC, DISC, MC, V. Open: Daily 11:30 a.m.–3 p.m. and 4:30 p.m. until park closing.*

Dexter's at Thornton Park
$–$$ Downtown Orlando   INTERNATIONAL

This popular cafe and neighborhood bar is just a few blocks from Lake Eola in the center of downtown. The creative fare features such fun foods as Cuban grilled swordfish topped with lime cilantro and blue crabmeat (talk about a taste explosion); and Thai-spiced filet mignon served with mashed potatoes and asparagus. Many of the seats are stools at high tables; if that's not for you, you may have a long wait. There's a modest wine list.

See map p. 147. 808 E. Washington St., at the corner of Hyer. ☎ **407-648-2777.** www. dexwine.com. *Reservations not accepted. Main courses: lunch $7–$12 ($5–$9 salads and sandwiches); dinner $15–$21. AE, DC, DISC, MC, V. Open: Mon–Sat 11 a.m. to midnight; Sun 5–10 p.m.*

Dux
$$$ International Drive Area   INTERNATIONAL

Think posh with a capital P — that's what comes to mind when you slip inside these walls. The restaurant's name honors the mallards that splash all day in the marble fountains in the Peabody's grandly formal lobby. (Staffers assure us that birds of the quacking variety will never appear on the menu.) Candlelit tables surround a large chandelier, and textured gold walls are hung with watercolors of the various duck species. Its eclectic menu changes with the seasons. Possibilities include a tender veal chop roasted medium rare with an artichoke-basil fricassee and garlic au jus; or steamed red snapper in tomato fricassee and fennel. Choose a wine from one of the best wine lists in the city. The service is impeccable; for most people, however, the prices make Dux a choice only for special nights or expense-account meals.

See map p. 139. 9801 International Drive in the Peabody Orlando, across from the Orlando Convention Center. ☎ **407-345-4550.** www.peabody-orlando.com. *Reservations recommended. Main courses: $26–$45. AE, DC, DISC, MC, V. Open: Mon–Sat 6–10 p.m. Jackets suggested for men and dresses for women.*

Earl of Sandwich
$ Downtown Disney   AMERICAN

In the spring of 2004, The Earl of Sandwich (the famous edible was invented by said earl in 1762 when he was too busy playing cards to eat a real meal) made its debut in Downtown Disney. It's a collaboration between Robert Earl, founder and CEO of Planet Hollywood, and John Montagu, the real 11th Earl of Sandwich. The eatery offers a great selection

International Drive & Dr. Phillips Area Restaurants

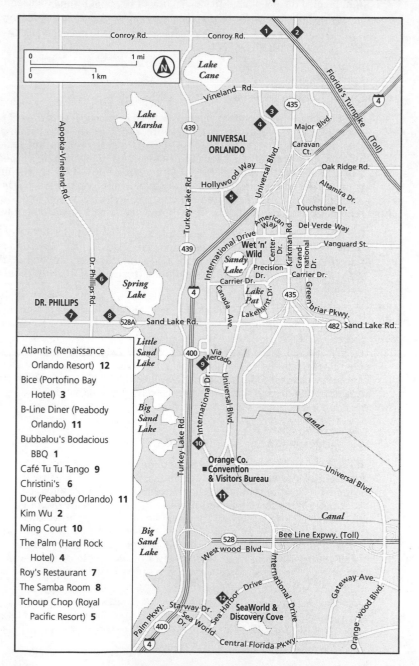

Atlantis (Renaissance
   Orlando Resort) **12**
Bice (Portofino Bay
   Hotel) **3**
B-Line Diner (Peabody
   Orlando) **11**
Bubbalou's Bodacious
   BBQ **1**
Café Tu Tu Tango **9**
Christini's **6**
Dux (Peabody Orlando) **11**
Kim Wu **2**
Ming Court **10**
The Palm (Hard Rock
   Hotel) **4**
Roy's Restaurant **7**
The Samba Room **8**
Tchoup Chop (Royal
   Pacific Resort) **5**

of hot and cold deli sandwiches, wraps, and salads for those looking for a light meal at a very decent price. It's one of the best dining deals at Disney.

1800 E. Buena Vista Drive. (in Downtown Disney Marketplace). ☎ **407-827-8500.** www.disneyworld.com. *Reservations not accepted. Main courses: $4–$6. AE, MC, V. Open: Daily 9:30 a.m.–11 p.m.*

Emeril's
$$–$$$ Universal Orlando   NEW ORLEANS

The Florida home of culinary genius Emeril Lagasse, star of *Emeril Live* on cable TV's Food Network (and, therefore, rarely on the premises), offers a feast for both the eyes and mouth. This two-story restaurant resembles an old warehouse, albeit one with pricey art on its walls. The second floor has a 12,000-bottle wine gallery. If you want a show, I highly recommend trying to get one of the eight counter seats where you can watch the chefs working their Creole-cuisine magic, but to get one, you'll need to make reservations *excruciatingly* early. (Reserve at least six weeks in advance.)

Best bets include the Texas redfish (an extremely moist white fish with roasted pecan-vegetable relish and meunière sauce) and a grilled-and-roasted half chicken served with rice pilaf. Though jackets are recommended for gents at dinner, you'll find a lot of diners, fresh out of the **Universal** theme parks, far less dressy.

Emeril's lunch menu is cheaper but has many of the same items as the one at dinner. It's also easier to get a reservation, and the dress code is more casual.

6000 Universal Studios Blvd. In CityWalk. ☎ **407-224-2424.** www.emerils.com/restaurants/index_Orlando.htm. *Reservations far in advance are a must. Main courses: lunch $18–$28; dinner $31–$50. AE, DISC, MC, V. Open: Daily 11:30 a.m.–2:30 p.m.; 5:30–10 p.m. (11 p.m. Fri–Sat). Jackets suggested for men.*

50's Prime Time Cafe
$$ Disney–MGM Studios   AMERICAN

If you yearn to go back to a time when life was simpler, this is the place for you. The décor is right out of the television sitcoms, and servers deliver comfort foods, including meatloaf, fried chicken, and pot roast. The food isn't quite the way mom used to make it, but the place offers enough fun that you may love it anyway. Black-and-white TVs air shows such as *Topper* and *My Little Margie* as servers zap you back to the days when you had to finish your vegetables if you wanted dessert. Mom, aka your server, may very well scold you if put your elbows on the table or don't clean your plate. Desserts like s'mores and sundaes top off the menu, and there's even a neat selection of specialty drinks.

Near the Indiana Jones Stunt Spectacular. ☎ **407-939-3463.** www.disneyworld.com. *Advanced Dining Reservations recommended. Main courses: $11–$20 lunch and dinner. AE, DC, DISC, MC, V. Open: 11 a.m. to park closing.*

Flying Fish Café
$$$ Walt Disney World Resorts   SEAFOOD

Welcome to Coney Island, circa 1940, à la Disney. The vibrant colorful décor here is almost as elaborate as the show kitchen, which puts the chefs at center stage where everyone can see meals being prepared. The seafood is among the freshest in town, so the menu changes frequently. Headliners may include potato-wrapped red snapper and oak-grilled salmon. You'll also find beef, poultry, and veggie options. If you can't get a table here, ask about sitting at the counter — you get a great view of the kitchen.

See map p. 130. At BoardWalk Inn Resort & Villas. ☎ *407-939-3463 or 407-939-2359.* www.disneyworld.com. *Advanced Dining Reservations recommended. Main courses: $28–$37. AE, DC, DISC, MC, V. Open: Daily 5:30–10 p.m.*

Fulton's Crab House
$$–$$$ Downtown Disney   SEAFOOD

Lose yourself in a world of brass, shining mahogany, and river charts as you dine on the city's best seafood while inside a moored Mississippi Delta-style paddlewheeler (just bring your bank account along). Lobster (Maine and Australian) and crab (stone, king, and Dungeness) dominate the menu. The grilled tuna mignon is served rare, and the Dungeness crab cakes are a real treat. One popular meal for two combines Alaskan king crab, snow crab, and lobster with potatoes and creamed spinach. You'll find a comprehensive wine list. You can dine on the outdoor deck if the weather's fair.

See map p. 130. Aboard the riverboat at Pleasure Island. ☎ *407-934-2628.* www.levy restaurants.com. *Advanced Dining Reservations recommended. Main courses: lunch $12–$45; dinner $17–$47. AE, DC, DISC, MC, V. Open: Daily 11:30 a.m.–4 p.m. and 5–11 p.m.*

Hemingway's
$$ Lake Buena Vista   SEAFOOD

If Papa were to eat at his namesake, he might dive into the beer-battered coconut shrimp with horseradish sauce and orange marmalade or the blackened swordfish with Cajun tartar sauce. No doubt, he would skip the wine list (there is a decent one) and opt for a few *Papa Dobles,* a potent rum concoction he invented and, according to legend, once downed 16 at one sitting! The interior of Hemingway's has a Key West air, and the walls are adorned with several sepia photographs of the famous author and his fishing trophies. The eatery has a romantic, indoor dining room lighted by hurricane lamps, and there's a wooden deck near a waterfall. It's usually childfree, although there is a kids' menu.

See map p. 130. 1 Grand Cypress Blvd. (off Hwy. 535). In Hyatt Regency Grand Cypress Resort. ☎ *407-239-3854.* www.hyattgrandcypress.com. *Reservations recommended. Main courses: $21–$36. AE, DC, DISC, MC, V. Open: Daily 6–10 p.m.*

Hollywood Brown Derby
$$ Disney–MGM Studios AMERICAN

The huge derby marks the entrance to this restaurant at **Disney–MGM.** Inside, this re-creation of the restaurant where Hollywood's stars gathered in the '30s and '40s is decorated with caricatures of the regulars on its walls and white linens on the tables. The food (on the pricy side) won't win an Academy Award, but the restaurant does have a respectable pan-seared black grouper with green beans al dente and mustard-crusted rack of lamb with acorn squash and sweet-and-sour cabbage. The restaurant's two signature dishes are the Cobb salad, invented by then-owner Bob Cobb in the 1930s, and the excellent grapefruit cake with cream-cheese frosting.

Hollywood Blvd. ☎ *407-939-3463.* www.disneyworld.com. *Advanced Dinner Reservations recommended. Main courses: lunch $13–$19; dinner $19–$28. AE, DC, DISC, MC, V. Open: Daily 11 a.m. until park closing.*

House of Blues
$$ Downtown Disney AMERICAN

Inside this Louisiana clapboard building, you find hearty portions of down-home Southern food served in an atmosphere literally pulsing with rhythm and blues. Exceedingly crowded on days of big concerts, the music in the nightclub next door is as much a draw as the food. Funky folk art with a voodooish feel covers the rustic walls from floor to ceiling. The back patio has seating and a nice view of the bay. Foodwise, the spicy Creole jambalaya (shrimp, chicken, ham, and andouille sausage) and pan-seared voodoo shrimp are good bets. Sunday's Gospel Brunch is a ton of foot-stomping fun, with plenty of southern favorites like chicken jambalaya, cornbread, and BBQ chicken alongside breakfast staples including omelets, sausage, and bacon. Brunch is the only time you can make reservations, and it sells out fast, so make them early.

See map p. 130. Located under the old-fashioned water tower at Disney's West Side. ☎ *407-934-2583.* www.hob.com. *Reservations not accepted (except for Gospel Brunch). Main courses: $10–$26; pizza & sandwiches $9–$11; brunch $30 adults, $15 kids 3–9. AE, DISC, MC, V. Open: Mon–Sat 11 a.m.–2 a.m.; Sunday brunch 10:30 a.m.–1 p.m.*

Jiko
$$–$$$ Walt Disney World Resorts AFRICAN

The signature restaurant (translation: most expensive) at **Disney's Animal Kingdom Lodge,** Jiko has a show kitchen, sporting two wood-burning ovens, and turns out a unique menu of international cuisine with African overtones. Dishes, depending on the season, include Maylay shrimp curry, pan-roasted monkfish, and lemon-cumin marinated ahi tuna. The wine list features an extensive number of South African vintages. If you have an adventurous palette, it's well worth the trip.

See map p. 130. 2901 Osceola Pkwy., at Disney's Animal Kingdom Lodge. ☎ *407-939-3463.* www.disneyworld.com. *Advanced Dining Reservations recommended. Main courses: $18–$33. AE, DC, DISC, MC, V. Open: Daily 5:30–10 p.m.*

Jimmy Buffett's Margaritaville
$–$$ Universal Orlando   CARIBBEAN

The laid back atmosphere may take you to paradise, but after the parrot-heads have had enough to drink, the noise can make it hard to hear your table mates. You have your choice of three watering holes: the Landshark Bar, the 12-Volt Bar, and the Volcano Bar, which comes complete with a two-story, margarita-spewing mini mountain. Despite the renowned cheese-burgers in paradise (yes, they're on the menu at $9.95), the food has Caribbean leanings. And although it isn't contending for a critic's choice award, it's fairly tasty. Best bets include jerk chicken, jambalaya, and a Cuban meat loaf survival sandwich that's a cheeseburger of another kind. The "Porch of Indecision" offers the best spot for those with kids along.

Watch your tab. At up to $8 a pop for margaritas (the mango ones are best), the bill can climb to $50 or more for a routine lunch.

1000 Universal Studios Plaza, in CityWalk. ☎ *407-224-2155.* www.universalorlando.com. *Reservations not accepted. Main courses: $8–$22 (most less than $15). AE, DISC, MC, V. Open: Daily 11 a.m. to midnight.*

Kim Wu
$ Universal Orlando Area   CHINESE

Tucked away in a shopping center corner near Universal, you'll find this award-winning favorite, which offers traditional Chinese food done right. Dishes are flavorful and excellently presented. Best of all, most entrees are priced in the single digits. It's been around for over 20 years, and for good reason. Most nights, owner Tom Yuen works the floor greeting guests like family.

See map p. 139. 4904 S. Kirkman Rd. (just a few blocks north of Universal Orlando at the intersection of Kirkman and Conroy). ☎ *407-293-0752. Reservations not accepted. Main courses: $4–$13. AE, DISC, MC, V. Open: Mon–Fri 11:30 a.m.–11 p.m.; Sat 4 p.m.–11 p.m.; Sun 12 p.m.–11 p.m.*

Le Cellier Steakhouse
$$–$$$ Epcot   STEAKS

You'll feel welcome in this cozy steakhouse, which tends to be less crowded — and less manic — than some of Epcot's other restaurants. The dining room resembles a wine cellar, where you'll sit in tapestry-upholstered chairs under vaulted stone arches, with lanterns lighting the room. Although it doesn't compete with some of the better outside-world steak-and-chop houses, it has a surprisingly good selection of Midwest, corn-fed beef in the usual cuts: filet, porterhouse, prime rib, rib-eye, and so on. Wash your meal down with Canadian wine or beer.

See map p. 136. In Canada Pavilion, World Showcase. ☎ *407-939-3463.* www.
disneyworld.com. *Advanced Dining Reservations recommended. Main courses:
lunch $7–$20; dinner $16–$37. AE, DC, DISC, MC, V. Open: Daily noon to park closing.*

Liberty Tree Tavern
$$ **Magic Kingdom AMERICAN**

This sit-down restaurant's 18th-century colonial pub atmosphere (period
music plays and the décor features antiques, oak-plank flooring, and a
huge fireplace filled with copper pots) and good service help make it one
of the better places to dine in the **Magic Kingdom,** but few will be com-
pelled to visit a second or third time. The cuisine is traditional American,
and the vittles are basic: roast turkey, carved beef, and smoked pork with
all the trimmings. Lunch offers à la carte service, while dinner gives you a
character buffet (see "Dining with Disney Characters" later in this chap-
ter for more on the character meal). *Note:* Even though this place calls
itself a tavern, it does not serve alcohol.

See map p. 130. In Liberty Square. ☎ *407-939-3463.* www.disneyworld.com.
*Advanced Dining Reservations recommended. Main courses: lunch $12–$15; dinner
buffet $22 adults; $10 kids 3–11. AE, DC, DISC, MC, V. Open: Daily 11:30 a.m.–3 p.m. and
4 p.m. until park closing.*

Little Saigon
$ **Downtown Orlando VIETNAMESE**

Situated in the heart of a tiny Vietnamese neighborhood, this ethnic eatery
has been open since 1987 and thrives on regulars from the community.
The menu offers everything from appetizers to noodle dishes to stir-fries
that mix and match pork, beef, seafood, and vegetables. The combo plates
are a good deal. Service and attention depend on the traffic. Order food
by number; if you need a description of a dish, you may need to ask the
manager, whose English is better than that of some of the servers. Don't
miss the summer rolls with peanut sauce.

See map p. 147. 1106 E. Colonial Dr., just east of I-4 on Highway 50. ☎ *407-423-8539.
Reservations not accepted. Main courses: lunch under $5; dinner $5–$10. AE, DISC,
MC, V. Open: Daily 10 a.m.–9 p.m.*

L'Originale Alfredo di Roma
$$–$$$ **Epcot ITALIAN**

Sample southern Italian cuisine in a re-creation of Alfredo De Lelio's
famous eatery in Rome, including some lovely wall murals and an exhibi-
tion kitchen. It may be the **World Showcase**'s most popular restaurant
(Advanced Dining Reservations are a must), but Alfredo's servers can be
snooty and its pasta is *very* overpriced. Your best bets include the signa-
ture fettuccine Alfredo and the calamari in a white wine, garlic, and tomato
sauce served on fettuccine. The dining room noise level can be quite high,

so if you want a quieter meal and a more casual atmosphere, ask for a seat on the veranda.

See map p. 136. In Italy Pavilion, World Showcase. ☎ *407-939-3463 or 407-827-8418.* www.disneyworld.com. *Advanced Dining Reservations recommended. Main courses: lunch $10–$25; dinner $17–$38. AE, DC, DISC, MC, V. Open: Daily noon to park closing.*

Lotus Blossom Café
$ **Epcot   CHINESE**

The open-air cafe offers familiar favorites much like what you find in Chinese restaurants located in mall food courts. Expect slightly above fast-food quality stir-fry, hot-and-sour, lo mein, and pork-fried rice. The outdoor (though covered) seating is refreshing. You can buy Chinese beer and wine as well. Quality aside, it's still a bargain in pricey Epcot.

See map p. 136. In China Pavilion, World Showcase. ☎ *407-939-3463.* www.disney world.com. *Advanced Dining Reservations not accepted. Main courses: $4–$6.50. AE, DC, DISC, MC, V. Open: Daily 11 a.m. to park closing.*

Manuel's on the 28th
$$$ **Downtown Orlando   INTERNATIONAL**

Manuel's is, literally, the pinnacle of elegance, situated in a posh, panoramic enclave on the 28th floor of a downtown bank. Come here for a stunning after-dark view of the sparkling, sprawling metropolis that Orlando has become. To make sure you don't miss out on the view, the dining room has floor-to-ceiling windows. The best news: The food matches the scenery, despite the small kitchen. The dozen or more appetizers and entrees hit high notes with duck, lamb, yellowfin tuna, lobster, and filet mignon. One popular dish is miso-marinated Chilean sea bass. The service is very professional, and the restaurant has a great wine list.

See map p. 147. 390 N. Orange Ave., in the Nations Bank Building. ☎ *407-246-6580.* www.manuelsonthe28th.com. *Reservations required. Main courses: $26–$45. AE, DC, DISC, MC, V. Open: Tues–Sat 6–9:45 p.m. Jackets recommended for men.*

Marrakesh
$$ **Epcot   MOROCCAN**

For a spot of romance and truly authentic flavor, head for Marrakesh. Of all the **World Showcase** restaurants, this venue best typifies the international spirit of the park. Hand-laid mosaics in intricate patterns set the scene for lavish North African dining, complete with belly dancers. Marrakesh uses a long list of spices, including saffron, to enhance flavorful specialties. Most entrees come with the national dish, couscous (steamed semolina with veggies and sometimes other embellishments). Good bets include a marinated shish kebob of lamb roasted in its own juices, and a seafood medley.

See map p. 136. In Morocco Pavilion, World Showcase. ☎ *407-939-3463.* www. disneyworld.com. *Advanced Dining Reservations recommended. Main courses: lunch $12–$18; dinner $17–$26. AE, DC, DISC, MC, V. Open: Daily noon to park closing.*

Ming Court
$$–$$$ International Drive Area CHINESE

Dine in a romantic setting, graced by lotus ponds filled with colorful koi while you're entertained by — get this — zither music. One of O-Town's favorite Chinese restaurants, Ming Court lets you rub elbows with more locals than tourists thanks to innovative twists on traditional cuisine. The flavors are delicate and probably more balanced than at your neighborhood Chinese place. Try the grilled filet mignon with Szechuan seasoning or the lightly battered and deep-fried chicken breast with lemon-tangerine sauce. Portions are sufficient, there's a moderate wine list, and the service is excellent.

See map p. 139. 9188 International Drive (between Sand Lake and BeeLine Expressway). ☎ *407-351-9988.* www.ming-court.com. *Reservations recommended. Main courses: lunch $7–$13; dinner $13–$36. AE, DC, DISC, MC, V. Open: Daily 11 a.m.–2:30 p.m. and 4:30–10:30 p.m.*

Nine Dragons
$$–$$$ Epcot CHINESE

Nine Dragons shines in the décor department with carved rosewood paneling and an amazing dragon-motif ceiling. But the food doesn't match its surroundings, and portions tend to be smaller than what most expect in a Chinese restaurant. Main courses feature Mandarin, Shanghai, Cantonese, and Szechuan cuisines. The dishes include spicy beef stir-fried with squash in sha cha sauce, lightly breaded lemon chicken, and a casserole of lobster, shrimp, and scallops sautéed with ginger and scallions. You can order Chinese or California wines with your meal.

See map p. 136. In China Pavilion, World Showcase. ☎ *407-939-3463.* www.disney world.com. *Advanced Dining Reservations recommended. Main courses: lunch $8–$22; dinner $13–$38; sampler for two $43.98, for four $59.99. AE, DC, DISC, MC, V. Open: Daily 11:30 a.m. until park closing.*

'Ohana
$$ Walt Disney World Resorts PACIFIC RIM

This restaurant is a hit in the fun department, but the decibel level can climb pretty high. Servers will address you as "cousin," as 'Ohana means family in Hawaiian. As your luau is prepared over an 18-foot fire pit, the staff keeps your eyes and ears busy. A storyteller is followed by coconut races in the center aisle, and then you can find out how to shake your booty during a hula lesson. Soon after you're seated, the feeding frenzy begins in rapid succession. (Ask your waiter to slow down if the pace is too fast.) Included is a variety of skewers (think shish kebob), including

Dining Elsewhere in Orlando

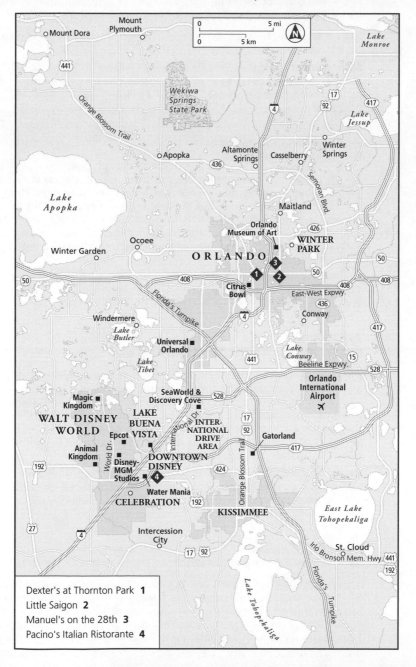

Dexter's at Thornton Park **1**
Little Saigon **2**
Manuel's on the 28th **3**
Pacino's Italian Ristorante **4**

turkey, shrimp, steak, and pork with veggies, stir-fried rice, and more. You'll also find lots of trimmings and a full bar with limited wine selections (tropical alcoholic drinks are available for an added fee).

Ask for a seat in the main dining room or you won't get a good view of the entertainment.

See map p. 130. 1600 Seven Seas Dr. at Disney's Polynesian Resort. ☎ 407-939-3463 or 407-824-2000. www.disneyworld.com. *Advanced Dining Reservations strongly recommended. Main courses: $25 adults; $11 kids 3–11. AE, DC, DISC, MC, V. Open: Daily 5–10 p.m.*

Pacino's Italian Ristorante
$$ Kissimmee ITALIAN

The ceiling of this restaurant contains fiber optics that create an aura of dining under the stars, but try the patio if you want the real thing. Some servers can be a little aloof, but the price and taste make up for it. Pacino's serves thick, juicy veal chops that are usually fork tender, a challenging 32-ounce porterhouse steak, and *fruitti di mare* (shrimp, calamari, clams, and scallops sautéed with white wine and herbs and heaped onto a mound of linguine).

See map p. 147. 5795 W. Hwy. 192/Irlo Bronson Memorial Pkwy. (2 miles east of I-4). ☎ *407-396-8022.* www.pacinos.com. *Reservations accepted. Main courses: $14–$27 (most are less than $20); pizza $9–$11. AE, MC, V. Open: Daily 4–10 p.m.*

The Palm
$$–$$$ Universal Orlando AMERICAN

This location is the 23rd member of a chain started more than 75 years ago in New York, and the food is good, if overpriced. The décor leans toward the upscale supper clubs of the '30s and '40s, and the walls are lined with caricatures of celebrities. Beef and seafood headline a menu that features a 36-ounce New York strip steak for two and a 3-pound Nova Scotia lobster. Smaller appetites and budgets can feast on salmon or veal chops. Validated parking is available.

See map p. 139. 5800 Universal Blvd. (in the Hard Rock Hotel). ☎ 407-503-7256. www. thepalm.com. *Reservations recommended. Main courses: lunch $9–$31; dinner $17–$38 (many less than $25). AE, DC, DISC, MC, V. Open: Mon–Fri 11:30 a.m.–11 p.m.; Sat 5–11 p.m.; Sun 5–10 p.m.*

Pastamore Ristorante
$$ Universal Orlando ITALIAN

This family-style restaurant greets you with display cases brimming with fresh mozzarella and other goodies lurking on the menu. Italian artifacts are scattered about, and the kitchen is open, allowing you a view of the cooks at work. The antipasto primo is a meal in itself. The mound includes bruschetta, eggplant Caponata, melon con prosciutto, grilled portobello mushrooms, olives, plum tomatoes with fresh mozzarella, a medley of Italian cold cuts, and more. The menu also has traditional features such as veal Marsala, chicken parmigiana, shrimp scampi, fettuccine Alfredo, lasagna, and pizza. The restaurant has a basic beer and wine selection. *1000 Universal Studios Plaza. In CityWalk.* ☎ *407-363-8000.* www.universal orlando.com. *Reservations accepted. Main courses: $7–$18. AE, DISC, MC, V. Open: Daily 5 p.m. to midnight.*

Pebbles
$$ Lake Buena Vista   AMERICAN

Pebbles is a local chain that has earned a reputation for great food, a provocative, though small, wine list, and creative appetizers. The laid-back Key West atmosphere is casual and comfortable. The Pebbles twin filets are seared, then bathed in the namesake lager, and delivered with caramelized onions and three-cheese potatoes. A sautéed double breast of chicken has a jacket of sour-orange sauce and sliced avocados. There's also a small selection of sandwiches ($7–$10).

See map p. 130. 12551 Hwy. 535 (in the Crossroads shopping center at the intersection of 535 and Hotel Plaza Boulevard). ☎ *407-827-1111.* www.pebbles worldwide.com. *Reservations not accepted. Main courses: $10–$28. AE, DC, DISC, MC, V. Open: Sun–Thurs noon to 11 p.m.; Fri–Sat 11 a.m.–11 p.m.; sometimes closed Sun.*

Plaza Restaurant
$ Magic Kingdom   AMERICAN

This 19th-century–inspired restaurant, located at the end of Main Street, offers a respite from the Magic Kingdom crowds — and the World's best hot-fudge sundae. If you insist on a meal before dessert, the menu offers tasty, but pricey, burgers, hot and cold sandwiches (try the Reuben or the double-decker hot roast beef), salads, and milkshakes. You can eat inside in an Art Nouveau dining room or on a veranda overlooking Cinderella Castle.

See map p. 130. On Main Street. ☎ *407-939-3463.* www.disneyworld.com. *Advanced Dining Reservations recommended. Main courses: $8–$11; ice cream: $4–$10. AE, DC, DISC, MC, V. Open: Daily 11 a.m. until park closing.*

Portobello Yacht Club
$$–$$$ Downtown Disney   ITALIAN

The pizzas here go beyond the routine to *quattro formaggio* (with four cheeses) and *margherita* (Italian sausage, plum tomatoes, and mozzarella). But it's the less casual entrees that pack people into this place. On the menu, you may find a wood-roasted Atlantic salmon or pasta with Alaskan king crab, scallops, shrimp, and clams in light wine sauce. Situated in a gabled Bermuda-style house, the Portobello's awning-covered patio overlooks Lake Buena Vista. Its cellar is small, but there's a nice selection of wines to match the meals.

See map p. 130. 1650 Buena Vista Drive. In Pleasure Island. ☎ *407-934-8888.* www.levyrestaurants.com. *Advanced Dining Reservations recommended. Main courses: $12–$50 (pizzas $9). AE, DC, DISC, MC, V. Open: Daily 11:30 a.m.–11 p.m.*

Rainforest Café
$$–$$$ Downtown Disney & Animal Kingdom AMERICAN

Set amid a jungle with tropical sounds of birds and waterfalls, this place is one that most kids love! The food's pretty respectable (with an extensive menu), but it's really the décor that makes this restaurant. As its name suggests, entering the Rainforest Café is like walking into a jungle — lifelike silk plants, chattering Animatronic monkeys and elephants, the occasional rain and thunder rumblings are all over. Fun dishes include Caribbean Coconut Shrimp (with a sweet mango sauce), and Maya's Mixed Grill (ribs, chicken breast, and shrimp) but there's just too many to list. The barstools resemble zebras, giraffes, and other wild-and-crazy critters.

Don't even think of showing up here without an Advanced Dining Reservation, or you could end up waiting hours to get in.

Also be aware you have to walk right by the souvenir shop to dine so keep little heads turned to the left if you can.

See map p. 130. 1800 E. Buena Vista Drive (in Downtown Disney Marketplace). ☎ *407-827-8500. Second location outside the entrance to Animal Kingdom.* ☎ *407-938-9100.* www.rainforestcafe.com. *Advanced Dining Reservations strongly recommended. Main courses: $11–$40 (most less than $25). AE, DISC, MC, V. Open: (at Downtown Disney) Sun–Thurs 10:30 a.m.–11 p.m., Fri–Sat 10:30 a.m. to midnight; (at Animal Kingdom) Daily 8:30 a.m.–6:30 p.m.*

Restaurant Akershus
$$ Epcot NORWEGIAN

This dining room, set inside a Disneyfied 14th-century castle, offers a 40-item smorgasbord of hot and cold dishes, making it a bargain for big eaters. Choices include venison stew, roast pork, cured salmon, smoked mackerel, mustard herring, an array of Norwegian breads and cheeses, smashed rutabaga, and more. Trimmings include red cabbage, potato salad, breads, and cheeses. The food is reasonably good, and the staff is friendly. Sweets and sandwiches are available across the courtyard at the **Kringla Bakeri Og Kafé.**

See map p. 136. In Norway Pavilion. ☎ *407-939-3463.* www.disneyworld.com. *Advanced Dining reservations recommended. Main courses: lunch buffet $14 adults, $9 kids 3–9; dinner buffet $20 adults, $9 kids 3–9. AE, DC, DISC, MC, V. Open: Daily noon to park closing.*

Rose & Crown Pub & Dining Room
$$ Epcot BRITISH

Visitors from the U.K. flock to this spot for a taste of home. The Rose & Crown has dark-oak wainscoting, a beamed Tudor ceiling, English folk music, and some spirited servers. Dine on such traditional dishes as fish-and-chips wrapped in newspaper, prime rib with Yorkshire pudding, and an English pie sampler (pork and cottage, and chicken and leek). On the lighter side, bar food includes sausage rolls, Cornish pasties (meat pies), and a Stilton cheese and fruit plate. You can order ale, lagers, and stouts by the pint or (designated-driver alert!) half-yard. The pub has an ale warmer to make sure Guinness is served at 55 degrees, just like its British guests prefer. If you only want to grab a pint or a snack at the bar, you don't need Advanced Dining Reservations.

The restaurant's outdoor seating (weather permitting) offers a fantastic view of IllumiNations (see Chapter 13 for more information), making this an excellent spot for a late dinner. These seats are first-come, first served, so ask the hostess when you arrive if a patio table is available.

See map p. 136. In United Kingdom Pavilion, World Showcase. ☎ 407-939-3463. www. disneyworld.com. Advanced Dining Reservations recommended for dining room. Main courses: lunch $11–$15; dinner $14–$20. AE, DC, DISC, MC, V. Open: Daily 11 a.m. until 1 hour before park closes.

Roy's Restaurant
$$–$$$ Dr. Phillips Area   PACIFIC RIM

Part of a small Hawaiian restaurant chain, this restaurant has an island theme and an atmosphere that allows for intimate conversation. Menus change often, but entrees may include wood-roasted lemon-grass shrimp with black-rice risotto, or a wood-grilled pork chop with ginger-pear sauce. Roy's also has a reasonably deep wine list.

See map p. 139. 7760 W. Sand Lake Rd. (1 mile west of I-4). ☎ 407-352-4844. www. roysrestaurant.com. Reservations suggested. Main courses: $16–$30. AE, DC, DISC, MC, V. Open: Daily 5:30–10 p.m.

The Samba Room
$$ Dr. Phillips Area   CUBAN

Given the almost ear-splitting decibel level, this place isn't one where you can whisper sweet nothings and expect to be heard. But if you like loud salsa sounds and an enterprising menu, the Samba Room may be the place for you. The kitchen turns out rum-raisin, plantain-crusted mahimahi on coconut rice with mango mojo; paella (chicken, mussels, fish, and sausage over rice); and sugarcane beef tenderloin with chipotle mashed potatoes and mushroom sofrito. A patio offers al fresco dining.

See map p. 139. 7468 W. Sand Lake Rd. (1 mile west of I-4). ☎ 407-226-0550. Reservations recommended. Main courses: $16–$30. AE, DC, DISC, MC, V. Open: Sun–Thurs 11:30 a.m.–11 p.m.; Fri–Sat 11:30 a.m. to midnight.

San Angel Inn
$–$$ Epcot MEXICAN

It's always night at the San Angel, where you'll eat at one of several roman-tic candlelit tables located in a hacienda courtyard surrounded by dense jungle foliage. The shadow of a crumbling Yucatán pyramid looms in the distance, and you hear the sound of faraway birds and faint rumblings of the volcano while you dine. The ambience of this restaurant, located inside the Mexico Pavilion, is exotic, and the fare is traditional — that's why you won't find nachos or Mexican pizza on the menu. Entrees include *mole poblano* (chicken simmered with more than 20 spices and a hint of choco-late) and *filete motuleño* (grilled tenderloin of beef served over black beans, melted cheese, pepper strips, and plantains). Your drinking options include Dos Equis beer and margaritas.

See map p. 136. In Mexico Pavilion, World Showcase. ☎ *407-939-3463.* www. disneyworld.com. *Advanced Dining Reservations recommended. Main courses: lunch $9–$18; dinner $18–$24. AE, DC, DISC, MC, V. Open: Daily 11:30 a.m. until park closing.*

Sci-Fi Dine-In Theater Restaurant
$$ Disney–MGM Studios AMERICAN

Horror flicks too hokey to be scary play on the screen while you dine in a replica of a 1950s Los Angeles drive-in movie emporium, complete with tables ensconced in flashy, chrome-trimmed convertible cars. Fun-loving carhops deliver free popcorn and your meal. Menu items have funny names but are basics like sandwiches, burgers, ribs, seafood, pasta, and steaks. The unique atmosphere definitely keeps the crowds and the kids coming.

Near Indiana Jones Epic Stunt Spectacular. ☎ *407-939-3463.* www.disneyworld. com. *Advanced Dining Reservations recommended. Main courses: lunch $12–$17; dinner $14–$17. AE, DC, DISC, MC, V. Open: Daily 10:30 a.m. until park closing.*

Spoodles
$$ Walt Disney World Resorts MEDITERRANEAN

Tapas, pizza, and pasta are the main items on the menu at this Mediterranean-style restaurant, which features an open exhibition kitchen and a lively atmosphere. The treats include sautéed chili-garlic shrimp, fried calamari, and a sampler platter. You can also choose from several conventional entrees, including Moroccan-spiced tuna and grilled pork porterhouse with goat cheese polenta. Table-side sangria presentations add something special to the evening. Although popular, the quality here doesn't rival Café Tu Tu Tango (reviewed earlier).

During the height of the summer, Spoodles gets crowded, and the wait can be long, even with Advanced Dining Reservations, so this restaurant isn't a good choice for famished families coming straight from the parks, and really not a great choice for families with young kids along either.

See map p. 130. 2101 N. Epcot Resorts Blvd. at BoardWalk Inn Resort & Villas. ☎ *407-939-3463 or 407-939-2380.* www.disneyworld.com. *Advanced Dining Reservations recommended. Main courses: tapas $6–$9; entrees $18–$28. AE, DC, DISC, MC, V. Open: Daily 7–11 a.m.; noon–2 p.m.; 5–10 p.m.*

Tchoup Chop
$$–$$$ Universal Orlando PACIFIC RIM

Pronounced "chop chop," Emeril Lagasse's second restaurant in Orlando opened in January 2003. The name comes from the location of Emeril's original restaurant — Tchoupitoulous Street in New Orleans. For its décor, the interior blends flowers, sculpted gardens, and mini waterfalls with Batik fabrics, carved-wood grilles, and glass chandeliers. The exhibition kitchen offers a look at the chefs making your meal in woks or on wood-burning grills. The Polynesian- and Asian-influenced menu offers temptations such as macadamia crusted Atlantic salmon with steamed rice and stir-fried vegetables and wok-fried filet mignon with vegetable chow mein and crispy oysters.

See map p. 139. 6300 Hollywood Way (in Universal's Royal Pacific Hotel). ☎ *407-503-2467.* www.emerils.com. *Reservations strongly recommended. Main courses: $13–$34. AE, DISC, MC, V. Daily 11:30 a.m.–2 p.m.; Sun–Thurs 5:30–10 p.m.; Fri–Sat 5:30–11 p.m.*

Teppanyaki Dining Room
$$–$$$ Epcot JAPANESE

If you've ever been to a Japanese steakhouse, then you know the drill: Diners sit around the large grill-tables while the chefs expertly and quickly dice, slice, stir-fry, and serve up your food to your plate with amazing dexterity. Kids especially enjoy watching the chef wield a cleaver and other utensils. Several parties are seated at teppanyaki tables, which makes for sociable dining, especially for single travelers looking for conversation. Expect the entrees to have chicken, steak, scallops, lobsters, or a combination. Kirin beer, plum wine, and sake are served.

The adjoining **Tempura Kiku** counter-restaurant offers sushi, sashimi, and tempura-battered shrimp and chicken.

See map p. 136. In Japan Pavilion, World Showcase. ☎ *407-939-3463.* www.disney world.com. *Advanced Dining Reservations recommended for Teppanyaki; reservations not accepted at Tempura Kiku. Teppanyaki main courses: lunch $12–$22, dinner $16–$35; Tempura Kiku: lunch $9–$14, dinner $13–$25. AE, DC, DISC, MC, V. Open: Daily 11 a.m. until 1 hour before park closing.*

Todd English's BlueZoo
$$–$$$$ Walt Disney World Resorts SEAFOOD

Celebrity chef Todd English put down roots, in 2004, at the Walt Disney World Dolphin with this restaurant, which serves innovative seafood in an unusually vibrant upscale setting. The food is served with an artistic flair almost as impressive as the décor. On the entree front, try the mizo-glazed Chilean sea bass or the catch of the day roasted on a rotisserie grill. There are a few non-marine items on the menu, but the emphasis here is on all dishes aquatic. Shellfish lovers will enjoy the raw bar (just be sure to bring your wallets!).

See map p. 130. 1500 Epcot Resorts Blvd., in the Walt Disney World Dolphin. ☎ *407-93934-1609.* www.thebluezoo.com. *Advanced Dining Reservations recommended. Main courses: $18–$54. AE, DISC, MC, V. Open: Daily 3:30–11 p.m.*

Victoria & Albert
$$$$ Walt Disney World Resorts   INTERNATIONAL

The setting is Victorian and a nostalgic reminder that dining out was once a treat to be savored in an evening-filling, relaxed, and stylish manner. The chef works wizardry with food from a diverse marketplace. This restaurant is the most memorable (and memorably expensive) in **WDW**. But if money's no object and you're serious about food and romance going hand in hand, head here. The intimate dining room has exquisitely appointed tables. The food is impeccable and presented with a flourish by an attentive and professional staff. (Each table has servers named Victoria and Albert.) The seven-course menu changes nightly. You may begin with roasted duck with candy-striped and golden beets, followed by Monterey abalone with lemon and baby spinach. Then, shrimp bisque may precede an entree such as Australian Kobe-beef tenderloin. English Stilton served with a poached pear sets up desserts such as vanilla-bean crème brûlée and Kona chocolate soufflé. Dinners are 2½- to 3-hour affairs, though the later sitting can run longer. If you want to try the chef's table experience (you actually dine in the kitchen and watch them prepare your meal), be sure to reserve it excruciatingly early (they begin taking Advanced Dining Reservations 180 days in advance). *Note: I don't recommend this restaurant for children.*

See map p. 130. 4401 Floridian Way, in Disney's Grand Floridian Resort & Spa. ☎ *407-939-3463.* www.disneyworld.com. *Advanced Dining Reservations required well in advance, especially for the Chef's Table. Main courses: fixed-price menu $95 per person, $145 with wine pairing; chef's table $125, $185 with wine. AE, DC, DISC, MC, V. Open: 2 dinner seatings daily Sept–June, 5:45–6:30 p.m. and 9–9:45 p.m.; 1 seating daily July–Aug, 6:45–8 p.m. Chef's Table 6 p.m. only. Jackets required for men.*

Wolfgang Puck Grand Café
$$–$$$ Downtown Disney   AMERICAN

This restaurant's sushi bar, an artistic copper-and-terrazzo masterpiece, delivers some of the best sushi in Orlando. You can eat gourmet pizza, with a thin crust and exotic toppings, on an outdoor patio or inside. Upstairs, the main dining room presents a seasonally changing menu that may feature Szechuan beef and crimini satay with a spicy vegetable stir fry or pumpkin ravioli with sage, hazelnut butter, and parmesan. The lower level can be noisy, making conversation difficult, and the downstairs wait for a table is excruciatingly long. Puck's also has a grab-and-go express restaurant that sells sandwiches, pizzas, desserts, and more.

See map p. 130. 1482 Buena Vista Drive. In Disney's West Side. 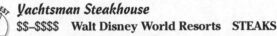 *☎ 407-938-9653.* www.wolfgangpuck.com/myrestaurants. *Advanced Dining Reservations recommended for lower-level dining room. Main courses (upstairs): $19–$38; $8–$40 pizza and sushi. AE, DC, DISC, MC, V. Daily 11 a.m.–1 a.m.*

Yachtsman Steakhouse
$$–$$$$ Walt Disney World Resorts   STEAKS

Regarded as one of Orlando's top steak-and-chop houses, Yachtsman Steakhouse is a good place to come if you love red meat. You can see the cuts age in a glass-enclosed room, and the exhibition kitchen provides a tantalizing glimpse of steaks, chops, and seafood being grilled over oak and hickory. The décor includes knotty-pine beams, plank floors, and leather-and-oak chairs. Steak options range from a 6-ounce filet to a 12-ounce bourbon-marinated strip to a belly-busting 24-ounce T-bone. The menu also includes salmon, chicken, and rack of lamb. The Steakhouse is prone to crowds, but most folks say that it's worth the wait.

See map p. 130. 1700 Epcot Resorts Blvd., in Disney's Yacht Club Resort. **☎ 407-939-3463.** www.disneyworld.com. *Advanced Dining Reservations recommended. Main courses: $21–$80. AE, DC, DISC, MC, V. Open: Daily 5:30–10 p.m.*

Dining with Disney Characters

The opportunity to chow down with Mickey, Donald, Cinderella, and many of the other major characters is the major dining experience in Orlando. The 8-and-under crowd usually gets starry-eyed when characters show up to say howdy, sign autographs, pose for photos, and encourage them to eat their broccoli. Character mealtime appearances at Disney parks, attractions, and resorts are incredibly popular. As a result, one-on-one interaction is somewhat brief, so be ready for that Kodak moment or hope a **WDW** photographer captures it for you (at a premium price).

You may not find a seat when you show up to a character appearance unannounced, so call ☎ **407-939-3463** to make Advanced Dinning Reservations as far in advance as possible (these reservations don't lock down a table, but they give you the next available table after you arrive at your appointed time). To take the guesswork out of figuring out how far in advance (60 days? 90? 180?) you need to make an Advanced Dining reservation, head online to the **PS Planning Guide** (www.pscalculator.net). This unofficial site does a very good job of keeping up-to-date on all the rules and reservation windows for every restaurant at Disney. But its best feature is a calculator that allows you to punch in your desired reservation date, and then tells you when the Advanced Dining Reservation window for your chosen restaurant will be open. Best of all, this service is free.

Character dining at Universal Orlando & SeaWorld

Though it's the recognized leader in the category, Disney doesn't have a lock on character dining in Orlando. At **Islands of Adventure,** you can have breakfast with Spider-Man, the Cat in the Hat, and other Marvel and Dr. Seuss characters Thursday through Sunday from park opening to 10:30 a.m. at the Confisco Grille. The cost is $16 for adults and $10 for children ages 3 to 9, plus tax and tip. Call ☎ **407-224-4012** for the mandatory reservations.

Shamu and a group of his marine friends (Penny Penguin and Seamore the Sea Lion, among others) welcome you at the **Shamu & Crew Character Breakfast** served from 8:45 to 10:15 a.m. at the park's Seafire Inn. The cost is $15 for adults and $10 for children ages 3 to 9 (children younger than 3 enter free, but must have a reservation). For the mandatory reservations, call ☎ **800-327-2420** or go to the park's Web site at www. seaworld.com.

The cost of catching characters

Prices for Disney character meals are pretty much the same no matter where you dine. Breakfast (most serve it) averages $17 to $20 for adults and $9 to $11 for children 3 to 11. Dinner, which is only available in some places, runs $22 to $27 for adults and $10 to $13 for children. In general, presentation at all the character meal listings here is high on the fun front but middle-of-the-road when it comes to the food.

Character meals accept American Express, Diners Club, Discover, MasterCard, Visa, and the Disney card. For more information on these meals, check Disney's Web site at www.disneyworld.com.

The most characters money can buy

Although I mention specific characters here, be advised that **WDW** frequently changes its lineups, so don't promise the kids a specific character or you may get burned. Also, keep in mind that you'll have to *add the price of admission* (and, if you aren't a Disney resort guest, the $8 parking fee) to meals that are served inside the theme parks. When bringing children to these meals, remember that some of the very young ones may actually end up scared of — and not delighted with — the larger-than-life characters.

Cape May Café

This delightful, New England-themed dining room offers buffet breakfasts (eggs, pancakes, bacon, pastries, and more) that are hosted by **Admiral Goofy** and his crew — **Chip 'n' Dale** and **Pluto.** Again, the characters that show up may vary.

See map p. 130. 1800 Epcot Resorts Blvd., in Disney's Beach Club Resort. Character breakfast: $18 adults, $10 children. Open: Daily 7:30–11:30 a.m.

Chef Mickey's

The whimsical Chef Mickey's welcomes your favorite cartoon characters twice a day: at buffet breakfasts (eggs, bacon, sausage, pancakes, fruit, and other items) and dinners. (Entrees change daily and are joined by a salad bar, soups, vegetables, and ice cream with toppings.) **Mickey and various pals** are there to meet and mingle.

See map p. 130. 4600 N. World Dr., in Disney's Contemporary Resort. Character breakfast: $18 adults, $10 children; character dinner: $27 adults, $12 children. Open: Daily 7:30–11:30 a.m.; 5–9:30 p.m.

Cinderella's Royal Table

This castle — the focal point of the park — is the setting for daily character breakfasts. The menu has standard fare: eggs, bacon, Danish, and fresh breads. Hosts vary, but **Cinderella** always makes an appearance. This meal is a great way to start your day in the **Magic Kingdom.**

Advanced Dining Reservations are a must here, and thanks to the crowds, the most difficult character breakfast to get. If this is a must-do breakfast, I suggest you begin trying as soon as the reservation window opens up 90 days in advance (call exactly at 7 a.m. and if — lucky you — you get through on your first try, don't get picky about your seating arrangements and dining times). *N*ote: Advanced Dining Reservations for this breakfast must be made with a guaranteed credit-card payment that will *cost you $10 for adults and $5 for kids if you don't cancel them at least 24 hours in advance.*

See map p. 130. In Cinderella Castle, Magic Kingdom. Character breakfast: $22 adults, $12 children. Open: Daily 8–10:30 a.m.

Crystal Palace

The real treats here are the characters, **Pooh and his pals,** who are on location throughout the day. The restaurant serves breakfast (eggs, French toast, pancakes, bacon), lunch, and dinner (a variety of beef, chicken, veggies, kids' favorites, a sundae bar, and more).

See map p. 130. On Main St., Magic Kingdom. Character breakfast: $18 adults, $10 children; character lunch: $20 adults, $12 children; character dinner $23 adults, $12 children. Open: Daily 8–10:30 a.m.; 11:30 a.m.–2:45 p.m.; 4 p.m. until park closing.

Donald's Prehistoric Breakfastosaurus

Here's another all-you-can-eat buffet of eggs, bacon, French toast and other favorites. **Donald Duck, Goofy,** and **Pluto** are on hand to entertain the little ones while they almost eat. *Note:* This is the only place in **Animal Kingdom** that offers a character breakfast.

See map p. 130. In Animal Kingdom, Restaurantosaurus, Dinoland U.S.A. Character breakfast: $17 adults, $9 children. Open: Daily from park opening until 10:30 a.m.

Garden Grill

There's a Mom's-in-the-kitchen theme at this revolving restaurant with comfortable, semicircular booths. **Mickey** and **Chip 'n' Dale** play host to family-style meals with a country theme. (Boy, that Mickey sure gets around.) Lunch and dinner (chicken, fish, steak, vegetables, and potatoes) are served.

See map p. 136. In The Land Pavilion, Epcot. Character lunch: $20 adults, $11 children; character dinner: $22 adults, $11 children. Open: Daily 11 a.m.–8 p.m.

Garden View Lounge

Every Thursday through Monday, **Princess Aurora** (aka **Sleeping Beauty**) hosts the *My Disney Girl's Perfectly Princess Tea Party* for all the little princesses. In addition to enjoying tea and cake with Aurora, guests age 3 to 11 will also receive a "My Disney Girl" collectible doll dressed in a matching Princess Aurora gown.

See map p. 130. 4401 Floridian Way, in Disney's Grand Floridian Beach Resort. $200 for one adult and one child age 3–11; $65 each additional adult, $135 for each additional child. Open: Thurs–Mon 10:30 a.m. to noon.

Liberty Tree Tavern

This colonial-style, 18th-century pub offers character dinners with hosts **Minnie, Goofy, Pluto,** and **Chip 'n' Dale.** The family-style meals include salad, roast turkey, pork, flank steak, cornbread, and apple crisp with vanilla ice cream.

See map p. 130. In Liberty Square, Magic Kingdom. Character dinner: $22 adults, $10 children. Open: Daily 4 p.m. until park closing.

1900 Park Fare

The exquisitely elegant Grand Floridian Resort hosts character breakfasts (eggs, French toast, bacon, and pancakes) and dinners (prime rib, pork loin, fish, and more) in the festive, exposition-themed 1900 Park Fare. Big Bertha — a 100-year-old French band organ that plays pipes, drums, bells, cymbals, castanets, and the xylophone — provides music. **Mary Poppins, Alice in Wonderland,** and **friends** appear at breakfast; **Cinderella** and **friends** show up for Cinderella's Gala Feast at dinner.

See map p. 130. 4401 Floridian Way, in Disney's Grand Floridian Beach Resort & Spa. Character breakfast: $17 adults, $10 children; character dinner: $26 adults, $11 children. Open: Daily 7:30–11 a.m.; 5–9 p.m.

'Ohana Character Breakfast

Traditional breakfast foods (eggs, pancakes, bacon, and more) are prepared on an 18-foot fire pit and served family style at this Polynesian-themed

restaurant. **Mickey and some of his pals** appear, and children can participate with musical instruments in a special parade.

*See map p. 130. 1600 Seven Seas Dr., in Disney's Polynesian Resort Character break-
fast: $17 adults, $9 children. Open: Daily 7:30–11 a.m.*

Princess Storybook Breakfast

Snow White, Mary Poppins, Princess Aurora, Pocahontas, or **Belle** might
show up at this character meal (scrambled eggs, French toast, sausage,
bacon, and potatoes). Because of its popularity the restaurant began offering a lunch (lamb, chicken, salmon, veggies, salads, kids' favorites, and
dessert) and dinner (lamb, salmon, venison stew, pasta, veggies, salads,
and dessert) in addition to the breakfast.

 Advanced Dining Reservations are a must here, and the second most difficult to get — every little girl at Disney has to meet her favorite princess.
If this is a must-do breakfast, I suggest you begin trying as soon as the
reservation window opens up 90 days in advance. *Note:* Advanced Dining
Reservations for this breakfast must be made with a guaranteed credit-
card payment that will cost you $10 for adults and $5 for kids if you don't
cancel them at least 48 hours in advance.

*See map p. 136. At Akershus Castle in Epcot's Norway Pavilion. Character breakfast:
$22 adults, $12 children; character lunch: $24 adults, $13 children; character dinner:
$28 adults, $13 children. Open: Daily 8:30–10:20 a.m., 11:40 a.m.–2:50 p.m., and
4:20–8:40 p.m.*

Index of Restaurants by Neighborhood

Downtown Disney

Earl of Sandwich (American, $)
Fulton's Crab House (Seafood, $$–$$$)
House of Blues (American, $$)
Portobello Yacht Club (Italian,
$$–$$$)
Rainforest Café (American, $$–$$$)
Wolfgang Puck Café (American,
$$–$$$)

Downtown Orlando

Dexter's at Thornton Park
(International, $–$$)
Little Saigon (Vietnamese, $)
Manuel's on the 28th (International,
$$$)

Dr. Phillips Area

Christini's (Italian, $$–$$$)
Roy's Restaurant (Pacific Rim, $$–$$$)
The Samba Room (Cuban, $$)

International Drive Area

Atlantis (Seafood/Steaks, $$$)
B-Line Diner (American, $–$$)
Bubbalou's Bodacious BBQ
(American, $–$$)
Café Tu Tu Tango (International,
$$–$$$)
Dux (International, $$$)
Ming Court (Chinese, $$–$$$)

Kissimmee

Pacino's Italian Ristorante (Italian, $$)

Lake Buena Vista

Arthur's 27 (International, $$$-$$$$)
Hemingway's (Seafood, $$)
Pebbles (American, $$)

Universal Orlando

Bice (Italian, $$-$$$)
Bob Marley — A Tribute to Freedom
(Caribbean, $)
Emeril's (New Orleans, $$-$$$)
Jimmy Buffett's Margaritaville
(Caribbean, $-$$)
The Palm (American, $$-$$$)
Pastamore Ristorante (Italian, $$)
Tchoup Chop (Pacific Rim, $$-$$$)

Universal Orlando Area

Kim Wu (Chinese, $)

Walt Disney World

Animal Kingdom

Rainforest Café (American, $$-$$$)

Disney–MGM Studios

50's Prime Time Café (American, $$)
Hollywood Brown Derby (American,
$$)
Sci-Fi Dine-In Theater Restaurant
(American, $$)

Epcot

Les Chefs de France (French, $$-$$$)

Coral Reef (Seafood, $$-$$$)
Le Cellier Steakhouse (Steaks, $$-$$$)
L'Originale Alfredo di Roma (Italian,
$$-$$$)
Lotus Blossom Café (Chinese, $)
Marrakesh (Moroccan, $$)
Nine Dragons (Chinese, $$-$$$)
Restaurant Akershus (Norwegian, $$)
Rose & Crown Pub & Dining Room
(British, $$)
San Angel Inn (Mexican, $-$$)
Teppanyaki Dining Room (Japanese,
$$-$$$)

Magic Kingdom

Cinderella's Royal Table (American,
$$-$$$)
Liberty Tree Tavern (American, $$)
Plaza Restaurant (American, $)

Walt Disney World Resorts

Boatwright's Dining Hall (New
Orleans, $-$$)
Boma (African, $$)
California Grill (American, $$-$$$)
Citricos (French, $$-$$$)
Flying Fish Café (Seafood, $$$)
Jiko (African, $$-$$$)
'Ohana (Pacific Rim, $$)
Spoodles (Mediterranean, $$)
Todd English's BlueZoo (Seafood,
$$-$$$$)
Victoria & Albert (International, $$$$)
Yachtsman Steakhouse (Steaks,
$$-$$$$)

Index of Restaurants by Cuisine

African

Boma (Walt Disney World Resorts, $$)
Jiko (Walt Disney World Resorts,
$$-$$$)

American

B-Line Diner (International Drive Area,
$-$$)

Bubbalou's Bodacious BBQ
(International Drive Area, $-$$)
California Grill (Walt Disney World
Resorts, $$-$$$)
Cinderella's Royal Table (Magic
Kingdom, $$-$$$)
Earl of Sandwich (Downtown
Disney, $)

50's Prime Time Café (Disney–MGM Studios, $$)

Hollywood Brown Derby (Disney–MGM Studios, $$)

House of Blues (Downtown Disney, $$)

Liberty Tree Tavern (Magic Kingdom, $$)

The Palm (Universal Orlando, $$–$$$)

Pebbles (Lake Buena Vista, $$)

Plaza Restaurant (Magic Kingdom, $)

Rainforest Café (Downtown Disney & Animal Kingdom, $$–$$$)

Sci-Fi Dine-In Theater Restaurant (Disney–MGM Studios, $$)

Wolfgang Puck Café (Downtown Disney, $$–$$$)

British

Rose & Crown Pub & Dining Room (Epcot, $$)

Caribbean

Bob Marley — A Tribute to Freedom (Universal Orlando, $)

Jimmy Buffett's Margaritaville (Universal Orlando, $–$$)

Chinese

Kim Wu (Universal Orlando Area, $)

Lotus Blossom Café (Epcot, $)

Ming Court (International Drive Area, $$–$$$)

Nine Dragons (Epcot, $$–$$$)

Cuban

The Samba Room (Dr. Phillips Area, $$)

French

Les Chefs de France (Epcot, $$–$$$)

Citricos (Walt Disney World Resorts, $$–$$$)

International

Arthur's 27 (Lake Buena Vista, $$$–$$$$)

Café Tu Tu Tango (International Drive Area, $$–$$$)

Dexter's at Thornton Park (Downtown Orlando, $–$$)

Dux (International Drive Area, $$$)

Manuel's on the 28th (Downtown Orlando, $$$)

Victoria & Albert (Walt Disney World Resorts, $$$$)

Italian

Bice (Universal Orlando, $$–$$$)

Christini's (Dr. Phillips Area, $$–$$$)

L'Originale Alfredo di Roma (Epcot, $$–$$$)

Pacino's Italian Ristorante (Kissimmee, $$)

Pastamore Ristorante (Universal Orlando, $$)

Portobello Yacht Club (Downtown Disney, $$–$$$)

Japanese

Teppanyaki Dining Room (Epcot, $$–$$$)

Mediterranean

Spoodles (Walt Disney World Resorts, $$)

Mexican

San Angel Inn (Epcot, $–$$)

Moroccan

Marrakesh (Epcot, $$)

New Orleans

Boatwright's Dining Hall (Walt Disney World Resorts, $–$$)

Emeril's (Universal Orlando, $$–$$$)

Norwegian

Restaurant Akershus (Epcot, $$)

Pacific Rim

'Ohana (Walt Disney World Resorts, $$)

Roy's Restaurant (Dr. Phillips Area, $$–$$$)
Tchoup Chop (Universal Orlando, $$–$$$)

Seafood

Atlantis (International Drive Area, $$$)
Coral Reef (Epcot, $$–$$$)
Flying Fish Café (Walt Disney World Resorts, $$$)
Fulton's Crab House (Downtown Disney, $$–$$$)

Hemingway's (Lake Buena Vista, $$)
Todd English's BlueZoo (Walt Disney World Resorts, $$–$$$$)

Steaks

Atlantis (International Drive Area, $$$)
Le Cellier Steakhouse (Epcot, $$–$$$)
Yachtsman Steakhouse (Walt Disney World Resorts, $$–$$$$)

Vietnamese

Little Saigon (Downtown Orlando, $)

Index of Restaurants by Price

$$$$

Arthur's 27 (International, Lake Buena Vista)
Victoria & Albert (International, Walt Disney World Resorts)

$$$

Atlantis (Seafood, International Drive Area)
Bice (Italian, Universal Orlando)
California Grill (American, Walt Disney World Resorts)
Les Chefs de France (French, Epcot)
Christini's (Italian, Dr. Phillips Area)
Cinderella's Royal Table (American, Magic Kingdom)
Citricos (French, Walt Disney World Resorts)
Coral Reef (Seafood, Epcot)
Dux (International, International Drive Area)
Emeril's (New Orleans, Universal Orlando)
Flying Fish Café (Seafood, Walt Disney World Resorts)
Fulton's Crab House (Seafood, Downtown Disney)
Jiko (African, Walt Disney World Resorts)
Le Cellier Steakhouse (Steaks, Epcot)
L'Originale Alfredo di Roma (Italian, Epcot)

Manuel's on the 28th (International, Downtown Orlando)
Ming Court (Chinese, International Drive Area)
Nine Dragons (Chinese, Epcot)
The Palm (American, Universal Orlando)
Portobello Yacht Club (Italian, Downtown Disney)
Rainforest Café (American, Downtown Disney & Animal Kingdom)
Roy's Restaurant (Pacific Rim, Dr. Phillips Area)
Tchoup Chop (Pacific Rim, Universal Orlando)
Teppanyaki Dining Room (Japanese, Epcot)
Todd English's BlueZoo (Seafood, Walt Disney World Resorts)
Wolfgang Puck Café (American, Downtown Disney)
Yachtsman Steakhouse (Steaks, Walt Disney World Resorts)

$$

Boatwright's Dining Hall (New Orleans, Walt Disney World Resorts)
Boma (African, Walt Disney World Resorts)
Café Tu Tu Tango (International, International Drive Area)

50's Prime Time Café (American, Disney–MGM Studios)

Hemingway's (Seafood, Lake Buena Vista)

Hollywood Brown Derby (American, Disney–MGM Studios)

House of Blues (American, Downtown Disney)

Jimmy Buffett's Margaritaville (Caribbean, Universal Orlando)

Liberty Tree Tavern (American, Magic Kingdom)

Marrakesh (Moroccan, Epcot)

'Ohana (Pacific Rim, Walt Disney World Resorts)

Pacino's Italian Ristorante (Italian, Kissimmee)

Pastamore Ristorante (Italian, Universal Orlando)

Pebbles (American, Lake Buena Vista)

Restaurant Akershus (Norwegian, Epcot)

Rose & Crown Pub & Dining Room (British, Epcot)

The Samba Room (Cuban, Dr. Phillips Area)

San Angel Inn (Mexican, Epcot)

Sci-Fi Dine-In Theater Restaurant (American, Disney–MGM Studios)

Spoodles (Mediterranean, Walt Disney World Resorts)

$

B-Line Diner (American, International Drive Area)

Bob Marley — A Tribute to Freedom (Caribbean, Universal Orlando)

Bubbalou's Bodacious BBQ (American, International Drive Area)

Dexter's at Thornton Park (International, Downtown Orlando)

Earl of Sandwich (American, Downtown Disney)

Kim Wu (Chinese, Universal Orlando Area)

Little Saigon (Vietnamese, Downtown Orlando)

Lotus Blossom Café (Chinese, Epcot)

Plaza Restaurant (American, Magic Kingdom)

Part IV
Exploring Walt Disney World

The 5th Wave   By Rich Tennant

@RICHTENNANT

"I __know__ these are your characters' names, but when you're around guests at the theme park, you're neither sleepy, dopey, nor grumpy."

In this part . . .

1 have some great news for you: You're going to visit the "Happiest Place on Earth" And now for the bad news: If you neglect to plan ahead, you may just be the unhappiest person there.

In an average year, more than 42 million people find their way to Disney's four major theme parks, and all are determined to ride the same rides and eat in the same restaurants as you (sometimes, it would seem, all at the same time!). You'll have much more fun if you arrive knowing which parks and attractions are best suited to your tastes as well as knowing which places aren't worth the effort. In this part, I guide you through matching up the parks' features to your tastes so that you can decide where you want to spend the majority of your time.

Chapter 11

Getting Acquainted with Walt Disney World

● ●

In This Chapter

▶ Familiarizing yourself with the Disney parks
▶ Getting to and around the Disney empire
▶ Pricing the cost of your visit
▶ Maximizing your fun and minimizing your wait
▶ Getting around the crowds

● ●

The first time I made a pilgrimage to the **Magic Kingdom,** I wandered in slack-jawed awe among the many marvels of Mickeyville.

Today, I marvel at a different wonder: growth. Walt Disney's legacy has exploded in the last three decades. It has truly become a world unto itself, with four theme parks, nearly a dozen smaller parks and attractions, clubs, hotels, restaurants, shopping districts, its own transit system, and two cruise ships. It's enough to fog your brain, but that's why I'm here — to defog and demystify the planning process.

In this and the next several chapters, I introduce you to the parks, tantalize you with ride descriptions, and offer you some suggested itineraries. With the many thanks to my own children and those of my sisters and friends, I also use a special ratings system to give you a kid's view ("KidRating") of the rides and shows in the parks. My reviews are based on those of my children: Ryan (12), Austin (10), Nicolas (8), Hailey (6), and Davis (4).

Introducing Walt's World

Disney's four main theme parks line the western half of this 30,500-acre world. The **Magic Kingdom** is the original attraction; with just over 15 million visitors in 2004, it was busier than any other U.S. theme park. **Epcot** was third busiest with 9.4 million visitors, followed by **Disney–MGM Studios** at 8.2 million, and **Animal Kingdom** with 7.8 million. (In case

Walt Disney World Parks & Attractions

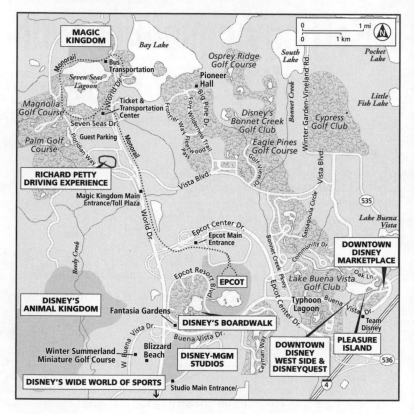

you're curious, Disneyland, in California, holds the No. 2 slot.) Here's a quick look at what you can find in all four Disney parks:

✔ **Magic Kingdom:** Built as Disney's flagship park, the **Magic Kingdom** is divided into seven themed lands. They're laid out like the spokes of a wheel, with the park's icon — *Cinderella Castle* — at the hub. Anyone with kids, or who is just young at heart, needs to give the Magic Kingdom at least one full day. It offers more for young children than any other Orlando theme park, but it has broad appeal for first-timers and Disney fans, too. If you fall into these categories, I recommend two days or more, provided you have the time and budget. (See Chapter 12 for more details about the **Magic Kingdom**.)

✔ **Epcot:** Built as an exposition of human achievement and new technology (albeit a somewhat commercialized version), **Epcot** is symbolized by *Spaceship Earth,* an attraction often described as "that big silver golf ball." *Future World,* the first of Epcot's two sections, has innovative exhibits and rides. This part of the park is also home to three of Disney's newest rides, *Soarin', Mission: Space,* and *Test Track.* The far end of the park, *World Showcase,* consists of a lagoon surrounded by pavilions showcasing the cultures of 11 countries. Allowing two days for the shows, rides, shops, and ethnic restaurants in Epcot is a good idea. (See Chapter 13 for more details about **Epcot.**)

This park is the least attractive for younger children, but the best one for inquiring minds and those who appreciate the world's unique cultures (as well as ethnic dining) (see Chapter 10).

✔ **Disney–MGM Studios:** This showbiz-themed park is reminiscent of the Tinseltown of the '30s and '40s. It blends working studios with shows such as the all new *Lights, Motors, Action! Extreme Stunt Show, Indiana Jones Epic Stunt Spectacular!,* and thrill rides such as the *Twilight Zone Tower of Terror* and *Rock 'n' Rollercoaster starring Aerosmith.* Young kids will find some cool things to occupy their time here, though they won't be able to do the two major thrill rides. And best of all for the foot-weary: You can tackle this part of **WDW** in only one day, and a more relaxed one at that. (See Chapter 14 for more details about **Disney–MGM Studios.**)

✔ **Disney's Animal Kingdom:** The newest Disney kid on the block is symbolized by the 14-story *Tree of Life,* which is to this park what Cinderella Castle is to the Magic Kingdom. At this park, guests explore Asia, Africa, and even the age of the Dinosaur. The wildlife exhibit, zoo, and theme park features shows such as *It's Tough to Be A Bug!* and *Festival of the Lion King,* as well as rides like *Kilimanjaro Safaris, DINOSAUR,* and *Expedition Everest* (debuting in 2006). You won't have trouble touring this park in one day, but keep in mind that this one's best seen early in the day. (See Chapter 15 for more details about **Disney's Animal Kingdom.**)

Have time for more?

In addition to the big four, a few other parks and attractions round out the Disney empire:

✔ **DisneyQuest** is a whole lot more than just a fancy video arcade. It's a virtual reality world unto itself, with top-flight games and simulators that put the game consoles you have at home to shame.

✔ **Disney's Wide World of Sports** is a 240-acre complex filled with an array of state-of-the-art sports facilities for football, soccer, baseball, softball, as well as other sports and activities. At the interactive *Multi-Sports Experience,* guests can participate in a variety of challenges that put their skills to the test. The complex also has a 7,500-seat baseball stadium that's the spring training home of the Atlanta Braves.

✔ **Walt Disney World Speedway** has a stock car–racing track that serves as host to the *Richard Petty Driving Experience,* where you can even drive a car or ride shotgun at 145 mph. (If you're from Talladega or Darlington, you probably can do that in your sleep.)

✔ **A pair of themed miniature golf courses** whose whimsical décor schemes (think "Santa goes to the beach" and "Disney classic film comes alive") entertain even as they challenge putters with all-too-realistic water hazards and tricky sand traps. To visit Santa in all his sunny glory, head for *Winter Summerland;* for Mickey's sorcerer's hat and dancing hippos, take your irons to *Fantasia Gardens.*

✔ **Two splashy parks** let you float along lazy streams, scream down gravity defying waterslides, and more. They're especially appealing in summer, when the heat and humidity both are above 90° and 90 percent. Kids and adults alike will enjoy cooling off at **Blizzard Beach** and **Typhoon Lagoon.**

I give you more info about these attractions in Chapter 16.

Planet Disney also has several shopping (see Chapter 17) and nightlife (see Chapter 25) venues. For example:

✔ **Disney's BoardWalk** is a good place to stroll the waterfront, dine, dance, or catch a game in the sports bar.

✔ **Downtown Disney** comprises **Pleasure Island,** an adult nightclub district; **Downtown Disney Marketplace,** which features dining and shopping; **Downtown Disney West Side,** with more shopping, dining, *Cirque du Soleil,* and the *House of Blues;* and **DisneyQuest,** a high-tech, interactive video arcade.

You can get additional information about all WDW properties by calling ☎ **407-934-7639** or visiting its Web site at www.disneyworld.com.

Palling around with Mickey

Introduced in 2003, **Pal Mickey** is a talking 10½-inch-tall stuffed digital Mickey Mouse who serves as a semi-amusing novelty guide to the Disney parks, telling guests about parades, show times, and so on when activated. Designed for kids, he nevertheless gets toted around by adults, too. (Pal Mickey comes with an attachable belt clip and most grown-ups, much to the amusement of their kids, often get confused and go for their pagers when he vibrates to let them know he's got a message for them). His computer chips pick up wireless signals throughout the park and dispenses pertinent fun and facts; after you leave, a few corny jokes are all that's left of his repertoire. Pal Mickey operates on three AA batteries — they're included! — and dispenses more than 700 bits of wisdom. He's available for purchase ($60) inside all Disney resort gift shops, and at select stores inside the theme parks. For that much money, I'd prefer the real Mickey to show me around instead of his little electronic brother, but at least you can take him home.

For a peek at the layout of Walt Disney World's various theme parks and other "lands," consult "The Lands" map earlier in this chapter.

Want to go behind the scenes?

If you'd like an insider's look at how the Wizards of Diz make magic, **Behind the Scenes Tours** are the way to go. So many options are available that the Disney folks sometimes have trouble remembering them all.

Reservations are recommended and, in many cases, essential for these tours. Call ☎ 407-939-8687 to make your reservations.

Note: Unless otherwise noted, you have to pay park admission, currently $60 for adults, $48 kids 3 to 9, in addition to the tour price. But ticket prices, times, and tours change often, so check before your trip by calling Disney's tour line at ☎ 407-939-8687; for custom guided tours call ☎ 407-560-4033.

Here's a sampling of the best offerings:

✔ **Family Magic Tour:** This two-hour scavenger hunt brings you face to face with Disney characters at the **Magic Kingdom** ($25 for ages 3 and older). It kicks off at 11:30 a.m. daily outside City Hall, but you need to book in advance.

✔ **Hidden Treasures of World Showcase:** This three-hour tour lets you explore the architectural and entertainment offerings at **Epcot's** 11 World Showcase nations. The tour costs $59 for ages 16 and older and begins at 9:45 a.m. on Tuesdays and Thursdays.

✔ **Keys to the Kingdom:** Receive a 4½-hour orientation to the **Magic Kingdom** and a glimpse into the high-tech systems behind Mickey's magic. It's $58 for ages 16 and older and includes lunch. The tour starts at 8:30, 9:30, and 10 a.m. daily.

✔ **Backstage Magic:** At the top of the price chain — $199 per person — Backstage Magic is a seven-hour, self- and bus-propelled tour through areas of **Epcot,** the **Magic Kingdom,** and **Disney–MGM Studios** that aren't seen by mainstream guests. If you must know how things work, this tour is for you. You may see mechanics repairing and building animatronic beings, and you venture into **Magic Kingdom** tunnels that aren't only work areas but also paths for the cast to get from one area to another without fighting tourist crowds. It is offered at 9:45 a.m. weekdays and is limited to 20 adults (age 16 or older), so book as early as possible (Disney recommends at least two months in advance). *Park admission isn't required.*

✔ **Custom guided tours:** Not satisfied with any of the standard tour offerings? Disney let's you can create your own itinerary. There are no age requirements, though be prepared for a minimum of 5 hours at $125 per hour (WDW resort guests pay only $95 per hour).

For those up to the task, not to mention the price tag, call ☎ **407-560-4033** to make tour arrangements. Photo ID's are required at check-in for all tours.

Finding Your Way to the Fun

If you're driving, Interstate 4's Disney exits are clearly marked (though the exit numbers periodically change thanks to construction). You can't miss them unless you close your eyes.

Interstate 4 is woefully crowded, especially during rush hour (7–9 a.m. and 4–6 p.m. daily). In addition to the thousands of people heading for a day at the parks, thousands of locals are heading to work. So remember to factor possible delays into your time schedule.

Parking in the Disney theme-park lots costs $8 per day (unless you're a WDW resort guest, and then it's free) and is a snap. Just do what the people in the yellow-striped shirts ask you to do. In the Size XXXL **Magic Kingdom** lot, you'll probably want to ride the tram to the front gate. (The trams are a hoot — the seats are made out of petrified plastic, so if you lack posterior padding, you'll probably remember the ride for a while. And don't forget a jacket if you plan on making a day of it; the ride back to your car at night can make you feel like you're one of those frozen Mickey pops.)

Getting from the parking lot to the action can take up to an hour at the **Magic Kingdom,** so be patient as you begin the day. The first stop after the tram ride is the Ticket and Transportation Station, where you transfer to the monorail or the ferry to get to the park.

At **Epcot, Disney–MGM,** and **Animal Kingdom,** trams are available, but walking can be faster — unless you have small children or sore feet — if you're parked in the front half of the lot.

Don't forget to make a note of your parking area, including your row and space number, or you may end up on an unfortunate scavenger hunt when you head home. After a day spent standing in lines, listening to screaming kids, and being tapped-out by cash registers, you'll have a hard time remembering your name, not to mention where you parked. And odds are that at least a few of the cars in the lot will be clones of your own, making it that much harder to spot your own.

If you don't have a car, or prefer to skip the drive, many area accommodations offer shuttles that are sometimes free but can also carry a fee. (Check the listings in Chapter 9 for hotels that offer shuttle service.)

Traveling within the World

If you're staying at a **WDW** resort, you can take the **Walt Disney World Transportation System** to get to the parks. The system also serves **Downtown Disney, Typhoon Lagoon, Blizzard Beach, Pleasure Island,** and **Disney's Wide World of Sports.** It's a thorough network that includes buses, monorails, ferries, and water taxis serving the major parks from two hours prior to opening until two hours after closing. On the downside, it doesn't always offer direct routes, and moving between locations can make for a long and complicated journey. For more on the pros and cons of using the transport system, see Chapter 8. Disney properties also offer transportation to other area attractions, but you have to pay for it.

 Ask at the *Guest Relations* desk in your hotel or at the theme parks for a copy of the *Walt Disney World Shopping, Dining & Recreation* guide, which includes a map of the entire transportation system. The map shows you everything in the empire and gives you an idea of where your hotel is in relation to places that you want to visit. You can also look at the map of WDW's areas in this chapter to help orient yourself.

Preparing for Park Admission Costs

The number of admission options — from one- to multiday tickets — offered at **Walt Disney World** is staggering, and they're all expensive. Deciding which option works best for you depends on the number of days you plan to spend in the parks, what parks and attractions you want to see, and whether you're staying at a WDW resort.

IIf you choose to buy a single-day admission pass, you're limited to seeing one **Disney** park; you can't hop to another one in the middle of the day without paying a separate admission. Most people get the best value from four- and five-day Magic Your Way passes with the Park Hopper option added on, which, as the name implies, let you move from park to park on the same day.

 Magic Your Way is an all new ticketing system at Disney, and it's designed to save you money the longer you stay and play and allows you add on several optional features.

If you plan on visiting **Walt Disney World** more than one time during the year, inquire about the no expiration option or money-saving annual passes ($395–$515 adults, $336–$438 children 3–9). For information on a host of WDW tickets and options, see the following tables.

Table 11-1 Magic Your Way Ticket Prices
(One theme park per day of your ticket)

No. of Days	1-Day	2-Day	3-Day	4-Day	5-Day	6-Day	7-Day
Ages 10+	$60	$119	$171	$185	$193	$196	$199
Cost/day		$59	$57	$46	$39	$33	$28
Ages 3–9	$48	$96	$137	$148	$155	$157	$160
Cost/day		$48	$46	$37	$31	$26	$23

Table 11-2 Magic Your Way Ticket Options
(additional cost)

	1-Day	2-Day	3-Day	4-Day	5-Day	6-Day	7-Day
Park Hopper Option	+$35	+$35	+$35	+$35	+$35	+$35	+$35

This option allows you to visit any combination of the 4 main theme parks on any given day.

	1-Day	2-Day	3-Day	4-Day	5-Day	6-Day	7-Day
Magic Plus Pack Option	+$45	+$45	+$45	+$45	+$45	+$45	+$45
	2 visits	2 visits	2 visits	3 visits	3 visits	4 visits	5 visits

This option allows you a specific number of visits (anywhere from 2–5, depending on what you choose) to your choice of Disney's Typhoon Lagoon, Disney's Blizzard Beach, DisneyQuest, Pleasure Island, and Disney's Wide World of Sports Complex.

	1-Day	2-Day	3-Day	4-Day	5-Day	6-Day	7-Day
No Expiration Option	N/A	+$10	+$10	+$15	+$35	+$45	+$55

This option allows you to use any unused portion of the ticket at any time in the future with absolutely no expiration date.

Table 11-3 Premium Tickets
(Combination of the Park Hopper
and Magic Plus Pack)

	1-Day	2-Day	3-Day	4-Day	5-Day	6-Day	7-Day
Ages 10+	N/A	N/A	N/A	N/A	$266	$267	$268
Ages 3–9	N/A	N/A	N/A	N/A	$229	$230	$230

Table 11-4	Other Walt Disney World Ticket Prices	
	Ages 3–9	*Ages 10+*
Typhoon Lagoon & Blizzard Beach	$28	$34
DisneyQuest	$28	$34
Pleasure Island	N/A	$21
Wide World of Sports Complex	$7.25	$9.80

WDW considers everyone 10 and older an adult, and the prices that I give you don't include 6.5 percent sales tax. Also, fluctuating attendance figures and new multimillion dollar rides continue to escalate the single-day admission fee. (It's now $60 for adults, $48 for kids 3–9, but I expect that price to continue rising, so check before your trip for up-to-the-minute costs.) You can save an average of 10 percent off the regular prices of all passes by ordering online in advance at www.disneyworld.com.

As with many of the attractions in the area and across the state, Florida residents can take advantage of additional and special savings. Inquire about these savings when ordering your tickets.

The average family will spend $100 to $125 per person per day on park admissions, midday food, snacks, and souvenirs alone.

Getting the Most Out of Your Trip to the World

The **Magic Kingdom, Epcot,** and **Disney–MGM Studios** usually open at 9 a.m. (sometimes earlier) throughout the year. They're open at least until 6 or 7 p.m. and often as late as 11 p.m. or midnight during peak periods (holidays and the summer months). **Animal Kingdom** usually opens at 8 or 9 a.m. and closes at 5 or 6 p.m. It's a safe bet that the longer a park stays open, the more people visiting that day, so planning your schedule before you get to the park is essential. Unfortunately, hours of operation vary greatly, so it's always wise to call ☎ **407-934-7639** ahead of time, or to check the official calendar on Disney's Web site at www.disneyworld.com. When you arrive at the park, pick up a *Times and Information* guide to use for the rest of your stay.

Beating the lines

Everyone's looking for a shortcut, and no wonder — lines at Disney and the other big parks can be incredibly long and irritating if you come at the wrong time. Twenty minutes is considered cruising when it comes to line time, and 45 minutes to one hour is common at the primo rides, unless you use FASTPASS. In peak periods — summer, holidays, weekends, and other times when kids are out of school — it can take an hour, sometimes longer, to reach the front of the line and in three or four minutes, the ride is over.

Here are the best tips I can give you to beat the long lines:

- ✔ Come during off-season periods.

- ✔ Arrive as early as possible — the crowds pour in beginning at around 11 a.m. and only get worse from there.

- ✔ Plan to spend the morning in one section, and the afternoon in another. That way, you won't waste time and energy running back and forth.

- ✔ Spend *two* days in the park if time and your budget allow.

- ✔ Ask about or read the health and height restrictions before you get in line to avoid wasting time on a ride that isn't for you.

- ✔ Disney parks have tip boards that provide up-to-the-minute information on show times and ride waits. You can find the boards at Main Street, U.S.A., near *Casey's Corner* in the **Magic Kingdom,** on Hollywood Boulevard near the entrance to Sunset Boulevard in **Disney–MGM Studios,** in the southwest quadrant of Innoventions Plaza near **Epcot**'s *Future World Fountain,* and in *Discovery Island* at **Animal Kingdom.**

Don't want to stand in line as long as other guests, yet not flush enough to hire a stand in? Disney parks have installed a ride-reservation system called **FASTPASS** where you go to the primo rides, feed your theme-park ticket into a small slot, and get an assigned time to return. When you do, you get into a short line and climb aboard. Here's the drill:

Hang on to your ticket stub when you enter and head to the hottest ride you want. If it's a FASTPASS attraction (they're noted in the guide map you get when you enter), feed your stub into the waist-level ticket taker. Retrieve your ticket stub and the FASTPASS stub that comes with it. Look at the two times stamped on the latter. You can return during that one-hour window and enter the ride with almost no wait. In the meantime, you can do something else until the appointed time.

Note: Early in the day, your one-hour window may begin 40 minutes after you feed the FASTPASS machine, but later in the day it may be hours, especially at **Epcot**'s *Test Track* (see Chapter 13). Initially, Disney allowed you to do this reservation system on only one ride at a time, but now, your FASTPASS ticket has a time when you can get a second FASTPASS, usually two hours later, even if you haven't yet used the first pass. And be prepared, FASTPASS tickets do run out. They are limited in quantity and often run out by noon so be sure to get yours as soon as you can.

Using E-Ride tickets

The **Magic Kingdom**'s *E-Ride Nights* — a three-hour window after regular closing time where you can ride that park's nine most popular rides, such as *Big Thunder Mountain Railroad, Space Mountain,* and *Buzz Lightyear's*

Space Ranger Spin, as many times as you want — are a bargain for Disney hotel guests who are persistent enough to track down tickets. Characters wander the park to pose with visitors, and some shops and fast-food restaurants stay open. Better still, Disney admits only 5,000 guests (about 20 percent of the normal day's park attendance) into the park on E-Ride Nights.

E-Ride tickets cost $12 adults, $10 kids 3 to 9 and are sold on a first-come, first-served basis at the *Guest Relations* desks in the Disney hotels and at the **Magic Kingdom** ticket window (the latter sells them only on the day of the E-Ride Night). In order to purchase an E-Ride ticket, you will be required to show a Disney Resort Guest ID or proof of stay at an Official Hotel, and a valid multiday admission pass. After 4 p.m. on the day of your E-Ride Night, take your ticket and park admission pass to one of three locations — City Hall on *Main Street, U.S.A.;* Splashdown Photo in *Frontierland;* or Tomorrowland Arcade — to get a special wristband that you must wear in order to remain in the park after closing. Call ☎ 407-934-7639 for details and dates when *E-Ride Nights* are scheduled.

Taking advantage of Extra Magic Hours

Each day a particular park offers either admittance one hour early or up to three hours after closing for Disney Resort Guests and those staying at an Official Hotel. To take advantage of the Extra Magic Hours, your ticket must be good for the participating park or you must have the Park Hopper option (allowing you to enter any of the four major parks). At press time, the Magic Hours schedule was: Magic Kingdom, Sunday and Thursday; Animal Kingdom, Monday and Friday; Disney–MGM Studios, Tuesday and Saturday; and Epcot, Wednesday. Get a show schedule when entering the park

Getting a show schedule (it's part of the handout guide map) as soon as you enter the park is essential. Spend a few minutes looking it over, noting where you need to be and when. Many of the attractions in **Walt Disney World** are nonstop, but others occur only at certain times or once a day. You can find maps and schedules at counters on one side or the other of the turnstiles; sometimes at both. They're also found at most Disney shops.

Avoiding the Crowds

Crowds are a fact of life at **Walt Disney World,** but that doesn't necessarily mean you'll have to stand in long lines at all the rides and attractions. Forward thinkers can definitely decrease their risk of encountering a major swarm of tourists. In addition to FASTPASS (see the section "Beating the lines," earlier in this chapter), here are some facts to keep in mind as you plan your crowd-avoiding strategy:

✔ Mondays, Thursdays, and Saturdays are the busiest days in **The Magic Kingdom.** Tuesdays and Fridays are the busy days at **Epcot.** Sundays and Wednesdays are crowded at **Disney–MGM Studios,** and Mondays, Tuesdays and Wednesdays are beastly at **Animal Kingdom.**

✔ Although it isn't guaranteed, the parks tend to be less crowded from mid-April (or after the Easter Holidays) to late May and from September through November, except for Thanksgiving. You also have a better chance of avoiding crowds if you go in the middle of the week. Also, while most people steer clear on rainy days, the parks can be less crowded, and you won't miss much other than parades. (There's plenty of good stuff indoors.)

✔ Finally, if you dine at **Disney,** make Advanced Dining Reservations early in the day, or before you arrive at the park, to lock in the time you want to eat. (See Chapter 10 for more on Advanced Dining Reservations.)

Chapter 12

Magic Kingdom

● ●

In This Chapter

▶ Locating resources and services in Magic Kingdom

▶ Checking out the fun: rides, shows, and attractions

● ●

*I*f you have kids or a soft spot for vintage or classic Disney, make your way to this WDW signature park first. Magic Kingdom is the most popular of Mickey's enterprises, attracting more than 40,000 people a day, with good reason. Be prepared for long lines, and lots of 'em.

Proof of the staying power of Magic Kingdom lies in the fact that the park has changed very little during its 30-plus years of existence. Most of its newer attractions, such as *Mickey's PhilharMagic,* are hardly the adrenaline generators you encounter at other theme parks, but Magic Kingdom remains the fairest of them all.

Managing Magic Kingdom Logistics

Yes, you can find rides, shows, and characters galore, but you also need to know some practical items about Magic Kingdom. This section gives you the lowdown on prices, hours, and services.

Buying tickets and making reservations

Ticket prices (at printing time) for a one-day admission are $60 for adults, $48 for kids 3 to 9, but these change frequently, so call ahead. (See Chapter 11 for more information on park admission prices.)

Tickets aren't the only thing you'll spend big bucks on. Magic Kingdom (and the other parks) nails you to the tune of $2 or more for a soda or milk, $1.25 to $2 for bottled water, $2.40 for an ice-cream bar, and $1.70 for a cup of coffee or cocoa. *Note:* If you're on a tight budget, whenever you can, bring bottled water from the outside world, where you can often get an entire six-pack of bottles (freeze them the night before so they're really cold) for less than just two bottles at the parks. A big bag of snacks costs far less and go a lot further as well.

When you first show up, make your Advanced Dining Reservations immediately (if you haven't done so before arriving) if you want to have

Magic Kingdom

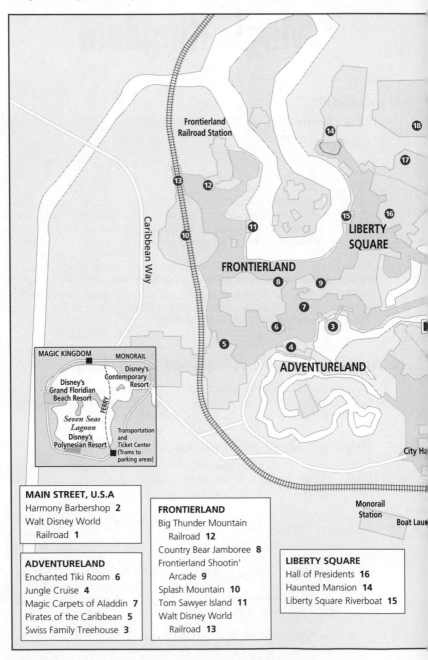

MAIN STREET, U.S.A
Harmony Barbershop **2**
Walt Disney World
   Railroad **1**

ADVENTURELAND
Enchanted Tiki Room **6**
Jungle Cruise **4**
Magic Carpets of Aladdin **7**
Pirates of the Caribbean **5**
Swiss Family Treehouse **3**

FRONTIERLAND
Big Thunder Mountain
   Railroad **12**
Country Bear Jamboree **8**
Frontierland Shootin'
   Arcade **9**
Splash Mountain **10**
Tom Sawyer Island **11**
Walt Disney World
   Railroad **13**

LIBERTY SQUARE
Hall of Presidents **16**
Haunted Mansion **14**
Liberty Square Riverboat **15**

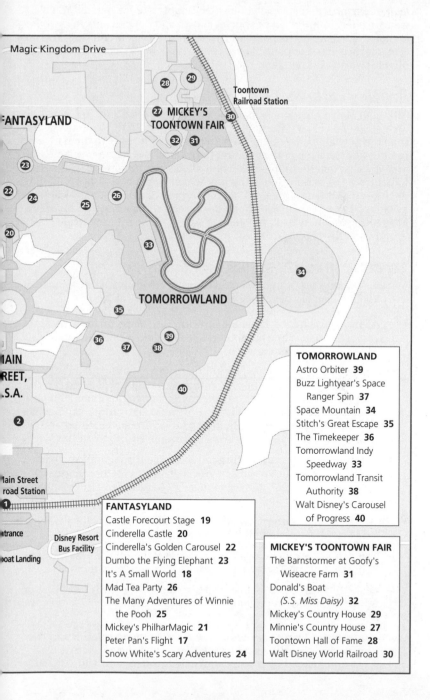

Magic Kingdom Drive

Toontown
Railroad Station

FANTASYLAND

㉗ **MICKEY'S
TOONTOWN FAIR**

TOMORROWLAND

MAIN
STREET,
U.S.A.

Main Street
Railroad Station

Entrance

Disney Resort
Bus Facility

Boat Landing

TOMORROWLAND
Astro Orbiter **39**
Buzz Lightyear's Space
Ranger Spin **37**
Space Mountain **34**
Stitch's Great Escape **35**
The Timekeeper **36**
Tomorrowland Indy
Speedway **33**
Tomorrowland Transit
Authority **38**
Walt Disney's Carousel
of Progress **40**

FANTASYLAND
Castle Forecourt Stage **19**
Cinderella Castle **20**
Cinderella's Golden Carousel **22**
Dumbo the Flying Elephant **23**
It's A Small World **18**
Mad Tea Party **26**
The Many Adventures of Winnie
the Pooh **25**
Mickey's PhilharMagic **21**
Peter Pan's Flight **17**
Snow White's Scary Adventures **24**

MICKEY'S TOONTOWN FAIR
The Barnstormer at Goofy's
Wiseacre Farm **31**
Donald's Boat
(S.S. Miss Daisy) **32**
Mickey's Country House **29**
Minnie's Country House **27**
Toontown Hall of Fame **28**
Walt Disney World Railroad **30**

a sit-down meal at a special venue. See Chapter 10 for details. You also want to check out the list of special shows and daily events in the *entertainment schedule* in the park guide-map you get upon entering. You may find information about special concerts, visits from Disney characters, plus fireworks and parades.

Arriving early and staying late

Although Magic Kingdom is usually open daily from 9 a.m. to 6 p.m., there are exceptions. In fact, the gates sometimes open 15 to 30 minutes earlier than the official opening time. I recommend trying to get to the park early, but not just because of the possibility of early opening hours. An early arrival helps beat morning traffic and allows you a more relaxed pace to get from the parking lot to the fun, which can take as long as an hour. At the end of the day, the park often closes later than 6 p.m., sometimes as late as 10 or 11 p.m., especially during the summer and on holidays. Magic Kingdom may even be open as late as midnight for certain special events. Call ☎ 407-934-7639 for more details.

Locating special services and facilities

In case you forget to bring essential items or need special assistance at the park, here's a list of services and facilities that can help:

✔ **ATMs** are located at the main entrance, in *Adventureland,* and in *Tomorrowland.* They honor cards from banks using the Cirrus, STAR, and Plus systems.

✔ **Baby-changing facilities,** including rocking chairs and toddler-size toilets, are next to the *Crystal Palace* at the end of *Main Street.* Of course, it isn't the most cost-effective place to buy them, but you can purchase disposable diapers, formula, baby food, and pacifiers in the **Baby Care Center.** Changing tables are also located at the center, as well as in all women's restrooms and some of the men's.

✔ **Disposable cameras and film** are available throughout the park, but Disney doesn't seem to have caught on to the popularity of digital cameras, as supplies such as rechargeable batteries and storage cards are limited.

✔ **The First Aid Center,** staffed by registered nurses, is located alongside *Crystal Palace* and the Baby Care Center.

✔ **You can access lockers** in an arcade underneath the Main Street Railroad Station. They cost $7, plus a $2 refundable deposit.

✔ **Lost children** are often taken to City Hall or the Baby Care Center, where lost children logbooks are kept. *Children under 7 should wear name-tags inside their clothing.*

✔ **You can send packages from any store to guest relations in the Plaza area,** so you can then pick them up at the service desk at day's end instead of hauling souvenirs around with you. Allow three hours for delivery. When you're staying at the Disney resorts, you can have your packages sent straight to your room at no charge, though it may take a day or two for them to get there.

✔ **Pets,** except service animals, are prohibited in the parks, but you can board yours at the Transportation and Ticket Center's kennels (☎ **407-824-6568**). Day rates are $6; overnighters cost $11 ($9 for Disney resort guests).

✔ **Rent strollers at the Stroller Shop near the entrance.** The cost is $8 for a single and $15 for a double, including a $1 deposit.

✔ **Rent wheelchairs** at the gift shop to the left of the ticket booths at the Transportation and Ticket Center or at the Stroller and Wheelchair Shop inside the main entrance to your right. Cost is $7 with a $1 deposit; $30 and a $10 deposit for battery-run chairs.

✔ **You can find some of your favorite characters at Mickey's Toontown Fair.** In *Fantasyland,* look for them in the *Fantasyland Character Fest* and *Ariel's Grotto.* In *Mickey's Toontown Fair* head to the *Judges Tent* and the *Toontown Hall of Fame.* Characters also appear in *Adventureland* (by *Pirates of the Caribbean*) and *Main Street* (near *City Hall*) as well as in *Liberty Square* at the *Diamond Horseshoe* and occasionally in *Tomorrowland* behind *Buzz Lightyear's Space Ranger Spin.* (See the guide map that you get when entering the park.)

You can get more information about WDW properties by calling ☎ **407-934-7639** or visiting Disney's Web site, www.disneyworld.com.

Making the Rounds: Magic Kingdom's Top Attractions

More than three-dozen attractions, an array of shops, and numerous eateries are located within Magic Kingdom's 107 acres. The following tour, complete with descriptions, begins at the front gates and takes you counterclockwise through the park's seven uniquely themed lands. To find all the listed attractions, see "Magic Kingdom" map on page 180.

Main Street, U.S.A.

Although it's considered one of the kingdom's lands, **Main Street** is more of an entry zone where you can easily lose yourself in the pleasant nostalgia of yesteryear. I recommend passing through it quickly when you arrive (so you can make a beeline for the more popular attractions before the lines get too long). You have to make a return voyage on *Main Street* when you cry "uncle" at the end of the day. At that time, stamina permitting, you can browse through the shops at a more leisurely pace before exiting the park. Here are a few of the highlights of *Main Street, U.S.A.:*

✔ **Walt Disney World Railroad:** This authentic steam-powered train makes a 15 to 20 minute **loop around the park,** with stops in *Frontierland* and at the far end of *Mickey's Toontown Fair.* During busy periods and parade times, this is a great way to get around the park without fighting your way through the crowds. It also gives the kids (and you) a well-deserved, albeit brief, break.

✔ **Harmony Barber Shop** on *Main Street* in Magic Kingdom is a real scissor shop where you can get your hair cut. The barbershop quartet might even take a break from entertaining guests along the street to serenade you. Hours are from 9 a.m. to 5 p.m. daily. Adult haircuts are $17; kids' are $14; colored gel will run you $5. If it's your child's very first haircut, Disney barbers will cut his or her hair for free and throw in a certificate and set of mouse ears. The shop is on *Main Street* near the firehouse, but it's a bit hidden so keep your eyes peeled.

Tomorrowland

This land attempts to focus on the future, but in 1994, the WDW folks realized that **Tomorrowland** (originally designed in the 1970s) was beginning to look a lot like "Yesteryear." As a result, Disney revamped the entire area to show the future as seen from the past (sometime around the 1920s or '30s) with a galactic, science fiction–inspired community filled with aliens, robots, and video games.

Here's a sampling of what you can find in *Tomorrowland:*

✔ *Astro Orbiter:* Future astronauts, especially those who are 7-years-old and younger, love whirling high (and I mean high — you have to take an elevator to get there) into the galaxy in the colorful rockets that circle around while gently rising and falling. Unfortunately, the orbiter lines can stretch for lightyears, so if you're on a tight timetable save it for later.

✔ *Buzz Lightyear's Space Ranger Spin:* On this ride you go to infinity and beyond in an interactive space adventure in which you help Buzz defend the Earth's supply of batteries from the evil Emperor Zurg. You fly an XP-37 space cruiser armed with twin lasers and a joystick that's capable of spinning the craft. (Space Rangers who get motion sickness should sit this attraction out. There's enough space debris flying around without your help.) While you cruise through space, you collect points by blasting anything that looks or smells remotely like Zurg (just look for all the neon "Z"'s and shoot). Your hits trigger light, sound, and animated effects. This ride is a tamer version of *Men in Black Alien Attack* at **Universal Studios Florida** (see Chapter 18). My 3-year old, 8-year old, and 10-year old all adore this ride.

✔ *Space Mountain:* Imagine a roller coaster. Then imagine it in the dark. This ride, plus *Big Thunder Mountain Railroad* (in the "Frontierland" section, later in this chapter) and *Splash Mountain* (also in the "Frontierland" section), are the three major Magic Kingdom attractions that tweens, teens, and thrill seekers alike head to first, so get here early or use FASTPASS. *Space Mountain* is a classic roller coaster with plenty of dramatic dips and drops, and the darkness makes it seem like it's going much faster than its top speed of 28 mph. Grab a front seat for the best ride.

"It was such a rush! In the dark you couldn't tell what was going to happen next." And: "The twists and turns happened really fast — it's definitely the coolest ride at Disney." It's recommended for those ages 10 and older, but because it was one of the first generation of modern, dark-side coasters, and is, therefore, somewhat outdated, it's a bit tamer than some of the more modern thrill rides at **Disney–MGM Studios.** Note, however, that *you must be 44 inches or taller* to ride, and there's a bailout area for those who decide at the last minute that they're not quite up to space travel. The seats and lap-bar restraints on *Space Mountain* may not fit some larger plus-size riders.

✔ **Stitch's Great Escape!:** Gone is the ultra-scary *ExtraTERRORestrial Alien Encounter,* and in its place is this slightly more family-friendly attraction based on the Disney hit film *Lilo & Stitch.* The storyline is a prequel to the movie, showing the mischief caused by rascally Experiment 626 (also known as Stitch) when he was originally captured. For those who experienced *Alien Encounter,* not that much has changed other than the characters, who are now far less frightening to look at. The state-of-the-art audio-animatronics are neat, but there are just too many gaps in between. There are long periods of darkness with no sound and really nothing going on — other than the screams of the scared little kids making their way to the door — and the multisensory effects, including an oderous burp belted out by Stitch, are a bit over the top. *You must be 38 inches or taller* to experience the great escape, a height restriction that keeps most of Stitch's fans from even entering.

✔ **The Timekeeper:** This seasonal attraction is a circlevision film hosted by none other than the very amusing Robin Williams. Upon entering you are greeted by a wacky animatronic robot who explains that he will be sending his assistant back through time, when, suddenly, everything starts to go awry, and you end up along for the ride. The journey takes you through various periods in time — when dinosaurs roamed the earth, the Ice Age, the Renaissance — where you meet famous figures such as H.G. Wells and Jules Vernes. While somewhat interesting for adults, it's a test of endurance for younger kids, who may not like standing (as is required) for the entire show.

✔ **Tomorrowland Resort Indy Speedway:** Kids, especially those ages 4 to 8, like slipping into these Indy-car knockoffs and taking them for a spin; but older children, teens, and adults (especially those with need for speed) generally hate them. The long lines and less-than-stellar steering, combined with an ultra-slow top speed of a mere 7 mph, add up to one giant snooze of an experience. Additionally, a thick iron rail separates your tires, so you're pretty much kept on track. This isn't a ride that will make you go *vroom*, even though *you have to be a minimum of 52 inches tall to drive alone.*

✔ *Tomorrowland Resort Transit Authority:* The small, five-car trains on this elevated people-mover are engineless. They work by electromagnets, create no pollution, and use little power. The environmentally friendly cars wind around *Tomorrowland* and into *Space Mountain* on a lazy ride that encourages you to nod off when it's late in the day, and you begin to realize that they've already covered 4 or 5 miles. There's usually no wait, but this ride is another one to skip if you're in a hurry. If you need to rest weary feet or have tired toddlers in tow, however, this one's a real winner. (It's also a good place to wait it out with your little ones when the older kids are riding *Space Mountain.*)

✔ *Walt Disney World Carousel of Progress:* Open only seasonally, this Disney oldie was refurbished to its original state in 1994. The 22-minute show takes you on a quasi-historical trip through time; hosted by an audio-animatronic family who explains how their lives have changed with the introduction of electricity and other technological advances of the past 50 years. Older guests may find it nostalgic, younger ones may wonder how anyone lived before the invention of video games. Although not particularly exciting, and definitely one to be skipped if you're pressed for time, it, nonetheless, is a good way to spend some down time waiting for the thrill seekers in the family to get through *Space Mountain.*

Mickey's Toontown Fair

Head off cries of "Where's Mickey?" by taking young kids (ages 2 to 8) to this two-acre site as soon as you arrive. It's by far the best place to meet the characters, including Mickey, Minnie, Donald Duck, Goofy, and Pluto. Magic Kingdom's smallest land is filled with a whimsical collection of rides, play areas, and candy-striped tents.

✔ *The Barnstormer at Goofy's Wiseacre Farm* is a mini roller coaster designed to look and feel like a crop duster that flies slightly off course and right through the Goofmeister's barn. It has a *35-inch height minimum,* and its tight turns and small dips even give some adults a rush.

✔ *Donald's Boat (The S.S. Miss Daisy)* is an interactive play area with fountains and water snakes that win squeals of joy (and relief on hot days). Unless you want to wear wet clothes for the rest of the day, bring along a dry change of clothes or a swimsuit.

✔ *Mickey's & Minnie's Country Houses* provide a lot of visual fun and some interactive areas for youngsters, though they're usually crowded and the lines flow like molasses. Mickey's place features garden and garage playgrounds. Minnie's lets kids play in her kitchen, where popcorn goes wild in a microwave, a cake billows up in the oven, and the utensils strike up a symphony of their own.

✔ **Toontown Hall of Fame** hosts meet and greets with various Disney characters as well as one of the largest souvenir shops in the park. You have to wait in line to meet the characters (each with his or her own separate line, so you'll have to decide which one is most worth the wait), but the payoff is that each family is allowed a few minutes with the character of their choice where hugs are exchanged and photos are snapped.

Fantasyland

Disney classics come to life in **Fantasyland,** where the rides are based on the movies you grew up with way back when, as well as a few of the more recent additions to the Disney treasure chest of films. The entire area is dedicated to the younger set, who would happily spend the entire day here; unfortunately, the seemingly endless lines eat up a good portion of your time unless you use FASTPASS. Here's a list of attractions in *Fantasyland:*

✔ **Cinderella Castle:** Modeled on several French châteaux, the fairy-tale Gothic-style castle sits at the end of *Main Street* in the center of the park. Its hard to miss the 189-foot landmark and its 18 towers, especially now as its decked out in golden adornments for the *Happiest Celebration on Earth* (an 18-month-long celebration to commemorate Disneyland's 50th birthday. Festivities are in full force at every Disney theme park around the world. For it's part, Walt Disney World has welcomed in new rides, shows, and special events, many of which are borrowed from its fellow Disney parks in California, Tokyo, and Paris.) The Castle is a favorite photo op, and if you land at the right time, you can meet Cinderella and a handful of other favorite characters at the Forecourt Stage just after the all new *"Cinderellabration"* production (a continuation of the Cinderella story set during her coronation pageant; the times guide will list the daily schedule of shows). Otherwise, the castle is mainly a visual attraction. The interior corridor is lined with beautiful murals and exquisite mosaics depicting the classic story of Cinderella. The upper level of the castle is also home to **Cinderella's Royal Table restaurant** (see Chapter 10).

✔ **Cinderella's Golden Carousel:** This old beauty was built in 1917 by the Philadelphia Toboggan Company and served tours in Detroit and New Jersey before it was discovered in the late 1960s by Disney Imagineers and brought to Magic Kingdom. A patriotic red, white, and blue in its first incarnation, it was restored and re-themed in time for the park's opening, and now tells the tale of Cinderella in 18 hand-painted scenes set above magnificent antique horses. It's a delight for kids and carousel lovers of all ages. The organ plays — what else? — Disney classics such as "When You Wish Upon a Star" and "Heigh Ho."

✔ **Dumbo The Flying Elephant:** This attraction doesn't do much for adrenaline-addicted older kids — or line-hating parents — but it's a favorite of kids ages 2 through 6. Dumbo's ears keep them airborne for a gentle, circular flight with some little dips. Except for the Disney theme, it's not all that different from the kiddie rides at most local carnivals. Most kids older than 6 will be humiliated if you even suggest they ride it. If your little ones are dying to ride Dumbo, get here early — wait times are brutal, and it doesn't have FASTPASS!

This ride is designed for the young ones, so plus-sized parents may have troubles getting their elephant to fly, and the taller among you may feel somewhat cramped.

✔ **"it's a small world":** Young kids and most parents love this attraction; teens and most other adults however may find it a real gagger. Nevertheless, pay your dues — it's an initiation rite every Disney visitor needs to undergo, and the sun-sheltered line isn't usually too long. You glide around the world in small, slow moving boats, meeting children (audio-animatronic, of course) from around the world, including Russian dancers, Chinese acrobats, and French cancan girls, and every one of them sings the tune that eats its way into your brain and refuses to stop playing for months.

A 10-year-old's take: "It was annoying with all the dolls, and the song just kept playing over and over." A 6-year-old: "It was so pretty with all the fancy costumes and lights in the sky, and nothing was scary." Either way, it's a cool place to rest for a while if you need a break from the summer heat.

Those of you who have ridden this attraction in the past may have noticed the recent refurbishments. This attraction, one of the original few that opened with the park in 1971 (and originally built by Walt Disney for the 1964 World's Fair) underwent a major renovation in 1994 that included painting and repairing the animatronics figures, as well as replacing the sound system and lights.

✔ **Mad Tea Party:** You make this tea party mild or wild, depending on how much you choose to spin the steering wheel of your gigantic teacup, though the cup does a little spinning of its own as well. This ride is suitable for ages 3 and older. Teens and older kids seem to enjoy this ride's potential for turning unwary passengers green. The woozy mouse who pops out of a big teapot in the center of the platform would no doubt sympathize with those left spinning.

✔ **The Many Adventures of Winnie the Pooh:** Pooh inadvertently created a small storm of protest when Disney used this ride to replace the popular *Mr. Toad's Wild Ride* in 1999. *The Many Adventures of Winnie the Pooh* features the cute-and-cuddly little fellow along with Eeyore, Piglet, and Tigger. You board a golden honey pot and ride through a storybook version of the Hundred Acre Woods, keeping an eye out for Heffalumps, Woozles, blustery days, and the Floody Place. This ride has become a favorite of kids 2 to 8 and their parents, so a FASTPASS is often needed.

✔ *Mickey's PhilharMagic:* Mickey, Donald, Ariel, Aladdin, and a handful of other favorites appear in this animated and impressively 3-D–enhanced adventure (it's projected on a 150-foot screen — the largest wraparound screen on the planet) in which a mischievous Donald has not so surprisingly gotten into a spot of trouble. This show is similar to *Jim Henson's Muppet*Vision 3-D* (see Chapter 14) at **Disney–MGM Studios,** but is far more engaging in its combination of music, animated film, puppetry, and special effects that tickle several of your senses. Kids love the effects, and if you're a sucker for the classic Disney films, you will absolutely adore it.

✔ *Peter Pan's Flight:* Another popular ride among visitors younger than 8, it begins with a nighttime flight over London (even adults ooh and aah here) in search of Captain Hook, Tiger Lily, and the Lost Boys. It's one of the old glide rides dating back to the limited technology that was available when Magic Kingdom was born, but the simplicity is part of what makes it so popular. Terribly long lines are almost a signature of this ride, so plan on using a FASTPASS to avoid the worst of it. My younger kids wouldn't miss it no matter how long they have to wait.

✔ *Snow White's Scary Adventures:* Your journey takes you to the dwarfs' cottage and the wishing well, ending with the prince's kiss to break the evil spell. This version of the Grimm's fairy tale is much less grim than it was years ago, when the focus was inexplicably on the wicked witch, though she still makes several appearances. Snow White now appears in several more-friendly scenes, though kids younger than 4 will likely still get scared. I can't recommend it if your time schedule is tight; for those young enough to want to ride, it's not worth the tears and screams, and those who won't get frightened are too old to get much pleasure out of it.

Liberty Square

Located between *Fantasyland* and *Frontierland,* **Liberty Square** is a re-creation of Revolutionary War–era America that infuses you with colonial spirit. Younger guests may not appreciate the historical touches (such as the 13 lanterns symbolizing the original 13 colonies that hang from the gigantic live Oak), but they'll delight in the chance to pose for a picture while locked in the stocks or march along with the fife-and-drum corps that sometimes makes an appearance along the cobblestone streets. Although it is one of the smallest lands in all Magic Kingdom, *Liberty Square* has an impressive number of attractions, including the following:

✔ *Liberty Square Riverboat:* The steam-powered paddlewheeler *Liberty Belle* departs *Liberty Square* for scenic cruises along the Rivers of America. The passing landscape recalls the Wild West, with an occasional Indian village, and a large wooden fort peeking through the trees. It makes a restful interlude for foot-weary park-stompers.

✔ *The Hall Of Presidents:* American-history buffs ages 10 and older most appreciate this show, which can be a real squirmer for younger children. The Hall is an inspiring production based on painstaking research, right down to the clothes — each president's costume reflects his period's fashion, fabrics, and tailoring techniques. The show begins with a film on the importance of the Constitution projected on an immense 180-degree screen, then the curtain rises on America's leaders, from George Washington through George W. Bush. Pay special attention to the roll call of presidents. The animatronic figures are incredibly lifelike and amazingly impressive: they fidget, whisper, and talk to the audience.

✔ *The Haunted Mansion:* Although this attraction has changed little through the years, the mansion continues to be a favorite and even has a cult following. (My editor makes a pilgrimage here every time she hits the park, as do I.) It has detailed special effects (this was one of the last rides Walt Disney actually had a hand in designing) and an atmosphere that's far more fun than creepy. You may chuckle at the corny tombstones lining the entrance before you hop aboard your Doom Buggy and are whisked past a ghostly banquet and ball, a graveyard band, weird flying objects, and more. And don't forget the 999 spirits of the house, one of whom may try to hitch a ride home with you. I always get a kick out of the fact that Disney has to continually add dust and cobwebs to keep up this attraction's old and decrepit appearance.

"The ghosts are really cool, but it's not all that scary. The best part is at the end when you see the ghost right next to you." I wholeheartedly agree with Ryan (age 12). The ride doesn't get much scarier than spooky music, eerie howling, and things that go bump in the night. It's best for those ages 6 and older however. FASTPASS is recommended, as this attraction usually has a long line, though you might be able to sneak right in at parade time.

Frontierland

Frontierland is located behind *Adventureland* and the rough-and-tumble Old West architecture runs to log cabins and rustic saloons, while the landscape is Southwestern scrubby with mesquite, cactus, yucca, and prickly pear. Attractions in *Frontierland* include the following:

✔ *Big Thunder Mountain Railroad:* The lines don't lie: This rocking railroad is a favorite in Magic Kingdom. *Thunder Mountain* bounces you around an old mining site, where you dodge floods, a bridge collapse, rock slides, and other mayhem. The ride is something of a low-grade roller coaster with speed and a lot of corkscrew action. It has enough of a reputation that even first-time visitors make a beeline for it. So if you can't get to it as soon as the park opens, FASTPASS is your best bet. Or give it a try late in the day, or when a parade pulls most visitors away from the rides. Most Disney coaster veterans maintain the ride is at its best after dark.

"So Cool . . . you really whip around the mountain, I loved this ride." "It's really fast and it kind of jerks you around when you are turning, that's so fun." Austin and Nicolas are both right on the money — the action is fast and a bit jerky, especially compared to some of the newer monster rides. The ride can be too intense for kids younger than 6 (and for those with neck problems); riders *must be at least 40 inches* tall.

✔ ***Country Bear Jamboree:*** The stars of this 15-minute animatronic show are the gigantic bumbling country bears, crooning country-and-western tunes and completely corny jokes. The Jamboree is a park standard — a show that's been around since Disney invented dirt — but it's still a huge hit with Disney buffs and little kids. The audience gets caught up in the hand-clapping, knee-slapping, foot-stomping fun as Trixie laments lost love while she sings "Tears Will Be the Chaser for Your Wine." Teddi Beara descends from the ceiling in a swing to perform "Heart, I Did All That I Could," and Big Al moans "Blood in the Saddle." It's a great way to cool off with tired toddlers, so sit back and relax for a spell.

"You can't be serious," were the words uttered by my 12-year-old as he rushed past in search of *Splash Mountain.* Unless you have an affinity for all things Disney or have younger children (5 and under), this might be best saved for those really hot days when you need a break inside. Most teens, young adults, and repeat visitors won't want to do it, even then.

✔ ***Frontierland Shootin' Arcade:*** Combining state-of-the-art electronics with a traditional shooting-gallery format, this arcade offers 97 targets (slow-moving ore cars, buzzards, and gravediggers) in an 1850s boomtown scenario. If you hit a tombstone, it may spin around and mysteriously change its epitaph. Coyotes howl, bridges creak, and skeletal arms reach out from the grave. To keep things authentic, newfangled electronic firing mechanisms with infrared bullets are concealed in genuine buffalo rifles. When you hit a target, you set off sound and motion gags. Fifty cents fetches 25 shots. Younger kids may find this more frustrating than fun.

✔ ***Splash Mountain:*** If I had to pick one ride as the Kingdom's most popular, *Splash Mountain* would be it (that should properly prepare you for the lines — sometimes longer than 2 hours — you will most definitely end up experiencing). It's on par with **SeaWorld**'s *Journey to Atlantis* (see Chapter 20), though half a click below *Jurassic Park River Adventure* at **Islands of Adventure** (see Chapter 19). Still, it has a flair that only Disney can deliver. *Splash Mountain* is a nifty voyage through the world of Disney's classic film *Song of the South,* past 26 colorful and delightful scenes that include backwoods swamps, bayous, some spooky caves, and waterfalls. You ride in a hollow log flume as Brer Fox and Brer Bear chase the ever-wily Brer Rabbit and end your journey with a 52-foot, 45-degree, 40 mph finish, with an impressively high splash factor (around 200 mega-tons worth of wet) that thoroughly soaks you and anyone remotely close by. If you're lucky enough to have some real heavyweights in the front seat, look for a little extra explosion on the five-story downhill. While FASTPASS is available, this is one that runs out early.

In summer, this ride can provide sweet relief from the heat and humidity, but in cool weather, parents may want to protect their kids (and themselves) from a chill. *Splash Mountain* is recommended for ages 8 and older. If they're unsure if they want to ride, let them watch from the bridge for a few minutes — they'll make up their minds after they see one or two logs make the drop. *Riders must be at least 40 inches tall.*

On warmer days, the ride shoots out a spray of water onto the viewing bridge in front of the big drop. If you want to catch your friends unaware for a good soaking, count the log drops: Every third one emits a good spray.

✔ **Tom Sawyer Island:** Board Huck Finn's raft for a 2-minute float across a river to this densely forested island, where kids can explore *Injun Joe's Cave* (complete with such scary sound effects as whistling wind), navigate a swinging bridge, and explore an old wooden fort. Narrow, winding dirt paths lined with oaks, pines, and sycamores create an authentic backwoods atmosphere. It's easy to get briefly lost and stumble upon some unexpected adventure. It's a great place for kids to lose a little excess energy and for moms and dads to relax and maybe indulge in lunch or a snack at Aunt Polly's, which overlooks the river.

"It fun just being able to run around, not wait in all the lines." "The caves and the bridges were really cool but so was the whole island." Nicolas and Austin, ages 10 and 8, weren't the only ones who gave it great reviews — everyone in the family concurred.

Adventureland

Adventureland is a left turn just at the end of *Main Street*. Kids can engage in swashbuckling behavior while walking through dense tropical foliage (complete with vines) or marauding through bamboo and thatch-roofed huts. The architecture here is a combination of the Caribbean, Southeast Asia, and Polynesia Walt Disney wanted this section of the park to exude romance, mystery, and (duh!) adventure. There's plenty of the latter here, especially for kids, though you may have more trouble finding the first two. Here is a list of some of the most popular attractions in *Adventureland:*

✔ **The Enchanted Tiki Room:** Upgraded over the years, the show's newest cast member is Iago of *Aladdin* fame. This attraction is set in a Polynesian-style building with thatched roof, bamboo beams, and tapa-bark murals. Other players include 250 tropical birds, chanting totem poles, and singing flowers that whistle, tweet, and warble. The show runs continuously throughout the day. Young children are most likely to appreciate this one (though beware the very young, under 2, may be frightened by the loud noises), but so will nostalgic adults. Otherwise, consider this only as a respite from the heat.

✔ ***Jungle Cruise:*** Give Disney 10 minutes, it gives you four famous rivers on three different continents. This narrated voyage on the Congo, Amazon, Mekong, and Nile rivers offers glimpses of animatronic animals, tropical and subtropical foliage (most of it real), a temple-of-doom–type camp, and lots of surprises. The ride passes animatronic pythons, elephants, rhinos, gorillas, and hippos that pop threateningly out of the water and blow snot — well, it could've been snot if they weren't robots — on you. This exhibit is about 30 years old, which means it's pretty hokey at times, but it's still a nice way to relax if the lines don't stretch too long (though the waiting area for this ride does offer some amusing moments — check out the prop menus on the walls).

✔ ***The Magic Carpets of Aladdin:*** The first major ride added in Adventureland since 1971 delights wee ones and even some older kids. Its 16 four-passenger carpets circle the giant genie's bottle while camels spit water at unsuspecting riders in much the same way riders are spritzed at *One Fish, Two Fish* at **Islands of Adventure** (see Chapter 19). As the fiberglass carpets spin, you can move them up, down, forward, and back.

If the lines are too long at *Dumbo* (see the "Fantasyland" section, earlier in this chapter), this is a good alternative, as the rides are similar and the lines here aren't nearly as sluggish.

✔ ***Pirates of the Caribbean:*** This oldie-but-goodie is another cult favorite (a Disney archivist confessed to me that it's still his favorite, which should be no great surprise given that this is another ride that Walt Disney had a hand in creating). After walking through a long, and somewhat eerie, grotto, you board a boat headed into a dark cave where you are warned that "Dead men tell no tales." Therein, elaborate scenery and hundreds of incredibly detailed (some of Disney's best) animatronic figures re-create an almost refreshingly non-P.C. Caribbean town overrun by buccaneers. To a background of cheerful yo-ho-ho music, the sound of rushing waterfalls, squawking seagulls, and screams of terror, passengers pass through the line of fire into a raging raid and panorama of almost fierce-looking pirates swigging rum, looting, and plundering. This ride, in addition to being one of the best in the park, is another great place to cool off on a hot day.

"The drop takes you by surprise — that's pretty cool, and the pirates are great, it's almost like being in the middle of the movie." Kids ages 5 and younger may find a pirate's life a bit too scary, especially with the small drop in the dark. Most kids 6 or older, though, will enjoy it. The recent Oscar-nominated film based on the ride (alas, there's no Johnny Depp to be found here) has made it even more popular with the young and teen set, who have fun spotting the scenes appropriated by the movie.

Offer a tip of your head to the parrot who sits above the ride's entrance plaza and you may get a hearty greeting in response.

✔ *Swiss Family Treehouse:* The story of the shipwrecked Swiss Family Robinson (via the 1960 Disney film of the same name) comes alive in this attraction made for swinging, exploring, and crawling fun. The "tree," designed by Disney Imagineers, has 330,000 polyethylene leaves sprouting from a 90-foot span of branches; although it isn't real, it's draped with actual Spanish moss. It's simple and void of all that high-tech stuff that's popular in today's parks, but that's what makes it so fun.

Be prepared to stand in a slow-moving line on busy days — the only thing that moves on this one are your feet, so the experience is only as fast paced as the people ahead of you make it. The attraction is also difficult for travelers with limited mobility to navigate. My younger kids (those under 8) thought it was neat, while the older ones moved onward to bigger adventures.

Parades and fireworks

Disney excels at producing fanfare, and its parades and fireworks displays are among the best of their kind in the world. Note, however, that some productions are staged only on a limited basis or during certain times of the year. Grab a times guide when you arrive. It includes an entertainment schedule that lists special goings-on for the day, including concerts, encounters with characters, holiday events, and other major happenings. If you want to know whether a specific parade or fireworks show will be staged when you're in town, consult the calendar at www.disneyworld.com or call ☎ 407-934-7639.

During fireworks and parades, Disney ropes off designated viewing spots for travelers with disabilities and their parties. Consult your park map or a park employee at least an hour before the parade, or you may have trouble making it through the crowds to get to the designated spots. Additionally, if there are two showings of a parade, the later one is usually less crowded.

If nobody in your party is a huge parade fan, these are the best times to ride some of the more popular attractions — while everyone else is lined up along the parade route. You can also use the *Walt Disney World Railroad* (mentioned earlier in the chapter) to navigate around the various areas of the park when the parade route has blocked off most major routes through the park.

Here are Disney's best parades and fireworks displays:

✓ **Wishes Nighttime Spectacular:** This explosive display debuted in fall 2003 and is touched off nightly at closing, except during the summer and on holidays when extended park hours allow for the fireworks to be shown between two scheduled showings of *SpectroMagic* (see next in this list). Before the display, Tinker Bell flies magically from *Cinderella Castle*. Then as a cacophany of intricately choreographed fireworks fills the skies, and Jiminy Crickett narrates, images are projected onto the castle in time to the medley of Disney songs being broadcast parkwide. Suggested viewing areas include almost anywhere on the front side of Cinderella Castle, including the very front of Liberty Square and Frontierland. The back of Liberty Square, Frontierland, and Mickey's Toontown Fair offer views as well, though some of the spectacular effects get a bit lost from behind. Disney hotels close to the park (the **Grand Floridian, Polynesian, Contemporary,** and **Wilderness Lodge** — all reviewed in Chapter 9) also offer views, as the fireworks display is rather large. This show can make even the most blasé fireworks watcher say "wow!"

✓ **SpectroMagic Parade:** This after-dark parade combines fiber optics, holographic images, clouds of liquid nitrogen, old-fashioned twinkling lights, and a soundtrack featuring classic Disney tunes. Mickey, dressed in an amber and purple grand magician's cape, makes an appearance in a confetti of light. You'll also see the SpectroMen atop the title float, and Chernabog, *Fantasia*'s monstrous demon, who unfolds his 38-foot wingspan. It takes the electrical equivalent of seven lightning bolts (enough to power a fleet of 2,000 trucks) to bring the show to life.

SpectroMagic plays only *on limited nights,* when park closing extends past dusk (generally during busy periods and on weekends). When park hours are extended to 10 p.m. or later, there are often two chances to view the parade. Check your show schedule to determine availability.

✓ **Share a Dream Come True Parade:** This parade honors the 100th anniversary of Uncle Walt's birth (which has come and gone though the parade lives on). Loads of characters (over 110 cast members take part) march up *Main Street* and into *Frontierland* in gigantic snowglobes on a daily basis. It's one of the most popular parades in the park since it takes place during the height of the day.

Index of Attractions by Land

Adventureland
The Enchanted Tiki Room
Jungle Cruise

The Magic Carpets of Aladdin
Pirates of the Caribbean
Swiss Family Treehouse

Fantasyland

Cinderella Castle
Cinderella's Golden Carrousel
Dumbo The Flying Elephant
"it's a small world"
Mad Tea Party
Mickey's PhilharMagic
The Many Adventures
of Winnie the Pooh
Peter Pan's Flight
Snow White's Scary Adventures

Frontierland

Big Thunder Mountain Railroad
Country Bear Jamboree
Frontierland Shootin' Arcade
Splash Mountain
Tom Sawyer Island

Liberty Square

Liberty Square Riverboat
The Hall Of Presidents
The Haunted Mansion

Main Street, U.S.A.

Harmony Barber Shop
Walt Disney World Railroad

Mickey's Toontown Fair

The Barnstormer at Goofy's
Wiseacre Farm
Mickey's Country House
Minnie's Country House
Donald's Boat (S.S. Miss Daisy)
Toontown Hall of Fame

Tomorrowland

Astro Orbiter
Buzz Lightyear's Space Ranger Spin
Space Mountain
Stitch's Great Escape!
The Timekeeper
Tomorrowland Resort Indy Speedway
Tomorrowland Resort Transit Authority
Walt Disney's Carousel of Progress

Chapter 13

Epcot

. . . .

In This Chapter

▶ Highlighting Epcot basics

▶ Checking out Future World

▶ Touring the World Showcase

. . . .

Grab a big pot. Start with a theme park foundation, stir in a heaping helping of technology, and add splashes of global architecture, street performers, and interactive exhibits. What do you have? Epcot, a science field trip combined with a whirlwind tour of the world — without the jet lag, although some say it's just as draining when you try to experience it in one day.

Walt Disney wanted his "Experimental Prototype Community of Tomorrow" to be a high-tech city. But, when it opened 15 years after his death, it was a theme park, and the name was shortened to an acronym, **Epcot,** because, well, it looked good in the snazzy Disney brochures.

 While the **Magic Kingdom** is every child's dream, Epcot isn't. It's techno and worldly. Epcot is best suited for older children (over 8) and adults with vivid imaginations or cravings to know how things work — or will work in the future. It's the least friendly of the Disney parks for those younger than 8, even with Disney's relatively recent additions that were intended to keep the younger members of the family entertained. If you have wee ones, or if all your kids are under the age of 6, I recommend skipping it this time around. If, on the other hand, you have older kids or an inquiring mind yourself, I suggest at least a two-day visit because it's so vast and varied. In the **World Showcase,** you experience exotic, far-flung lands without a passport; you can visit *China's* Temple of Heaven, or *Italy's* St. Mark's Square. In **Future World,** you can jump into the third millennium as you explore cutting-edge technology and the latest and greatest thrill rides.

Discovering Epcot's Essentials

Before helping you dive into Epcot's attractions, I need to get a few practical matters out of the way.

Buying tickets and making reservations

Tickets to Epcot cost $60 for a one-day adult admission, $48 for kids ages 3 to 9, *but prices frequently change*. See Chapter 11 for other admission options.

Tickets aren't the only thing you'll find that deplete your stash of cash. The prices of consumables are pretty much standard among Disney parks. Epcot will put you out $2 or more for a soda or milk, $1.25 to $2 for bottled water, $2.40 for an ice-cream bar, and $1.90 for a cup of coffee or cocoa.

You can make **Advanced Dining Reservations** (see Chapter 10) at *Guest Relations* in the Plaza area, though it's best to make them ahead of time by calling ☎ 407-939-3463.

Future World usually is open from 9 a.m. to 7 p.m. and sometimes as late as 10 p.m. **World Showcase** usually opens at 11 a.m. or noon and generally remains open until 9 p.m., sometimes later.

Locating special services and facilities

In case you forgot to bring essential items, or if you need special assistance while at the park, here's a list of services and facilities that may come in handy:

- ✔ **ATM machines** accept cards from banks using Cirrus, STAR, and Plus. You can find them at the front of the park, in *The American Pavilion* (near the very back), and on the bridge between **World Showcase** and **Future World.**

- ✔ **The baby-changing area** for Epcot is located in the **Baby Care Center** near the Odyssey Center in **Future World.** It sells disposable diapers, formula, baby food, and pacifiers. Changing tables are in all women's and some men's restrooms.

- ✔ You can buy **disposable cameras and film** throughout the park, although supplies for digital cameras are few and far between.

- ✔ Registered nurses staff the **First Aid Center.** It's located near the Odyssey Center in **Future World.**

- ✔ **Lockers** are located west of *Spaceship Earth,* outside the Entrance Plaza, and in the Bus Information Center by the bus parking lot. The cost is $7 a day, plus a $2 deposit.

- ✔ **Lost children** are usually taken to Earth Center or the Baby Care Center. *Children under 7 should wear name-tags* on the inside of their clothing.

- ✔ You can send **packages** from any store in the park to *Guest Relations* in the Plaza area, where you can pick them up all at once at the end of the day. (This service is free.) Allow three hours for delivery. A package pickup also is located at the International Gateway entrance

Epcot

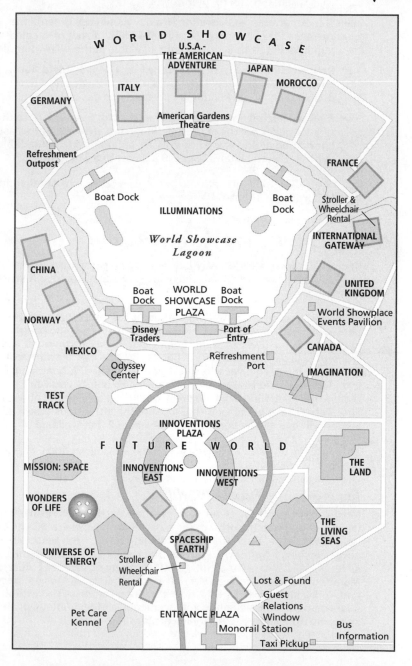

in the **World Showcase.** Disney resort guests can have their purchases sent directly to their hotels.

✔ You can arrange **pet care** for $6 a day at kennels outside the Entrance Plaza at Epcot (☎ 407-824-6568). Proof of vaccination is required. Four other kennels are available in the WDW complex.

✔ **Rent strollers** east of the Entrance Plaza and at **World Showcase**'s International Gateway. The cost is $8 for a single and $15 for a double. The prices include a $1 refundable deposit.

✔ **Rent wheelchairs** inside the Entrance Plaza to your left, to the right of ticket booths at the Gift Shop, and at **World Showcase**'s International Gateway. They cost $8, including a $1 refundable deposit. Electric chairs cost $40 a day with a $10 deposit.

Call ☎ 407-934-7639 or visit www.disneyworld.com to obtain additional information about **WDW** properties.

Touring Epcot's Top Attractions

Epcot's 300 acres are vibrantly landscaped, so enjoy the scenery on your way through its two very distinctive areas, **Future World** and **World Showcase.**

Epcot is big enough that walking around it can be exhausting (the **World Showcase** semicircle alone is 1.3 miles). That's why some people say Epcot stands for "Every Person Comes Out Tired." If you don't spend much time lingering in the World Showcase, you can see all Epcot in one day, but you'll need a vacation after you're finished. A boat launch runs from **Future World** to *Germany* or *Morocco* so unless you want the complete world tour, this may be a great way to get a sampling of World Showcase. The good news is that most of the attractions take a fair amount of time, giving you a break between all that walking.

To locate the attractions I discuss in the following sections, check out the "Epcot" map on p.199.

Experiencing Future World

Most visitors enter Epcot through the main entrance at **Future World** (there is, unlike at any other park, a back entrance where guests of the BoardWalk, Swan, Dolphin, Yacht Club, and Beach Club resorts have access by boat). *Spaceship Earth,* that thing that looks like the giant silver golf ball meant for a club to fit Paul Bunyan, centers Future World. Major corporations such as Hewlett Packard, General Motors, Nestlé, and Kodak sponsor Future World's nine themed areas. The exhibits focus on discovery, scientific achievements, and technology in areas spanning from energy to undersea exploration.

Innoventions: The Road to Tomorrow

The crescent-shaped buildings to your right and left, just beyond *Spaceship Earth,* showcase cutting-edge technology and future products in the *Innoventions* exhibit. The headliner in the building to the left **(Innoventions East)** as you enter the park is *House of Innoventions,* which offers a preview of tomorrow's smart house (including a refrigerator that can itemize and order groceries and a Jacuzzi with surround sound). A recent addition is *Plastic Works,* where kids can build their own robot and — bonus — they get to keep it for free. The *Test the Limits Lab* exhibit has six kiosks that let kids and fun-loving adults try out a variety of products. In one, you can pull a rope attached to a hammer that crashes into a TV screen to see whether it's shatter resistant. In another, you can push a button that releases a magnet that falls onto a firefighter's helmet. Other exhibits focus on communications, the new Segway transport device, and outer space.

Across the way at **Innoventions West,** crowds flock to *Video Games of Tomorrow,* which has nearly three dozen game stations, and the *Ultimate Home Theater,* which offers a look at the history of home entertainment and a futuristic home set-up that will have couch potatoes salivating. *ThinkPlace presented by IBM* looks at various interactive software programs (including voice recognition technology) and also features Internet Postcards that allow you to take a picture and send it via e-mail to family and friends back home. *Where's the Fire?* is America's largest fire-safety display, where kids can get an up-close look at a life-size fire truck and follow a lighted path through a burning house to safety. Other diversions include a virtual-reality playground and a display highlighting advances in the life sciences at *The Great American Farm.*

Journey into Imagination with Figment

Even the fountains in front of this pavilion are magical — shooting water snakes through the air. (The fountains are popular with kids, who like to try to catch water snakes and, in the process, get a good soaking.)

When the *Journey into Imagination* exhibit reopened in summer 2002 after a year-long refurbishment, it marked the return of an Epcot golden oldie — *Figment,* a crazy-but-lovable purple dinosaur, who was a fixture at Epcot until 1999 (his three-year disappearance was greeted with major boos by Disneyphiles, who abandoned ship until he returned). Things begin with an open house at the Imagination Institute, with Dr. Nigel Channing (played by Monty Python's Eric Idle) taking you on a tour of the labs that demonstrate how the senses capture and control one's imagination. Figment arrives at each of the areas to prove it's far, far better to set your imagination free. He invites you to his upside-down house, where a new perspective enhances your imagination. "One Little Spark," an upbeat ditty that debuted when the attraction opened in 1983, has also been brought back. This ride is best for the younger set as older kids may find it too tame.

After you disembark from the ride, head for *The Kodak "What If" Labs,* where your kids can burn lots of energy while exercising their imaginations at a number of interactive stations that allow them to conduct music, experiment with video, or transform themselves into animals. The lab can be accessed from the outside as well, so older kids can experiment while waiting for their younger siblings to ride along with Figment.

The pavilion's main attraction is the 3-D *"Honey, I Shrunk the Audience"* ride, based on the Disney film *Honey, I Shrunk the Kids,* in which you're caught up in all the mayhem of another shrinking experiment gone awry. Inside, mice terrorize you and, after you're shrunk, a large cat adds to the trauma; then a giant 5-year-old gives you a good shaking. Vibrating seats and sensory effects enhances all the 3-D action. In the end, everyone is returned to proper size — but not the dog, who offers up one final surprise. Kids under 4 may be frightened by some of the 3-D and special effects; most older kids will be utterly amused.

The Land Pavilion

The Land is Future World's largest pavilion (a whopping 6 acres) and showcases the wonders of food and the environment. *Living with the Land,* a 14-minute boat ride through a simulated rain forest, an African desert, and the Great Plains, may be a tad too dry for visitors not interested in agriculture. New farming methods and experiments ranging from hydroponics to plants growing in simulated Martian soil are showcased in real gardens.

 A 45-minute *Behind the Seeds* walking tour for gardeners and others who want a more detailed agricultural lesson is offered daily and costs $8 for adults and $6 for kids 3 to 9. Sign up at the Green Thumb Emporium to the right of the Sunshine Seasons food court area.

Live footage and animation mix in *Circle of Life,* a 15-minute, 70mm motion picture based on *The Lion King.* The story line has Timon and Pumbaa building a monument to the good life called Hakuna Matata Lakeside Village, but their project, as Simba points out, is damaging the savanna for other animals. It's a fun, but pointed, environmental message.

 The Land's newest attraction is *Soarin',* a ride borrowed from Disney's California Adventure park. The experience combines cinematic artistry and state-of-the-art motion technology as you are seated in mock-gliders and lifted 40 feet inside a giant projection screen dome. Completely surrounded with the beauty and wonder of the state of California, the elevated seats take you on a scenic tour over the Golden Gate Bridge, the Redwood forests, Napa Valley, and Yosemite, gliding and swooping over the changing landscapes. You can even feel the sweeping winds and smell fragrant orange blossoms and pine trees around you. The entire experience is absolutely one of the best in all of Disney. It makes me wonder if a version showcasing Florida's highlights may be up next . . . Epcot *is* in Florida after all. *You must be 40 inches tall to ride.* This is

Water-cooler conversations

Many an ordinary item at **Disney World** has hidden entertainment value. Take a sip of water at the drinking fountain in **Epcot**'s Innoventions Plaza (the one right next to the Mouse Gear shop close to Innoventions East) and it may beg you not to drink it dry. No, you haven't gotten too much sun — the fountain actually talks (much to the delight of kids and the surprise of unsuspecting adults). A few more talking fountains are scattered around Epcot.

The fountains aren't the only items at WDW that talk. I've kibitzed with a walking and talking garbage can (named PUSH) in Tomorrowland at the **Magic Kingdom** (he's been known to make appearances at Epcot as well). An assortment of sassy (if not mobile) garbage cans are also in place at the Magic Kingdom inside Cosmic Ray's Starlight Cafe. And a personable palm tree (who goes by Wes Palm) may strike up a conversation with you at **Animal Kingdom.** Ask a Disney employee to direct you if you want to meet any of these chatty contraptions.

definitely a good candidate for FASTPASS as the lines are lengthy with wait times of at least an hour, even during the slower seasons.

The Living Seas

The Living Seas pavilion has a 5.7 million-gallon aquarium filled with more than 4,000 sharks, barracudas, rays, dolphins, and other reef fish. It starts with a film, *The Seas,* demonstrating the formation of the Earth and the seas as a means to support life. You also can see other exhibits such as a diving barrel used by Alexander the Great in 332 B.C. and Sir Edmund Halley's first diving bell (1697). After the films, you enter "hydrolators" (a somewhat hokey elevator ride) and descend to the simulated ocean floor and Sea Base Alpha. The two-level base displays numerous exhibits dealing with various aspects of marine science and technology, and — most important of all — you get close-up views through acrylic windows of real denizens of the deep, as they swim amidst a man-made coral reef. Both kids and adults enjoy visiting the rescued manatees (sea cows), which reside on the second level.

In the past I've complained that *The Living Seas* could be a snoozer for younger kids unless they are fascinated by the sea. Disney must have been listening, because they've added a few attractions that are sure to keep kids younger than 10 entertained. **Turtle Talk with Crush,** an interactive theater presentation, captivates kids' attention as well as their hearts. In a small theater adults are seated on benches in the back while children are asked to sit on the floor right in front of the screen (which, for the moment, looks like a giant underwater viewing area). After a brief introduction, Crush, a 152-year old sea turtle from the film *Finding Nemo,* appears swimming around, chit-chatting to himself and, before you know it, with the kids — and I mean really conversing.

Through some amazing technology and animation the talking turtle can "see" the audience, pick out whose question he'd like to answer by describing their clothing, and actually respond to their questions. Kids love it.

Disney has also added a small play area where little ones can expend some of their extra energy. *Bruce's Sub House* features some larger than life (albeit animated) sharks to climb on, in, and around.

Epcot's **DiveQuest** program enables certified divers ages 10 and up (those between 10 and 14 are required to have an adult participate along with them) to take part in a three-hour program that includes a 30-minute dive in the Living Seas aquarium. The program costs $140. Call ☎ 407-939-8687 for details. Keep in mind, however, that that you get more dolphins for your money at **Discovery Cove** (see Chapter 20).

Spaceship Earth

Epcot's iconic, silvery geosphere houses an attraction of the same name, a slow-track journey back to the roots of communications. The 15-minute ride begins with Cro-Magnon cave painting and then advances to Egyptian hieroglyphs, the Phoenician and Greek alphabets, the Gutenberg printing press, and the Renaissance. Technologies develop at a rapid pace, through the telegraph, telephone, radio, movies, and TV. It's but a short step to the age of electronic communications. You're catapulted (though slowly) into outer space to see *Spaceship Earth* from a new perspective, returning for a finale that places the audience amid interactive global networks. Unfortunately, the presentation is not particularly engaging, and I recommend that you skip it unless it's a really hot day or you need time off your feet.

Test Track

Test Track is a $60 million marvel of a ride that combines GM engineering and Disney Imagineering. You can wait in line an hour or more during peak periods, so use FASTPASS. (See Chapter 11 for more information about beating the long lines.) During the last part of your wait, you snake through displays about corrosion, crash tests, and more. The 5-minute ride follows what looks to be an actual highway. It includes braking tests, a hill climb, and tight S-curves in a six-passenger "convertible." The left front seat offers the most thrills as the vehicle moves through the curves. There's also a 12-second burst of heart-pumping speed to the tune of 65 mph on the straightaway (with no traffic!). It's one of the best thrill rides in Epcot, and for those who can't stomach roller coasters, it offers a few thrills that you most likely can handle.

"The beginning is a lot of stopping and starting but once you hit 60 it's a blast." Ryan liked it, but it may be too intense for those younger than 10, and it has a *40-inch height minimum*. The single-rider line (which allows singles to fill in vacant spots in select cars) can speed up your wait time if all the FASTPASSES are gone — which really happens! — but you have to be willing to split up your party to use it. Also keep in mind that rain will shut it down, so head here early in the day if there's even the slightest chance of a sprinkle.

Mission: SPACE

The headliner for **Mission: SPACE** is a motion simulator like those used by astronauts training for space. (Think G-force and weightlessness.) You assume the role of commander, pilot, navigator, or engineer, depending on where you sit, and must complete related jobs vital to a flight to the Red Planet (don't worry if you miss your cue, you won't crash). The ride uses a combination of visuals, sound, and centrifugal force to create the illusion of a launch and trip to Mars. As the launch begins, your rocket rumbles under you, white clouds of steam billow around you, and you shoot into the galaxy. Of course, there are some unexpected twists and turns that require you to react pronto in order to complete your mission successfully. Even veteran roller-coaster riders who tried the simulator said the sensation mimics a liftoff, as riders are pressed into their seats and the roar and vibration tricks the brain during the launch portion of the 4-minute adventure.

In the pre-ride show, you go to the futuristic *International Space Training Center* and then proceed to the *Ready Room* where you learn your role as commander, pilot, navigator, or engineer from CapCom (played by actor Gary Sinese, who co-starred in *Apollo 13*).

This is probably one of the most physically intense rides at Disney. If you are prone to motion sickness from spinning, have a sinus infection, or experience severe claustrophobia, do not ride this attraction. There's a reason they put motion sickness bags in each capsule and post all the warnings. Once the door of your pod closes, that's it, there's no escape. You're going to Mars whether you like it or not. If the experience gets too much mid-trip, a Disney Imagineer told me that focusing straight ahead can help minimize the effects, and he warned against closing your eyes as that actually enhances the ride's intensity.

So you know, if you're taller (or shorter, in the case of younger kids) than average, you may have difficulties seeing the screen from the optimum perspective or handling the controls from the optimum angle.

"It was awesome — the whole ride was intense, but awesome." 12-year-old Ryan, who has an intense hatred for roller coasters, survived and was even smiling after the ride, but be aware that it may be too intense for those younger than 10 and has a *44-inch height minimum*.

Universe of Energy

Sponsored by Exxon, **Universe of Energy** has a roof full of solar panels and a goal of bettering your understanding of America's energy problems and potential solutions. *Ellen's Energy Adventure,* the pavilion's 32-minute ride, features comedienne Ellen DeGeneres tutored by Bill Nye the Science Guy to be a *Jeopardy!* champ. An animated movie depicts the Earth's molten beginnings, its cooling process, and the formation of fossil fuels. You then move back 275 million years into an eerie, storm-wracked landscape of the Mesozoic Era. Giant audio-animatronic dragonflies, pterodactyls, dinosaurs, earthquakes, and streams of molten lava threaten before you enter a misty tunnel deep in the bowels of a volcano. When you emerge into a giant space that looks like a NASA control room, a 70mm film projected on a massive 210-foot wraparound screen depicts the challenges of the world's increasing energy demands and the emerging technologies that will help meet them. The show ends on an upbeat note — a vision of an energy-abundant future and Ellen as a new *Jeopardy!* champion. The ride itself is a bit slow moving (literally), but the bits featuring Ellen are funny, and it's a good place to escape the heat. Younger kids may find brief parts of the film a bit intense and the fleeting appearance of the dinosaurs a tad too lifelike.

Wonders of Life

The focus of the ***Wonders of Life*** pavilion (you can't miss the giant DNA strand that marks its entrance) is on health and biology.

The entire *Wonders of Life* pavilion began opening on a limited schedule (mostly during peak crowds to alleviate long lines on other rides) in January 2004, prompting speculation that a new exhibit may be installed here within the next few years.

The *Making of Me,* starring Martin Short, is a 15-minute film combining live action with animation and spectacular in utero photography to create a sweet introduction to the facts of life. Short travels back in time to witness his parents as children, their meeting at a college dance, their wedding, and their decision to have a baby. Alongside him, *Making of Me* visitors view his development inside the womb and witness his birth.

The presentation may prompt some pointed questions from young children — if you're not ready for them, think about heading them off and heading elsewhere; I recommend it for ages 10 and older.

Didn't get your fill of being shrunk at *Imagination?* Haven't been shaken up enough on a simulator? Try *Body Wars,* where you're reduced to the size of a cell for a rescue mission inside a human's immune system (it reminds many sci-fi fans of the Isaac Asimov classic novel *Fantastic Voyage*). This motion-simulator takes you on a wild ride through gale-force winds in the lungs and pounding heart chambers. It's nowhere near as cool as the similar *Star Tours* attraction at **Disney–MGM Studios** (see Chapter 14), but is still fun.

Engineers designed this ride from the last row of the car, so that's the best place to sit to get the most bang for your buck. Riders must be *at least 40 inches tall* to climb aboard.

In the hilarious *Cranium Command,* Buzzy, an animatronic brain-pilot-in-training in the Cranium Commando Squad, is charged with the daunting task of controlling the brain of Bobby, a 12-year-old boy, during adolescent traumas that include meeting a girl and a run-in with the principal. The audience is seemingly seated inside Bobby's head as Buzzy guides him through his day — and gets chewed out every now and then by his animated C.O., General Knowledge. Well-known actors and comedians, including Charles Grodin, Jon Lovitz, and Dana Carvey, play the boy's body parts. This must-see attraction has a very loyal fan following and is good for all ages.

Don't skip the very funny pre-show film at this attraction, as it sets up the action that happens inside.

At *The Fitness Fairgrounds,* you can have your tennis, golf, or baseball swing analyzed by experts. You can also get a computer-generated evaluation of your health habits or ride the exercycles, touring through Disney via video.

Traveling through the World Showcase

World Showcase is enjoyed mainly by adults or older kids with an appreciation of world history and cultural shows. Its 11 miniature nations, each re-created with meticulous detail, open at 11 a.m. daily and surround the parks 40-acre lagoon. All the showcase's countries have authentically indigenous architecture, landscaping, background music, restaurants, and shops. The nations' cultural facets are explored in art exhibits, song and dance performances, and innovative rides, films, and attractions. And all the employees at each of the pavilions are natives of the country represented.

Most of these nations offer some kind of live entertainment throughout the day. You may see acrobats, bagpipers, mariachi bands, storytellers, belly dancers, and stilt walkers. Characters regularly appear in the Showcase Plaza. Check your guide map/show schedule when you enter the park. You can also find schedules posted near the entrance to each country.

Those with kids should grab a copy of the *Epcot Kids' Guide* at *Guest Relations* upon entering the park; it uses a "K" in a red square to note **Kidcot Fun Stops** inside the World Showcase. These play and learning stations are for the younger set and allow them to stop at various World Showcase countries, do crafts, get autographs, have Kidcot passports stamped (these are available for purchase in most Epcot stores and make a great souvenir), and chat with cast members native to those countries. Your kids will get the chance to learn about different countries and make a souvenir to bring home. For more information, stop in at *Guest Relations* when you get into the park. The stations open at 1 p.m. daily.

Finally, excellent shopping and dining opportunities are available at all the pavilions. For details on dining inside the World Showcase, see Chapter 10; shopping information can be found in Chapter 17.

Canada

The pavilion's highlight attraction is *O Canada!* — a dazzling, 18-minute, 360-degree CircleVision film that shows Canada's scenic wonders, from sophisticated Montréal to the thundering flight of thousands of snow geese departing the St. Lawrence River.

The theater has no seats and you stand for the entire production (though there are lean rails).

The architecture and landscape in **Canada** include a mansard-roofed replica of Ottawa's 19th-century Château Laurier (here called the *Hôtel du Canada*) and an Indian village complete with 30-foot replicas of Ojibwa totem poles. The Canadian wilderness is reflected by a rocky mountain (really made of concrete and chicken wire); a waterfall cascading into a whitewater stream; and a mini forest of evergreens, stately cedars, maples, and birch trees. Don't miss the stunning floral display inspired by Victoria's world-renowned Butchart Gardens. *Off Kilter* entertains visitors with New Age Celtic music.

China

You enter Epcot's version of **China** through a triple-arched ceremonial gate inspired by the Temple of Heaven in Beijing, a summer retreat for Chinese emperors. Passing through the gate, you'll see a half-size replica of this ornately embellished red-and-gold circular temple, built in 1420 during the Ming dynasty. Gardens simulate those at Suzhou, with miniature waterfalls, lotus ponds, and bamboo groves.

Inside the temple, you can watch *Reflections of China,* a 20-minute 360-degree CircleVision film that explores the culture and landscapes in and around seven Chinese cities. It visits Beijing, Shanghai, and the Great Wall (begun 24 centuries ago!), among other places.

Like Canada, the theater here has no seats and you stand for the entire production (though there are lean rails).

Land of Many Faces is an exhibit that introduces China's ethnic peoples, and entertainment is provided daily by the amazing *Dragon Legend Acrobats.*

France

This pavilion focuses on **France**'s Belle Époque (Beautiful Age) — the period from 1870 to 1910 — when art, literature, and architecture ruled. You enter via a replica of the beautiful cast-iron Pont des Arts footbridge over the Seine and find yourself in a park with bleached sycamores, Bradford pear trees, flowering crape myrtle, and sculptured parterre flower gardens inspired by Seurat's painting *A Sunday Afternoon on the Island of La Grande Jatte.* The grounds also include a 1/10-scale model of the Eiffel Tower, which was built from Gustave Eiffel's original blueprints.

The premiere attraction here is *Impressions de France*. Shown in the palatial Palais du Cinema, a sit-down theater à la Fontainebleau, this 18-minute film is a journey through diverse French landscapes projected on a vast, 200-degree wraparound screen. Outside, grab a French pastry and watch the antics of *Serveur Amusant,* a comedic waiter, or the visual comedy of *Le Mime Roland.*

Germany

Enclosed by castle walls, **Germany** offers 'wursts, oompah bands, and a rollicking atmosphere. The clock tower in the central *platz* (plaza) is embellished with a glockenspiel that heralds each hour with quaint melodies. The Biergarten was inspired by medieval Rothenberg, while 16th-century building façades replicate a merchant's hall in the Black Forest and the town hall in Frankfurt's Römerberg Square.

If you're a model-train fanatic or visiting with young kids, don't miss the exquisitely detailed version of a small Bavarian town, complete with working train station, located between *Germany* and *Italy.*

Italy

Italy lures visitors over an arched stone footbridge to a replica of Venice's intricately ornamented pink-and-white Doge's Palace. Other architectural highlights include the 83-foot Campanile (bell tower) of St. Mark's Square, Venetian bridges, and a piazza enclosing a version of Bernini's Neptune Fountain. A garden wall suggests a backdrop of provincial countryside, and citrus, cypress, pine, and olive trees frame a formal garden. Gondolas are moored on the lagoon.

In the street entertainment department, the seemingly lifeless forms of *Imaginum, A Statue Act* fascinate visitors young and old daily, and the hilarious *World Showcase Players,* who, at press time, were seen spoofing Shakespeare's Italian-set *Taming of the Shrew* here.

Japan

A flaming red *torii* (gate of honor) on the banks of the lagoon and the graceful blue-roofed Goju No To pagoda, inspired by an 8th-century shrine built at Nara, welcome you to the **Japan** pavilion, which focuses on Japan's ancient culture. If you have some leisure time, enjoy the exquisitely cultivated Japanese garden — it's a haven of tranquility in a place that's anything but, and 90 percent of the plants you see are actually native to Japan. The Shishinden, inspired by the ceremonial and coronation hall found in the Imperial Palace grounds at Kyoto, is home to Mitsukoshi's department store (discussed in Chapter 17). The *Bijutsu-kan Gallery* offers rotating exhibits ranging from 18th-century Bunraki puppets to Japanese baseball.

Make sure that you include a performance of traditional Taiko drumming by *Matsuriza,* which entertains guests daily. Japanese storytellers offer up native tales every now and then.

Mexico

The music of mariachi bands greets you at *Mexico*'s festive showcase, fronted by a Mayan pyramid modeled on the Aztec temple of Quetzalcoatl (God of Life) and surrounded by dense Yucatán jungle landscaping. Just inside the pavilion's entrance, a museum exhibits rare Oaxacan wood sculptures. Also inside the pyramid you'll find an open-air marketplace filled with artisans peddling their wares under the star-filled skies above (it's always nighttime here) behind which is *El Rio del Tiempo* (River of Time), an eight-minute cruise through Mexico's past and present (the audio-animatronic dolls you encounter en-route may remind you of those in **Magic Kingdom**'s *It's a Small World*). Along the river route, passengers get a close-up look at the Mayan pyramid and the erupting Popocatepetl volcano.

 Mariachi Cobre, a 12-piece mariachi ensemble, performs Tuesday through Saturday.

Morocco

A replica of the world famous Koutoubia Minaret, the prayer tower of a 12th-century mosque in Marrakesh, overlooks the very atmospheric pavilion of *Morocco,* featuring the architectural styles of several cities inside the North African kingdom. The exotic ambiance is enhanced by geometrically patterned tile work, hand-painted wood ceilings, and brass lighting fixtures. The Medina (old city), entered via a replica of an arched gateway in Fez, leads to a traditional Moroccan home and the narrow, winding streets of the *souk,* a bustling marketplace where authentic handicrafts are on display. The Medina's courtyard centers on a replica of the ornately tiled Najjarine Fountain in Fez.

The *Gallery of Arts and History* contains ever-changing exhibits of Moroccan art. A guided tour of the pavilion, *Treasures of Morocco,* runs three times daily. (Check your show schedule.) Speaking of shows, the band *Mo'Rockin'* kicks things up with Arabian rock music.

Norway

The *Norway* pavilion's stave church, located off a charming cobblestone plaza and styled after the 13th-century Gol Church of Hallingdal, features changing exhibits focusing on Norwegian art and culture. A replica of Oslo's 14th-century Akershus Castle is the setting for the pavilion's restaurant (see Chapter 10). Other buildings simulate the red-roofed cottages of Bergen and the timber-sided farm buildings of the Nordic woodlands.

Norway includes a two-part attraction. *Maelstrom,* a boat ride in a dragon-headed Viking vessel, travels Norway's fjords and mythical forests to the music of Peer Gynt. Along the way, you see polar bears prowling the shore and are turned into frogs by trolls that cast a spell on your boat. The watercraft crashes through a narrow gorge (two small separate drops) and spins into the North Sea, where a storm is in progress. (Don't worry — this is a relatively calm ride, though some of mthe thunder elements may frighten the very young.) The storm abates, a princess's kiss turns you into a human again, and you disembark to a 10th-century Viking village to view the 70mm film *Norway,* highlighting history and culture (you can proceed through the theater to the exit if you don't want to watch the film).

Spelmanns Gledje plays lively Norwegian folk music.

United Kingdom

The **United Kingdom** pavilion evokes Merry Olde England through its *Britannia Square* — a London-style park complete with copper-roofed gazebo bandstand, a stereotypical red phone booth (it really works!), an old-fashioned pub, a thatched cottage, and a statue of the Bard. Four centuries of architecture — from the Tudor era all the way through the English Regency period — line cobblestone streets. In the horticulture department, there's a formal garden with low box hedges in geometric patterns, and the flagstone paths and a stone fountain replicate the landscaping of 16th- and 17th-century palaces.

Don't miss *The British Invasion,* a group that impersonates the Beatles; vivacious pub pianist Pam Brody; and Jason Wethington, a pub magician who offers up Disney magic of the sleight-of-hand variety.

U.S.A. — The American Adventure

This flagship pavilion's main building is a 108,000-square-foot Georgian mansion and occupies the central spot in the **World Showcase.** Notable U.S. landmarks that inspired Disney's Imagineers in the design of the building include *Independence Hall, Monticello,* and *Colonial Williamsburg.* The action takes place in an elegant colonial-style 1,024-seat theater loaded with Corinthian columns, chandeliers, and 12 marble statues symbolizing the 12 "Spirits of America." The flags you pass under as you enter the theater — 44 in all — include every one that has flown over the United States throughout its history.

The actual production, a 29-minute CliffsNotes version of U.S. history, utilizes a 72-foot rear-projection screen, rousing music, and a large cast of lifelike audio-animatronic figures, including narrators Mark Twain and Ben Franklin. You follow the voyage of the *Mayflower,* watch Jefferson writing the *Declaration of Independence,* and witness Matthew Brady photographing a family that the Civil War is about to divide. You can also witness Pearl Harbor and the *Eagle* going to the moon. Teddy Roosevelt discusses the need for national parks; Susan B. Anthony speaks out on women's rights; Frederick Douglass discusses slavery; and Chief Joseph talks about the plight of Native Americans. It's one of Disney's best historical productions.

Entertainment includes the *Spirit of America Fife & Drum Corps* and the *Voices of Liberty* a cappella group, which sings patriotic songs in the lobby of the main theater between shows. Large-scale outdoor productions are often staged in the *America Gardens Theatre,* a 1,800-seat outdoor venue across from the main pavilion building.

Ending your day at Epcot

Epcot's end-of-day celebration, **IllumiNations,** is a moving blend of fireworks, lasers, and fountains in a display that's signature Disney. The show is worth the crowds that flock to the parking lot when it's over.

You can find tons of good viewing points around the lagoon (one excellent spot is the terrace at the **Rose & Crown Pub** in the United Kingdom — see Chapter 10 for more on the pub). That said, it's best to stake your claim at least a half-hour or so before show time, which is listed in your entertainment schedule.

Index of Attractions by Land

Future World

Innoventions
Journey into Imagination
The Land
The Living Seas
Mission: SPACE
Spaceship Earth
Test Track
Universe of Energy
Wonders of Life

World Showcase

Canada
China
France
Germany
Italy
Japan
Mexico
Morocco
Norway
United Kingdom
U.S.A. — The American Adventure

Chapter 14

Disney–MGM Studios

Disney touts Disney–MGM Studios as "the Hollywood that never was and always will be." Its movie- and TV-themed shows and props set the stage, so to speak, but this little park is also home to two of the biggest thrill rides in Orlando — *The Twilight Zone Tower of Terror* and *Rock 'n' Roller Coaster Starring Aerosmith*. Its neighborhoods include Hollywood and Sunset boulevards, where Art Deco movie sets evoke the Golden Age of Hollywood. *Streets of America* is lined with miniature renditions of the cityscapes of New York City and San Francisco, including re-creations of actual city streets and buildings. You can find some of the best street performing in the Disney parks here. More importantly, it's a working movie and TV studio where shows are occasionally produced. The new *Lights, Motors, Action! Extreme Stunt Show* lets you experience the thrills of a high-speed chase and other dramatic movie stunts as well as gives you insight into how such effects are created, designed, and filmed for the movies.

Unlike the Magic Kingdom and Epcot, you can pretty much see Disney–MGM's 154 acres of attractions relatively easily in a single day; that is if you arrive reasonably early and keep up a brisk pace. If you don't get a *Disney–MGM Studios Guidemap* and entertainment schedule as you enter the park, be sure to grab one at *Guest Relations*.

 Check show times as soon as you arrive and work out an entertainment schedule that works for you. Likewise, take a second to plan ahead for mealtimes and make your Advanced Dining Reservations immediately if you haven't already; many of the park's rather unique restaurants fill up quickly.

Acquainting Yourself with Disney–MGM Studios

Before I head off for a closer look at the park's rides and attractions, I must first deal with some mundane matters that you may very well appreciate once you're there:

Buying tickets and making reservations

Admission prices to Disney–MGM are $60 for a one-day adult ticket, $48 for children ages 3 to 9. See Chapter 11 for other ticket options.

Tickets aren't the only thing you spend your hard-earned money on. The prices of consumables are pretty much standard among Disney parks. Disney–MGM Studios nails you to the tune of $2 or more for a soda or milk, $1.25 to $2.50 for bottled water, $2.40 for an ice-cream bar, and $1.70 to $1.90 for a cup of coffee.

If you have not done so in advance by calling ☎ 407-939-3463 (the preferred course of action), **make Advanced Dining Reservation arrangements** the minute you enter the park if you care to eat a sit-down meal at one of the park's unique dining venues. See Chapter 10 for details on Disney–MGM's best restaurants.

Park hours are generally from 9 a.m. to 6 or 7 p.m., with extended hours — sometimes as late as 10 p.m. — during holidays and summer.

Locating special services and facilities

In case you forgot to bring essential items or if you need special assistance while at the park, here's a list of services and facilities that may come in handy:

- ✓ **ATMs** accept cards from banks using Cirrus, STAR, and Plus and are located to the right of the main entrance and next to Toy Story Pizza Planet, across from *Jim Henson's Muppet*Vision 3-D*.

- ✓ **The Baby Care Center** is to the left of the main entrance and includes places for nursing and changing. You can buy disposable diapers, formula, baby food, and pacifiers. Changing tables also are in all women's restrooms and some men's rooms.

- ✓ You can find disposable **cameras** and **film** throughout the park, although digital camera supplies are extremely limited.

- ✓ **The First Aid Center,** staffed by registered nurses, is in the Entrance Plaza adjoining *Guest Relations*.

- ✓ **Lockers** are located near Oscar's Classic Car Souvenirs, to the right of the entrance. They cost $7 a day, plus a $2 refundable deposit.

Disney–MGM Studios

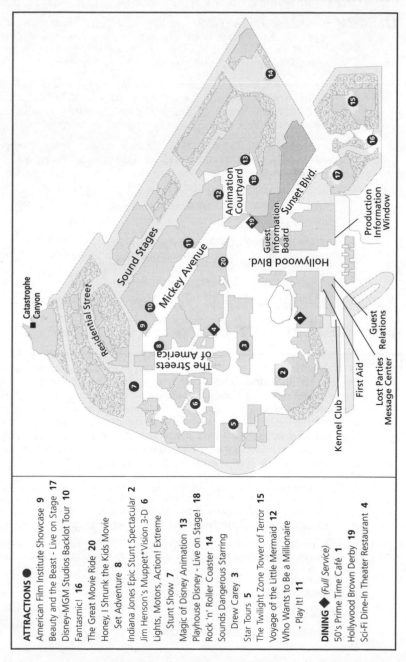

ATTRACTIONS ●

American Film Institute Showcase **9**
Beauty and the Beast - Live on Stage **17**
Disney-MGM Studios Backlot Tour **10**
Fantasmic! **16**
The Great Movie Ride **20**
Honey, I Shrunk the Kids Movie
   Set Adventure **8**
Indiana Jones Epic Stunt Spectacular **2**
Jim Henson's Muppet*Vision 3-D **6**
Lights, Motors, Action! Extreme
   Stunt Show **7**
Magic of Disney Animation **13**
Playhouse Disney - Live on Stage! **18**
Rock 'n' Roller Coaster **14**
Sounds Dangerous Starring
   Drew Carey **3**
Star Tours **5**
The Twilight Zone Tower of Terror **15**
Voyage of the Little Mermaid **12**
Who Wants to Be a Millionaire
   - Play It! **11**

DINING ◆ *(Full Service)*
50's Prime Time Café **1**
Hollywood Brown Derby **19**
Sci-Fi Dine-In Theater Restaurant **4**

- **Lost children** at Disney–MGM Studios are taken to *Guest Relations*. Children younger than 7 should wear name-tags inside their clothing.

- Shop clerks can send your **packages** to *Guest Relations* near the entrance. Allow three hours for delivery. If you're staying at a Disney resort, you can have your package shipped directly to your room. Both services are free.

- For **pet care,** day accommodations ($6) are offered at kennels to the left and just outside the entrance (☎ **407-824-6568**). Proof of vaccinations is required, and you're responsible for walking and feeding your pet.

- You can rent **strollers** at Oscar's Super Service, inside the main entrance. A single costs $8, $15 for a double, including a $1 refundable deposit.

- **Rent wheelchairs** at Oscar's Super Service inside the main entrance. Your cost is $10 for a standard wheelchair; $35 plus a $5 deposit for battery-run chairs.

Call ☎ **407-824-4321** or visit Disney's Web site, www.disneyworld.com, to get more information on WDW properties.

Pitting Disney–MGM Studios Against Universal Studios Florida

If you love the movies, Broadway-style productions, or the Golden Age of Hollywood, you'll enjoy wandering the streets, shops, and sets of **Disney–MGM Studios. Universal Studios Florida** (see Chapter 18) caters more to visitors with children thanks to *Nickelodeon Studios, Fievel's Playland,* and *Woody Woodpecker's KidZone.* But is this town big enough for two studios? Both offer unique experiences and a flair all their own, so if you can swing it, it's well worth your time to experience both. I genuinely feel for the visitor who has time to visit only one of these stellar parks.

Both have a variety of good shows and, alas, unavoidably long lines. Universal has an edge in the number and diversity of rides, but MGM's *Tower of Terror* is, arguably, the best thrill ride in either park (even with the addition of Universal's *Revenge of the Mummy*) and *Rock 'n' Roller Coaster Starring Aerosmith* is nothing to sneeze at either. Universal is larger, which means you wear out more shoe leather, but it isn't as congested.

My overall evaluation is that MGM Studios has some great shows and rides, mainly the *Indiana Jones Epic Stunt Spectacular!, The Twilight Zone Tower of Terror, Star Tours — the ultimate Star Wars thrill ride, Jim Henson's Muppet*Vision 3-D,* and the *Disney–MGM Studios Backlot Tour,* but I give Universal a microscopic edge.

The following sections divide attractions in Disney–MGM Studios into two categories. Rides and shows rated G will assuredly entertain the youngest visitors and, in many cases, the older ones as well. PG-rated rides are those geared toward adults and teens (and may bore or frighten children). For a look at the park, turn to the "Disney–MGM Studios" map on page 215.

Entertaining the Whole Family: G-Rated Attractions and Rides

Rides and attractions listed in this category are suitable for everyone, although a few in particular may not appeal to teens or adults.

Beauty and the Beast — Live on Stage

A 1,500-seat, covered amphitheater provides the stage for this 30-minute, live production of *Beauty and the Beast,* adapted from the movie version. Musical highlights include the rousing "Be Our Guest" opening number and the poignant title song featured in a romantic waltz-scene finale. Sets and costumes are lavish, and the production numbers are spectacular. Arrive early to get a good seat. The park usually hosts four or five shows a day.

"Honey, I Shrunk the Kids" Movie Set Adventure

In this 11,000-square-foot playground, everything is larger than life. A thicket of grass is 30 feet tall, mushroom caps are three stories high, and a friendly ant makes a suitable seat. Play areas include a massive cream cookie, a 52-foot garden hose with leaks, cereal loops 9 feet wide and cushioned for jumping, and a waterfall cascading from a leaf to a dell of fern sprouts. (The sprouts form a musical stairway, activated when you step from sprout to sprout.) There's also a root maze with a flower-petal slide, a filmstrip slide in a giant film canister, and a huge spider web with 11 levels. This attraction is a great place for children ages 2 to 8 to work off their excess energy, while you regain some of your sanity.

Indiana Jones Epic Stunt Spectacular!

Spectacular barely begins to describe this 35-minute rock 'em, sock 'em extravaganza guaran-double-teed to keep you entertained and on the edge of your seat. The show is held in a big, open-air stadium and recruits a handful of adult volunteers to help out. It begins with Indy rappelling down from the rafters, and the amazing special effects soon have him dodging spikes, falling into a pit of molten something-or-other, surviving two ax-wielding gargoyles, grabbing a priceless amulet, and then outrunning fire, steam, and a tremendous boulder that nearly flattens him. The actors, special effects folks, and director use the breaks to explain what you just saw or are about to see, including stunt secrets. In later scenes, Indy battles the evil Nazis in a Cairo marketplace and at an airport-munitions dump. Shots are fired and flames are bursting all around the set. For some stunts, adult victims . . . err . . . volunteers are chosen from the audience.

 The closer to the front of the theater you are, the more likely you are to feel the extreme heat from the explosions, so if you have young kids along you may want to sit a few rows back.

 "It looked just like the movie — how cool is that!" It's definitely an adrenaline booster, though loud noises may make this show a little too intense for kids under 5. There usually are five or six shows a day.

Jim Henson's Muppet*Vision 3-D

 This must-see production stars Kermit and Miss Piggy in a delightful marriage of Jim Henson's puppets and Disney audio-animatronics, special-effects wizardry, 70mm film, and cutting-edge 3-D technology. The action takes place in a pretty darn accurate reproduction of the theater most of you grew up watching on TV. In the show, you encounter flying Muppets, cream pies, cannonballs, high winds, fiber-optic fireworks, bubble showers, and even an actual spray of water. Kermit is host, Miss Piggy sings "Dream a Little Dream of Me," Statler and Waldorf heckle the action from the balcony, and Nicki Napoleon and his Emperor Penguins (a full Muppet orchestra) provide music from the pit. Kids of all ages will enjoy this whimsical attraction and adults will be just as delighted. The 25-minute show (including a 12-minute video pre-show) runs continuously.

Lights, Motors, Action! Extreme Stunt Show

Inspired by the popular Stunt Show Spectacular at Disneyland Paris, this high-octane stunt show takes places on the set of a spy thriller in progress, with a quaint Mediterranean village as the backdrop. The show features specially designed stunt cars, motorcycles, and jet skis, plus some rather amazing special effects and even more spectacular driving — with an audience member pulled in for a bit of the fun. Much like the *Indiana Jones Epic Stunt Spectacular!*, insiders reveal industry secrets, detailing how stunts are created, designed, and filmed for the movies. Filmed images are shown on an oversized screen, illustrating how the use of different camera angles can add drama to filmed scenes.

 Seating is in a large outdoor stadium with a degree of cover from the sun, but a late-afternoon show may be the best way to avoid the direct rays and heat. The only bad seats in the house are the few rows in the center just above an entry to the set used by some of the vehicles.

The Magic of Disney Animation

The new *Drawn to Animation* tour opens with a live artist interacting with Mushu from Disney's *Mulan* and a cute video on the making of that film. Alas, Disney's real-life Florida animators were all laid off in 2004, so the inspection of their former working quarters strikes a somewhat sour chord. The tour ends on an up note, however, as visitors attempt their own Disney character drawings under the supervision of a working animator. Just before exiting, be sure to have the kids head to an animation station. The short computerized program photographs your children's faces and asks a few questions to determine which Disney character they are most like.

Playhouse Disney — Live on Stage!

Younger audiences (2–8 years old) love this 20-minute show, where they meet characters from *Bear in the Big Blue House, The Book of Pooh, Jo Jo's Circus,* and other favorite Disney stories. The show encourages preschoolers to dance, sing, and play along with the cast. It happens several times daily. Check your show schedule.

Sounds Dangerous — Starring Drew Carey

Drew Carey (on film) provides laughs while dual-audio technology provides some incredible hair-raising effects during a 12-minute mixture of movie and live action at ABC Sound Studios. You feel like you're right in the middle of the action of a TV pilot featuring undercover police work and plenty of amusing mishaps. Even when the picture disappears, you continue the chase via headphones that demonstrate "3-D" sound effects such as a roomful of angry bees, a herd of galloping elephants, and a deafening auto race.

Most of the show takes place in total darkness, and the sound and sensory effects may be frightening to younger ears, so think twice before bringing younger children.

Voyage of The Little Mermaid

Hazy lighting helps paint a picture of an underwater world in a 17-minute show that combines live performances, movie clips, puppetry, and special effects. Sebastian sings "Under the Sea," Ariel performs "Part of Your World," and the evil Ursula, 12 feet tall and 10 feet wide, belts out "Poor Unfortunate Soul." The Voyage has some scary scenes, but most little kids don't mind because, just like the movie, they know the show has a happy ending. You get spritzed with water during the show, making this an especially good experience during hot days.

Exploring PG-Rated Attractions and Rides

Rides and attractions in this category appeal to older children and adults. In some cases, they have age, height, or health restrictions — most of them well deserved.

The American Film Institute Showcase

More of a shop than anything, the showcase includes an exhibit area where you can waltz through Hollywood history, learning about the folks behind the movies — editors, cinematographers, producers, and directors whose names roll by in the blur of credits. It also spotlights some of the institute's lifetime-achievement winners, including Bette Davis, Jack Nicholson, and Elizabeth Taylor. A special exhibit here, *Villains: Movie Characters You Love to Hate,* features the costumes and props of several notable bad guys, including Darth Vader.

Disney–MGM Studios Backlot Tour

This fun, 35-minute special-effects show starts on foot and finishes in a tram. You get a behind-the-scenes look at the vehicles, props, costumes, sets, and special effects used in some of your favorite movies and TV shows. On most days, you see costume makers at work in the wardrobe department (the largest of its kind, with around 2 million garments). But the real fun begins when the tram heads for *Catastrophe Canyon,* where an earthquake in the heart of oil country causes canyon walls to rumble. A raging oil fire, massive explosions, torrents of rain, and flash floods threaten you and other riders before you're taken behind the scenes to see how filmmakers use special effects to make such disasters.

Groans at the thought of enduring a tour of the backlot gave way to screams after Austin, Ryan, and Nicolas experienced *Catastrophe Canyon,* where the "earthquake" shook the tram and a very large, *very wet* wave threw 70,000 gallons of water our way. All in all, this ride is very similar in type to *Earthquake — The Big One* at **Universal Studios Florida** (see Chapter 18). Sit on the left side of the tram if you want to get wet.

The Great Movie Ride

Set inside a replica of Los Angeles's famous Grauman's Chinese Theatre, this 22-minute journey down MGM's memory lane starts in the 1930s and moves forward from there, using lifelike audio-animatronic versions of famous actors to re-create some memorable movie moments. The line/waiting area features film clips from various classic films, and several cinematic artifacts to gawk at, including a set of Dorothy's ruby slippers from the *Wizard of Oz.* Then, you're off to watch Bogey say goodbye to Bergman, Tarzan (the Johnny Weismuller version) swing through the jungle, James Cagney act tough, and Gene Kelly dance — and sing — in the rain. A live outlaw enhances the action when he kidnaps you and your mates, but — revenge is so sweet, isn't it? — he goes the wrong way, hopping onto a set that has an uncanny resemblance to one in *Raiders of the Lost Ark.* After a narrow escape from the space thing from *Alien,* your bank-robbing buddy gets incinerated when he tries to steal the sphinx's jewel. You survive to follow the yellow brick road to Oz, where a remarkable likeness of the witch warns, "I'll get you my pretty, ahahahaha!"

Even though this ride was recently refurbished, the older kids expressed zero interest in it, so we split up. They headed for the heart-pounding thrills down on Hollywood Boulevard while my two youngest (ages 3 and 5) and I enjoyed the slow moving trip (with a brief moment or two of excitement thrown in for good measure) through Tinseltown. Movie buffs and nostalgic adults will love it.

Rock 'n' Roller Coaster Starring Aerosmith

It takes a lot to really wow anyone anymore but this ride is sure to do the trick. This inverted roller coaster is one of the best thrill rides that WDW has to offer, definitely not a ride for younger kids or anyone with neck or back problems, faint hearts, a tendency toward motion sickness, or fear of the dark.

Rock 'n' Roller Coaster is a fast-and-furious indoor ride that puts you in a 24-passenger stretch limo, outfitted with 120 speakers that blare Aerosmith at 32,000 watts! A flashing light warns you to "prepare to merge as you've never merged before," and faster than you can scream "Stop the music!" (around 2.8 seconds, actually), you shoot from 0 to 60 mph and into the first gut-tightening inversion at 5Gs. The ride's beginning is a real test of your courage as you blast into a wild journey through a make-believe California freeway system. One inversion cuts through an "O" in the Hollywood sign, but you won't feel that you're going to be thrown out because the ride's too fast and too smooth for that. It's so fast, the Disney hype says, that it's similar to sitting atop an F-14 Tomcat. The ride lasts 3 minutes and 12 seconds, the running time of Aerosmith's hit, "Sweet Emotion," which is one of the tunes played in the limos. Similar to *Space Mountain,* the entire ride takes place indoors and in the dark, but this one packs far more of a punch. Riders must be *at least 48 inches tall.*

Plus-size guests with larger chests may not be able to pull the shoulder harness fully closed and, therefore, may not be able to ride this.

"Lets do it again!" 8-year-old Nicolas screamed while playing air guitar. Austin (age 10) screamed back in agreement. I wasn't sure if they were screaming from the excitement or as a result of the loud music being pumped from the speaker behind their heads on the ride. People with sensitive ears should probably bring earplugs for this ride.

Star Tours — the ultimate Star Wars thrill ride

Star Tours, like the slightly lesser *Body Wars* at **Epcot** (see Chapter 13), is a virtual ride where you go nowhere, but you feel like you do. Your journey to a place far, far away begins with a pre-ride warning about high turbulence, sharp drops, and sudden turns, and a winding walk (a line) through the woodlands, where you see an Ewok village in the trees overhead and a humungous Imperial Walker standing guard near the entry. The pre-ride, which is expected to be updated eventually with characters from the prequels, now has R2-D2 and C-3PO running a galactic travel agency of sorts. After boarding your StarSpeeder, the ride itself starts kind of slow, but it finishes fast as you soar through space as the good-guy fighter, with R2-D2 and C-3PO helping you make passes through the canals of a Death Star. The special effects include hitting hyperspace speed (you feel like you're going up against a very small G-force) and falling. All things considered, though, this ride isn't quite up to modern rides here and at Orlando's other theme parks, including *Back to the Future* at **USF** (see Chapter 18), but it's still highly enjoyable. Sit in the last row to feel the motion best. If you feel a twinge of motion sickness there are plenty of stationary objects you can look at to get your bearings.

 "That was so awesome!" Austin, a *Star Wars* fan, was definitely impressed. It's not nearly as threatening or active as the *Rock 'n' Roller Coaster Starring Aerosmith,* but *Star Tours* still carries a *40-inch height minimum.*

The Twilight Zone Tower of Terror

 A truly stomach-lifting (and dropping) ride, Disney continues to fine-tune the *Tower of Terror* to make it even better. That includes a January 2003 upgrade that added random drop sequences, meaning you get a different fright every time you ride. Its legend says that during a violent storm on Halloween night 1939, lightning struck the Hollywood Tower Hotel, causing an entire wing and an elevator full of people to disappear. And you're about to meet them as you star in a special episode of *The Twilight Zone* (cue that television show's famously creepy music). En route to this formerly grand hotel, guests walk past overgrown landscaping and faded signs that once pointed the way to stables and tennis courts; the vines above the entrance trellis are dead, and the hotel is a crumbling ruin. Eerie corridors lead to a dimly lit library, where you can hear a storm raging outside. The detailing on this ride is some of the best around. After various ghostly apparitions, blasts of chilling air, and creepy experiences, your ride ends in a dramatic climax: a terrifying 13-story fall into *The Twilight Zone!* From there it's anyone's guess as to what happens next — not even the bellhops operating the elevator know what the ride is going to do. At 199 feet, it's the tallest WDW attraction, and it's a cut (or two or three) above its rival *Dr. Doom's Fearfall* at Universal's **Islands of Adventure** (see Chapter 19).

 "Absolutely the best ride ever!" 10-year-old Austin couldn't get enough, but my 8- and 12-year-olds wouldn't get near the ride. I have no way of knowing whether it was from the screams coming from the building or the semi-green faces on a family that came out as we were about to get in line. They aren't alone, though: One of the Disney Imagineers who helped design the attraction is too afraid to ride his own creation. Note, however, that there were plenty of other kids ready for more at the ride's end. This ride carries a *40-inch height minimum.*

Who Wants to Be a Millionaire — Play It!

Forget about winning $1 million — it ain't happening here — but contestants can win points toward prizes ranging from collectible pins to a leather jacket to a three-night cruise on a Disney cruise ship (see Chapter 16 for more on Disney cruises). Based on Disney-owned ABC TV's game show, the theme-park version features the same dramatic music and lighting that made the TV version so famous. Lifelines (such as asking the audience or calling a stranger on two phones set up in the park) are available for contestants who need a little help answering up to 15 multiple-choice questions in the climb to the top. It's great fun to play along, but you soon realize it isn't as easy as it looks when you're under the gun (the audience is timed as well). Games run continuously in the 600-seat studio.

 Unlike the TV show, the entire audience competes to get in the hot seat by answering questions on keypads; the fastest to answer qualifying questions become the contestants.

Taking Time Out for Fantastic Parades and Fireworks

In addition to its assortment of rides, Disney–MGM also offers its own daily parade and an exceptional evening fireworks display.

Fantasmic!

 It's hard not to be in awe of the choreography, laser lights, and fireworks that are the core of this 25-minute extravaganza held once — sometimes twice — a night, weather permitting. Shooting comets, great balls of fire, and animated fountains, and projection animation are among the many special effects that entrance the audience. The cast includes 50 performers, a gigantic dragon, a huge king cobra, and 1 million gallons of water. The entire show represents Mickey's dream, filled with fanciful songs and fantastic visuals. The dream turns into a nightmare thanks to the mischievous magic of some of Disney's more infamous villains. Surprisingly, much of the show is rather dark, with foreboding music and frightening creatures, with Mickey taking on some evil villains. The magical mouse of course triumphs, and the show ends on a festive note. Younger children might be frightened.

 If you want to avoid a real traffic jam after the show, arrive up to 60 minutes early and sit on the right (the theater empties right to left) side of the amphitheater. When there are two shows per night, especially during peak periods, finding a seat at the later show is usually easier.

 At press time, Disney was offering preferred seating at the end-of-the-day spectacular, *Fantasmic!,* along with a fixed-price dinner at one of Disney–MGM's sit-down restaurants. All you need to do is make Advanced Dining Reservation arrangements (☎ **407-939-3463**) and request the *Fantasmic!* package for the **Hollywood Brown Derby** ($37 adults, $10 kids 3–11), **Mama Melrose's Ristorante Italiano** ($29 adults, $10 kids 3–11), or **Hollywood & Vine** ($23 adults, $11 kids 3–11). *Note:* You must tell the reservation agent you want the *Fantasmic!* package. You'll get your line pass at the restaurant and instructions on getting to the special entrance to the preferred-seating area of the show.

Be aware that the prices above are for a fixed-price meal and don't include sales tax, tip, or alcoholic beverages; ordering off the menu costs you more. The prices also don't include a reserved seat at *Fantasmic!*, only a pass that gets you into the preferred seating area (you must arrive at least 30 minutes in advance — a much shorter wait than usual).

Disney's Stars and Motor Cars Parade

This motorcade includes a fun, highly recognizable procession of Disney characters and their chariots. The parade is popular enough that if you decide to skip it, you can find *far* shorter lines at the park's most popular rides and shows. (Check the parade schedule in your park map.)

Index of Attractions and Rides

G-Rated

Beauty and the Beast — Live on Stage
"Honey, I Shrunk the Kids" Movie Set Adventure
Indiana Jones Epic Stunt Spectacular!
Jim Henson's Muppet*Vision 3-D
Lights, Motors, Action! Extreme Stunt Show
The Magic of Disney Animation
Playhouse Disney — Live on Stage!
Sounds Dangerous — Starring Drew Carey
Voyage of The Little Mermaid

PG-Rated

The American Film Institute Showcase
Disney–MGM Studios Backlot Tour
The Great Movie Ride
Rock 'n' Roller Coaster Starring Aerosmith
Star Tours — the ultimate Star Wars thrill ride
The Twilight Zone Tower of Terror
Who Wants to Be a Millionaire — Play It!

Chapter 15

Animal Kingdom

● ●

In This Chapter

▶ Acquainting yourself with Animal Kingdom
▶ Comparing Animal Kingdom to Busch Gardens
▶ Exploring the attractions in Animal Kingdom

● ●

Disney's fourth major park combines exotic animals, elaborate landscapes, and a handful of rides and shows to create yet another
reason why many WDW resort-goers don't venture outside this World.
The $800 million park opened in 1998; its most recent land, Asia, was fin-
ished in 1999. Speaking of Asia, it will be the home of Animal Kingdom's
first and long-awaited thrill ride. Expected to debut in 2006, *Expedition
Everest,* will be a high-speed, coasterlike train ride through glaciers,
waterfalls, and canyons, climaxing with an encounter with a yeti. Even
with this addition, and although the park offers some unique experiences, an expedition here requires only a half to three-quarters of a day,
leaving some visitors (and I'm among them!) to believe there isn't enough
there to justify the $60 admission charge per adult or $48 per child (3–9).

But don't go canceling that safari vacation just yet. Animal Kingdom is a
theme park after all — even if the exotic wildlife can move out of your
view. It's filled with some amazing experiences and some of the most
remarkable landscaping and architectural recreations in all of Disney
(after Epcot's World Showcase pavilions, that is). In this chapter, I give
you helpful information about Animal Kingdom and its marvels, as well
as basic info for visiting the park.

Finding Helpful Services in the Kingdom

Before trekking through the jungle of attractions at Animal Kingdom, you
need to know some basic information, key to your survival when on
safari about the park.

Buying tickets and making reservations

A one-day ticket costs $60 for adults, $48 for children 3 to 9. See Chapter 11 for other ticket options.

Animal Kingdom

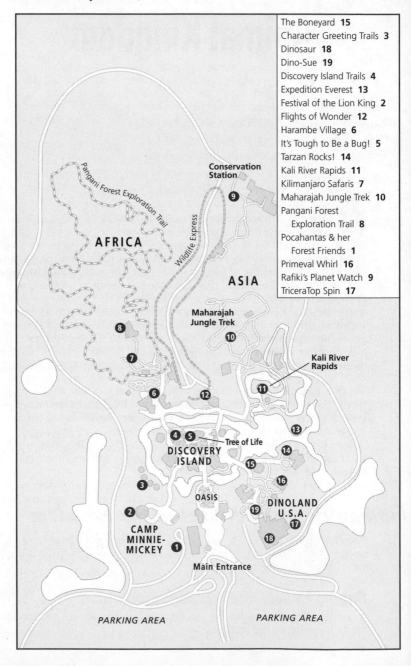

The Boneyard **15**
Character Greeting Trails **3**
Dinosaur **18**
Dino-Sue **19**
Discovery Island Trails **4**
Expedition Everest **13**
Festival of the Lion King **2**
Flights of Wonder **12**
Harambe Village **6**
It's Tough to Be a Bug! **5**
Tarzan Rocks! **14**
Kali River Rapids **11**
Kilimanjaro Safaris **7**
Maharajah Jungle Trek **10**
Pangani Forest
   Exploration Trail **8**
Pocahantas & her
   Forest Friends **1**
Primeval Whirl **16**
Rafiki's Planet Watch **9**
TriceraTop Spin **17**

Conservation Station

Pangani Forest Exploration Trail

AFRICA

Wildlife Express

ASIA

Maharajah
Jungle Trek

Kali River
Rapids

Tree of Life

**DISCOVERY
ISLAND**

OASIS

**DINOLAND
U.S.A.**

**CAMP
MINNIE-
MICKEY**

Main Entrance

PARKING AREA   *PARKING AREA*

Tickets aren't the only things to cut down on your cash. You'll pay the Disney park standard of $2 and up for a soda, $1.25 to $2.50 for bottled water, $2.60 for an ice-cream bar, and $1.80 for a cup of coffee. If you buy a soda, note that the park doesn't provide lids or straws with its fountain drinks. They're not trying to make it difficult for you to walk around with your soda — these items are banned because, in the hands of litterbugs, they can become deadly to the wildlife. Another no-no: chewing gum.

You can make Advanced Dining Reservations (see Chapter 10 for details on call-ahead dining) at *Guest Relations* just inside the entrance, though it's best to make them in advance by calling ☎ **407-939-3463**.

Hours at Animal Kingdom are from 8 a.m. to 5 or 6 p.m., but they're sometimes extended to 7 a.m. to 7 p.m. (though it's rare).

Locating special services and facilities

In case you forgot to bring essential items, or if you need special assistance while at the park, here's a list of services and facilities that may come in handy:

- ✔ You can find **ATMs** in Animal Kingdom near *Garden Gates Gifts* to the right of the park entrance. Cards from banks using the Cirrus, STAR, and Plus systems are accepted.

- ✔ **The Baby Care Center** is located near *Creature Comforts* on the west side of the *Tree of Life*. As in the other Disney parks, you can also find changing tables in women's restrooms and some men's rooms. You can also buy disposable diapers at *Guest Relations*.

- ✔ **Disposable cameras and film** are available throughout the park, but digital supplies are limited.

- ✔ **The First Aid Center,** which is staffed by registered nurses, is located near *Creature Comforts* near the *Tree of Life*.

- ✔ **Lockers** are located in *Garden Gate Gifts* to your right as you enter the park. You can also find them to the left, near *Rainforest Café*. Rent lockers for $7 a day, plus a $2 deposit.

- ✔ **A lost children center** is located near *Creature Comforts* near the *Tree of Life*. This area also is the site of same-day lost and found. *Kids age 7 and younger should wear name-tags.*

- ✔ Shop clerks can send your **packages** (at no charge) to the front of the park at *Garden Gate Gifts*. Allow three hours for delivery. If you're staying at a Disney resort, you can have your packages shipped there, though it may take a day or two to get to your room.

- ✔ **Pet care** facilities are just outside the park entrance to the right. You can board your pet for $6 a day (☎ **407-824-6568**). The Transportation and Ticket Center at the **Magic Kingdom** has overnight boarding available for $11 ($9 for Disney resort guests). Proof of vaccination is required.

- ✔ **Rent strollers** at the *Garden Gate Gifts* shop to the right as you enter the park ($8 for a single, $15 for a double, including a $1 refundable deposit). Satellite locations are also throughout the park. Ask a Disney employee to steer you in the right direction.

- ✔ **Rent wheelchairs** at the *Garden Gate Gifts* shop that's on your right as you enter the park. Rentals cost $10 for a standard wheelchair, and $35 (plus a $5 deposit) for electric carts. Ask Disney employees for other locations in the park.

You can call ☎ **407-934-7639** or visit Disney's Web site, www.disney world.com, to find out more about WDW properties.

Deciding between Animal Kingdom and Busch Gardens

When Disney's fourth theme park opened, it raised two questions: Is it a first-rate park worthy of the same sticker shock as Orlando's other major parks, and when does the area have too many parks?

Well, when it comes to visitor volume and diversity of things to do, **Animal Kingdom** ranks as one of the top two animal parks in Florida. **Busch Gardens** ($56 per adult, $46 per child entry) in Tampa is the other. Although I discuss Busch Gardens in Chapter 23, I'm going to talk about it briefly here so that I can draw a few comparisons.

Animal Kingdom is as much a park for animals, a conservation venue, as it is an attraction. The short of it is that its creatures aren't as easy to see; they're given much more cover than at Busch Gardens, so when they want to avoid your probing eyes and the heat, they can. Even in high-profile areas, such as *Pangani Forest Exploration Trail,* Disney goes to great lengths to protect resident lowland gorillas, including a magnificent silverback, from prying eyes. The beautiful foliage used to create that cover also means that Animal Kingdom is a lot prettier than its Tampa rival.

 Although I'm all for protecting wildlife, Animal Kingdom can do a much better job of providing shade for the only species that doesn't get much consideration in the park — the homo sapiens who paid to get in. The amount of cover given to tourists waiting in line is decidedly unimpressive (a problem in all of Disney's parks, in my opinion). Arriving early at both parks, especially in summer, saves you the unpleasant experience of languishing under a blistering sun.

 The best time to catch the animals out and about at Animal Kingdom is in the early morning just after the park opens — usually 7 or 8 a.m. (depending on the season) — or at closing as the day begins to cool. Most animals are on the prowl at those times, not at midday (especially during the summer). Busch's animals are far easier to see, regardless of the time of day, as they have fewer places to take cover.

Animal Kingdom wins the battle of shows with humdingers such as *Festival of the Lion King.* Although the Animal Kingdom has three — soon to be four — thrill rides (and I'm being kind in including two of them in the thrill category), Busch Gardens pulls ahead with six roller coasters including *SheiKra,* the incredible new dive coaster, and *Gwazi,* a set of dueling wooden coasters.

Busch is the better all-around park. New additions aside, many criticize Animal Kingdom — fairly, in my opinion — for not offering enough to justify a ticket price comparable to Busch Gardens and the other Orlando theme parks. But geographically speaking, you may not have or want a choice between the two. Animal Kingdom is located right in the center of the Orlando action, where you can find a ton of other things to do. Alas, Busch Gardens is at least a 75-minute drive or shuttle trip from O-Town, and the Tampa Bay area simply doesn't have the draw of Orlando, though it does offer cultural centers, museums, aquariums, and sandy beaches. If you're considering a trip to the Tampa Bay area, I recommend buying a copy of *Florida For Dummies* or *Frommer's Florida* (both published by Wiley); both books have a wealth of information about attractions, accommodations, and restaurants on the state's Suncoast.

Checking Out Animal Kingdom's Top Attractions

The overall conservation theme in this state-of-the-art park is simple but not subtle. Everywhere you turn, you find an environmental message, including the park's signs and the narratives of the tour guides on rides such as *Kilimanjaro Safaris.* It's this underlying theme that connects the park's rather diverse sections, where you'll encounter everything from a dinosaur-themed thrill ride to a kid-friendly zone where Disney characters hang out.

Animal Kingdom, like WDW's **Magic Kingdom,** is set up on a hub-and-spoke format with the Tree of Life (in Discovery Island) as its hub and five other sections scattered around it. The following sections provide you with a closer look at the six lands of Animal Kingdom. You can find all the Kingdom's attractions on the "Animal Kingdom" map on page 226.

The Oasis

The Oasis Exhibits is your introduction to Animal Kingdom, but a lot of folks, itching to get to the action, launch their way through it, overlooking the fact that this is one of the better places to see not-so-rare animals early in the day. The lush vegetation, streams, grottoes, and

waterfalls on either side of the walkway are good places to spot walla-
bies, miniature deer, anteaters, sloths, iguanas, tree kangaroos, otters,
and macaws. But a misty fog and the landscaping also give them room
to escape your eyes whenever they choose.

Discovery Island

After you pass through *The Oasis,* **Discovery Island** lies directly ahead,
with the park's signature icon, the *Tree of Life,* in the center of it all.
Although you will find only three attractions, they are among the park's
most unique features.

Discovery Island Trails

The *Discovery Island Trail* is another of the park's animal-viewing areas,
a leisurely path through the root system of the *Tree of Life* (Animal
Kingdom's 145-foot man-made tree described in detail later in this section) and a chance to see real, but not-so-rare, critters such as axis deer,
red kangaroos, otters, flamingos, lemurs, galapagos tortoises, ducks,
storks, and cockatoos.

The best viewing times are early or late in the day, though I'd save this
one for later and head to the park's few thrill rides first.

It's Tough to Be a Bug!

Take the walkway through the *Tree of Life*'s 50-foot base, grab a pair of
3-D glasses, and settle into a sometimes creepy-crawly seat. Based on the
Disney-Pixar film, *A Bug's Life,* the special effects in this multimedia adventure are pretty impressive. Although it may not be a good choice for kids
younger than 4 (it's dark and loud) or bug haters. The attraction offers a
fun and sometimes-poignant look at life from a smaller perspective. After
you put on your bug-eye glasses, all your senses are awakened by the
stars, including ants, beetles, spiders, and — oh, no! — a stink bug.

I won't say who, but more than one of my kids came out in tears, but for
reasons you may not expect. The simple sensory effects, mostly because
they occur unexpectedly and in the dark, terrorized even some of the
older ones. The issue my youngest had was with the bugs — he HATES
them.

On the other hand, Katie (a cousin), thought the show was "really
funny." Viewers experience some spritzes of water, blasts of air, and a
foul smell when the stink bug gets its revenge. The show's finale, when
the on-screen insects run amok, definitely leaves you buzzing.

The Tree of Life

Like *Cinderella Castle* at **Magic Kingdom** (see Chapter 12 for more
details) and *Spaceship Earth* in **Epcot** (described in Chapter 13), the
14-story *Tree of Life* is a park icon. The man-made tree, and its carved
animals, are the work of Disney artists, teams of which worked for more
than a year on its carved, free-form animal sculptures. It isn't as tall or

imposing as those other icons, but it is certainly impressive. It has 8,000 limbs, 103,000 leaves, and 325 mammals, reptiles, amphibians, insects, birds, dinosaurs, and Mickeys carved into its trunk, limbs, and roots. Different animals appear or vanish depending on the angle from which you view the *Tree.* One of the creators says he expects it to become one of the most photographed works of art in the world.

 Although passing up a detailed inspection of the tree as you enter the park is hard to do (it is awesomely difficult to ignore), I recommend gawking only while standing in line for *It's Tough to Be a Bug!* You'll have time for a more detailed look at the tree — if you so desire — on the way out.

Camp Minnie–Mickey

Youngsters love this place, though I don't share their enthusiasm. It's a favorite hangout for Disney characters from the forest and jungle, including Simba from *Lion King* and Baloo from *The Jungle Book.* Mickey, Minnie, Goofy, Pluto, Donald, Daisy, and other stars also make appearances from time to time around this woody retreat, which was designed to resemble an Adirondack summer camp. The lines for the meet and greets are often excruciatingly long, and unless the kids insist on visiting, I recommend avoiding waiting to meet with Disney characters here.

In addition to the characters, this land is also home to some of Disney World's best stage shows, including *Festival of the Lion King,* an exhilarating extravaganza.

Character Greeting Trails

If you're traveling with children, this attraction is probably a must-do, but be prepared for a long wait. A variety of Disney characters from Timon and Winnie the Pooh to Pluto and Donald Duck shake your hand, give hugs, allow photos to be taken, and sign autographs. Mickey and Minnie, in recognition of their star status, get their own shaded pavilions.

Festival of the Lion King

 This Broadway-style production at the Lion King Theater is the best in Animal Kingdom and one of the top three productions in all of Walt Disney World. The extravaganza celebrates nature's diversity with a talented, colorfully attired cast of singers, dancers, and life-size critters who lead you to an inspiring sing-along. Based loosely on the animated movie, this stage show combines the pageantry of a parade with a tribal celebration. The action takes place on the center stage and even around the audience. Even though the pavilion has 1,000 seats, arrive at least 20 minutes early to ensure you get a spot. The show lasts just under a half-hour.

Pocahontas and Her Forest Friends

 The wait to see *Pocahontas and Her Forest Friends* can be nightmarish, and the 15-minute show isn't remotely close to the caliber of *Festival of the Lion King.* In this presentation, Pocahontas and Grandmother Willow, with the help of some of the forest creatures (a raccoon, turkey, porcupine, rat, and more), bring to light the importance of treating nature with respect and protecting our forests. Young fans of the movie and of little creatures will be most appreciative of the performance. If you must go, go early. The theater has a mere 350 seats, but standing-room crowds are admitted.

Africa

Enter through the town of Harambe, which means "coming together" in Swahili. This area of *Africa* is a re-creation of an African coastal village poised on the edge of the 21st century. The impressive whitewashed structures, built of coral stone and thatched with reed brought from Africa, surround a beautifully landscaped central marketplace that's rich with local wares and colors. After passing through the town, the various trails lead you to Africa's other rides and attractions.

Kilimanjaro Safaris

This attraction is one of the few rides and the best animal-viewing venue in the kingdom. But remember: The animals are scarce during the middle of the day, especially in the heat of summer.

You can wait 45 minutes or more in line at this attraction. Yes, using FASTPASS (see Chapter 11) is an option, but it virtually eliminates the chance of riding during the best viewing times. My advice: Skip FASTPASS, get to the park a bit before its scheduled time to open, and make your way straight here. If you simply aren't a morning person, your next best shot is to get a FASTPASS that lets you ride as close to the park's closing as you can get (so know ahead of time you will have to check back every so often to get a pass that doesn't have you returning mid-day!).

After you reach the end of the very long and winding line, you'll board a rather large truck specially made for such an expedition, and set off on a bouncy ride through the African landscape. Animals in the *Safari* include black rhinos, hippos, antelopes, Nile crocodiles, zebras, wildebeests, and lions that, if your timing is right, may offer a half-hearted roar toward some gazelles that are safely out of reach. The animals roam freely, occasionally crossing the path of the truck allowing a really up-close view, but again, it's far more likely to occur in the morning or evening hours. Predictably, the theme is conservation. There's even a little drama — this, after all, is a theme park ride — as you and your mates will help pursue some park poachers.

"The bumpy ride was fun and way better than having to walk around to see the animals. Looking over railings isn't nearly as fun." I agree with Nicolas — several giraffe came practically within arms length on this ride. This one's fun for the whole family, although very small infants shouldn't ride because of the bumps.

Pangani Forest Exploration Trail

You can get a good look at hippos, mole rats, and African birds on the *Pangani Falls Exploration Trail,* but lowland gorillas are the main feature. The trail has two gorilla-related areas: One is home to a family comprised of a 500-pound silverback, his ladies, and kids; the other has five bachelors. Most people tend to rush through the trails, missing out on the chance to see the giant apes, and the animals are not always cooperative, especially in hot weather when they tend to spend most of the day in shady areas out of view. But visitors who have good timing or who make return visits are truly rewarded with up-close views (through Plexiglas) of these magnificent creatures. A new *Endangered Animal Rehabilitation Centre* that includes Colobus and Mona monkeys is one of the latest additions to the trail.

Rafiki's Planet Watch

This area of Africa includes *Conservation Station,* which offers a behind-the-scenes look at how Disney cares for animals inside the park, as you walk past a series of nurseries and veterinary stations. The problem is that these facilities need staff members present to make them interesting, and that isn't always the case. *Affection Section* gives you a chance to cuddle some friendly animals (including goats and potbellied pigs), while *Habitat Habit!* has a trail that's home to some smaller animals, such as cotton-topped tamarins. ***Note:*** Take heed of the signs in the Affection Section that instruct you to put all paper, including maps, away. Goats love paper and will cause a stampede in an attempt to snatch your paper products from you.

Asia

Disney's Imagineers outdid themselves in creating the mythical kingdom of *Anandapur* (place of delight) in the ***Asia*** section of the Kingdom, with an exotic atmosphere enhanced by the crumbling ruins of an ancient village, its temples, and even a maharajah's palace, all decorated with intricate carvings and artwork.

Expedition Everest

Animal Kingdom's newest thrill ride is scheduled to make its debut in 2006. Guests will board an old mountain railway bound for Mount Everest which, at 200 feet, will be one of Florida's highest peaks. Passing through bamboo forests, thundering waterfalls, and glacier fields, the train ascends higher and higher to the snow-capped peaks of the mountain. As you might expect, what starts out as a relaxing tour turns into an exciting expedition as the train hits tracks that are mangled and twisted. The train races frantically through the icy canyons and caverns as you suddenly find yourself face-to-face with the Yeti (also known as the abominable snowman). FASTPASS will be a necessity when the expedition opens. There will be height and health restrictions, although no information was available at the time this book went to press.

Flights of Wonder

This live-animal action show is a low-key break from the madness and offers a few laughs, including Groucho the African yellow-nape, who entertains the audience with his op-*parrot*-ic a cappella solos, and the just-above-your-head soaring of a Harris hawk and a Eurasian eagle owl. Other feathered stars include an American bald eagle and a crowned crane.

Kali River Rapids

Whitewater fanatics may scoff, but for a theme-park raft ride, the *Kali River Rapids* ride is pretty good — slightly better than *Congo River Rapids* at **Busch Gardens** (see Chapter 23), but not as good as *Popeye & Bluto's Bilge-Rat Barges* at **Islands of Adventure** (see Chapter 19); though the theme is more alluring here. This ride's churning water mimics realistic rapids and its optical illusions make you wonder whether you're about to go over the falls. The ride begins with a peaceful tour of lush foliage, but soon you're dipping and dripping as your tiny raft tosses and turns through the jungles. You *will* get wet (or, more precisely, soaked). The lines are long, but keep your head up, and enjoy some of the marvelous art overhead and on the beautiful murals. This ride has a *38-inch height minimum.*

Maharajah Jungle Trek

Disney keeps its promise to provide up-close views of animals with this exhibit, whose setting is almost an attraction in its own right. Lush tropical foliage and bamboo grow amidst the ruins, architecture, and carvings of Nepal, India, Thailand, and Indonesia. It's some of Disney's best thematic work.

If you don't show up in the midday heat, you'll probably see Bengal tigers roaming an abandoned maharajah's palace through a thick glass barrier. Nothing but air separates you from dozens of giant fruit bats hanging in what appears to be a courtyard. Some of the bats have wingspans of six feet. (If you have a phobia, you can bypass this, but know that the bats are harmless.) Guides are on hand to answer questions, and you also get a brochure that lists the animals you may spot. You also have chances to see Komodo dragons, tapirs, playful gibbons, and acrobatic siamangs, whose calls have been likened to someone in the throes of pain or passion.

DinoLand U.S.A.

Located to the right, or east side, of *Discovery Island* as you enter, **DinoLand U.S.A.** is Disney's attempt to capitalize on the dinosaur craze inspired by *Jurassic Park* and (ugh) *Barney.* You enter beneath Olden Gate Bridge, a 40-foot-tall brachiosaurus reassembled from excavated fossils. Speaking of which, until late summer 1999, *DinoLand* had three paleontologists working on the very real skeleton of *Sue,* a monstrously big tyrannosaurus rex unearthed in the Black Hills of South Dakota in

1990. The paleontologists patched and assembled the bones here, mainly because Disney helped pay for the project. Alas, *Sue* has moved to her permanent home at The Field Museum in Chicago, but a cast replica of her 67-million-year-old bones, called *Dino-Sue* on the handout guide maps, is on display.

The Boneyard

The Boneyard is a great place for parents to catch a second wind. Kids absolutely love the prehistoric playground, and there are plenty of activities to wear them down a bit. They can slide and climb over a paleontological dig site and squeeze through the fossils and skeletons of a triceratops and a brontosaurus. They can even search the sands for skeletal remains.

 You have to be vigilant about keeping track of your kids here. *The Bone Yard* is a large area, and although Disney staff monitors them at both ends, kids play in a multilevel arena where tube slides can take them from one level to the next in a heartbeat.

DINOSAUR

This ride hurls you through darkness in a CTX Rover time machine, past an array of snarling audio-animatronic dinosaurs. Some kids may find the dinosaurs (and darkness) frightening; adults might find them a bit hokey. However, after Expedition Everest, *DINOSAUR* is as close as Animal Kingdom comes to a thrill ride — a twisting-turning, and very jerky, adventure in which you and 20 other passengers try to save the last Iguanadon on Earth from an asteroid. Evolution, nature's fragility, and potential catastrophe are the punch lines in this lip-biting, armrest-clenching ride against time. It features some very large lizards (such as a 33-foot carnotaurus, named for its favorite food — meat).

 Plus-size riders may find the seats uncomfortably narrow, especially with the jerky motions of the ride.

 "You felt like you were really being thrown around," Ryan announced after he got off. Austin called it "Awesome!" but added that it wasn't as scary as he thought it would be. Riders *must be at least 40 inches tall*. *DINOSAUR* also has a list of warnings aimed at folks with neck and back ailments. If you've ever wondered what it feels like aboard a bucking bronco, this rough ride is probably pretty comparable.

Primeval Whirl

Sometimes criticized for being too passive, Animal Kingdom jumped into the coaster craze with Primeval Whirl. *Primeval Whirl* is a bit tame, and it doesn't have inversions, but it does have plenty of spinning action in carnival-style, rider-controlled cars that whirl by asteroids and hokey dinosaurs that pop up along the track. The ride has tight loops, short dips, and a final spin that sends you into the gaping jaws of a fossilized dinosaur.

Though this ride was originally supposed to enlarge the park's appeal to the kid set, *Primeval Whirl* has a *48-inch height minimum.*

TriceraTop Spin

The principle behind this kiddie favorite is pretty much the same as *The Magic Carpets of Aladdin* and *Dumbo The Flying Elephant* at **WDW's Magic Kingdom** (see Chapter 12). Cartoonish dinosaurs take riders up, down, and all around. To the delight of the kids, a dinosaur occasionally pops his head in and out of the central hub. Most young children, especially those ages 2 to 6, love it. Parents loathe the long lines.

Index of Attractions by Land

The Oasis

Discovery Island
Discovery Island Trails
It's Tough to Be a Bug!
The Tree of Life

Camp Minnie–Mickey
Character Greeting Trails
Festival of the Lion King
Pocahontas and Her Forest Friends

Africa
Kilimanjaro Safaris
Pangani Forest Exploration Trail
Rafiki's Planet Watch

Asia
Expedition Everest
Flights of Wonder
Kali River Rapids
Maharajah Jungle Trek

DinoLand U.S.A.
The Boneyard
DINOSAUR
Primeval Whirl
TriceraTop Spin

Chapter 16

Enjoying the Rest of Walt Disney World

● ●

In This Chapter

▶ Playing in an interactive adventure park

▶ Experiencing a sports fan's nirvana

▶ Golfing, Disney-style

▶ Splashing into the Disney water parks

▶ Enjoying holiday happenings

▶ Cruising with Disney

● ●

*I*n Chapters 12 through 15, I acquaint you with the major parks of Walt Disney World. But the House of Mouse is home to much, much more. In this chapter, I introduce you to the smaller, second-tier attractions, as well as a few holiday happenings and the Disney Cruise Line.

Playing It Up at DisneyQuest

The minute you step inside you realize this is no ordinary arcade — throughout the five levels are some of the most unique and cutting edge games ever created. Disney has taken the state of the art technology of virtual reality, added a spirit of adventure, and has shaken it all up with some of that magical pixie dust for good measure. The result is the World's most interactive game complex. From kids just old enough to work the controls to teens, reactions to **DisneyQuest** are pretty much the same: "Awesome!" And although many adults enter the arcade thinking that they're only going to find kids' stuff, many bite the hook as hard as their offspring when they get a gander at the electronic wizardry — everything from old-fashioned pinball with a newfangled twist to virtual-reality adventure rides.

Here are just some of the entrees that you can find at **DisneyQuest:**

▶ *Aladdin's Magic Carpet Ride:* straddling the magic carpet you'll fly through the 3-D Cave of Wonders, the alleys and streets of Agrabah, in search of the magic lamp. This is definitely fun, but your head may get hot from the virtual-reality helmets.

✔ *Pirates of the Caribbean: Battle for Buccaneer Gold* outfits you and up to three mates in 3-D helmets so you can battle pirate ships virtual-reality style. One of you volunteers to be the captain, steering the ship, while the others assume positions behind cannons to blast the black hearts into oblivion — maybe. Each time you do, you're rewarded with some doubloons, but beware of sea monsters that can gobble up you *and* your treasure. In the game's final moments, you come face to face with the ghost of Davey Jones. It's great fun for all ages.

✔ The *Mighty Ducks Pinball Slam* is an interactive, life-size game in which the players ride platforms and use body English to try to score points. It's your opportunity to explore life as a pinball — from the ball's perspective. Just try to stop the quivering in your arms after this.

✔ If you have an inventive mind (and a steel stomach), stop in at *Cyberspace Mountain,* where Bill Nye the Science-Turned-Roller-Coaster Guy helps you create the ultimate loop-and-dipster, which you then can ride in a very real-feeling simulator. It's a major hit with the coaster-crazy crowd. (I know some adrenaline junkies who spent hours here constructing, then riding, one heart-stopper after another.) Bring your own motion-sickness medicine (though you can choose slow, medium, or quick death).

✔ If you need some quiet time, sign up at *Animation Academy* for a mini course in Disney cartooning. The academy also has snack and food areas; a typical theme park–style meal and drink runs from $12 to $15 per person.

Crowds really start building after lunch when the heat of the day begins to truly kick in, and they're simply maddening after dark.

While there are some rides and games appropriate for a variety of ages, Disney Quest is by far most appealing to those over 8 or even 10 (some attractions also have height requirements so be sure to check ahead of time to avoid disappointments). If you have toddlers in tow, be aware that strollers are not allowed in the building.

See map p. 168. In Downtown Disney West Side (off Buena Vista Drive). ☎ *407-828-4600.* www.disneyquest.com. *Admission: $34 adults, $28 kids 3–9 for unlimited play. Open: Sun–Thurs 11:30 a.m.–11 p.m., Fri–Sat 11:30 a.m. to midnight.*

Fielding the Fun at Disney's Wide World of Sports

Disney's Wide World of Sports is a 200-acre, megacomplex that has a 7,500-seat baseball stadium, 10 other baseball and softball fields, 6 basketball courts, 12 lighted tennis courts, a track-and-field complex, a golf driving range, and 6 sand volleyball courts.

If you're a true sports fan, call for a package of information about the facilities and a calendar of events (see the listing data below). You can also consult the facility's Web site for up-to-date information.

Here's a sampling of the options at **Disney's Wide World of Sports:**

- ✔ The **Atlanta Braves** play 16 spring training games in the stadium during a one-month season that begins in early March. Tickets for the stadium's two seating areas cost $12 to $21. For tickets call Ticketmaster (☎ **407-839-3900**). *Note:* In addition to the Braves, the facility also hosts the NFL's **Tampa Bay Buccaneers'** spring-training camp.

- ✔ The **Multi-Sports Experience,** which is included in Wide World's general admission price, is open on select days. It challenges guests with activities covering many sports: football, baseball, basketball, hockey, soccer, and volleyball.

- ✔ The **NBA, NCAA, PGA,** and **Harlem Globetrotters** also stage events, sometimes annually and sometimes more frequently, at the complex.

See map p. 168. On Victory Way, just north of U.S. 192 (west of I-4). ☎ *407-828-3267 or 407-939-4263, the sports information line is 407-939-1500* www.disneysports.com. *Admission: $10.75 adults, $8 kids 3–9 (tax included). Open: Daily 10 a.m.–5 p.m., but hours may vary by venue.*

Gearing Up at the Richard Petty Driving Experience

Compared to the ***Richard Petty Driving Experience*** at the Walt Disney World Speedway, Epcot's thriller *Test Track* is for sissies. This is your chance to race like a pro in a 600-horsepower NASCAR race car. How real is it?

 You must sign a two-page waiver with words such as *Dangerous, Calculated Risk,* and *Update Your Will!* before getting into a car. At one end of the spectrum, you can ride shotgun for a couple of laps at 145 mph ($99). At the other end, you can spend from three hours to two days learning how to drive the car yourself and racing other daredevils in 8 to 30 laps of excitement (for a cool $349 to $1,249, not including tax). You must be 18 or older to ride in the car.

See map p. 168. At Walt Disney World Speedway on World Drive at Vista Boulevard just off U.S. 192, south of the Magic Kingdom. ☎ *800-237-3889.* www.1800bepetty.com. *Admission varies by seasons and hours, so call ahead. The speedway is open daily 9 a.m.–4 p.m., though hours may vary.*

Preparing for the PGA at Disney Golf

The Magic Mickey offers **99 holes of golf:** five 18-hole, par-72 courses and a 9-hole, par-36 walking course. All WDW courses are open to the public and offer pro shops, equipment rentals, and instruction. For tee times and information, call ☎ **407-939-4653** up to 60 days in advance. (Disney resort guests can reserve up to 90 days in advance.) Golf packages are also available (with select packages available only 7 days in advance), and you can call ☎ **407-934-7639** to make reservations.

Greens fees for Disney hotel guests can range from $69 to $159 per 18-hole round (it's $10 more if you're not a resort guest), though rates are subject to change at any time and do vary by season and by course. Special pricing may also available for play after 10 a.m., after 3 p.m., and after 5 p.m. Here's a rundown of Disney's courses:

- ✔ **Palm Course (18 holes):** By PGA standards, the Palm is Disney's toughest course. Set among natural Florida woodlands, the elevated greens, water, and sand traps offer more hazards than Interstate 4. Good luck with the 18th hole; it's rated among the toughest holes on the PGA Tour.

- ✔ **Magnolia Course (18 holes):** The longest course on Disney property is designed in classic PGA style. Wide fairways are deceiving; you've got to hunker down and whack the ball, but take care: Eleven holes have water hazards, and 97 bunkers are on the course. The 6th hole has a special hazard — a Mickey Mouse–shaped sand trap.

- ✔ **Lake Buena Vista Course (18 holes):** This course has a classic country-club style, with many pines spread across a residential area. Well-bunkered, it's also a challenge that demands accuracy. This course is one of a few that have played host to PGA, LPGA, and USGA events.

- ✔ **Eagle Pines Course (18 holes):** Expansive traps and sloping fairways follow the natural lay of the land. Rough pine straw and sand replace grass on this course, and 16 holes feature water hazards.

- ✔ **Osprey Ridge Course (18 holes):** This Fazio-designed course combines rolling fairways cut through forests of scrub oak, pine, palmetto, cypress, and bay trees. The Osprey course is ranked as one of the best courses in Florida by *Golf Digest*.

- ✔ **Oak Trail Course (9 holes):** If you can't go a day without getting in a few holes, but don't have time for the 18-hole courses, this course is the place to spank the ball. This 9-hole walking course is designed for families or for a quick golf fix.

Disney occasionally offers discounted twilight tee times after 3 p.m. and 5 p.m., and often, it's during the summer season. To find out whether a discount is available during your visit, call ☎ **407-939-4653** up to seven days in advance or consult the golf section (it's under the "Recreation" link) on Walt Disney World's Web site at www.disneyworld.com.

If you want more golfing options or want to get out of Disney for a bit, two excellent sources of information and tee time reservations are **Golfpac** (☎ **888-848-8941** or 407-260-2288; www.golfpacinc.com), and **Tee Times USA** (☎ **888-465-3356;** www.teetimesusa.com).

Puttering Around at Disney Miniature Golf

Those too timid to tee off at Disney's majors — or whose big games aren't yet up to par — can try their putters on the World's miniature golf courses. Thanks to four whimsically themed courses, everyone, from novices to master minigolfers, should find at least one course to their liking.

Fantasia Gardens

Fantasia Gardens Miniature Golf, located across from **Disney–MGM Studios,** offers two 18-hole miniature courses drawing inspiration from the Walt Disney classic cartoon of the same name. On the *Fantasia Gardens* course, hippos, ostriches, and gators appear, and the Sorcerer's Apprentice presides over the final hole. This is a good course for beginners and kids. Seasoned minigolfers will probably prefer the tougher *Fantasia Fairways,* a scaled-down golf course complete with sand traps, water hazards, tricky putting greens, and holes ranging from 40 to 75 feet — as for the kids, only those who can actually golf may find the *Fairways* any fun.

See map p. 168. On Buena Vista Drive, just east of World Drive. ☎ *407-560-4582.* www.disneyworld.com. *Admission: $10 adults, $8 kids 3–9. Open: Daily 10 a.m.–11 p.m.*

Winter Summerland

Santa Claus and his elves supply the theme at **Winter Summerland,** a well-designed miniature-golf spread that has two 18-hole courses. The *Winter* course takes you from an ice castle to a snowman to the North Pole. The *Summer* course is pure Florida, from sand castles to surfboards to a visit with Santa on the Winternet.

See map p. 168. East off Buena Vista Drive, across from Blizzard Beach. ☎ *407-60-3000.* www.disneyworld.com. *Admission: $10 adults, $8 kids 3–9. Open: Daily 10 a.m.– 11 p.m.*

Making a Splash at Disney's Water Parks

Disney's two water parks are great places to chill out for all or part of a day. Here are a few things to keep in mind before you head off for a swim:

- ✔ Go in the afternoons — about 2 p.m., even in summer — if you can stand the heat that long and want to avoid crowds. The early birds are usually gone by then, and lines are far shorter.

- ✔ Another way to enjoy the smallest crowds is to go early in the week when most week-long guests are filling the lines at the theme parks.

- ✔ Kids can get lost just as easily at a water park, and the consequences can be worse. All Disney parks have lifeguards, usually wearing bright red suits, but, to be safe, ask how to identify an on-duty lifeguard, and keep an eye on your little ones. Life jackets are available, at no charge, for an added measure of safety but are limited in availability and are in no way a substitute for adult supervision.

- ✔ If modesty is your policy, women should remember to bring a one-piece bathing suit for the more daring slides. All bathers should remember the wedgie factor on the more extreme rides, such as *Summit Plummet.* You may enter the park wearing baggies, but, thanks to high-speed water pressure, find yourself in a thong.

Blizzard Beach

The youngest of Disney's water parks is also tops in the country in attendance. **Blizzard Beach** is a 66-acre "ski resort" set in the midst of a tropical lagoon beneath 90-foot, uh-oh, *Mount Gushmore.* The base of *Mount Gushmore* has a sand beach and several other attractions, including a wave pool and a smaller, kids' version of the mountain.

Here are brief descriptions of other **Blizzard Beach** attractions:

- ✔ *Cross Country Creek* is a 2,900-foot tube ride around the park and through a cave where you get splashed with melting ice.

- ✔ *Runoff Rapids* allows you and your tube to careen down your choice of three twisting-and-turning runs, one of which plunges you into darkness.

- ✔ *Ski Patrol Training Camp* is designed for preteens. It features a rope swing, an airborne water drop from a T-bar, slides, such as the wet and slippery *Mogul Mania,* and a challenging ice-flow walk along slippery floating icebergs.

- ✔ *Slush Gusher* is a speed slide that shoots you along a snow-banked gully. It packs a *48-inch minimum height* requirement.

- ✔ *Melt Away Bay* is a one-acre, relatively calm wave pool.

- ✔ *Snow Stormers* has three flumes that descend from the top of *Mount Gushmore* along a switchback course through ski-type slalom gates.

✓ *Summit Plummet* is wild! Read *every* speed, motion, vertical-dip, wedgie, and hold-onto-your-breastplate warning in this guide. Then test your bravado in a bull ring, a space shuttle, or dozens of other death-defying hobbies as a warm-up. This one starts out pretty slow, with a lift ride (even in Florida's 100° dog days) to the 120-foot summit. Once you're at the top, kiss any kids or religious medal you may carry with you because, if you board, you *will be on the world's fastest body slide*. It's a test of your courage and your swimsuit as you'll be headed virtually straight down and moving, *sans* vehicle, at 60 mph by the time you reach the *catch pool* (the stop zone). Even the hardiest of riders may find this slide hard to handle; a veteran thrill-seeker has described the experience as "15 seconds of paralyzing fear." *Minimum height requirement is 48 inches.*

✓ *Teamboat Springs* is the World's longest white-water raft ride. Your six-passenger raft twists down a 1,200-foot series of rushing waterfalls.

✓ *Tike's Peak* is a mini version of **Blizzard Beach** for mini visitors. It offers short slides, a squirting ice pool, a fountain play area, and a snow castle.

✓ *Toboggan Racers* is an eight-lane slide that sends you racing, head first, over exhilarating dips into a "snowy" slope.

See map p. 168. On World Drive, north of the All-Star resorts and across from Winter Summerland. ☎ *407-560-3400.* www.disneyworld.com. *Admission: $34 adults, $28 kids 3–9. Open: Daily 10 a.m.–5 p.m., with extended hours during peak times, such as summer.*

Typhoon Lagoon

Typhoon Lagoon is the ultimate in water theme parks. Its fantasy setting is a palm-fringed tropical island village of ramshackle, tin-roofed island shacks, the entire area strewn with cargo, surfboards, and other marine wreckage left by the great typhoon. The storm-stranded fishing boat (the *Miss Tilly*) dangles precariously atop the 95-foot *Mount Mayday,* the steep setting for several rides. Every 30 minutes, *Tilly's* stack blows shooting a 50-foot geyser even higher into the air.

Here are some other park highlights:

✓ *Castaway Creek* is a 2,100-foot lazy river that circles most of the park. Hop onto a raft or an inner tube and meander through a misty rain forest and then past caves and secluded grottoes. *Water Works,* its theme area, is where jets of water spew from shipwrecked boats, and a Rube Goldberg assemblage of broken bamboo pipes and buckets soak you. Tubes are included in the admission.

✓ *Crush 'n' Gusher* is the newest addition to the park. Coaster crazies will appreciate its gravity defying drops between which powerful jets of water propel riders back uphill, through twists and turns, only to drop them again. The Banana Blaster, Coconut Crusher, and Pineapple Plunger offer a unique, out-of-control experience, each sending riders careening on a different route through the remains of a ramshackle fruit exporting plant. Roughly the same length (410–420-ft. long) the three spillways feature varying degrees of slopes and turns to keep you coming back for more.

✔ *Humunga Kowabunga* consists of three 214-foot *Mount Mayday* slides that propel you down the mountain on a serpentine route through waterfalls and bat caves and past nautical wreckage at up to 30 mph before depositing you into a bubbling catch pool; each slide offers slightly different views and thrills. Seating also is available for non-Kowabunga folks whose kids have commissioned them to "watch me." Women should wear a one-piece on the slides (unless you don't mind putting on a different sort of show for gawkers). This attraction has a *48-inch height minimum*.

✔ *Ketchakiddie Creek* is a kiddie area designed exclusively for the kiddie set (2–5 years). An innovative water playground, it has bubbling fountains in which kids can frolic, mini waterslides, a pint-size white-water tubing run, spouting whales and squirting seals, rubbery crocodiles on which to climb, grottoes to explore, and waterfalls under which to loll.

✔ *Typhoon Lagoon* is the park's main swimming area. This large (2.75 million gallons) and lovely lagoon (one of the world's largest inland wave pools) is the size of two football fields and is surrounded by a white sandy beach. The chlorinated water has a turquoise hue much like the waters of the Caribbean. Large waves hit the shore every 90 seconds. A foghorn sounds to warn you when a wave is coming. Young children can wade in the lagoon's more peaceful tidal pools — *Blustery Bay* and *Whitecap Cove*.

You can catch a wave at popular **early-bird surfing sessions** that take place at the lagoon on select mornings before the park officially opens. For those not brave enough to learn in the ocean, this controlled environment may be a good alternative. For more information on the surfing program, see Chapter 27.

✔ *White-Water Rides,* found in *Mount Mayday,* is the setting for three white-water rafting adventures — *Keelhaul Falls, Mayday Falls,* and *Gang Plank Falls* — all of which offer steep drops coursing through caves and passing lush scenery. *Keelhaul Falls* has the most spiraling route, *Mayday Falls* has the steepest drops and fastest water, and the slightly tamer *Gang Plank Falls* uses large tubes so that the whole family can pile on.

See map on p. 168. Located off Buena Vista Drive between the Downtown Disney Marketplace and Disney–MGM Studios. ☎ *407-560-4141.* www.disneyworld.com. *Admission: $34 adults, $28 kids 3–9. Open: Daily 10 a.m.–5 p.m., with extended hours during some holiday periods and summer.*

Enjoying the Holiday Season at Disney

Disney uses extra pixie dust during the holidays as the parks and resorts are decked out even more spectacularly than you can even imagine. They bring out the holiday spirit in a way only Disney can. Lights, trees, caroling, and special activities begin around Thanksgiving and last until the first of the new year. For more information on all of the events in this section, call ☎ 407-934-7639 or check out www.disneyworld.com.

Three of the best Yuletide attractions include the following:

- ✔ *Mickey's Very Merry Christmas Party,* an after-dark ticketed event (7 p.m. to midnight), takes place on select nights at **Magic Kingdom** and offers a traditional Christmas parade and a breathtaking fireworks display. The charge ($44 adults, $35 kids 3–9; if purchased in advance you will save $5 per ticket) includes cookies, cocoa, and a souvenir photo. The best part? Shorter lines for the rides that are open.

- ✔ *The Candlelight Procession* at **Epcot** features hundreds of candle-holding carolers, a celebrity narrator telling a Christmas story, a 450-voice choir, and a 50-piece orchestra. Also held on select nights, this moving event features several celebrities during its five-week run. Normal theme park admission ($60 adults, $48 kids 3–9) is charged.

- ✔ *The Osborne Family Spectacle of Lights* came to **Disney–MGM Studios** in 1995, when an Arkansas family ran into trouble with hometown authorities over their multimillion-light display. It seems they'd committed the ultimate Little Rock sin, taking to heart the old hymn that says, "You can't be a beacon if your light don't shine." Their Christmas-light collection of 2-million-plus blinkers, twinklers, and strands was so bright that their neighbors complained. (Imagine it next to your bedroom window!) After the flow of faithful spectators in cars caused mile-long backups, the neighbors, finally seeing the light, went to court. Disney came to the rescue and, in 1995, moved the whole thing to Orlando, adding a million or so bulbs to the display. You can see it all for the normal park admission ($60 adults, $48 kids 3–9).

- ✔ For those 21 and over, Downtown Disney's **Pleasure Island** features an *Island Wide New Year's Eve* celebration featuring big name performers (in the past acts have included Cheap Trick, Tone Loc, Kurtis Blow, and Kim Waters among others). Tickets include entrance to all the P.I. clubs and a spectacular midnight fireworks display — not to mention all the loud music your ears can handle.

The other Orlando parks and many of the WDW resorts hold their own holiday festivities featuring special activities, spectacular decorations, holiday-themed parades, and more. Be sure to ask in advance or check with your concierge or at guest services when you arrive.

Sailing the Seas with Disney

It took them a while to catch on, which is unusual for the Disney folks, but they finally discovered another place to expand their empire — the high seas. Despite delays, the **Disney Cruise Line** launched the *Disney Magic* and the *Disney Wonder* in 1998 and 1999, respectively.

The two ships have small differences. The *Magic* is Art Deco, with a giant Mickey in its three-level lobby and a *Beauty and the Beast* mural in its top restaurant, Lumiere's. The *Wonder* is Art Nouveau; Ariel commands its lobby, and its featured eatery, Triton's, sports a mural from *The Little Mermaid*. Both ships have recently been refurbished.

The restaurants, nightlife, shows, and other onboard activities on both vessels are very family-oriented (indeed, the Disney ships are the best in all cruisedom for kids). One of the ships' unique features is a dine-around option that lets you move among main restaurants (each ship has four) from night to night while keeping the same servers. Disney also offers **Castaway Cay,** its own private Bahamian island featuring water sports and other activities.

The *Disney Magic* sails seven-day eastern Caribbean (St. Thomas, St. Maarten, and Castaway Cay) and seven-day western Caribbean (Key West, Grand Cayman, Cozumel, and Castaway Cay) itineraries on an alternating basis year-round. A special 10-day Caribbean cruise is scheduled for the end of December 2006; call for details and rates. The *Disney Wonder* offers shorter three- and four-day Bahamas cruises that are often (though not necessarily) sold as part of seven-day vacation packages, combining the sailings with a **Walt Disney World** land experience. Subtle differences aside, these two ships are nearly identical twins. Both are 83,000 tons with 12 decks, 875 extra large cabins, and room for up to 1,755 guests (when each ship's children's berths are filled to capacity, that total can reach as high as 3,325). The ships have some adults-only areas, but no casinos.

Recently updated, the line's free kids' programs are some of the best at sea. Just like at Disney World, costumed Disney characters are available at scheduled times during the voyage, so that passengers can line up for hugs and photos. The children's program is divided into four age groups: the **Flounder's Reef Nursery** for ages 3 months to 3 years; **Disney's Oceaneer Club** for ages 3 to 7; **Disney's Oceaneer Lab** for ages 8 to 12; and **The Stack** for ages 13 to 17. Each program offers numerous age-appropriate activities and diversions.

Especially important to parents with young kids, Disney has expanded its **Flounder's Reef Nursery** on both ships to hold as many as 30 children with a child/counselor ratio of four to one. Extended hours are featured on seven-night cruises so parents can dine alone, try a spa treatment, or sneak off for a shore excursion. Best of all, unlike other cruise lines, the nursery welcomes infants from as young as 12 weeks old to 3-year-old toddlers. The space has cribs and counselors do change diapers (though you must supply them). The price is $6 per child per hour with a two-hour minimum.

 You can get discounted fares if you book well in advance and go during non-peak periods. The line also offers special fares for kids 3 to 12 traveling as a third, fourth, or fifth passenger sharing a cabin with two adults.

All cruises depart from Port Canaveral, which is about an hour east of Orlando by car. If you buy a Land and Sea package, transportation to and from Orlando is included. For more information, call Disney Cruise Line or check out its very informative Web site, which also allows you to plan and reserve shore excursions before you go.

Hwy. 528 at A1A, Cape Canaveral. ☎ *800-951-3532.* www.disneycruise.com. *Seven-day land-sea packages include three or four days afloat with the rest of the week at a WDW resort. Prices range from $799–$5,199 for adults, $399–$2,199 for kids 3–12, and $139 for kids younger than 3, depending on your choice of resort and stateroom. Some packages include round-trip air, and unlimited admission to Disney parks, Pleasure Island, and other attractions. Cruise-only options for three nights are $399–$2,849 for adults, $229–$1,099 for kids 3–12, and $99 for those younger than 3; four-night cruises are $499–$3,249 for adults, $329–$1,199 for kids 3–12, and $99 for kids younger than 3.*

Chapter 17

Shopping in Walt Disney World

. . . .

In This Chapter

▶ Getting money-saving tips
▶ Shopping inside the parks
▶ Cruising the shopping districts outside of Disney
▶ Taking advantage of airport options

. . . .

*P*art of the fun of going on vacation is stocking up on souvenirs. A trip to Walt Disney World shouldn't be any different — unless you want to arrive home with money in your wallet. In this chapter, you discover the ins and outs of shopping for Walt Disney World mementos.

Money-Saving Tips for Top-Notch Take-Homes

The kids are tugging at your shirt, begging you for 14-carat mouse ears and the biggest stuffed Mickey on the planet, your mother just has to have a pair of Goofy slippers, and you've always wanted a crystal Cinderella clock for the den. Then you see the price tags. *Gasp!* Are they kidding? No, unfortunately, they are not.

You're an emotional and physical captive of a commercial enterprise sprinkled with feel-good pixie dust when you're at Disney. Now I'm just guessing and don't know this for sure, but I think Disney uses a simple formula for setting prices: Start with reasonable retail and then multiply . . . by three. Don't panic just yet, not everything is so completely out of reach, and if you keep reading I'll point you in the right direction.

But no matter how much I warn you, most of you probably won't escape without a sizable contribution to the stockholders' fund, especially if it's your first trip to Walt Disney World or you have kids in tow. So before you start spending, here are a few things to think about:

> ✔ If there's a **Disney Store** near your hometown, some of what's sold in the Disney parks likely is sold in there as well. You can also get a fairly large selection of it on the Internet through the shopping link

at www.disney.com. So there's no need to rush into a purchase. (Notable exceptions however are goods sold in the **World Showcase** pavilions at **Epcot** and **Walt Disney World** logo merchandise sold throughout the parks.)

✔ At the other end of the spectrum, many **WDW** shops sell products themed to their particular area of the park (such as the shops found at the exit of many rides or the kiosks found throughout the different lands), and finding the identical item elsewhere in the parks (let alone outside the parks) may be difficult at best. (You do get an eleventh-hour shot at the airport, but the selection is limited. See "Last Chance: Shopping for Disney Doodads at the Airport," at the end of this chapter.)

✔ Don't be fooled the discount stores offering you a "bargain." You usually won't find bargains or discounts on true or authentic **WDW** merchandise anywhere. If someone offers you one (especially outside the parks), beware. The bargain or discount may be a cheap imitation or knock off — or worse, "hot."

✔ Theme park shops keep the same hours as the attractions: usually 9 a.m. to 6 p.m. (or whatever time the park happens to close that day) though the main shops near the parks' entrances often remain open at least a few minutes extra for those last minute shoppers on their way out.

✔ Don't forget to account for the 6.5 percent sales tax on purchases.

Loading Up Your Cart at Walt Disney World

In general, you'll find three categories of merchandise in the WDW parks. Souvenirs that scream "Disney!" are the most common. (The number of choices — from Ariel to Winnie the Pooh and beyond — can, and will, fog your brain.) Collectibles, including some not related to Disney, are another. You find these items in some of the **Main Street** shops in the **Magic Kingdom,** as well as around the **World Showcase** in **Epcot** and at the **Downtown Disney Marketplace.** The last category, merchandise native to the 11 countries showcased throughout Epcot's World Showcase, and is completely unrelated to Disney whatsoever, is aptly considered a **World Showcase** specialty.

Why lug all your bulky purchases around? You can send your purchases from any store to designated areas near the entrance, where you can pick them up as you leave the park that day. In the **Magic Kingdom,** you can pick up packages at *Guest Relations* next to *City Hall* in the Plaza area. In **Epcot,** you can send your packages to *The Gift Stop* in the Entrance Plaza or the *World Traveler* at the International Gateway in World Showcase. **Disney–MGM Studios** shop clerks will send your goodies to the package pickup next to Oscar's Super Service in front of the park. And you can pick up your **Animal Kingdom** purchases at *Garden Gate Gifts* near the Entrance Plaza. (Allow at least three hours for delivery.) If you're a Disney resort guest, you can have your packages delivered to your room for free — ask the shops about this service. Packages, however, may not arrive until the next afternoon if purchased prior to 7 p.m.; if purchased after 7 p.m. they will arrive the second afternoon after your purchase was made.

Magic Kingdom

The Emporium along **Main Street, U.S.A.**, has a large selection of *Disneyana* including pricey collectibles such as Minnie Mouse cookie jars and vintage Mickey Mouse wristwatches, as well as apparel, toys, and trinkets. The **Fantasy Faire** inside *Cinderella Castle* sells family crests, tapestries, suits of armor, and other medieval wares, as well as miniature carousels.

Pirates Bazaar in **Adventureland** peddles hats, Captain Hook T-shirts, ships in bottles, toy muskets, and loads of other yo-ho-ho buccaneer booty, in addition to jewelry and a small selection of resort wear. It's outside the *Pirates of the Caribbean* ride. Also look for the tiny little shack (selling mostly camera supplies) just up the way before you get to **Frontierland** — it sells Mickey and Minnie two-way radios, which are a great way to communicate in the parks.

The **Frontier Trading Post** in **Frontierland** hawks cowboy hats, western shirts, coonskin caps, turquoise jewelry, belts, and toy rifles.

The **Yankee Trader** in **Liberty Square** is a charming country store that sells Lion King and Pooh cookie jars, Disney cookie cutters, and fancy food items. **Ye Olde Christmas Shoppe** features plenty of holiday ideas, some Disney, some not.

Sir Mickey's in **Fantasyland** is supply central for a variety of Disney-motif trinkets. Wares at **Tinker Bell's Treasures** include Peter Pan merchandise, costumes (Tinker Bell, Snow White, Cinderella, Pocahontas, and others), and collector dolls. And just at the exit of **Mickey's PhilharMagic**, you'll find a collection of trinkets, toys, and T's that feature Donald Duck.

Pooh's Thotful Shop in **Fantasyland** is dedicated to 100 Acre gang merchandise, including plenty of Pooh and Tigger items.

Inside the **Toontown Hall of Fame** you'll find a large array of toys, T's, candy, and other Disney-themed trinkets.

Mickey's Star Traders and **Merchants of Venus** in **Tomorrowland** is another place to get a look at Disney collectibles along with just about anything else Disney, and the spaceship shaped kiosk just outside **Buzz Lightyear's Space Ranger Spin** has enough Toy Story toys to fill any kid's toy chest.

Epcot

World Showcase pavilions carry unique and unusual items that represent their respective pavilion's country. Following are some of the shopping highlights.

Heritage Manor Gifts in **The American Adventure** sells autographed presidential photographs, needlepoint samplers, quilts, pottery, candles, Davy Crockett hats, books on American history, historically costumed dolls, classic political campaign buttons, and vintage newspapers with banner headlines such as "Nixon Resigns!" You can also buy Disney art and character merchandise, as well as popular Disney pins.

The **Canada** pavilion's **Northwest Mercantile** carries sandstone and soapstone carvings, fringed leather vests, duck decoys, moccasins, an array of stuffed animals, Native American dolls and spirit stones, rabbit-skin caps, knitted sweaters, and, of course, maple syrup.

China's Yong Feng Shangdian Department Store is a bustling marketplace filled with an array of merchandise including silk robes, brocade pajamas, lacquer and inlaid mother-of-pearl furniture, jade figures, cloisonné vases, tea sets, silk rugs and embroideries, dolls, fans, wind chimes, and clothing. Artisans demonstrate calligraphy here, too.

Emporia is the covered shopping area filled with several little boutiques found in **France**. Merchandise includes art, cookbooks, cookware, wines (there's a tasting counter), Madeline and Babar books and dolls, perfumes, and original letters written by famous Frenchmen, such as Napoleon. This is one of only two locations in the entire world to feature signature Guerlain fragrances (cosmetics and accessories are available as well).

Germany's shops feature Hümmel figurines (one of only eight worldwide locations to carry a complete collection), crystal, glassware, cookware, cuckoo clocks, cowbells, Alpine hats, German wines (there's a tasting counter) and foods, books, and toys (German Disneyana, teddy bears, dolls, and puppets). An artisan sometimes demonstrates molding and painting Hümmel figures; another paints detailed scenes on eggs.

La Cucina Italiana and **Il Bel Cristallo** in **Italy** stock cameo and delicate filigree jewelry, fine-leather goods, Armani figurines, cookware, Italian wines and foods, Murano and other Venetian glass, alabaster figurines, inlaid wooden music boxes, and festive Carnivale masks.

The **Mitsukoshi Department Store** (Japan's answer to Sears) stocks lacquerware, kimonos, kites, fans, dolls in traditional costumes, origami books, samurai swords, Japanese Disneyana, bonsai trees, Japanese foods, Netsuke carvings, pottery, and electronics. Artisans in the courtyard demonstrate the ancient arts of *anesaiku* (shaping brown rice candy into dragons, unicorns, and dolphins), *sumi-e* (calligraphy), and *origami* (paper folding). Kids interested in the *Hello Kitty* gang or anime cartoons will find plenty to ask you to buy.

Great things to buy at Epcot

Epcot's **World Showcase** shines in the shopping department. Although the selections here change from time to time and may not necessarily represent bargains — **Disney** never quits trying to lighten your wallet — they are the kind of unique and unusual items you may not find anywhere else.

- ✔ If you're into silver jewelry, don't miss the *Mexico* pavilion. You can find trinkets ranging from simple flowered hair clips to stone-and-silver bracelets.

- ✔ The shops in *Norway* have great sweaters and Scandinavian trolls that are so ugly, you're likely to fall in love with them.

- ✔ In *China*, browse through jade teardrop earrings, Disney art, and more. Its merchandise is among the most expensive and most fetching in **Epcot.**

- ✔ *Italy's* 100-percent silk scarves and ties come in several patterns.

- ✔ Style-conscious teenagers may love a Taquia knit cap, something of a colorful fezlike chapeau, that's available in *Morocco.* You can also find beautifully painted pottery.

- ✔ Wimbledon shirts, shorts, and skirts are among the hard-to-find items in the *United Kingdom,* which also has an assortment of tea accessories, sweaters, and Beatles memorabilia.

Given Tokyo's notorious astronomical prices, this store may be one of the few places in **WDW** where you can actually score a relative bargain.

Shops in and around the **Plaza de Los Amigos** (a Mexican *mercado* market with a tiered fountain and street lamps) display an array of leather goods, baskets, sombreros, piñatas, pottery, embroidered dresses and blouses, maracas, jewelry, serapes, paper flowers, colorful papier-mâché birds, and blown-glass objects (an artisan gives glass-blowing demonstrations).

Morocco's streets lead to the **souk,** a bustling marketplace where handcrafted pottery, brassware, hand-knotted Berber carpets, colorful Rabat carpets, ornate silver and camel-bone boxes, straw baskets, and prayer rugs are sold. You can also catch weaving demonstrations during the day.

Norway's shops sell hand-knitted wool hats and sweaters (including a collection by Dale of Norway), toys (there's a LEGO table where kids can play), trolls, woodcarvings, Scandinavian foods, pewterware, jewelry, and Christmas items. There's also a nice selection of fragrances, body creams, and candles.

High Street and **Tudor Lane shops** in the **United Kingdom** display a broad sampling of British merchandise, including toy soldiers, Paddington bears, Thomas the Tank Engine wooden train sets, personalized coats of arms, Scottish clothing (cashmere and Shetland sweaters, golf wear, tams, knits, and tartans), Wimbledon sportswear, fine English china, Waterford crystal, and pub items such as tankards and dartboards. A tea shop occupies a replica of Anne Hathaway's thatch-roofed 16th-century cottage in Stratford-upon-Avon. Other stores represent the Georgian, Victorian, Queen Anne, and Tudor periods.

Disney–MGM Studios

The **Animation Gallery** carries collectible animation cels, books about animation, arts-and-crafts kits for future animators, and collector figurines. **Sid Cahuenga's One-of-a-Kind** sells autographed photos of the stars, original movie posters, and star-touched jewelry and other memorabilia. Over at **The Darkroom/Cover Story,** you can have your photograph put on the cover of your favorite magazine, anything from *Forbes* to *Psychology Today* to *Golf Digest.* **Celebrity 5 & 10,** modeled after a 1940s Woolworth's, is filled with unique Disneyesque housewares, MGM Studio T-shirts, and movie posters.

Many of the park's major attractions also have shops or kiosks filled with items such as *Indiana Jones* adventure clothing, *Little Mermaid* stuffed characters, *Star Wars* light sabers and LEGO sets, and so on.

Animal Kingdom

The **Oasis's Outpost Shop** deals in T-shirts, sweatshirts, hats, toys, and other souvenir items.

Beastly Bazaar in *Safari Village* has a wide selection of items related to *The Tree of Life* and the show, *It's Tough to Be a Bug!* Along with chocolates, candies, and home décor items. **Creature Comforts** sells clothing, stuffed animals, and toys, and is mostly geared for kids. **Island Mercantile** offers theme merchandise that represents the park's lands with a plentitude of character merchandise. They also have a hair-braiding service and are a pin-trading location.

Mombasa Marketplace/Ziwani Traders in *Africa* sells *Kilimanjaro Safaris* apparel and gifts, as well as realistic animal items, including beautiful wood carvings, and other authentic African gifts.

Chester & Hester's Dinosaur Treasures in **DinoLand U.S.A.** has wild and wacky dinosaur souvenirs, tons of toys, and T-shirts.

Other shopping ops include **Mandala Gifts** in *Asia* just beyond *Kali River Rapids* and the **Dino Institute Shop** just beyond *DINOSAUR* in *DinoLand U.S.A.*

Disney Shopping Outside the Theme Parks

Don't think that the enticement to spend money magically disappears when you step outside the theme parks. Walt Disney World also encompasses some shopping districts that house a multitude of shops — some of which carry merchandise you can't get anywhere else — that offer you the chance to blow your budget.

Disney West Side

Disney West Side has many rather unique specialty stores where you can find plenty of unusual gifts and souvenirs.

Guitar Gallery tempts string-strokers with custom guitars, including one-of-a-kind and rare collectibles with a selection of accessories, books, and clothing. **Hoypoloi Gallery** is a New Age store offering artsy glass, ceramics, sculptures, and other decorative doodads made from metal, stone, and wood. **Magnetron** is — well, wow! Can there be a market for this many refrigerator magnets? **Magic Masters,** a re-creation of Harry Houdini's private library, is the place for magic tricks and illusions, and the magic experts here often entertain guests with a few tricks of their own. Smoking may be on the way to sayonara-ville, but **Sosa Family Cigars** beckons with sweet smells and a tradition reaching back to yesterday's Cuba. Over at **Starabilias,** the main events are jukeboxes, Coke machines, and other lost treasures.

Disney West Side (☎ 407-828-3800; www.disneyworld.com) is on Buena Vista Drive. From I-4, exit on Highway 536 or Highway 535 and follow the signs. Some shop times vary, but the complex is open daily from 9:30 a.m. to 11 p.m.

Downtown Disney Marketplace

Basin offers a cornucopia of fresh-made bath products, including glycerin soaps and wonderful bath bombs. **The Art of Disney** is a one-of-a-kind gallery that also includes sculpture, crystal, and more. **EUROSPAIN** comes calling with products that crystal and metal artists make before your eyes. **Once Upon a Toy** has Disney-themed versions of many popular games, including Mr. Potato Head and Monopoly.

The newly-renovated **LEGO Imagination Center** is one of the best shops around. This spot is fabulous for moms and dads to relax while your young whippersnappers unwind in a free LEGO building play area beside the store. **World of Disney** comes with the (don't-hold-it-to-them) promise that if it exists, and it's Disney, it's on their shelves.

Downtown Disney Marketplace (☎ 407-828-3800; www.disneyworld.com) is on Buena Vista Drive at Hotel Plaza Boulevard. From I-4, exit on Highway 536 or Highway 535 and follow the signs. It's open daily from 9:30 a.m. to 11 p.m.

Part V

Exploring the Rest of Orlando

The 5th Wave   By Rich Tennant

"Since we lost the dolphins, business hasn't been quite the same."

In this part . . .

*M*ickey may be the toughest mouse around, but he doesn't own Orlando anymore. Yes, this is still the town that Disney built, but the fact is, half of the eight big-league attractions in Orlando don't belong to Disney.

This part of the book explores the rest of Orlando, including the exciting attractions at Universal Orlando as well as what you find at SeaWorld, Discovery Cove, the smaller attractions, and some of the best shopping venues outside the parks. It also includes information on great day trips to two of the most popular attractions outside of the immediate Orlando area: Busch Gardens and the Kennedy Space Center.

Chapter 18

Universal Studios Florida

● ●

In This Chapter

▶ Discovering helpful Universal facts

▶ Seeing the best things at Universal Studios Florida

▶ Eating at USF

▶ Shopping for souvenirs

● ●

*W*ith two studios in Orlando, you soon get the picture, literally and figuratively, about which studio produces what films in the movie business. Both **Universal** and **Disney–MGM Studios** (see Chapter 14) have plenty to offer, and they both spend plenty of money plugging their movies and characters. At Universal, that investment means you'll encounter the *Mummy, Twister, Terminator, Jaws, E.T., Shrek, Barney,* and many more. You'll also find plenty of grown-up, cutting edge, hurl-'em-and-twirl-'em rides, such as *Back to the Future, Men in Black Alien Attack,* and *Earthquake.* Universal has recently made great strides to appeal to younger kids as well, especially with *Woody Woodpecker's KidZone* and its pint-size rides, shows, and play areas.

As a plus, Universal is a working television and movie studio, so occasionally there's some live filming done at Nickelodeon's sound stages or elsewhere in the park. You can also see reel history displayed in the form of actual sets exhibited along Hollywood Boulevard and Rodeo Drive. A talented troupe of actors portraying Universal stars, such as the Blues Brothers, or a wide range of not-so-recognizable characters, often wander the park chatting with guests along the way. And park shows, such as *Terminator 2: 3D Battle Across Time* and *Fear Factor Live* deliver heart-pumping excitement.

In this chapter, I give you helpful hints and basic information about visiting Universal Studios Florida and experiencing its attractions.

Finding Out Important Park Information

Before I get on to the good stuff of USF, I first need to get the logistical information out of the way; believe me, you'll appreciate it when you get there.

Universal Studios Florida

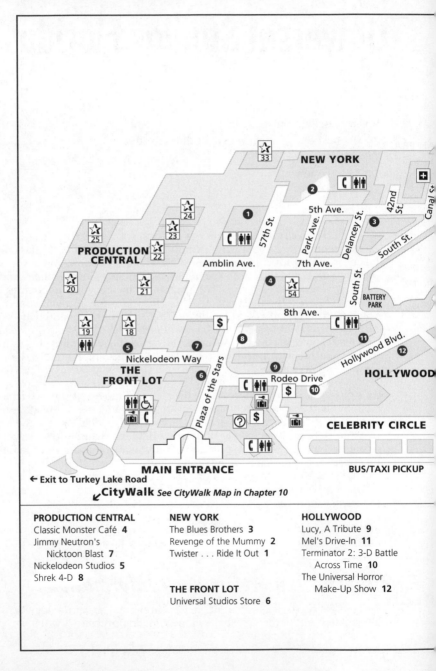

← Exit to Turkey Lake Road

CityWalk See CityWalk Map in Chapter 10

PRODUCTION CENTRAL
Classic Monster Café **4**
Jimmy Neutron's
    Nicktoon Blast **7**
Nickelodeon Studios **5**
Shrek 4-D **8**

NEW YORK
The Blues Brothers **3**
Revenge of the Mummy **2**
Twister . . . Ride It Out **1**

THE FRONT LOT
Universal Studios Store **6**

HOLLYWOOD
Lucy, A Tribute **9**
Mel's Drive-In **11**
Terminator 2: 3-D Battle
    Across Time **10**
The Universal Horror
    Make-Up Show **12**

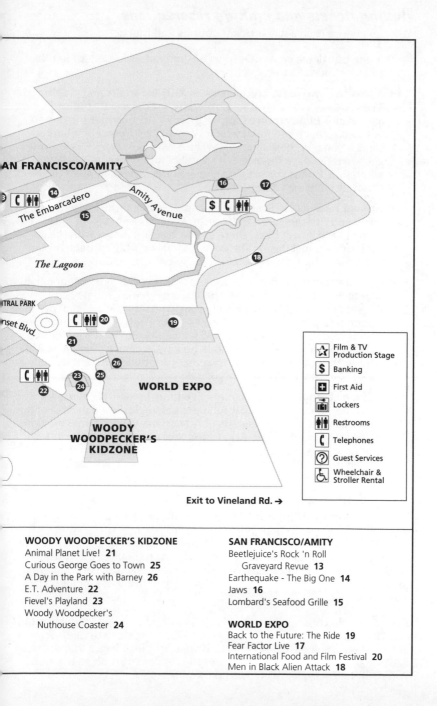

Exit to Vineland Rd. →

Legend:
- Film & TV Production Stage
- $ Banking
- First Aid
- Lockers
- Restrooms
- Telephones
- Guest Services
- Wheelchair & Stroller Rental

WOODY WOODPECKER'S KIDZONE
Animal Planet Live! **21**
Curious George Goes to Town **25**
A Day in the Park with Barney **26**
E.T. Adventure **22**
Fievel's Playland **23**
Woody Woodpecker's Nuthouse Coaster **24**

SAN FRANCISCO/AMITY
Beetlejuice's Rock 'n Roll Graveyard Revue **13**
Earthequake - The Big One **14**
Jaws **16**
Lombard's Seafood Grille **15**

WORLD EXPO
Back to the Future: The Ride **19**
Fear Factor Live **17**
International Food and Film Festival **20**
Men in Black Alien Attack **18**

Buying tickets and making reservations

You can choose from several ticket options and tours:

- ✔ A **one-day ticket** costs $60 (plus 6.5 percent sales tax) for adults, $48 for children 3 to 9.

- ✔ A **two-day, two-park, bonus pass,** is $105 for adults and children. These passes enable you to move between Universal Studios Florida and Islands of Adventure (see Chapter 19) throughout the day so you can go back and forth whenever you like. *Note:* For a limited time, if you buy them online (www.universalorlando.com), you get two more days for free, for a total of four consecutive days of admission. Bonus passes also give you free access at night to select CityWalk clubs (see Chapter 25).

- ✔ **Annual Passes** (the **Preferred Annual Pass** and the **Power Pass**) allow entry to the park for an entire year (some blackout dates apply to the Power Pass; there are no blackout dates with the Preferred Annual Pass). The cost is $180 and $120 respectively. For more details check out www.universalorlando.com.

- ✔ The **FlexTicket** multiday, multipark option is the most economical way to see the various "other-than-Disney" parks. You pay one price to visit any and all of the participating parks during a 14-day period. A four-park pass to Universal Studios Florida, Islands of Adventure, Wet 'n Wild, and SeaWorld is $185 for adults and $151 for children 3 to 9. A five-park pass, which adds Busch Gardens in Tampa, is $225 for adults and $190 for kids. You can order the FlexTicket by calling ☎ 407-363-8000 or online by going to www.universalorlando.com.

- ✔ **Universal Studios Florida** offers five-hour, guided **VIP tours** for $100 per person for just USF, $125 per person for a two-park, six-hour tour that also includes Islands of Adventure. Guided tours include line-cutting privileges and preferred seating at several attractions, and they start at 10 a.m. and noon daily. For more information on the VIP tour, call ☎ 407-363-8295. *Note:* The price of the VIP tour includes neither the 6.5 percent sales tax *nor admission to the park!*

The park prices are not the only place you'll wish you'd left your wallet behind. Expect to spend up to $2.50 for a coke, $1.80 for a cup of coffee, about $5 for a beer, $2.60 for popcorn, and $2.50 for bottled water. However, you can save 10 percent on your purchases at any gift shop or on a meal by showing your **AAA (American Automobile Association) card.** This discount isn't available at food or merchandise carts. Likewise, tobacco, candy, film, collectibles, and sundry items aren't included in discounts.

For information about new travel packages and theme-park information, call ☎ **800-711-0080,** 800-224-4233, or 407-363-8000; write to *Guest Services* at Universal Studios Florida, 1000 Universal Studios Plaza, Orlando, FL 32819-7601; or visit its Web site at www.universalorlndo.com. Once you're at the park, just head over to *Guest Services.*

Universal Orlando is located about half a mile north of I-4's Kirkman Road/ Highway 435 exit. You may find construction in the area, so keep an eye out for the road signs directing you to Universal Orlando.

The park is open 365 days a year. **Park hours** generally are from 9 a.m. to 6 or 7 p.m., though they vary seasonally and might close as late as 10 p.m. during the summer and on holidays. Call or check online before you go for exact times.

Locating special services and facilities

In case you forgot to bring essential items, or if you need special assistance while at the park, here's a list of services and facilities that may come in handy:

- **ATMs** accepting cards from banks using the Cirrus, STAR, and Plus systems are on the outside and just inside Universal's entrance and in San Francisco/Amity near Lombard's Seafood Grille restaurant.

- You can find **baby-changing tables** in all men's and women's restrooms; **nursing facilities** are at **Family Services,** just inside the main entrance and to the right. (*Family Services* doesn't sell diapers or infant supplies of any kind, so be sure that you bring enough of your own.)

- Disposable **cameras** and **film** (and limited digital supplies) are available at the **On Location** shop in the Front Lot, just inside the main entrance. One-hour photo developing is available, but I don't recommend paying park prices. You can find many cheaper one-hour or overnight places around town, including many near tourist-area motels.

- Universal has its own version of Disney's FASTPASS, called **Universal EXPRESS.** The system operates much the same as Disney's does. You feed your admission ticket into the machine at the EXPRESS Distribution Center for a given ride (they're usually located close to the entrance of rides that accept EXPRESS passes) and you get a second pass (along with your park ticket) stamped with a designated time window in which you can return to ride. At any time within the window you can head straight for the shorter EXPRESS line (usually no more than 15 minutes) and off you go. You can only get one EXPRESS pass at a time, but similar to Disney, you can get a second pass just two hours after the first one is issued — the time you can obtain your next EXPRESS pass is printed on the first pass.

  If you're not willing to chance that there will be an EXPRESS pass left (and they do run out, sometimes as early as noon during peak periods) you can purchase the **Universal EXPRESS Plus Pass.** It allows access to the Express line at each and every attraction that accepts the Universal Express Pass without having to continually obtain separate passes or wait for any time limits to expire before heading to Universal Express line at the next attraction. The price varies with the season, and I have seen prices as high as $39 during peak periods. In addition, it is only good for one day at one park, regardless of what type of park tickets you hold, and it can only be used once at each of the attractions.

✔ Universal offers a separate line-beating option as a perk for those visitors staying at its resorts. All guests of the **Portofino Bay, Hard Rock,** and **Royal Pacific** hotels have to do is to show their room keys to get at or near the front of the line for most of the rides and even most of the restaurants.

✔ You can find **first aid centers** between New York and San Francisco, next to Louie's Italian Restaurant, and just inside the main entrance next to *Guest Services.*

✔ **Rent lockers** for $8 and $10 a day plus a $2 refundable deposit across from *Guest Services,* near the main entrance.

✔ **Report lost children** to any staff member and then go to *Guest Services* near the main entrance or Security (behind Louie's Italian Restaurant, between *New York* and *San Francisco*). *Make sure children younger than 7 wear name-tags inside their clothing for easy identification in case they get lost.*

✔ When **parking** in multilevel garages, write down your location, including the character, level, row, and space number so you can find your car later. Parking costs $9 for cars and trucks. Valet parking is available for $16. After 6 p.m., parking is free. Universal's garages are connected to its parks by walkways and a series of moving sidewalks, but reaching the gates can take a while.

✔ The park provides **car assistance,** including battery jumps. If you need assistance with your car, raise the hood and tell any parking attendant your location. Use the call boxes located throughout the parking garage to call for security.

✔ **Pet care** for your small animals is available at the shelter in the parking garages for $10 a day (no overnight stays), but you'll have to feed and walk your animals yourself. Ask the parking attendant where you pay for parking to direct you to the kennel.

✔ **Rent strollers** in Amity and at *Guest Services,* just inside the entrance to the right. The cost is $10 for a single and $16 for a double.

✔ You can rent regular **wheelchairs** for $12 per day in Amity and at *Guest Services* just inside the main gate. Electric wheelchairs are $40 per day. Both require a $50 deposit and a signed contract.

✔ **Package delivery** is available for purchases made at park stores (though not at the kiosks and carts). You can have your purchases sent to the Universal Studios Store near the entrance to be picked up on your way out. If you are a guest at one of the three Universal Resorts you can have your purchased delivered to your room (though delivery will be the following day, so don't try this if it's your last day).

If you find you have arrived home without that essential USF T-shirt or all-important blaster gun, you can call ☎ **407-224-5800** and the **Universal Mail Order Department** will help. Just let them know what the item is, where it is located, and they can arrange to have it shipped to you house (for a fee, of course).

Exploring the Top Attractions

Universal matches Disney stride for stride, and in some cases is a half-step ahead, when it comes to cutting-edge rides. Real and virtual thrills, terrific special effects, mammoth screens, and 3-D action are all part of its successful mix.

The rides and shows at Universal are located in six distinctive sets: **Hollywood, New York, Production Central, San Francisco/Amity, Woody Woodpecker's KidZone,** and **World Expo.** The Front Lot serves as the parks main entrance. Universal is much better than Disney at keeping you occupied while you're standing in line. There are entertaining preshows, some of which are just as amusing or interesting as the main event, and elaborate surroundings intended to create the feeling that you've already begun your experience. Most of the lines are under cover from the sun, with the occasional water spritzer or drinking fountain nearby. Although these extras may not initially seem like a big deal, it makes your time in line far more tolerable.

The "Universal Studios Florida" map, found on page 258, will help you visualize the layout of the park.

Hollywood

Hollywood is to the right of the Front Lot, and its main streets include Rodeo Drive, Hollywood Boulevard, and Sunset Boulevard, all lined with ornate buildings in soft hues, much like you would have found in Hollywood's heyday so many years ago. Here's a list of the best that Hollywood has to offer:

✔ *Lucy — A Tribute.* This show is a remembrance of America's queen of comedy, Lucille Ball. If you love Lucy, it's a must, filled with memorabilia and a really neat interactive trivia game, but if you're pressed for time or have a handful of smaller kids along, it's skippable.

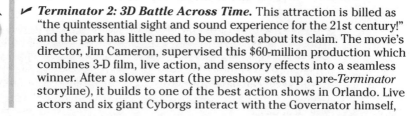

✔ *Terminator 2: 3D Battle Across Time.* This attraction is billed as "the quintessential sight and sound experience for the 21st century!" and the park has little need to be modest about its claim. The movie's director, Jim Cameron, supervised this $60-million production which combines 3-D film, live action, and sensory effects into a seamless winner. After a slower start (the preshow sets up a pre-*Terminator* storyline), it builds to one of the best action shows in Orlando. Live actors and six giant Cyborgs interact with the Governator himself, who appears on-screen (actually three huge screens). The crisp 3-D effects are among the best in Orlando. (When liquid mercury falls from the screen, cold water really hits your legs.)

"All the action was so cool, and the motorcycle and special effects were amazing. I thought for sure the hand that came out into the audience was going to grab me," says 12-year-old Ryan. The show, however, is rated **PG-13,** Universal's way of saying violence and loud noises may make it unsuitable for preteens. Younger children may find the crashing and flying 3-D effects (in conjunction with a few of the sensory effects) too intense.

 ✔ *Universal Horror Make-up Show.* This show (loaded with corny humor) gives you a behind-the-scenes look at the wizardry behind Hollywood's monster makeup. It also takes an up-close look at some cinematic make-up masterpieces, including the transformation scenes from such movies as *The Fly* and *The Exorcist.* It, too, is rated **PG-13,** mostly due to the scary on-screen characters.

New York

New York is near the back of the park and includes rides and shows set among mock-ups of 42nd and 57th streets, Park Avenue, and Delancey Street. The premiere attractions in this section are:

 ✔ *The Blues Brothers.* This foot-stomping revue takes to the street (Delancey Street, actually) five times a day. Clap along as Jake and Elwood, the "bad boys of the blues," belt out a medley of their greatest hits.

 ✔ *Twister . . . Ride it Out.* This windy incarnation of *Earthquake —
The Big One* (discussed later in this chapter) packs quite a wallop. Based on the hit film, the curtain rises on the movie town of Wakita, where Universal engineers have created a five-story funnel cloud by injecting 2 million cubic feet of air per minute. (That's enough to fill four full-size blimps.) The sensory elements are pretty incredible. Power lines spark and fall, an oak tree splits, and the storm rumbles at rock-concert level as cars, trucks, and a cow fly about while the audience watches from only 20 feet away. In the finale, the floor begins to buckle at your feet. The only downside is that you tend to get way too much water whipped at your face (it is a tornado, after all).

"You don't really ride anything as much as walk through it, but it was pretty intense," Nicolas offered. It's similar to the *Backdraft* attraction at **Universal Studios Hollywood,** though that California attraction is (sacrilege!) actually a bit better than this one. *Twister* doesn't have a minimum height, but it carries Universal's **PG-13** rating, meaning it may be a little too intense for younger children.

Hello Mummy!

Kongfrontation, long a fixture at **Universal Studios Florida,** closed in September 2002 to make room for the spring 2004 opening of *Revenge of the Mummy* in the New York section of the park. Billed as a "psychological thrill ride," the new $40-million indoor roller coaster relies on speed, pyrotechnics, and robotics to induce screams as riders hurtle through the elaborate Egyptian sets, passageways, and tombs in cars that move forward and even in reverse. Even the preshow for the waiting victims — riders, I mean riders — lends to the ominous atmosphere and includes several surprise interactive areas and a storyline that plays out as you get closer to boarding the ride.

The five-minute journey aims to prey on one's inner phobias via encounters with overhead flames, pitch-black darkness, insects, and a skeletal warrior that hops aboard your coaster. Does it work? Yes — and how. Even the most-manly man in my coaster car was screaming, though you'd have a fat chance of getting him to admit it afterwards. The best confession I got was when a friend admitted that he hasn't freaked out on a ride like that since the first time he rode the *Twilight Zone Tower of Terror* (see Chapter 14) over ten years ago (and that was before the random sequencing). So if you have any severe phobias or medical conditions, pay attention to the warnings posted, and don't even think about getting aboard. Coaster-lovers of all ages will likely make this one tops on their list. *You must be at least 48 inches tall to ride.*

Production Central

Production Central is directly behind and to the left of the Front Lot. Its main thoroughfares are Nickelodeon Way, Plaza of the Stars, and 7th and 8th avenues. Here are some of the area's highlights:

✔ *Jimmy Neutron's Nicktoon Blast.* Launched in 2003, this ride is based on the movie *Jimmy Neutron: Boy Genius.* Here, you climb aboard a Mark IV rocket and motion-simulator technology and sophisticated computer graphics send you on a spinning, careening adventure that includes a battle against Yokians — evil, egg-shaped aliens. The attraction also features characters from several popular cartoons, including Rugrats and Fairly Odd Parents. If you feel any twinge of motion sickness, simply look at any stationary object within the large theater.

"It was cool, just like being part of the TV show. The Chicken Dance was pretty funny, too," Nicolas (age 8) and his younger sister, Hailey (age 6), were impressed with this very kid-friendly ride. That having been said, kids *do need to be at least 40 inches tall to ride.* There is a small area near the front for those who would prefer to skip the moving spaceships.

✔ **Nickelodeon Studios.** Tour the soundstages where Nick shows are produced, view concept pilots, visit the kitchen where Gak and green slime are made, and try new Sega video games at the *Game Lab*. This 45-minute behind-the-scenes tour is a fun escape from the hustle of the midway, and there's plenty of audience participation. One child volunteer always gets slimed.

The studio usually doesn't open until 10 or 10:30 a.m. *The Slime Fountain* is what the kids love to see, and it erupts every 30 minutes or so (stuff tastes like applesauce from what I'm told — I couldn't stomach the idea of trying it). Occasionally Nickelodeon does shoot here, so if your kids want to be on TV, call ☎ 407-224-4233 to find out how you can become a contestant or get tickets to a taping.

✔ **Shrek 4-D.** In spring 2003, Universal opened this 4-D fractured fairy-tale based on the hit movie *Shrek*. A 15-minute show, it can be seen, heard, felt, and smelled thanks to 3-D film, motion simulators, OgreVision glasses, and other special effects, including water spritzers. The attraction picks up where the movie leaves off — enabling you to join Shrek and Princess Fiona on their honeymoon (which, predictably, gets interrupted by the evil Lord Farquaad). Fractured or not, you know this one will have a happy ending, and it's similar in style to Disney's *It's Tough to Be a Bug* (see Chapter 15) and "*Honey, I Shrunk the Audience*" (see Chapter 14). But, as with all of the Universal rides, it's a bit edgier all around. The preshow is one of the funniest in the park and is as good as the show itself. The line can stretch for miles — and the show doesn't accept EXPRESS passes — but at least you'll wait under cover from the sun.

"Awesome! Except the spiders freaked me out," 10-year-old Austin giggled. Kids not into sensory effects may get freaked out as well. This ride can also be rather bumpy, but the front row has stationary seats for those who need them.

San Francisco

San Francisco faces the waterfront, and its attractions line The Embarcadero and Amity Avenue.

✔ **Beetlejuice's Rock 'n' Roll Graveyard Revue.** Dracula, Wolfman, the Phantom of the Opera, Frankenstein and his bride, and Beetlejuice show up to scare you silly. Their funky rock musical has pyrotechnic special effects and MTV-style choreography. It's loud and lively enough to aggravate some older adults and scare small children, and it carries Universal's **PG-13** rating. Young teens seem to like it the most.

✔ **Earthquake — The Big One.** Sparks fly shortly after you board a Bay Area Rapid Transit (better known as BART) train ostensibly running from San Francisco (the real one) to Oakland. The whopper — 8.3 on the Richter scale! — hits as you pull into the Embarcadero Station, and you're left trapped as vast slabs of concrete collapse around you, a propane truck bursts into flames, a runaway train comes hurtling at you, and the station floods (65,000 gallons of water cascade down the steps). Prior to the ride, you find out how *Earthquake,* the Oscar-winning movie, was made and take a look at a $2.4-million set model. You then shuffle off to a soundstage where seven adult volunteers help re-create the big one for you.

✔ *Jaws.* As your boat heads into a 7-acre, 5-million-gallon lagoon, an ominous dorsal fin appears on the horizon (and the blockbuster film's famous score starts to run through your brain). What follows is a series of attacks by a 3-ton, 32-foot-long, mechanical great white shark that tries to sink its urethane teeth into your hide — or at least into your boat's hide. A 30-foot wall of flame caused by burning fuel surrounds your ride, and you'll truly feel the heat at this $45-million attraction.

The effects of this ride are definitely more startling after dark; during the day, it's too easy to see the shark coming. And though the attraction doesn't have any height limitations, you may want to think twice before bringing along the 5-and-younger crowd.

Woody Woodpecker's KidZone

Woody Woodpecker's KidZone contains rides and attractions sure to please the littlest members of your party. When you're traveling with young children, plan on spending plenty of time here. Highlights include:

✔ *A Day in the Park with Barney.* This musical is Universal's sadistic answer to Disney's *It's a Small World;* one of those attractions that eats the brains and ignites the nerves of anyone but 2- to 6-year-olds and their loving parents. Set in a parklike theater-in-the-round, this 25-minute musical stars the Purple One, Baby Bop, and BJ. It uses song, dance, and interactive play to deliver an environmental message. This show can be the highlight of your youngster's day. The playground next door has chimes to ring, tree houses to explore, and more.

✔ *E.T. Adventure.* You soar with E.T., who is on a mission to save his ailing planet, through the forest and into space aboard a star-bound bicycle. You also meet some new characters Steven Spielberg created for the ride, including Botanicus, Tickli Moot Moot, Horn Flowers, and Tympani Tremblies. It's a family-friendly charmer. A cool, wooded forest serves to create one of the most pleasant waits for any ride in central Florida, although you have to endure two lines before you actually make it onto the ride.

✔ *Woody Woodpecker's Nuthouse Coaster.* This ride is the top attraction in the *KidZone,* an 8-acre concession Universal Studios made after being criticized for having too little for young visitors. Sure, it's a kiddie coaster, but the *Nuthouse Coaster* will thrill some moms and dads, too. Although it's only 30 feet at its peak, this ride offers quick, banked turns while you sit in a miniature steam train. It's very much like *The Barnstormer at Goofy's Wiseacre Farm* in **Magic Kingdom** (see Chapter 12).

The ride lasts only 55 seconds, and you can wait as long as 40 minutes, but your children probably won't let you skip it if they see it. It has a *36-inch height minimum,* and kids have to be 48 inches or taller to ride without an adult.

✔ **More to Do in Woody Woodpecker's KidZone.** *Fievel's Playground* is a wet, western-themed playground with a house to climb and a small water slide. *Curious George Goes to Town* has water- and ball-shooting cannons, plus a huge water tower that empties (after an alarm), drenching anyone who doesn't run for cover.

World Expo

The smallest zone in Universal Studios Florida packs a bunch of punch in its two rides. **World Expo** is on Exposition Boulevard, between San Francisco/Amity and KidZone. The top attractions here are:

✔ *Back to the Future: The Ride.* This ride has more warnings than a centipede has legs. Topping the list, of course: If you have a problem with motion sickness, don't get on. If you don't have a problem with motion sickness, but do have a problem with other people getting motion sick on you, you may want to invest in one of the rain ponchos sold at most Universal souvenir stands. (No sense ruining your new Mickey — um, Barney — shirt, right?) Other warnings are posted for would-be riders who are pregnant or become dizzy, and for those who are claustrophobic or have neck, heart, or back problems. These warnings are all justified.

Back to the Future offers you a chance at time travel in a simulator made to look like the movie's famous DeLorean. You are herded into your car after a video briefing from Dr. Emmett Brown (actor Christopher Lloyd). Biff the Bully has stolen another DeLorean, and you have to catch him. The fate of the universe is in your hands. Along the way, you'll dive into blazing volcanic tunnels, collide with Ice Age glaciers, thunder through caves and canyons, and briefly get swallowed by a dinosaur in an eye-crossing multi-sensory adventure. You twist, you turn, you dip, you dive — all the while feeling like you're really flying.

"Wow," Ryan said, adding that he noticed that the taller people were hitting their heads in the back row. If this describes you, request one of the front seats that don't have overhead cover. By the way, riders *must be 40 inches or taller* to get aboard.

✔ *Fear Factor Live.* Taking center stage at World Expo is the all-new *Fear Factor Live.* Based on the hit NBC reality TV show, contestants (who are actual Universal Studios guests age 18 and older and who meet certain height, weight, and health restrictions) face some of their greatest fears in front of thousands of people. They'll go head to head with other competitors, each trying to outdo the other in order to be proclaimed the winner. The wild stunts, similar to what you've seen on the television show, will test both their physical and emotional limits — not to mention their stomachs. Leave it to

Universal to be the first to transform a blockbuster reality-TV show into the hottest new attraction around.

BEST OF THE BEST

✔ ***Men in Black Alien Attack.*** You and your mates have to blast the bug-eyes, or the end of the world may be at hand. You buzz the streets of New York in six-passenger cruisers, using your "zapper" to splatter up to 120 bug-eyed targets. You have to contend with return fire and distractions (noise, clouds of liquid nitrogen, and such), any of which can send you spinning out of control. Your laser tag–style gun fires infrared bullets. Earn a bonus by hitting Frank the Pug (to the right, just past the alien shipwreck). The four-minute ride relies on 360-degree spins and some scary looking insects rather than speed for its thrill factor. Near the end, you're swallowed by a giant roach (it's 30 ft. tall with 8-ft. fangs and 20-ft. claws) that explodes — dousing you with bug guts (actually warm water) — as you blast your way to safety and into the pest-control hall of fame. After you survive unscathed (well, maybe a trifle wet), Will Smith rates you anywhere from a galaxy defender to bug bait. (There are 38 possible scores.)

TIP

Men in Black often has a *much* shorter line for single riders. If you're not alone but are willing to be split up, get in this line and you will usually be able to hop right on a vehicle that has fewer than six passengers.

KID RATING

"I loved blasting those gigantic bugs and the spinning made it even more fun." Twelve-year-old Ryan clearly didn't end up as bug bait. This $70-million ride-through video game has a *42-inch height minimum.*

Grabbing a Bite to Eat

Universal Studios Florida has more than a dozen places to eat, with offerings that range from lobster to corn dogs. Quality-wise, things inside the park are on the same level as those found in the Disney parks (see Chapters 11–15), meaning that they are generally over-priced for the quality you receive. Here are our favorites by category:

✔ **Best sit-down meal:** Lombard's Seafood Grille, across from *Earthquake,* has a hearty fried clam basket, lobster, steak, pasta, and burgers ($11–$30).

✔ **Best counter service:** Universal Studios' Classic Monsters Café is one of the newer eateries in the park and serves salads, pizza, pasta, and rotisserie chicken ($6–$15). It's off 7th Avenue near *Shrek 4-D.*

✔ **Best place for hungry families:** Similar to a mall food court, the International Food and Film Festival offers a variety of food in one location. With options ranging from stir-fry to fajitas, this is a place where a family can split up and still eat under one roof. The food is far from gourmet but a cut above regular fast food ($6–$11). It's located near the back of *Animal Planet Live!* near the lagoon and the entrance to *Back to the Future.*

> ✔ **Best places for snacks:** Grab a malt ($4) and enjoy the classic atmosphere of Mel's Drive-In, located across from *The Universal Horror Make-up Show.* **The San Francisco Pastry Co.,** located across from *Earthquake,* has a glass case full of sweet treats, including a large and decadent chocolate brownie. **Brody's Ice Cream,** in Amity near *Jaws,* and **Schwab's Pharmacy,** about halfway along Hollywood Boulevard, both offer plenty of ice cream treats to cool you off on a hot day.

See Chapter 10 for the best places to grab a bite at **Universal's CityWalk.**

Shopping at Universal Studios Florida

If Disney can do it, Universal can, too. Most major attractions at Universal have a theme store attached. Just as at Disney, the prices are high, when you consider you're just buying a T-shirt, mug, or whatever.

More than 25 other shops in the park sell souvenirs ranging from *I Love Lucy* collectibles to *Men in Black* souvenirs. Be warned, however, that, unlike WDW, these shops are even more specific to individual attractions — if you see something you like, buy it. You probably won't see it in another store even throughout the park itself. Here's a sampling of the more unusual gifts available at some of the Universal stores:

> ✔ **Back to the Future — The Store.** Real fans of the movie series find plenty of intriguing stuff here. One of the more interesting is a miniature version of the *Back to the Future* DeLorean.

> ✔ **E.T.'s Toy Closet and Photo Spot.** This is the place for plush, stuffed animals, including a replica of the alien namesake.

> ✔ **MIB Gear.** Clothes, T-shirts, and everything else the well-dressed alien should own. Oh, and the cool shades that are the staple of the *Men in Black* uniform.

> ✔ **Quint's Surf Shack.** This is the place to go if you plan on hanging ten in the future. It's got all of the latest surfing apparel.

> ✔ **Sahara Traders.** A wide range of Egyptian-themed items and *Revenge of the Mummy* souvenirs near, you guessed it, the *Mummy* ride.

> ✔ **Silver Screen Collectibles.** Fans of *I Love Lucy* will adore the small variety of collector dolls. There's also a Betty Boop line. And how can you pass up a Bates Motel shower curtain?

> ✔ **Universal Studios Store.** This store, near the entrance, sells just about everything when it comes to Universal apparel. It's also the spot to pick up your packages if you've had them delivered from another store.

Index of Top Attractions by Area

Hollywood
Lucy — A Tribute
Terminator 2: 3D Battle Across Time
Universal Horror Make-up Show

New York
The Blues Brothers
Revenge of the Mummy
Twister . . . Ride It Out

Production Central
Jimmy Neutron's Nicktoon Blast
Nickelodeon Studios
Shrek 4-D

San Francisco
Beetlejuice's Rock 'n' Roll Graveyard
Revue

Earthquake — The Big One
Jaws

Woody Woodpecker's KidZone
A Day in the Park with Barney
Animal Planet Live!
Curious George Goes to Town
E.T. Adventure
Fievel's Playground
Woody Woodpecker's Nuthouse
Coaster

World Expo
Back to the Future: The Ride
Fear Factor Live
Men in Black Alien Attack

Chapter 19

Islands of Adventure

● ●

In This Chapter

▶ Getting the lowdown on IOA info
▶ Exploring the Islands
▶ Tasting the native cuisine
▶ Taking home souvenirs

● ●

*U*niversal's second theme park opened in 1999 with a vibrantly colored, cleverly themed collection of edgy, fast, and fun rides. Heart-pounding roller coasters thunder above (and, in one case, dives below) its pedestrian walkways, water rides careen through the center of the park, and uniquely themed restaurants are camouflaged to match their surroundings, adding to your overall immersion in the various "islands" in this adventure.

From the wobbly angles and day-glo colors of *Seuss Island* to the lush foliage and distant rumblings of gigantic beasts in *Jurassic Park,* Universal does an incredible job of differentiating between the various islands. As if you've been transported through a portal, each island completely envelops you in its theme, and within only steps, you've no idea any of the other islands exist. Navigation is far easier than at its sister park (Universal Studios Florida) where the studio's sets often times blend together, making it difficult to tell when you've left *New York* and entered *San Francisco.* At **Islands of Adventure,** almost the entire park, save the Port of Entry, surrounds the central sea. Between each island, a simple walkway creates a bridge from one island to the next.

This billion dollar park is divided into six islands; beginning with the **Port of Entry,** you find a marketplace filled with shops, bazaars, and eateries all occupying a street designed to recall ancient far off lands and exotic ports of call. The remaining islands include: **Seuss Landing,** where you feel as if you've jumped into the pages of the good Doctor's whimsical classic tales; **The Lost Continent,** which combines mythical and mystical enchantments; **Jurassic Park,** where you enter through a massive stone gateway, are surrounded by towering dense foliage, and can hear the rumblings of gigantic prehistoric beasts off in the distance;

Toon Lagoon, which takes you on an amusing lighthearted stroll through the classic Sunday comic strips of the past; and **Marvel Super Hero Island,** where super heroes and their arch nemeses jump off the pages of comic books to entertain and impress with their super powers. Each of the islands is listed in further detail throughout this chapter.

 Islands of Adventure boasts an incredible collection of thrill rides and coasters, with a more modest selection of play areas and somewhat tamer rides for younger adventurers. It's unquestionably the best park in town for tweens, teens, and adrenaline junkies. The trade-off is that the park features only a few shows and stage productions.

Knowing Essential Park Information

Before you embark on your journey through the park's rides and attractions, here are some mundane matters that you may need to know.

Buying tickets and making reservations

You can choose from several ticket options and tours:

- ✔ A **one-day ticket** costs $60 (plus 6.5 percent sales tax) for adults, $48 for children 3 to 9.

- ✔ A **two-day, two-park, bonus pass** is $100 for adults and kids alike, with kids younger than the age of 3 admitted free. These passes enable you to move between Islands of Adventure and Universal Studios Florida (see Chapter 18) throughout the day so you can go back and forth whenever you like. *Note:* For a limited time, if you buy your bonus pass online (www.universalorlando.com), you get 2 more days for free, for a total of 4 consecutive days of admission. Bonus passes also give you free access at night to select CityWalk clubs (see Chapter 25).

- ✔ **Annual Passes** (the **Preferred Annual Pass** and the **Power Pass**) allow entry to the park for an entire year (some blackout dates apply to the Power Pass; there are no blackout dates with the Preferred Annual Pass) The cost is $180 and $120 respectively. For more details check out www.universalorlando.com.

- ✔ The **FlexTicket** multiday, multipark option is the most economical way to see the various "other-than-Disney" parks. You pay one price to visit any and all of the participating parks during a 14-day period. A four-park pass to Islands of Adventure, Universal Studios Florida, Wet 'n Wild, and SeaWorld is $185 for adults and $151 for children 3 to 9. A five-park pass, which adds Busch Gardens in Tampa, is $225 for adults and $190 for kids. You can order the FlexTicket by calling ☎ 407-363-8000 or online by going to www.universalorlando.com.

✔ **Islands of Adventure** offers five-hour, guided **VIP tours** for $100 per person for just Islands of Adventure, $125 per person for a two-park, six-hour tour that also includes Universal Studios Florida. Guided tours include line-cutting privileges and preferred seating at several attractions, and they start at 10 a.m. and noon daily. For more information on the VIP tour, call ☎ **407-363-8295.** Note that the price of the VIP tour includes neither the 6.5 percent sales tax *nor admission to the park!*

The park prices are not the only place you'll wish you'd left your wallet behind. Expect to spend upwards of around $2.50 for a coke, $1.80 for a cup of coffee, about $5 for a beer, $2.60 for popcorn, and $2.50 for bottled water. However, you can save 10 percent on your purchases at any gift shop or on a meal by showing your **AAA (American Automobile Association) card.** This discount isn't available at food or merchandise carts. Likewise, tobacco, candy, film, collectibles, and sundry items aren't included in discounts.

For information about new travel packages and theme-park information, call ☎ **800-711-0080** or 800-224-4233; write to *Guest Services* at **Universal Studios Florida,** 1000 Universal Studios Plaza, Orlando, FL 32819-7601; or visit its Web site, www.universalorlndo.com. Once you're at the park, just head over to *Guest Services.*

Universal Orlando's Islands of Adventure is about half a mile north of I-4's Kirkman Road/Highway 435 exit. You may find construction in the area, so keep an eye out for the road signs directing you to Universal Orlando.

Islands of Adventure is open 365 days a year, generally from at least 9 a.m. to 6 or 7 p.m. Closing hours vary seasonally with peak season and holiday hours extended later into the evening, with special activities inside the park often extending the hours as well. For example, during Halloween Horror Nights, which is celebrated at both parks, the park closes around 5 p.m., reopens at around 7 p.m. (with a new admission fee), and remains open until at least midnight.

Locating special services and facilities

In case you forgot to bring essential items, or if you need special assistance while at the park, here's a list of services and facilities that may come in handy:

✔ **ATMs.** You can find machines accepting cards from banks using the Cirrus, STAR, and Plus systems outside and to the right of the park's entrance and in **The Lost Continent** near the bridge to **Jurassic Park.**

✔ **Baby-changing and nursing facilities.** Diaper-changing stations are located in all the restrooms. You can find nursing facilities at the *family services* located in the *Guest Services* building at the **Port of Entry,** but they don't sell any infant or toddler supplies like diapers, formula, or pacifiers, so make sure you come prepared with enough provisions.

Islands of Adventure

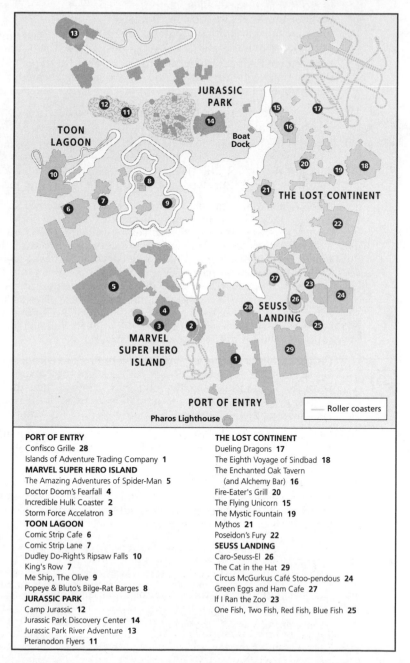

PORT OF ENTRY

MARVEL SUPER HERO ISLAND

TOON LAGOON

JURASSIC PARK

Boat Dock

THE LOST CONTINENT

SEUSS LANDING

PORT OF ENTRY

Pharos Lighthouse

—— Roller coasters

✔ **Cameras and film.** Buy film and disposable cameras at *De Foto's Expedition Photography,* inside the main entrance to the right. Digital supplies are rather limited.

✔ Universal has its own version of Disney's FASTPASS, called **Universal EXPRESS.** The system operates much the same as Disney's does. You feed your admission ticket into the machine at the EXPRESS Distribution Center for a given ride (they're usually located close to the entrance of rides that accept EXPRESS passes), and you get a second pass (along with your park ticket) stamped with a designated time window in which you can return to ride. At any time within the window, you can head straight for the shorter EXPRESS line (usually no more than 15 minutes) and off you go. You can only get one EXPRESS pass at a time, but like at Disney, you can get a second pass just two hours after the first one is issued — the time you can obtain the next EXPRESS pass is printed right on the first pass.

If you're not willing to chance that there will be an EXPRESS pass left (and they do run out, sometimes as early as noon during peak periods) you can purchase the **Universal EXPRESS Plus Pass** option. It allows access to the Express line at each and every attraction that accepts the Universal EXPRESS Pass without having to continually obtain separate passes or wait for any time limits to expire before heading to a Universal EXPRESS line at the next attraction. The price varies with the season, and I have seen prices as high as $39 during peak periods. In addition, it is only good for one day at one park, regardless of what type of park tickets you hold, and it can only be used once at each of the attractions.

✔ **Universal** offers a separate line-beating option to visitors staying at any of the three Universal resorts. All guests of the **Portofino Bay, Hard Rock,** and **Royal Pacific** hotels have to do is show their room keys to get at or near the front of the line for most of the rides and even most of the restaurants.

✔ You can find **first aid centers** just inside and to the right of the main entrance in the Port of Entry as well as in The Lost Continent, across from Oasis Coolers.

✔ **Rent lockers** for $8 and $10 a day plus a $2 refundable deposit across from *Guest Services,* near the main entrance. Lockers are a smart place to keep valuables you might lose on the wilder rides, and Islands of Adventure even provides lockers near the entrances to *The Hulk, Dueling Dragons,* and the *Jurassic Park River Adventure;* the first 45 minutes are free and every hour thereafter is $2 (with a $14 max).

✔ **Lost children.** If you lose a child, grab the nearest staff member, and he or she will direct you to the "found children" area, usually the *Guest Services* or Security area. *Make children younger than 7 wear name-tags inside their clothing for easy identification.*

✔ **Parking.** If you park in the multilevel garages, be sure to write down the level, character, row, and space number so you can find your car later. Parking costs $9 for cars and trucks. Valet parking is available for $16. If you arrive after 6 p.m., parking is free. Universal's garages are connected to its parks by walkways and a series of moving sidewalks; reaching the gates can take a while.

✔ **Car assistance.** If you need assistance with your car, raise the hood and tell any parking attendant your location, or use the call boxes located throughout the garage to call for security. The park provides battery jumps for free.

✔ **Pet care.** You can leave your small animals at the shelter in the parking garages for $10 a day (no overnight stays), but you'll have to feed and walk them throughout the day. Ask the parking attendant to direct you to the kennel.

✔ **Strollers.** Look to the left as you enter the park through the turnstiles. Stroller rental costs $10 for a single, $16 for a double, tax included.

✔ **Wheelchairs.** You can rent wheelchairs for $12 per day in the parking garage concourse. Electric wheelchairs are $40 per day. Both require a $50 deposit and a signed rental agreement. Prices include taxes.

Practical Advice for Island Adventurers

If you want to get the most out of your adventure, you would do well to keep the following tips in mind when you're exploring the Islands of Adventure:

✔ **Short visitors.** Of the 14 major rides at Islands of Adventure, 13 of them have minimum-height restrictions between *40 and 54 inches.* You can find a child-swap service at all major attractions, enabling you or your partner to ride while the other watches over your tikes, but sitting in a waiting room isn't much fun for them. Take your child's height into consideration before visiting the park, or consider splitting up for part of the day. Islands has actually a few great play areas that will keep younger kids entertained while older kids and parents ride some of the wilder rides.

In July 2000, Universal added two notable attractions to its lineup as an answer to criticism that Islands of Adventure had too little for young guests. *The Flying Unicorn* is a small roller coaster that travels through a mythical forest. (It's comparable to *The Barnstormer at Goofy's Wiseacre Farm* in Disney's **Magic Kingdom,** Chapter 12, and *Woody Woodpecker's Nuthouse Coaster* at **Universal Studios Florida,** Chapter 18, though it still has plenty of zip.) *Storm Force* is a spinning attraction in which guests help the *X-Men's* Storm harness the weather to fight her archenemy, Magneto. It's a bit wilder and definitely edgier in its theme than the *Tea Cups* at **Magic Kingdom** (Chapter 12), but the idea's the same.

✔ **Jittery or health-restricted visitors.** See the preceding note about short visitors and add the warning that height isn't the only limiting factor. If you're pregnant, prone to dizziness or motion sickness, or have heart, back, or other health problems, this may not be the best choice of parks for you. Consider heading to a tamer park, like Disney's **Magic Kingdom** (see Chapter 12), Disney's **Animal Kingdom** (see Chapter 15), Disney's **Epcot** (see Chapter 13), and **Disney–MGM Studios** (see Chapter 14), **SeaWorld** (see Chapter 20), or even **Universal Studios Florida** (see Chapter 18).

✔ **Cruising the Islands.** If you hauled your stroller on your vacation, bring it to the park. The walk from your car is a long one, through the parking garage and the entertainment district's **CityWalk,** before you get to the attractions. Carrying a young child and all their accompanying paraphernalia, even on moving sidewalks, can make the long trek seem even longer.

✔ **Beat the heat.** Several rides have lengthy pathways outside that offer no cover to protect you from the sizzling Florida sun. Bring some bottled water with you for the long waits (a bottle that costs $2.50 here is less than $1 in the outside world) or take a sip from fountains placed in the waiting areas. Alcohol is more readily available at this park than at Disney, so remember that liquor, roller coasters, and sweltering heat can make for a *very messy mix*.

Exploring the Top Attractions at Islands of Adventure

Islands of Adventure features more than 20 rides and attractions, as well as numerous uniquely-themed restaurants and shops, all surrounding its central sea. (It's similar in layout of the **World Showcase** at **Epcot,** Chapter 13.)

See the "Islands of Adventure" map on page 275 to locate all the attractions in the sections that follow.

Port of Entry

Beyond the gigantic, crumbling-stone archway you'll find the **Port's** numerous souvenir shops, bazaars, and eateries lining the exotic streetscape. Save this area for last, spending only a few minutes now to take in your surroundings, as the architecture and attention to detail is striking. I suggest you begin your adventure just beyond the second stone archway by heading to either **Seuss Landing** (to the right) or **Marvel Super Hero Island** (to the left). Your direction will likely be determined by the age of your children, or whether you're willing to start out by riding one of the most intense and thrilling rides in the entire park.

Seuss Landing

Within these 10 fanciful acres you step onto the pages of Dr. Seuss' classic tales, complete with Seussian signature color swirls and whimsical architecture and a cast of classic characters. The main attractions in **Seuss Landing** are aimed at the younger set, although anyone who loved the good Doctor as a child will enjoy some nostalgic fun.

✔ *Caro-Seuss-El.* This not-so-ordinary carousel replaces the traditional wooden horses with seven whimsical Seussian characters (a total of 54 mounts), including Cowfish, the elephant birds from *Horton Hatches an Egg,* and Mulligatawnies. They move up and down and in and out. Pull the reins to make their eyes blink or heads bob.

This ride has a rocking-chariot platform and a wheelchair-loading system that makes it a fun attraction for guests with disabilities.

✔ *The Cat in the Hat.* All aboard the couch! In this case, the couches are six-passenger futons that steer you through 18 silly scenes, retelling the tale of a day gone terribly south. Seuss fans will recognize the giant candy-striped hat looming over the entrance as well as the chaotic journey itself. The ride's highlight is a revolving 24-foot tunnel that alters your perceptions and leaves you feeling a bit woozy.

✔ "It's just not very fast and the Cat in the Hat is a little-kids' story," was 12-year-old Ryan's verdict. *The Cat in the Hat* is one of the signature "young" experiences of **Islands of Adventure,** and because of this, you — as well as your older children — may find it a bit tame. Small children may be slightly frightened by pop-up characters, although most kids ages 4 to 7 will find it a winner.

✔ *If I Ran the Zoo.* At this small interactive play area, kids can dodge flying water snakes and tickle the toes of a Seussian creature. The area is filled with 19 play stations that include slides, wheels to spin, caves to explore, and other things geared to burning off some of the excited energy of tinier tots. Just plan on them getting wet, as that's half the fun.

✔ *One Fish, Two Fish, Red Fish, Blue Fish.* You move "up, up, up" and "down, down, down" on this attraction, where you ride in a funky flying fish whose controls enable you to ascend or descend 15 feet as you spin around on an arm attached to a hub (much like Magic Kingdom's Magic Carpets of Aladdin, see Chapter 12). Watch out for squirt posts, which spray unsuspecting riders who don't follow along with the ride's little rhyme (and sometimes even the ones who do follow it).

Marvel Super Hero Island

Thrill-ride junkies love the twisting, turning, stomach-churning rides on this island. The streets are filled with giant-sized murals of Marvel Super Heroes, making you feel as if you've stepped onto the pages of a gigantic comic book. The larger-than-life scenery was created using a special effect that mimics Marvel's style. The hard rockin' music here is loud; definitely a reflection of the island's overall personality.

✔ **The Amazing Adventures of Spider-Man.** This primo ride combines moving vehicles, 3-D action, and an array of special effects themed around the original web master. The script: While you're on a ho-hum tour of the *Daily Bugle* newspaper — *yikes!* — the boys in black hats (Doc Oc, Hobgoblin, and the rest of the Sinister Syndicate) filch the Statue of Liberty. You have to help Spidey get it back. Unlike the many roller coasters and stationary motion simulators in Orlando, this ride offers a unique experience. Passengers squeal as real and computer-generated objects alternately fly toward their 12-person cars, which plunge and spin through a comic-book universe. A simulated 400-foot drop feels an awful lot like the real thing.

Expectant mothers or those with heart, neck, or back problems shouldn't ride *The Amazing Adventures of Spider-Man.* For those who can, know that lines here can get ridiculously long, so use Universal EXPRESS, or, if you don't mind splitting up your party, use the single-rider line when it's available.

"This was the coolest ride ever!" exclaimed Austin, age 10. Ryan (age 12) echoed that sentiment, adding, "You gotta do this one a couple times at least!" Dark scenes, the motion of the car, the in-your-face 3-D effects and the simulated motion make this ride unsuitable for extremely young kids and even some preteens. Most of the rest of you will probably want to give it another spin — a number of Universal employees rate it the best in the park (and my ride-addicted editor thinks it's the best in town). Keep in mind that you can close your eyes if a scene is too intense, as the motion of the car, without the combined effects, isn't overwhelming by itself. There's a *40-inch height minimum.*

✔ **Doctor Doom's Fearfall.** Look! Up in the sky! It's a bird, it's a plane . . . uh, it's you falling 200 feet if you're courageous enough to climb aboard. This towering metal skeleton provides screams that you can hear far into the day and night. The plot: You're touring a lab when — are you sensing a theme here? — something goes horribly wrong as supervillain Doctor Doom tries to drain you of fear in order to power his latest evil scheme. You're fired to the top of the ride (pulling 4Gs in the process), with feet dangling, and then dropped in intervals, leaving your stomach at several levels.

If you're an expectant mother or you experience heart, neck, or back problems, you shouldn't ride *Doctor Doom's Fearfall.* Make sure all items are secured well — or better yet, give them to someone not riding for safe keeping. Plenty of riders have ended up watching their sunglasses fly off into the wild blue yonder upon lift off. _Minimum height is 52 inches._ Though it's actually less nightmarish than the _Twilight Zone Tower of Terror_ (see Chapter 14), I recommend kids be a minimum 10 years of age before even attempting this one.

✔ _**Incredible Hulk Coaster.**_ Bruce Banner is working in his lab when — yes, again — something goes wrong. This coaster rockets from a dark tunnel into the sunlight, while accelerating from 0 to 40 mph in two seconds. **Universal**'s scriptwriters insist that it has the same thrust as an F-16. Although it's only two-thirds the speed of **Disney–MGM**'s _Rock 'n' Rollercoaster,_ this ride is in broad daylight, and you can _see_ the asphalt! After you're launched, you spin upside down 128 feet from the ground, feel weightless, and career through the center of the park over the heads of other visitors. If you're a coaster lover, you'll be pleased to know that this ride, which lasts 2 minutes and 15 seconds, includes seven rollovers and two deep drops. As a nice touch, the 32-passenger metal coaster glows green at night. The ride is surprisingly smooth, making it much more comfortable than coasters that are far less intense.

Expectant mothers or those with heart, neck, or back problems shouldn't ride. I've seen people ignore the warnings, only to turn the same shade as the coaster. This is also another one where you should heed warnings to store all loose items in a locker before you get on . . . or finding your car at the end of the day may become a moot point when your car keys go flying.

Mixed reviews for this "monster" of a coaster from my young reviewers. "No way. Uh-uh, you go upside down — you won't even get me on it," were 12-year-old Ryan's final words on the subject.

But Nicolas (age 8) and Austin (age 10) both said it was "the most amazing roller coaster ever — you think you're going to hit the pavement, but then you don't — it's fast and really smooth." From another coaster crazy — this one an adult — who rides them all (and I mean all), he felt it was one of the best he had ever ridden, mostly because it was so smooth. This is another ride that I think is best for riders 10 to 12 years and older. Riders must be _at least 54 inches tall_ to climb aboard.

✔ _**Storm Force Accelatron.**_ This ride is a 22nd-century version of **Magic Kingdom**'s _Mad Tea Party_ and its spinning teacups. While aboard, you and the _X-Men_'s superheroine, Storm, try to defeat the evil Magneto. To do that, you need to spin faster and faster to give the mistress of weather a little boost in the energy department. In addition to some upset stomachs, your motion creates a thunderstorm of sound and light, which gives Storm all the power she needs to blast Magneto. Some young kids (5 and under) may find the characters, lights, and sounds a bit too intense.

This ride is closed during some off-peak periods.

Toon Lagoon

More than 150 life-size sculpted cartoon images — characters range from Betty Boop and Flash Gordon to Bullwinkle and Cathy — let you know you've entered an island dedicated to your favorites from the Sunday funnies.

✔ **Dudley Do-Right's Ripsaw Falls.** The heroic Dudley stars on this adrenaline-pumping, splashy flume ride that drops 75 feet at 50 mph. Your mission is to save the fair Nell from Snidely Whiplash. The boats take you around a 400,000-gallon lagoon and plunge you 15 feet below the water's surface, but this is mainly hype — the waters is contained on either side of you. That said, you *will* get very wet anyway. Though it beats out *Splash Mountain* (see Chapter 12) in the adrenaline department, the latter offers better effects and a nicer atmosphere.

Expectant mothers or people with heart, neck, or back problems shouldn't ride this attraction. It has a *44-inch height minimum*. Tall folks should note that the boats on this ride offer legroom on par with that in an airline's coach section.

✔ **Me Ship, The Olive.** This three-story boat offers dozens of interactive activities. Kids can toot whistles, clang bells, or play the organ. *Sweet Pea's Playpen* is a favorite of younger guests. Kids 6 and older love *Cargo Crane,* where they can use water cannons to drench riders on *Popeye & Bluto's Bilge-Rat Barges* (see the following bullet).

✔ **Popeye & Bluto's Bilge-Rat Barges.** Here's another water special — a churning, turning, twisting, listing raft ride with the same kind of vehicle as *Kali River Rapids* at Disney's **Animal Kingdom** (see Chapter 15), but this one's a bit faster and bouncier (though not nearly as scenic). You'll get wet from mechanical devices and from the water cannons fired by guests at *Me Ship, The Olive* (see the preceding bullet). The 12-passenger rafts bump and dip their way along a course lined with villains, including Bluto and Sea Hag.

"That water is freezing, but it really feels good when it's hot, and I loved bouncing up and down on the waves." Nic's right; the water is *c-c-cold,* which is a blessing on hot summer days but less so in January, and trust me — you can get completely soaked. Riders must be *at least 42 inches tall* to ride.

✔ Along **Kings Row** and **Comic Strip Lane** you'll find Beetle Bailey, Dudley, and plenty of other classic comic characters out and about.

Jurassic Park

All the basics from Steven Spielberg's wildly successful films (you'll hear the score from the movies pretty much everywhere you go), and some of the high-tech wizardry, are incorporated into this lushly landscaped locale, which includes a replica of the visitor's center from the movie and one of the best themed attractions in the park.

✔ **Camp Jurassic.** This amazingly entertaining prehistoric play area, designed along the same lines as *The Boneyard* in Disney's **Animal**

Kingdom (see Chapter 15), has everything from lava pits with dinosaur bones to amber mines to a tropical rain forest where the bushes occasionally rustle and you can hear dinosaurs off in the distance. Watch out for the spitters that often lurk in the dark caves. The multilevel area offers plenty of places for kids to climb, crawl, explore, and wear down their batteries eventually.

While there's only one way in and out of this attraction, keep a close eye on young children because it's easy to get lost inside the caverns.

✔ *Jurassic Park Discovery Center.* Inside this air-conditioned spot, you can relax for the moment while you and your kids discover something new. The center has life-size dinosaur replicas, including a massive skeleton, a handful of interactive games, including a sequencer that lets you combine your DNA with a dinosaur's, and the *Beasaur* exhibit, where you can see and hear as the dinosaurs did. You can also play the game show *You Bet Jurassic* (bet you wouldn't see an attraction name like this at Disney), watch a tiny Velociraptor "hatch" in the lab, and turn your voice into a dinosaur screech.

Austin (10), Nicolas (8), and Hailey (6) all give this one high marks, but because there are a limited number of interactive stations, this attraction can consume a lot of time on busy days.

✔ *Jurassic Park River Adventure.* Your adventure cruise begins slowly but soon throws you into a world of jungle plants and stormy skies, where you literally come face-to-face with five-story "breathing" inhabitants of Jurassic Park. At one point, a *Tyrannosaurus rex* decides you look like a tasty morsel; at another, spitters launch venom your way. To escape, you take a breathtaking 85-foot plunge in a flume that's steep and quick enough to lift your fanny from the seat. (When Spielberg rode it, he made them stop the ride and let him out before the plunge.) Oh, yeah — you'll get soaked. If you can only stomach the thought of getting on one flume ride at Islands, make it this one — both the atmosphere and comfort level far exceed that of *Dudley Do-Right's Ripsaw Falls.*

"That was amazing — the dinosaurs looked real and the waterfall at the end was fun!" Austin could have gone back for more, though people with height issues may not be as happy. Ryan on the other hand said "the drop at the end was definitely too long and way, *way* too steep." Riders must be *at least 42 inches tall.*

✔ *Pteranodon Flyers.* The line for this one is simply ridiculous! For an 80 second ride, neat as it may be, you'll often wait up to an hour, sometimes more. This high-flying ride swings from side-to-side and, unlike traditional gondolas in sky rides, on *Pteranodon Flyers,* your feet dangle free from a two-seat skeletal flyer with little more than a restraining belt between you and the ground. Now that I've scared you, this is a kiddie ride — *single passengers must be between 36 and 56 inches;* adults can ride *only* when accompanying someone that size. For what it's worth, I wouldn't put my young squirmers on it even if the wait weren't so long.

The Lost Continent

Universal has created a foreboding mood in this section of the park, whose entrance is marked by menacing stone griffins and fire-lit torches. This uniquely themed area combines various mythical and mystical elements, including ancient Greek gods, crumbling ruins, and medieval magicians and a magical forest.

✔ **Dueling Dragons.** This ride has a scream factor of 11 on a 10-point scale. True coaster crazies love this intertwined set of leg-dangling racers that climb to 125 feet, invert five times, and, on three occasions, come within only 12 inches of each other as the two dragons battle it out; you prove your bravery by tagging along. The *Fire Dragon* can reach speeds of up to 60 mph, while the *Ice Dragon* makes it to only 55 mph. It, of course, comes with the usual health warnings.

For the best ride, try to get one of the two outside seats in each row. Also, pay attention because the lines for both coasters split near the loading dock so that daredevils can claim the very first row, which many hard-core thrill junkies claim offers the city's ultimate adrenaline rush. And, yes, that line is even longer!

"That was so scary — but so, so cool." Austin barely took time to give his review as he headed back for another battle. After riding it several times, he added, "The best seat is the front seat on *Ice*." You shouldn't ride this ride if you're an expectant mother or if you have heart, neck, or back problems. (Why aren't you surprised?) Riders must be *at least 54 inches tall*.

✔ **The Eighth Voyage of Sindbad.** The mythical sailor Sindbad is the star of a stunt demonstration that includes six water explosions and 50 pyrotechnic effects, which includes a 10-foot circle of flames. It doesn't, however, come close to the quality of the *Indiana Jones* stunt show at **Disney–MGM Studios** (see Chapter 14), and some of the characters are far scarier for young kids.

✔ **The Flying Unicorn.** This small roller coaster is similar to *Woody Woodpecker's Nuthouse Coaster* at **Universal Studios Florida** (see Chapter 18) and *The Barnstormer at Goofy's Wiseacre Farm* in **Magic Kingdom** (see Chapter 12). That means a fast, corkscrew run sure to earn squeals, but probably not at the risk of someone losing their lunch. The ride travels through a mythical forest next to *Dueling Dragons*. Younger kids love it, but riders must be *at least 36 inches tall*. I'd have them watch for a few minutes before they commit to getting on.

✔ **The Mystic Fountain.** This interactive smart fountain delights younger guests. It can see, hear, and spit water, leading to plenty of kibitzing with those who stand before the stone fountain, suitably named Rocky. (A staff member viewing the action through cameras is at the helm, which makes for a personable experience.) It's a real treat for 3- to 8-year-olds.

✔ ***Poseidon's Fury.*** Clearly, *Poseidon's Fury* is the park's best show, but that may be a backhanded compliment because it's one of the park's only shows. It exposes you to fire and water in the same manner that *Earthquake* does at **Universal Studios Florida.** You pass through a 42-foot vortex — where 17,500 gallons of water swirl around you, barrel-style — and then get a front-row seat at a battle royale, where Zeus and Poseidon hurl 25-foot fireballs at each other. However, some of the special effects are not up to the usual Universal standards. If the line is short, I recommend that you check it out, but if the lines are long, as is often the case, it's not worth waiting for.

Children younger than 7 may find the flaming fireballs, explosive sounds, and rushing water a little too intense. Also, if you wear eye glasses, take them off before you walk through the water vortex or they will fog up completely and you won't see much of anything.

Dining at Islands of Adventure

After riding rides and visiting attractions, you're probably hungry. You can get a quick bite to eat at a number of stands in the park, as well as a handful of full-service restaurants — any and all of which are well above the standards at most other theme-park eateries. The park's creators have taken some extra care to tie in restaurant offerings with the theme of the island they're in. For example, the **Green Eggs and Ham Cafe** in Seuss Landing may be one of the few places on Earth where you're willing to eat tinted *huevos*. (They're sold in the form of an egg-and-ham sandwich for $6.)

✔ **Best sit-down restaurant.** At **Mythos Restaurant in The Lost Continent,** diners are transported to a mythical underwater world. This upscale restaurant offers selections ranging from wood-fired oven pizzas, burgers, and simple bowls of greens, to elaborate entrees of fish, seafood, and steaks. You can dine here without a park ticket, however there's a time limit and you need to leave a credit-card number at the gate. If you're running late, the restaurant can call the gate to let them know so you won't be charged. This restaurant is best suited for adults, although older kids may be okay. Entrees range from $10 to $24. Open daily from 11:30 a.m. to park closing.

✔ **Best atmosphere for adults.** Also in **The Lost Continent, The Enchanted Oak Tavern (and Alchemy Bar)** looks like a mammoth tree from the outside; the interior is brightened by a blue skylight with a celestial theme. The tables and chairs are thick planks, and the servers are clad like wenches. Try the chicken/ rib combo with waffle fries for $13. You can also choose from 45 brands of beer.

✔ **Best atmosphere for kids.** The fun never stops under the big top at **Circus McGurkus Cafe Stoo-pendous** in **Seuss Landing,** where animated trapeze artists swing from the ceiling. Kids' meals, including a souvenir cup, are $6 to $7. The adult menu features fried chicken, lasagna, spaghetti, and pizza. Try the fried chicken platter for $8 or the lasagna for $7.

✔ **Best vegetarian fare.** Fire-Eater's Grill, located in **The Lost Continent,** is a fast-food stand that offers a tasty veggie falafel for $6. You can also get a tossed salad for about $4.

✔ **Best diversity.** Comic Strip Cafe, located in **Toon Lagoon,** is a four-in-one, counter service–style eatery offering burgers, Chinese food, Mexican food, and pizza and pasta ($6–$9).

You can also find several restaurants (see Chapter 10) and clubs (see Chapter 25) just a short walk from Islands of Adventure at the new entertainment complex, **CityWalk.** If you get your hand stamped, you can leave the park and return after eating.

Shopping at Islands of Adventure

The park's 20-something shops have plenty of theme merchandise. You may want to check out *Cats, Hats & Things* and *Dr. Seuss' All the Books You Can Read* for special Seussian material. *Jurassic Outfitters* offers an array of stuffed and plastic dinos, plus safari-style clothing. If you're a superhero fan, check out *The Marvel Alterverse Store.*

Remember that you may find theme- or character-specific merchandise in only one store. Here's a sample of some of the more unusual wares available:

✔ **Betty Boop Store.** You name it, this store in **Toon Lagoon** has her famous mug on it.

✔ **Spider-Man Shop.** This shop specializes in its namesake's paraphernalia, including red Spidey caps covered with black webs and denim jackets with logos.

✔ **Toon Extra.** Where else can you buy a miniature stuffed Mr. Peanut beanbag chair, an Olive Oyl and Popeye frame, or a stuffed Beetle Bailey?

✔ **Historic Families.** Here's your chance to get your own coat of arms made in a shop that looks just like King Arthur's armory. It's a must for the knight wannabe.

Index of Attractions by Area

Seuss Landing
Caro-Seuss-El
The Cat in the Hat
If I Ran the Zoo
One Fish, Two Fish, Red Fish, Blue Fish

Marvel Super Hero Island
The Amazing Adventures of Spider-Man
Doctor Doom's Fearfall
Incredible Hulk Coaster
Storm Force Accelatron

Toon Lagoon
Dudley Do-Right's Ripsaw Falls
Me Ship, The Olive
Popeye & Bluto's Bilge-Rat Barges

Jurassic Park
Camp Jurassic
Jurassic Park Discovery Center
Jurassic Park River Adventure
Pteranodon Flyers

The Lost Continent
Dueling Dragons
The Eighth Voyage of Sindbad
The Flying Unicorn
The Mystic Fountain
Poseidon's Fury

Chapter 20

SeaWorld & Discovery Cove

· ·

In This Chapter

▶ Understanding the basics
▶ Checking out attractions at SeaWorld
▶ Exploring Discovery Cove
▶ Deciding where to eat and shop

· ·

*W*hile I have always included SeaWorld on my must-see list of parks, not everyone gives it the chance it deserves. This modern, marine-adventure park focuses more on discovery than on thrill rides, but it offers its share of excitement with *Journey to Atlantis,* a steep flume-like ride, and the thundering *Kraken,* a floorless roller coaster. SeaWorld's more than 200 acres of educational fun features stars such as Shamu and his expanding family of performing killer whales, polar bears Klondike and Snow, and a supporting cast of seals, sea lions, manatees, penguins, dolphins, walruses, and more. You can also feed some nonperforming critters and feel the crushed-velvet texture of a gentle ray in various pools throughout the park — something Disney and Universal just don't offer.

SeaWorld's sister park, **Discovery Cove,** opened in summer 2000. It lets guests swim with a dolphin in an adventure that, at $229 to $259 per person (plus 6.5 percent sales tax), goes off the price chart; you can also just swim with the fishes for a lower, though still stiff, ticket price of $129 to $159. The payoff is that you only have to share the park with 999 other people, not the tens of thousands you find at the other parks. A day here offers a tranquil and relaxing experience where you can sit in the sand or swim with the sea life — a refreshing way to spend the day in Orlando.

In this chapter, I tell you all you need to know to make the most out of SeaWorld and Discovery Cove.

Gathering Important SeaWorld Information

Before I start wading through the park's attractions and shows, here are some helpful, though possibly mundane, matters that you may find helpful to know.

Buying tickets and making reservations

You have a couple different options when buying your tickets at SeaWorld. A one-day ticket costs $60 for adults, $48 for kids 3 to 9 (plus 6.5 percent sales tax). Buy your tickets online to avoid long lines and save 10 percent off the regular admission price. SeaWorld sometimes offers online specials, such as a second day free.

If you're planning to see a number of non-Disney parks during your stay, consider the **FlexTicket.** This pass enables you to pay one price to visit any of the participating parks during a 14-day period. A four-park pass to Universal Studios Florida, Islands of Adventure, Wet 'n Wild, and SeaWorld is $185 for adults and $151 for children 3 to 9. A five-park pass, which adds Busch Gardens in Tampa, is $225 for adults and $190 for kids. You can order the *FlexTicket* through SeaWorld by calling ☎ **407-351-3600** or heading to www.seaworld.com on the Web.

SeaWorld's Adventure Express Tour ($89 for adults and $79 for kids 3–9 plus park admission fees) is a six-hour guided excursion that includes front-of-the-line access to *Kraken, Journey to Atlantis,* and *Wild Arctic;* reserved seating at two animal shows; lunch; and a chance to touch or feed penguins, dolphins, sting rays, and sea lions. It's the only way to dodge park lines. SeaWorld doesn't have an equivalent to FASTPASS or Universal EXPRESS, although its lines aren't nearly as long as the ones at **Disney** and **Universal** parks. Advanced reservations are recommended for this tour and can be made by calling ☎ **800-406-2244.**

Additionally, you have three one-hour tour options: **Polar Expedition Guided Tour** (touch a penguin), **Predators** (touch a shark!), and **Saving a Species** (see manatees and sea turtles). Each tour costs $16 for adults and $12 for kids 3 to 9 (plus park admission fees) and you have to sign up for them at the *Information Center* just inside the park's entrance. Call ☎ **800-406-2244** or 407-351-3600 for information.

To gather park information before you leave home, write to **SeaWorld Guest Services** at 7007 SeaWorld Dr., Orlando, FL 32801; call ☎ **407-351-3600;** or visit www.seaworld.com. Once inside the park, head for the *Information Center,* which is on your left as you enter the park.

If you're arriving on I-4, just look for the signs pointing the way to the SeaWorld exit. You also can reach it on International Drive. (It's located on the southern third of I-Drive.)

The park usually is open from 9 a.m. to 6 p.m., 365 days a year, and later during summer and holidays.

Locating special services and facilities

In case you forgot to bring essential items, or if you need special assistance while at the park, here's a list of services and facilities that may come in handy:

- ✓ **ATMs.** You can find an ATM machine that accepts cards from banks using the Cirrus, STAR, and Plus systems at the front of the park, near *Atlantis Bayside Stadium,* and across from the *Sea Lion & Otter Stadium* near the *Friends of the Wild* gift shop.

- ✓ **Baby-changing and nursing stations.** Changing tables are in or near most women's restrooms and at the men's restroom at the front entrance near *Shamu's Emporium.* You can buy diapers in machines located near all changing areas and at *Shamu's Emporium.* Likewise, a special area for nursing mothers is located near the women's restroom at *Friends of the Wild* gift shop, near the center of the park.

- ✓ **Cameras and film.** You can purchase film and disposable cameras at stores throughout SeaWorld, although digital supplies are limited.

- ✓ **First aid center.** Registered nurses staff centers behind *Stingray Lagoon* and near *Shamu's Happy Harbor.*

- ✓ **Lockers.** You can rent them for $8 a day plus a $2 refundable deposit at *Shamu's Emporium,* just inside the park entrance.

- ✓ **Lost children.** Lost kids are taken to the *Information Center,* where a park-wide paging system helps reunite them with their families. Children younger than 7 should wear name-tags inside their clothing.

- ✓ **Parking.** Parking costs $8 for cars, pickups, and vans. The parking lots aren't huge, so most people can walk to the park, but trams also run most times. Remember to note the location of your car, too. SeaWorld characters, such as Wally Walrus, mark sections, but forgetting where you parked is still easy after a long day in the park.

- ✓ **Pet care.** Board your pet for the day at the kennel between the parking lot and main gate. The cost is $6 a day (no overnight stays). Proof of vaccination is required.

- ✓ **Strollers.** Rent dolphin-shaped strollers at the *Information Center* near the entrance. They cost $10 for a single, $17 for a double.

- ✓ **Wheelchairs.** Regular wheelchairs are available at the *Information Center* for $8; electric chairs are $32; no deposits are required.

SeaWorld and **Busch Gardens** in Tampa (see Chapter 23), both owned by Anheuser-Busch, have a shuttle service that provides $10 round-trip tickets to get you from Orlando to Tampa and back. The 1½- to 2-hour one-way shuttle runs daily and has five pick-up locations in Orlando,

SeaWorld

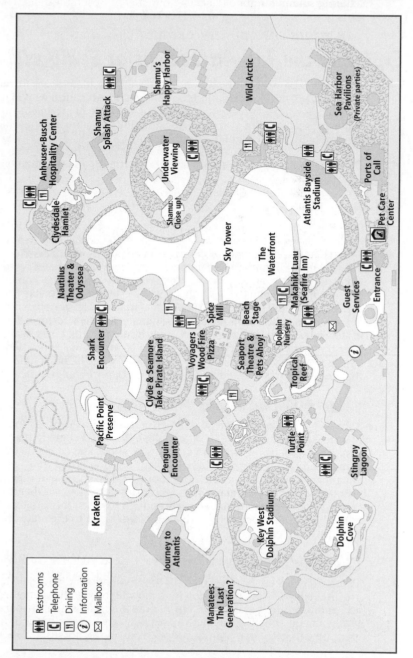

including one at Universal and one on I-Drive (☎ **800-221-1339**). The schedule allows for about a seven-hour stay at Busch Gardens. The service is free if you have a five-park **FlexTicket.**

Exploring the Top Attractions at SeaWorld

SeaWorld explores the mysteries of the deep in a theme-park format that combines wildlife-conservation awareness and education with simple laid-back fun. Up-close encounters with a montage of marine life are the major draws here, but you can also find plenty of amusing shows and a handful of thrill rides added into the mix.

To get a good look at the park's layout, see the "SeaWorld" map on page 291.

Blue Horizons

Blue Horizons, SeaWorld's newest and most spectacular show to date, made its debut in the summer of 2005 and replaced the Key West Dolphin Fest. This unique show combines the grace and power of SeaWorld's most famous inhabitants, its dolphins and false killer whales, with the pageantry of a Broadway production. The show transports you into the dreams of an imaginative young girl, whose dream is to fly like the birds and swim like the dolphins. Bringing the story to life, aerialists twirl high in the air, while dolphins, whales, and bungee jumpers perform acrobatics in the water. Adding to the drama are brightly-colored birds, which fly over the audience. The entire show is set to an original score performed by the Seattle Symphony Orchestra. This is by far the most unique show that SeaWorld has created and one that certainly shouldn't be missed.

Clyde & Seamore Take Pirate Island

A lovable and amusing sea lion-and-otter duet, with a supporting cast of walruses and harbor seals, stars in fish-breathed comedy that comes with a swashbuckling series of stunts. The show, staged inside the aptly named *Sea Lion & Otter Stadium,* is corny, but don't hold that against the animal actors who are predictably adorable. The show also serves as a welcome change from all the high-tech rides and shows at the other theme parks. Be sure to arrive early enough to catch the mime as he pokes fun at the guests who arrive a bit late, much to the amusement of the entire audience.

Clydesdale Hamlet

Twice a day except Fridays, eight of the tremendous Clydesdale horses are hitched to the big red wagon for a parade through the park, beginning and ending at their stables, where visitors also can watch the parade tack going on and off. Daily petting sessions are scheduled, and they're a great time to get a snapshot of you with one of the horses. In late winter and spring, you may get to see a mare and foal that aren't part of the Clydesdale team.

Journey to Atlantis

Taking a cue from Disney's Imagineers, SeaWorld created a part-flume, part-coaster ride that carries the customary surgeon-general's warning about heart problems, neck or back ailments, pregnancy, dizziness, and claustrophobia. The story line involves a fisherman, Hermes (the Greek god), and wicked Sirens in a fierce battle between good and evil, but what really matters is the drop — a wild, 60-foot plunge, with a bunch of luge-like twists and turns and a shorter drop thrown in for good measure. There's no hidden lesson here, just a splashy thrill when you least expect it. Oh, and it goes without saying that you will get totally soaked.

Key West at SeaWorld

Although not quite the way Hemingway saw Key West, this 5-acre, tree-and flower-lined, Caribbean-style village has food, street vendors, and entertainers. It has three animal habitats: *Stingray Lagoon,* where you get a hands-on encounter with harmless southern diamond and cownose rays, an absolute favorite for younger kids; *Dolphin Cove,* a habitat for bottlenose dolphins where you can sometimes feed or pet them as they pass by; and *Turtle Point,* home to endangered and threatened species. Shortly after this area opened, the dolphins often teased visitors by swimming just out of arm's reach. But they soon discovered the advantages to human interaction — namely smelt.

Speaking of smelt, it's real easy to be melted by the dolphins' begging, and you can easily burn $20 buying trays of their favorite snack to feed to your newfound aquatic friends. I once spent half a park admission feeding them before coming to my senses, so set a limit to your spending (and feeding) ahead of time.

Kraken

Launched in summer 2000, this coaster is SeaWorld's deepest foray into the world of thrill-ride battles. *Kraken* is named for a massive, mythological, underwater beast that Poseidon kept caged. This 21st-century monster has floorless and open-sided 32-passenger trains that plant you on a pedestal high above the track. When the coaster breaks loose, you climb 151 feet, fall 144 feet, hit speeds of 65 mph, go underground three times (spraying bystanders with water — or worse, if you're weak of stomach), experience a moment of weightlessness, and make seven loops over a 4,177-foot course. This ride may be the longest 3 minutes, 39 seconds of your life; according to a coaster fanatic friend who lives for adrenaline, this is the best coaster in Central Florida (take that, Disney and Universal!). *Kraken* carries a *54-inch height minimum.* This is not a coaster for beginners or youngsters — even if they meet the height requirement.

Manatee Rescue

This exhibit is as close as most people get to endangered West Indian manatees. There are as few as 3,200 of them currently remaining in the wild. Underwater viewing stations, innovative cinema techniques, and interactive displays combine for a tribute to these gentle marine mammals. It's a nicer and roomier (for the manatees) exhibit than the tight quarters their cousins have at *The Living Seas* in **Epcot** (see Chapter 13). Kids especially like the more natural outdoor viewing area near the entrance to the exhibit.

Marine Mammal Keeper Experience

Expect to invest a sizable chunk of your day and budget in this nine-hour program (it runs from 6:30 a.m.–3:30 p.m., so you'll also need to be an early riser). You get to work side by side with a trainer, preparing meals and feeding the animals, learning basic training techniques, and sharing lunch. It costs $399 (tax inclusive), which also includes 7 days of consecutive admission to SeaWorld, lunch, a career book, and a T-shirt. The program is limited to two people per day, so make the required reservations very early. You must be 13 or older, *at least 52 inches tall,* able to climb, and able to lift and carry 15 pounds of vittles. Call ☎ **407-432-1178** for more information.

Odyssea

Inside the Nautilus Theater, a cast of acrobats, mimes, dancers, musicians, and comics put on a undersea show called *Odyssea* that, at times, is artistic and funny (and always entertaining). The sets and costumes focus on a whimsical underwater world. It's similar in style to the *Cirque du Soleil* production at **Downtown Disney** (see Chapter 25), but on a much smaller scale. It's also a great spot to give your feet a break and to cool off, making it a good stop in the afternoon.

Penguin Encounter

The *Penguin Encounter* transports you via a 120-foot-long moving sidewalk through Antarctic Tuxedoville. The stars of the show — four different species of penguins — are on the other side of a Plexiglas shield. You get a quick look at them as they preen, socialize, and swim at bullet speed in a 30-degree habitat. You can also see puffins and murres (shorebirds) in a similar, but separate, area.

Though you get a nice view of the penguins (and they are always a hit with the kids), the viewing area surroundings leave a bit to be desired.

Pets Ahoy!

A veritable menagerie of cats, dogs, pot-bellied pigs, skunks, and a horse are joined by birds and rats (nearly 100 animals in all) to perform comic relief in a 25-minute show held several times a day inside the SeaWorld Theater. Almost all of the performers were rescued from animal shelters.

Stick around after the show and your kids can have an up-close
encounter with a couple of the featured animal stars.

Shamu Adventure Show

Everyone comes to SeaWorld to see Shamu, and believe me the show
never disappoints. The *Shamu Adventure Show,* held inside Shamu
Stadium, is a well-choreographed show, planned and carried out by very
good trainers and very smart Orcas. Performing stunts with and without
their trainers, the whales jump and dive into the depths of the gigantic
pool, impressing the audience every time. The fun builds until the video
monitor flashes an urgent "Weather Watch," and one of the trainers utters
the warning, "Uh-oh! Hurricane Shamu is about to make landfall!" At this
point, many folks remember the splash-area warnings posted throughout
the grandstand (seats in the first 14 rows may get drenched). Those who
didn't pay attention when they arrived get one last chance to flee to higher
and drier areas of the stadium. The Orcas then race around the edge of
the pool, creating huge waves of icy water that profoundly soak everyone
and everything within range. Veteran animal handler Jack Hanna makes a
cameo appearance on overhead monitors, compliments of ShamuVision.

Shamu: Close Up! is an adjoining exhibit that lets you get close to killer
whales and learn about breeding programs. Don't miss the underwater
viewing area. You may get to see a mother with her big baby.

A nighttime version of this show, *Shamu Rocks America,* offers more of
a party atmosphere and less of an educational experience. The whales
perform to the beat of blaring rock music, and special effects are more
predominant against the nighttime sky. It adds up to a very entertaining
show for all ages.

Eating with the fish

In May 2002, **SeaWorld** opened a restaurant program called *Dine with Shamu*
(☎ **800-327-2420** or 407-351-3600 for information and reservations). This reservations-
only seafood buffet is served poolside with Shamu as a special guest. While eating,
guests can mingle and question SeaWorld trainers. The menu also includes chicken,
beef, and salads and a children's buffet offering mac 'n' cheese, chicken, hot dogs,
and other kiddie favorites. The cost is $34 for adults and $18 for kids 3 to 9, in addition
to park admission. Reserving a spot two to three weeks in advance is usually more
than enough unless you're coming in one of the crunch periods (summer, holidays).

The park also opened **Sharks Underwater Grill** (☎ **407-363-2559** for reservations),
where diners can dig into Floridian and Caribbean treats while watching denizens
swim by in the *Shark Encounter* exhibit — almost the entire back wall of the restaurant serves as a gigantic viewing area. Menu prices are $16 to $30 for adults and $6
to $12 for kids 3 to 9 (pasta, hot dogs, chicken breast, steak, and popcorn shrimp), and
theme-park admission is required.

Shamu's Happy Harbor

This 3-acre play area has a four-story net tower with a 35-foot crow's-nest lookout, water cannons, remote-controlled vehicles, a ship, and a water maze. It's one of the most extensive play areas at any park and a great place for kids to unwind. Because of its size, smaller kids can easily get lost and could easily escape to the other areas of the park if you're not paying close attention.

 Bring extra clothes for the tots (or for yourself) because the *Harbor* isn't designed to keep you dry.

Shark Encounter

 This attraction was expanded to include 220 species of aquatic predators. Pools out front have small sharks and rays. (Feeding isn't allowed.) Eerie background music sets the mood for viewing big eels, beautiful lionfish, hauntingly still barracudas, and the fat, bug-eyed pufferfish in large indoor aquariums.

 This attraction isn't for the claustrophobic: You walk through a Plexiglas tube beneath hundreds of millions of gallons of water. Small children may find the swimming sharks a little too much to handle.

Sharks Deep Dive gives snorkelers and divers a chance to have limited, hands-off contact with the 58 sharks, including a nearly 9-foot sand tiger, in the *Shark Encounter* area. Two at a time, guests don wetsuits for a close up encounter inside an actual shark cage that rides a 125-foot track. Part of the cage is above water, but participants can dive up to 8 feet underwater for a close-up look at the inhabitants. The cost is $150 for certified divers, $125 for snorkelers (minimum age 10). The price includes a souvenir booklet, T-shirt, and snorkel gear, but does not include the required park admission fee.

Wild Arctic

Wild Arctic combines a high-definition adventure film with flight-simulator technology to envelop guests in the beauty, exhilaration, and danger of a polar expedition. After a hazardous, simulated helicopter flight over the frozen north, visitors emerge at a remote research base, home to star residents and polar bear twins Klondike and Snow, seals, walruses, and white beluga whales. A separate walk-through line is available for those who want to skip the bumpy simulator ride.

More SeaWorld fun

Other SeaWorld attractions include **Pacific Point Preserve,** a 2½-acre natural setting that duplicates the rocky northern Pacific Coast home of California sea lions and harbor seals (yes, there are smelt opportunities here!), and **Tropical Rain Forest,** a bamboo and banyan-tree habitat that's home to cockatoos and other birds.

The **Anheuser-Busch Hospitality Center** next to the Clydesdale Hamlet has the "Label Stable" gift shop and a deli and offers free samples of Anheuser-Busch beers. At the **Budweiser Beer School,** guests age 21 and over can learn how Anheuser-Busch brews the world's top-selling beer.

SeaWorld's new 5-acre **Waterfront** area, which debuted in late spring 2003, added a 5-acre, seaport-themed village to the park's landscape. On High Street, look for a blend of shops and the Seafire Inn restaurant, where lunch includes a cute musical revue celebrating family, food, and fun called *Rico and Roza's Musical Feast.* At Harbor Square, the funny *Groove Chefs* orchestra has chefs making music with pots and pans. The park has also added street performers, including a crusty old sea captain, who tells fish tales and makes music with bottles and brandy glasses. Other eateries include Voyager's Wood Fired Pizza and The Spice Mill.

Dining and Shopping at SeaWorld

For details on SeaWorld's *Makahiki Luau,* a full-scale dinner show featuring South Seas food (mahimahi, chicken, and pork) and entertainment, see Chapter 24. For the lowdown on Sharks Underwater Grill, see the *Terrors of the Deep* review earlier in this chapter.

SeaWorld also has several counter-style eateries offering the usual burgers, fajitas, salads, and so on. Most fast-food meals cost about $7 or $8 per person, and this doesn't include the cost of a drink, which will set you back another $2.50 or so.

The **Waterfront** is home to a number of full-service dining options with decent cuisine, including:

- ✔ **The Seafire Inn.** Choose from a number of burgers (about $8–$9) stir fry, sandwiches, and salads, or try a jumbo baked potato served with your choice of several toppings for $7.

- ✔ **Voyager's Wood Fired Pizzas.** The pizza- and parmesan fries–combo platter here offers good value at $8, with seafood, pasta, chicken, sandwiches, and salads and a huge kid's menu to choose from as well.

- ✔ **The Spice Mill.** This eatery specializes in the spices of famous seaport cities. Try the jambalaya or the jerk-grilled chicken sandwiches or an array of other more unique offerings. An entree will set you back about $12.

SeaWorld doesn't have nearly as many shops as the other major theme parks, but the stores offer plenty of surprisingly cuddly sea creatures. For example, you can buy a stuffed manatee at **Manatee Cove.** The **Friends of the Wild** gift shop near *Penguin Encounter* is also nice, as is the shop attached to *Wild Arctic.* Because of the Anheuser-Busch connection, the gift shop outside the entrance to the park offers a staggering array of Budweiser- and Busch-related items. There are a handful of unique boutiques featuring items from garden art to unique toys and T-shirts at the **Waterfront.**

Checking Out Discovery Cove

SeaWorld's second theme park opened in summer 2000. Its $100-million construction cost may be one-tenth the sticker price of **Islands of Adventure,** but **Discovery Cove**'s admission price is four times higher. The options: $229 to $259 per person plus 6.5 percent sales tax if you want to swim with a dolphin *(minimum age 6),* or $129 to $159 if you can simply settle for the fishes. The prices vary seasonally, so double check when you make your reservations (which are a requirement to enter this park).

A perk of the higher price tag is that it includes a 7-day consecutive pass to either **SeaWorld** or **Busch Gardens** (see Chapter 23). You can upgrade this feature to a 14-day combination pass for both parks for an additional $30. If you plan on visiting all three parks, that's actually a pretty good deal.

Almost everyone who does the dolphin encounter finds it exciting — just the kind of thing that makes for a most memorable vacation. If, however, your kids are younger than age 6, or you decide to skip the dolphin swim, it's hard to imagine that you'll get your $129 worth. The atmosphere here isn't tailored to toddlers and is, instead, meant to be a relaxing oasis, quiet and serene. I can't really recommend this park for those of you with very young children in tow.

The park has more than two-dozen dolphins, and each works from two to four hours a day. They're pretty incredible animals, and, although their size may be a bit intimidating to some, they're very people-friendly. Many of them are mature critters that have spent their lives in captivity, around people. Most of them love getting their bellies, backs, and flukes rubbed. They also have an impressive bag of tricks. Given the proper hand signals, they can mimic the sound of a human passing gas, chatter in dolphin talk, and do seemingly effortless 1½ gainers in 12 feet of water. They also take guests for piggyback rides.

The dolphin experience lasts 90 minutes, about 35 to 40 minutes of which is actually spent in the lagoon. Trainers use the rest of the time to teach visitors about these remarkable mammals.

The rest of your day won't be nearly as exciting, but it is wonderfully relaxing. Discovery Cove doesn't deliver thrill rides, water slides, or acrobatic animal shows; that's what **SeaWorld, Disney,** and **Universal** are for. This is where you come to get away from all that!

Discovery Cove is an all-inclusive park, so in addition to the dolphin experience, your fee tosses in

✔ Elbow room — there's a limit of 1,000 guests per day. (To give you an idea of how little that is, the normal daily attendance at Disney's **Magic Kingdom** is 41,000.) This ensures your experience will be more relaxing and private, which is essentially what you're paying for.

✔ Lunch (entrees include items such as fajitas, salmon, stir-fry, and pesto chicken), a towel, sunscreen, snorkeling gear including a flotation vest, a souvenir photo, and free parking are also part of the deal.

✔ Activities that include:

  • Swimming near (but on the other side of Plexiglas from) barracudas and black-tip sharks.

  • Snorkeling around a huge pool containing a coral reef with colorful tropical fish and another area with gentle rays.

  • Touching and feeding 300 exotic birds in an aviary hidden under a waterfall.

  • Cooling off under foaming waterfalls.

  • Soaking up the sun on the beaches.

  • Enjoying the soothing waters of the park's pools and rivers (freshwater and saltwater).

✔ Seven days of unlimited admission to **SeaWorld** or **Busch Gardens** in Tampa.

 Reservations are required far in advance, but you have at least a chance of getting in as a walk-up guest as the park reserves a small number of tickets daily for folks whose earlier dolphin sessions were canceled due to bad weather. Your best chance for last-minute tickets comes during any extended period of good weather.

To get to Discovery Cove, follow the directions to SeaWorld given in the "Gathering Important SeaWorld Information" section, earlier in this chapter.

For up-to-the-minute information about this park, call ☎ 877-434-7268 or go to www.discoverycove.com.

Index of SeaWorld Main Attractions

Blue Horizons
Clyde & Seamore Take Pirate Island
Clydesdale Hamlet
Journey to Atlantis
Key West at SeaWorld
Kraken
Manatee Rescue
Marine Mammal Keeper Experience

Odyssea
Penguin Encounter
Pets Ahoy!
Shamu Adventure Show
Shamu's Happy Harbor
Shark Encounter
Waterfront
Wild Arctic

Chapter 21

Discovering Orlando's Other Attractions

In This Chapter

▶ Exploring Orlando's best smaller attractions

▶ Getting wet outside Walt's World

*I*n Chapters 11 through 20, I covered the major theme parks in and around Orlando. But you're probably wondering if there's *anything* that's more relaxed, a little — and I do mean little — cheaper, and still offers a memorable experience.

The answer is yes.

In this chapter, I explore the city's best alternatives to the mega parks. To further help you out, I've divided them into two categories: those in which you stay dry and those in which you get wet — the latter are very popular options in the midst of Orlando's summer heat and humidity (for more about the weather, see Chapter 3).

Checking Out the City's Best Attractions

For a list of bargain-basement priced attractions, even easier on your wallet than the ones I mention here, see Chapter 26.

Flying Tigers Warbird Restoration Museum
Kissimmee

A guided tour through this working restoration and museum facility allows visitors to see, smell, and touch numerous historic warplanes, mainly from the World War II era. The museum's fleet — many of which are still flightworthy — includes a B-17 Flying Fortress, a Kestrel Harrier, a P-38

Lightning, a Corsair, and three dozen others. The museum also has a number of armament and memorabilia displays. It's a great outing for aviation buffs. Plan on spending about two hours.

See map p. 303. 231 N. Hoagland Blvd. (south of U.S. 192), Kissimmee. ☎ 407-933-1942. www.warbirdmuseum.com. Admission: $9 adults, $8 seniors 60 and older and children 7–12, children younger than 7 enter free. Parking: Free. Open: Daily 9 a.m.–5 p.m.

Gatorland
North of Kissimmee

It's hard to miss the gigantic green jaws — a perfect vacation photo op, by the way — marking this park's entrance. Founded in 1949, with just a handful of alligators living in huts and pens, Gatorland, still privately owned and operated, now houses thousands of alligators (including a rare blue one) and crocodiles on 110-acre grounds that do dual duty as a wildlife preserve and theme park. Gatorland has survived the arrival of Disney, Universal, and SeaWorld in part because of its old-Florida charm and resistance to becoming overly commercialized (though it hasn't escaped entirely). Breeding pens, nurseries, and rearing ponds are scattered throughout the densely landscaped property, which also displays monkeys, snakes, birds, Florida turtles, and a galapagos tortoise. Its 2,000-foot boardwalk winds through a cypress swamp and breeding marsh with an observation tower for those who prefer an overhead view. The park's four shows include *Gator Wrestlin',* where, at the same time wrestlers are wrangling the reptilians, they're educating the audience about their opponents and how they live; the *Gator Jumparoo,* which features the giant reptiles lunging 4 to 5 feet up out of the water to snatch a dead chicken right from a trainer's hand; *Up Close Encounters,* which showcases a variety of the park's wildlife, including some venomous snakes; and *Jungle Crocs of the World,* which features even more of the park's toothy reptiles. There's an open-air restaurant where you can try smoked gator ribs and nuggets, though more-familiar favorites, such as burgers and hot dogs, are available as well, and a shop where you can buy gator-leather goods and souvenirs. (Gatorland also operates a breeding farm for meat and hides.) Younger guests will appreciate the park's water play area, petting zoo, and train ride. The atmosphere here is laid back. It's always been a huge hit with my family, and it serves up the best half-day experience in the area.

Gatorland's **Trainer for a Day** program lets up to five guests get up close and personal with the gators for a day (or part of it, anyway). The $100, two-hour experience puts you side by side with trainers and includes a chance to wrangle some alligators (minimum age 12). Advanced reservations are required, and admission to the park is included.

See map p. 303. 14501 S. Orange Blossom Trail/U.S. 441 (between Osceola Parkway and Hunter's Creek Boulevard). ☎ 800-393-5297 or 407-855-5496. www.gatorland.com. Admission: $20 adults, $9.95 kids 3–12; advance online purchase price $17 adults, $7.95 kids 3–12. Parking: Free. Open: Daily 9 a.m.–6 p.m., sometimes later.

Orlando Area Attractions

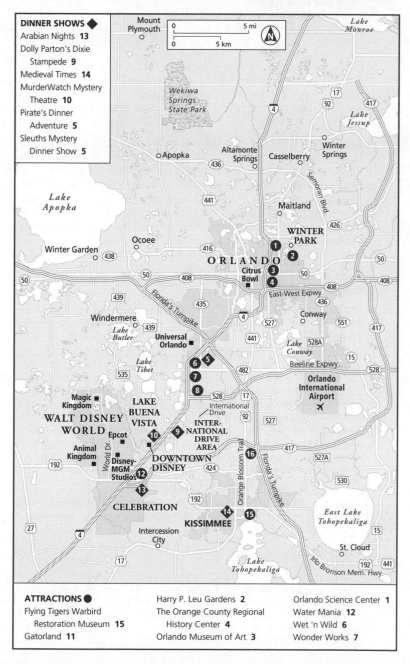

DINNER SHOWS ◆
Arabian Nights **13**
Dolly Parton's Dixie
　Stampede **9**
Medieval Times **14**
MurderWatch Mystery
　Theatre **10**
Pirate's Dinner
　Adventure **5**
Sleuths Mystery
　Dinner Show **5**

ATTRACTIONS ●
Flying Tigers Warbird
　Restoration Museum **15**
Gatorland **11**

Harry P. Leu Gardens **2**
The Orange County Regional
　History Center **4**
Orlando Museum of Art **3**

Orlando Science Center **1**
Water Mania **12**
Wet 'n Wild **6**
Wonder Works **7**

Harry P. Leu Gardens
Near Winter Park

This serene, 50-acre botanical garden on the shores of Lake Rowena offers a delightful break from the theme-park razzle-dazzle. Meandering paths lead through camphors, oaks, and palms. The camellia collection is one of the world's largest, blooming October through March. The formal rose gardens are the largest in Florida and contain 75 varieties. Italian fountains, statues, and a gazebo enhance the gardens. Other highlights include orchids, azaleas, desert plants, beds of colorful annuals and perennials, a butterfly garden, and a 50-foot floral clock.

Businessman Harry P. Leu, who donated his estate to the city in the 1960s, created the gardens. There are $6 guided tours of his house, built in 1888, on the hour and half-hour (advance reservations suggested). The interior has Victorian, Chippendale, and Empire furnishings and pieces of art.

See map p. 303. 1920 N. Forest Ave. (between Nebraska Street and Corrine Drive), Orlando. ☎ *407-246-2620.* www.leugardens.org. *Admission: $5 adults, $1 children grades K–12. Admission is free Mon 9am–noon. Parking: Free. Open: Daily 9 a.m.–5 p.m. except Christmas. Leu House is closed July.*

The Orange County Regional History Center
Downtown

Located within a beautifully restored and historic courthouse built back in 1927, the history center is filled with a multimedia experience that takes visitors on a tour of the Florida and Orlando of long ago to the thriving urban community it is today. The interactive and multisensory experience makes for a unique walk through history. Among the five stories of exhibits are a Florida back porch where the sights and sounds of central Florida's natural environment surround you; a Paleo and Seminole Indian settlement; pioneer cabins; and Florida Crackers. There is also an old courtroom where Ted Bundy is said to have scratched his name into the defendants' table. For those who believe, it is said that ghosts have been known to roam the hallways, causing supernatural disturbances that have induced more than a few letters of resignation over the years. Guided tours are available on Saturdays at 11 a.m. Allow two hours.

See map p. 303. 65 E. Central Blvd. ☎ *407-836-8595.* www.thehistorycenter.org. *Admission: $7 Adults, $6.50 students and seniors, $3.50 children 3–12. Parking: Free at the Orlando Public Library. Open: Mon–Sat 10 a.m.–5 p.m., Sun noon–5 p.m.*

Orlando Museum of Art
Downtown

This local heavyweight handles some of the most prestigious traveling exhibits in the nation. The museum, founded in 1924, hosts special exhibits throughout the year, but even if you miss one, it's worth a stop to see its rotating permanent collection of 19th- and 20th-century American art, pre-Columbian art dating from 1200 B.C. to A.D. 1500, and African art. Allow two to three hours.

See map p. 303. 2416 N. Mills Ave. (in Loch Haven Park). ☎ 407-896-4231. www.omart. org. *Admission: $8 adults, $7 seniors, $5 children 6–18. Parking: Free. Open: Tue–Fri 10 a.m.–4 p.m., Sat–Sun noon to 4 p.m.*

Orlando Science Center
Downtown

This modern, four-story center — the largest of its kind in the Southeast — has 10 halls in which visitors can explore everything from the swamps of Florida to the arid plains of Mars. One of the big attractions is the Dr. Phillips CineDome, a 310-seat theater that features films, planetarium shows, and laser-light presentations. In KidsTown, small fries wander in a mini version of the world around them. Science City, located nearby, has a power plant and suspension bridge, and 123 Math Avenue uses puzzles and other things to make math fun. This option is a great change of pace, especially if you're traveling with children. Allow three to four hours (more if you have an inquiring mind). If you stomach gets the better of you, there's a very casual open cafe area that serves burgers and other familiar favorites.

Strollers are available at no extra charge.

See map p. 303. 777 E. Princeton St. (between Orange and Mills in Loch Haven Park), Orlando. ☎ 407-514-2000 or 888-672-4386. www.osc.org. *Admission (includes exhibits, CineDome film, and planetarium show): $15 adults, $14 students with valid ID and seniors 55 and older, $9.95 children 3–11. After 4 p.m. Fri and Sat admission is reduced $5 for all rates. Parking: $3.50 in a garage across the street. Open: Mon–Thurs 9 a.m.–5 p.m., Fri–Sat 9 a.m.–9 p.m., Sun noon to 5 p.m.*

Go Orlando!

The newly introduced **Go Orlando Card** is a great way to see the "best of the rest" that Orlando has to offer, with admission to attractions like **Gatorland, Ripley's, Watermania, WonderWorks, Kennedy Space Center,** and discounts at area restaurants and shops. Here's how it works: You purchase the all-inclusive Go Card instead of individual tickets to each venue. You then have two weeks in which to use the card at any of the participating venues. They are available in two-, three-, five-, or seven-day increments; the card is activated with the first use and is good for up to 14 days after activated (For example a two-day ticket can be used any two days during the two-week time frame).

Depending on the number of attractions you plan to visit, the Go Card may very well save you some bucks. For details go to www.goorlandocard.com. When you purchase a Go Orlando Card, you'll receive maps and a free guidebook with information on the included attractions. The cost of a two-day card is $99 for adults, $79 for kids ages 3 to 12; a three-day card costs $149 for adults, $109 for kids; a five-day card is $199 for adults, $149 for kids; and a seven-day card runs $259 for adults and $179 for kids.

Ripley's Believe It or Not! Odditorium
International Drive

Do you crave weird science? If you're a fan of the truly bizarre, come here to see lots of oddities. Among the hundreds of exhibits in its 16 galleries: a shrunken head, a two-headed calf, a 1,069-pound man, a five-legged cow, a three-quarter-scale model of a 1907 Rolls-Royce made of 1 million matchsticks, a mosaic of the Mona Lisa created from toast, torture devices from the Spanish Inquisition, and a Tibetan flute made of human bones — you're getting the idea right? You'll also find exhibits on Houdini, films of people swallowing coat hangers, and other human oddities. Visitors are greeted by a hologram of Robert Ripley himself. There are 27 Odditoriums throughout the world, and no two are alike. The tour makes for a fun rainy afternoon or late-night activity. Allow two hours.

8201 International Drive (1½ blocks south of Sand Lake Road). ☎ **407-345-4501.** `www.ripleys.com/orlando2.htm`. *Admission: $17 adults, $12 children 4–12. Parking: Free. Open: Daily 9 a.m.–1 a.m.*

WonderWorks
International Drive

On an uncharted island somewhere in the Bermuda Triangle, a tornado was inadvertently created by scientists experimenting with some seriously weird science. In the midst of the storm, the gigantic building where they were working was swept up and carried off, dropping right in the middle of Orlando — amazingly, the building is fully intact, but it is now upside down. This attraction is educational and fun, just don't come expecting things to be as glitzy as they are in some of the major parks. Throughout the three levels you'll feel the tremble of an earthquake, experience the rush of hurricane-force winds, create massive bubbles, lie on a bed of nails, walk across the bridge of fire — a hair-raising, electrical experience — and even ride the rails via a simulator on a create-your-own-coaster ride. You'll learn dozens of fun and interesting facts. (Where are a cricket's ears? On its knees.) And experience plenty of mind-boggling visual effects. More than 100 exhibits are included, but if you're not a good shot, steer clear of the Laser Tag game: It costs $5 above regular admission and can make for a frustrating few minutes — and while you're at it, skip the arcade extras as well.

The attraction also features a nightly combination of magic and comedy in the dinner show called *The Outta Control Magic Show.* The 90-minute show features magic and improvisational comedy, as well as unlimited pizza, popcorn, soft drinks, and beer. It's a fun time for the kids, and not too bad for adults either. Call to reserve a spot for the show.

Combination tickets are available for discounted admission to WonderWorks, Laser Tag, and the dinner show and are a good buy. Discount coupons are also available on the attraction's Web site, so check it out before you arrive.

See map p. 303. 9067 International Drive, Orlando ☎ **407-351-8800.** `www.Wonder WorksOnline.com`. *Admission: regular admission $19 adults, $13 kids 4–11 and seniors 55 and older; combination ticket offering admission to WonderWorks, Laser*

Tag, and Outta Control $38 adults, $27 kids 4–12 and seniors 55 and older. Outta Control alone is $22 adults, $15 kids 4–11 and seniors. Parking: $2 an hour next door at the Pointe Orlando parking garage. Open: Daily 9 a.m. to midnight. Dinner show nightly at 6 p.m. and 8 p.m.

Getting Wet at Orlando's Water Parks

For more aquatic fun, see Chapter 16 for information on **Disney World's** pair of water parks: *Typhoon Lagoon* and *Blizzard Beach*.

Water Mania
Kissimmee

This 36-acre water park offers a variety of aquatic thrill rides and attractions. You can boogie board or body surf in the wave pools, float lazily along an 850-foot river, enjoy a white-water tube run on *Riptide,* and spiral down the *Twin Tornadoes* water slide. If you dare, ride *The Screamer,* a 72-foot freefall speed slide, or the *Abyss,* an enclosed tube slide that corkscrews through 380 feet of darkness, exiting into a splash pool. There's a rain forest–themed water playground and a pirates' lagoon for children; a miniature golf course; and picnic area with arcade games, a beach, and volleyball. Allow four to five hours. Tubes, towels, and lockers are all available for rent for a small fee and a $1 deposit ($2.15 for a towel, $5–$6.40 for a tube, $4.30–$6.40 for a locker; a child-size life vest can be rented at no charge).

This park offers fewer thrill rides than the city's other water parks and, therefore, attracts fewer teens and young adults, which may make it a little more attractive to families with smaller children.

See map p. 303. 6073 W. Irlo Bronson Memorial Hwy./U.S. 192, Kissimmee. ☎ *800-527-3092 or 407-396-2626.* www.watermania-florida.com. *Admission: $30 adults; $27 kids 3–9. Parking: $6. Open: Daily 10 a.m.–5 p.m. Mar–early Sept; Mon–Fri 11 a.m.– 5 p.m., Sat–Sun 10 a.m.–5 p.m. mid- to late Sept. Call for hours during the month of Oct.*

Wet 'n Wild
International Drive

Unlike Water Mania (see the preceding entry), this 25-acre Universal-owned water park is in the same league as *Typhoon Lagoon* and *Blizzard Beach*. In terms of popularity, it ranks third in the country, right behind the two **Disney** parks. It has several first-rate water rides, including *The Flyer,* a six-story, four-passenger toboggan ride packing 450 feet of banked curves; *The Surge,* which offers 580 feet of greased curves and is billed as the fastest tube ride in the Southeast; *Black Hole,* where two-person rafts shoot through 500 feet of twisting, sometimes dark passages; and the new *Disco H2O,* which takes riders back in time on a four-person raft through an enclosed and rather wild flume ride. Riders eventually end up floating about in the *Aqua Club,* giving a whole new meaning to the phrase Disco Duck. Laser lights and disco balls flash all around as you move and groove to the sounds of the '70s. *All three require that kids 36- to 48-inches tall have an adult with them.*

You can also ride *Raging Rapids,* a simulated white-water run with a waterfall plunge; *Blue Niagara* with its 300 feet of loops and dips *(48-inch height minimum); Knee Ski,* a cable-operated knee-boarding course only open in warm weather *(56-inch height minimum);* and *Mach 5,* which consists of a trio of twisting, turning flumes. The park also has a large kids' area with miniature versions of some of the grown-up rides. If you enjoy the water, plan on spending a full day here. You can rent tubes ($4), towels ($2), and lockers ($5); or a combination of all three ($9); each rental requires a $2 refundable deposit.

If you're considering visiting several of the non-Disney theme parks, the most economical way to see **Wet 'n Wild, Universal Studios Florida, Islands of Adventure,** and **SeaWorld** is with a FlexTicket. It enables you to pay one price to visit any of them during a 14-day period. The four-park pass costs $185 for adults and $151 for children 3 to 9. A five-park pass, which adds **Busch Gardens,** in Tampa (see Chapter 23), is $225 for adults and $190 for kids. You can order the *FlexTicket* through Wet 'n Wild.

See map p. 303. 6200 International Drive (at Universal Boulevard), Orlando. ☎ *800-992-9453 or 407-351-9453.* www.wetnwild.com. *Admission: $34 adults, $28 kids 3–9. Parking: $6. Open: Hours vary seasonally, but the park is open at least 10 a.m.–5 p.m., sometimes as late as 11 p.m., weather permitting.*

Chapter 22

Shopping in Orlando

● ●

In This Chapter

▶ Getting acquainted with Orlando's shopping districts

▶ Checking out the malls, the outlets, and more

▶ Exploring the antiques district

● ●

*I*n this chapter, I provide you with a rundown of some of the better spots outside the Disney district where you can shop to your heart's content, if you've anything left in your bank account after the theme parks have wangled their share. Because **Walt Disney World** is so expert at separating you from your money, you'll find the lowdown on shopping (and spending) at Disney in Chapter 17 . . . yes, it actually requires its very own chapter.

Surveying the Scene

Orlando is a shopper's paradise, offering everything from antiques to souvenirs to upscale one-of-a-kind boutiques. Bargains, however, are few and far between. If you're the kind of person who prides yourself on unearthing a good buy, you'll be doing a lot of digging before you find any noteworthy deals. Orlando hosts an array of indoor multilevel malls, many of them with a fine collection of upscale department stores and unique specialty stores. There are also a few factory outlets, but the bargains there are often not much better than the sale prices offered at many department stores. The city proper has an antiques district where its lots of fun to window shop, but unless you're a serious collector, the prices tend to be prohibitive. Most of Central Florida's tourist areas (Orlando, Kissimmee, and the surrounding territory included) are riddled with T-shirt shacks, jeans joints, and souvenir stands promising bargains that don't (or rarely) exist.

The same is true of the theme parks. If you line up at the registers at Disney, Universal, and the other parks, you pay more than what the merchandise is worth. But if you must have those mouse ears, check out the Disney shopping options in Chapter 17 with the other major theme parks' merchandise mentioned in Chapters 18, 19, and 20.

You can actually get cheaper authentic theme park merchandise outside of the parks than you can within them. Both Disney and Universal operate outlet stores in some of the city's most popular malls (though selections are often very limited, so don't expect to find any unique merchandise). See "Checking Out the Big Names," later in this chapter for more details on these rare opportunities.

Here are three shopping heads-ups before you get started:

- ✔ **Sales tax:** In Orange County, which includes the International Drive area and most of the parks, sales tax is 6.5 percent. Kissimmee and the rest of Osceola County charge 7 percent sales tax.

- ✔ **Store hours:** Most of the stores I mention in this chapter are open seven days a week, from 9 or 10 a.m. until 9 p.m. (6 p.m. on Sun). Small stores, including those in the antiques district, usually close around 5 or 6 p.m. and often aren't open on Sunday. Be sure to call before you head out; the hours are subject to change.

- ✔ **Money:** Most stores accept major credit cards, traveler's checks, and, of course, cash (U.S. currency only). An ATM may not be handy in some areas, and none of the stores listed in this chapter accept foreign currency or personal checks. So be prepared before heading out.

All the places listed in this chapter can be found on the "Orlando Area Shopping" map on page 311.

Finally, know that because Orlando is geared toward travelers, many retailers offer to ship packages home for a few dollars more. So, if you're pondering an extra-large or a fragile purchase you don't want to drag home on the plane, train, or in the car, ask. If a retailer doesn't offer this service, check with your hotel. Many either have a business center where you can mail it yourself, or they can arrange a pick-up by United Parcel Service, the slow-but-good-old U.S. Postal Service, or another carrier to keep you from dragging a 6-foot stuffed Pluto into the Friendly Skies.

Exploring Great Shopping Neighborhoods

Orlando doesn't have a central shopping district or districts. Instead, most shops are sprinkled throughout and around the tourist hot spots and in retail areas where locals shop, such as malls and so on. The following is a list of some of the more frequented shopping zones:

- ✔ **Celebration:** Think *Pleasantville* à la Disney. Created by Disney, the town of 25,000 is more of a charming diversion than a good place to power shop. The downtown area has a dozen or so stores and boutiques, a handful of art galleries, a grocer, and a parfumerie among others. The storefronts are filled with enticing displays, while inside they peddle interesting and, often, unique — though highly priced — merchandise; but, the real attraction is the mid-20th-century, Main Street atmosphere. Those nostalgic for yesteryear, or in search of

Orlando Area Shopping

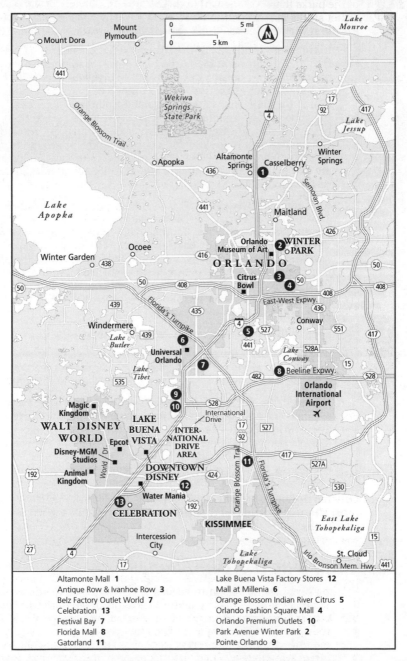

Altamonte Mall **1**
Antique Row & Ivanhoe Row **3**
Belz Factory Outlet World **7**
Celebration **13**
Festival Bay **7**
Florida Mall **8**
Gatorland **11**

Lake Buena Vista Factory Stores **12**
Mall at Millenia **6**
Orange Blossom Indian River Citrus **5**
Orlando Fashion Square Mall **4**
Orlando Premium Outlets **10**
Park Avenue Winter Park **2**
Pointe Orlando **9**

a quieter, more sophisticated afternoon out on the town, love it, and . . . look, over there! Is that Ozzie and Harriet? From **WDW,** take U.S. 192 east 5 miles, past Interstate 4. The entrance to Celebration is on the right. Call ☎ 407-566-2200 for more information.

✔ **Kissimmee:** Southeast of the Disney parks, Kissimmee straddles U.S. 192/Irlo Bronson Memorial Highway — a sometimes tacky, too-often-under-construction stretch of highway lined with budget motels, smaller attractions, and a branch of every fast-food restaurant in the known universe. Although Kissimmee has recently begun to evolve and now includes more family-oriented attractions and better hotels and eateries, the town's shopping merit remains negligible unless you're looking for a cheap T-shirt, or seashells not sold by the seashore, or the like. That said, cowboy lovers may appreciate the area's Western shops, a sign the city is still mindful of its cowboy roots.

✔ **International Drive area:** This tourist magnet is east of, and extends 7 to 10 miles north of, the Disney parks between Highway 535 and the Florida Turnpike. The southern end offers a little elbow room, the midsection is somewhat upscale, but the northern part is a tourist strip crowded with small-time attractions (including bungee jumping for those who have a death wish), fast fooderies, and souvenir shacks. Its most redeeming shopping draws: **Pointe Orlando** and the **Orlando Premium Outlets.** (See listing under "The Malls," later in this chapter.)

Locally, International Drive is better known as *I-Drive.*

✔ **Downtown Orlando:** Orlando's downtown is actually northeast of the theme parks along I-4. The biggest draws here are the shops along **Antique Row.** (See "Antiquing Downtown," later in this chapter.)

✔ **Winter Park:** Just north of Downtown Orlando, Winter Park began as a haven for the wealthy Yankees escaping the cold Northeast. Today, Winter Park's centerpiece is **Park Avenue,** a collection of upscale shops, art galleries, and restaurants along a cobblestone, tree-lined street. Ann Taylor, Talbot's, Williams-Sonoma, and Crabtree & Evelyn are among the dozens of specialty shops. No matter which end of Park Avenue you start at, there are more shops than most can survive, but you're bound to find something here you won't find anywhere else. For more information on Winter Park, call ☎ 407-644-8281.

Checking Out the Big Names

Orlando's reputation wasn't built on shopping. In fact, it isn't even the No. 1 shopping area in Florida, falling well short of Miami–Fort Lauderdale. But Orlando has attracted some big names, including a very small *Saks,* as well as *Neiman Marcus, Nordstrom, Bloomingdale's,* and Macy's. Some of the better specialty stores include *Tiffany & Co.* and *Charles David,* while some of the more unique retailers include *Ron Jon's Surf Shop* and *Hilo Hattie.* It also has a growing stable of discount centers.

Factory outlets

In the last decade, the tourist areas have bloomed with outlets where shoppers can find plenty of name brands, but not always big bargains. Although many of the stores claim savings of 50 to 75 percent, a discount on a heavily marked-up or overpriced item doesn't always mean you're actually getting a deal. And more often than not, only a few items are as heavily marked down as the outlets maintain. What you will find (at least in most cases anyway) is a decent selection of designer and name-brand merchandise at slightly lower prices than you would normally pay at the malls.

If you're a smart outlet shopper, you know the suggested retail prices for items before you hit the stores. Therefore, you'll know just what is — and what *isn't* — a bargain.

Here's a list of outlet stores and centers in and around Orlando:

- ✔ **Belz Factory Outlet World:** Belz (☎ **407-352-9611;** www.belz.com) is the granddaddy of all Orlando outlets. Located at 5401 W. Oak Ridge Rd. (at the north end of International Drive), it has 170 stores in two huge, enclosed malls and four annexes. The outlet offers more than a dozen shoe stores (including Bass, Nike, and Timberland), many housewares stores (such as Fitz & Floyd, Oneida, and Mikasa), and more than 60 clothing shops (London Fog, Adidas, Tommy Hilfiger, Danskin, Izod, Liz Claiborne, Guess Jeans, Kasper, and Geoffrey Beene, for example). You'll also find records, electronics, sporting goods, health and beauty aids, jewelry, toys, gifts, accessories, lingerie, hosiery, and so on.

  The two main buildings, Mall 1 and Mall 2, each have discount outlets for *Disney World* merchandise (*Character Premier* and *Character Warehouse*), as well a store for *Universal Orlando.* You have to dig for some of the bargains, but if you don't mind your item saying 2005 instead of 2006, you can save 50 percent or more on select items.

- ✔ **Lake Buena Vista Factory Stores:** The three dozen or so outlets here include Big Dog, Casuals (Ralph Lauren and Tommy Hilfiger), Gap, Old Navy, Nike, Eddie Bauer, Carters, Liz Claiborne, Fossil, Osh Kosh, and Reebok. Savings are modest, but the plaza itself is quiet and inviting. There's also a food court and a salon. You can find these stores at 15591 S. Apopka–Vineland Rd.; ☎ **407-238-9301;** www.lbvfs.com.

✔ **Orlando Premium Outlets:** This is my favorite outlet mall in Orlando, and it's also the only true upscale outlet in the city. The center's 110 tenants include Coach, DKNY, Kenneth Cole, Nike, Hugo Boss, Ralph Lauren, Nautica, Timberland, and Tommy Hilfiger. In contrast to most of the outlet centers in the city, it's character is more of an open-air outdoor mall. Some of the best buys here are at Banana Republic and a second location of Disney's discount *Character Premier* store. It's at 8200 Vineland Ave. (just off the southern third of I-Drive, next to *Dolly's Dixie Stampede*); ☎ **407-238-7787;** www.PremiumOutlets.com.

The Malls

The Orlando area is also home to several traditional shopping malls. As in malls throughout the country, good buys are often elusive. Arguably, a mall's best bargain is the people-watching, which is free. Here's a list of Orlando's malls:

✔ **Altamonte Mall:** Built in the early 1970s, this is the area's second largest mall, behind the Florida Mall (see later in this list). Altamonte Mall's major-league tenants include Macy's, JCPenney, and Sears, as well as 175 specialty shops. Major renovations have added a food court; a new indoor, soft-play area for younger kids; rides for toddlers; and a new 18-screen AMC movie theater with stadium seating. You can find it at 451 E. Altamonte Dr. (about 15 miles north of downtown Orlando). For information call ☎ **407-830-4422** or surf over to www.altamontemall.com.

✔ **Festival Bay:** One of the newest additions to the shopping scene, Festival Bay's tenants include a Ron Jon Surf Shop, Hilo Hattie, Bass Pro Shops, and several other specialty stores. Restaurants include a handful of fast-food eateries as well as Murray Bros. Caddy Shack, Fuddruckers, and the brand new Dixie Crossroads, with a Cold Stone Creamery to top off your meal. Some of the area's more unique recreational venues can be found here as well, including Vans (indoor) Skatepark; The Putting Edge, a glow-in-the-dark mini golf park; and a 20-screen Cinemark Theater. Plans are in the works for an indoor Ron Jon Surf Park where surfers, beginners and experts alike, can ride the waves and hang ten all day long. This one can be found at 5250 International Drive (the far north end of I-Drive across from the Belz Outlets). For information call ☎ **407-351-7718** or go to www.belz.com.

✔ **Florida Mall:** The exciting news at this popular shopping spot is the arrival of Nordstrom and Lord & Taylor to combat the opening of Mall at Millenia (see below). Other anchors include Macy's, Dillard's, JCPenney, Sears, and Saks to go along with an Adam's Mark Hotel and more than 250 specialty stores (Abercrombie & Fitch, Harry & David, Sharper Image, and Benetton, to name a few), restaurants (the Salsa Taqueria and Tequila Bar, California Pizza Kitchen, and Bucca Di Beppo are just three of the choices), and entertainment venues. You can find the Florida Mall at 8001 S. Orange Blossom Trail (at Sand Lake Road, 4 miles east of International Drive). For details, call ☎ 407-851-6255 or check out www.shopsimon.com.

✔ **Mall at Millenia:** This 1.3 million-square-foot upscale center made quite a splash when it debuted in October 2002 with anchors that include Bloomingdale's, Macy's, and Neiman Marcus. In addition to the heavyweight anchors, Millenia offers 200 specialty stores that include Burberry, Chanel, Crate & Barrel, Godiva, Gucci, Lladro, Swarovski, and Tiffany & Co. Restaurants include The Cheesecake Factory, P.F. Chang's China Bistro, Johnny Rockets, and Panera Bread among others. The recently-opened Blue Martini is an upscale bar featuring a tapas menu and 29 designer martinis and is a good place to celebrity watch or just pretend to be famous. The mall is 5 miles from downtown Orlando at 4200 Conroy Rd. (at I-4 near Universal Orlando). For details, call ☎ 407-363-3555 or visit www. mallatmillenia.com.

✔ **Orlando Fashion Square Mall:** This city-side mall has marbled walkways, indoor palm trees, and tenants that include Macy's, JCPenney, Sears, 165 specialty shops, and an extensive food court. The mall is 5 miles from downtown Orlando at 3201 E. Colonial Dr.; ☎ 407-896-1132.

✔ **Pointe Orlando:** Although it's set up like a mall, this complex's two levels of stores, restaurants, and a 21-screen IMAX theater aren't under one roof, making it a mall with an open top. Headliners among the 60 shops include Bath & Body Works, Foot Locker, and Victoria's Secret. Plans are underway to renovate the complex to include even more shops and restaurants and create a more-inviting streetscape. Parking is $5 in the attached garage, but most restaurants, night-clubs, and the movie theater will validate with a purchase. Pointe Orlando (☎ 407-248-2838; www.pointeorlandofl.com) is located at 9101 International Drive.

Antiquing Downtown

If you can think of nothing better than a relaxing afternoon of sifting through yesterday's treasures, check out **Antique Row** and **Ivanhoe Row** on North Orange Avenue in downtown Orlando.

Flo's Attic (☎ 407-895-1800; www.flosattic.com) and *A.J. Lillun* (☎ 407-895-6111) sell traditional antiques. *Fredlund Wildlife Gallery* (☎ 407-898-4544; www.fredlundwildlife.com) sells pricey, original works of art, including sculpture. And *The Fly Fisherman* (☎ 407-898-1989; www.fly fishermaninc.com) sells — no surprise here — fly-fishing gear. You can sometimes watch people taking lessons in the park across the street.

Homegrown souvenirs

Given Orlando's history as a major citrus producer, oranges, grapefruit, and other citrus products rank high on the list of local products. **Orange Blossom Indian River Citrus,** 5151 S. Orange Blossom Trail, Orlando (☎ **800-624-8835** or 407-855-2837; www.orange-blossom.com), is one of the top sellers during the late-fall-to-late-spring season. It also makes a great place to shop for anyone left in charge of your pets, house, or other such duties while you're off vacationing in the sunshine state.

And if you have a love affair with leather, alligator-skin leather goods are a specialty of the gift shop at **Gatorland,** 14501 S. Orange Blossom Trail (☎ **407-855-5496;** www.gatorland.com). For more details on this classic Florida theme park, see Chapter 21.

All the stores I mention in this section are spread over 3 miles along Orange Avenue. The heaviest concentration is between Princeton Street and New Hampshire Avenue, although a few are scattered between New Hampshire and Virginia avenues. The more upscale shops extend a few blocks beyond Virginia Avenue. To reach the area from the theme parks, take I-4 east to Princeton Street (Exit 43). Turn right on Orange Avenue. Parking is limited, so stop wherever you find a space.

As for hours of operation, most of the stores are open from 9 or 10 a.m. to 5 p.m., Monday through Saturday. (Storeowners usually run the stores, so hours can vary; call before you head out. A small number of shops are open Sunday, but it isn't worth the trip from the resorts.)

If you decide to do your antiquing on a Saturday, you can also shop for fresh produce, plants, baked goods, and crafts every Saturday from 8 a.m. to 2:30 p.m. at a downtown **farmers' market.** It's located at the intersection of North Magnolia and East Central. Get more information at www.downtownorlando.com.

Chapter 23

Going Beyond Orlando: Two Day Trips

• •

In This Chapter
▶ Going on safari at Busch Gardens
▶ Lifting off at the Kennedy Space Center

• •

*E*ven with all Orlando has to offer (and if you've read chapters 12–20 you know there's plenty), you may want to drive to the coast for a day to enjoy a change of pace, some sugary sand beaches, and warm waters. In addition to Florida's spectacular beaches, two places are worth going out of your way to visit: **Busch Gardens** in Tampa Bay and the **Kennedy Space Center** at Cape Canaveral. The first is a combination of SeaWorld, with its lush landscaping, relaxing atmosphere, and eco-educational themes (see Chapter 20), Disney's Animal Kingdom, with its array of African wildlife; (see Chapter 15), and Universal's Islands of Adventure's heart-pounding thrill rides. Kennedy Space Center is a unique experience that you just can't get in Orlando (unless Disney starts developing a space-shuttle program, which would be a stretch, even for them).

Trekking to Busch Gardens

When this Tampa theme park grew out of a brewery in the '60s, the main (and only) attractions were a bird show and free beer. (Some of you may be wondering, who could ask for anything more?) Both are alive and well, but Busch Gardens has grown into one of Florida's top theme parks, filled with coasters that can out-thrill even Universal Orlando, and wildlife, eco-educational themes, and landscaping that all give the park a unique and fascinating allure.

Getting there

If you're driving from Orlando, head west on I-4 to I-75. Go north on I-75 to Exit 265 (Fowler Avenue/University of South Florida). Bear left on the exit ramp, and it will lead you directly onto Fowler Avenue. Proceed west on Fowler Avenue to McKinley Avenue. (McKinley Avenue is the first light past the main entrance to the University.) Turn left on McKinley. Proceed south on McKinley to the parking lot and the main entrance to the park. Parking costs $7 per day. The drive should take a little more than an hour, depending on traffic.

SeaWorld (see Chapter 20) and **Busch Gardens** in Tampa, both owned by Anheuser-Busch, have a shuttle service (☎ **800-221-1339**) that offers $10 round-trip tickets to get you from Orlando to Tampa and back. The 1½- to 2-hour one-way shuttle runs daily and has five pick-up locations in Orlando, including at Universal Orlando and on I-Drive (call for schedules, reservations, and pick-up locations). The schedule allows about seven hours at Busch Gardens. The service is free if you have a 5-park FlexTicket. For more on the FlexTicket, see "Admission options," which follows.

Most Orlando shuttle services will also take you to Busch Gardens. See Chapter 8 for details on the city's shuttle companies.

Visitor information

You can get information in advance of your visit by calling ☎ **888-800-5447** or 813-987-5283 or heading online to the park's excellent Web site, www.buschgardens.com. Once inside the park, you can obtain information from several visitor centers, or you can try the **Expedition Africa Gift Shop.** Be sure to grab a guide map of the park when you enter.

Busch Garden is open daily, generally from 10 a.m. to 6 p.m. (though hours can range from 9 a.m.–9 p.m. during peak season). The park's hours change seasonally, and seemingly on a whim, so be sure to confirm the hours for the day you're going by either calling or checking the Web site before you depart.

You can get information, save a few dollars, and avoid waiting in long lines by buying your tickets to Busch Gardens at the privately owned **Tampa Bay Visitor Information Center,** opposite the park at 3601 E. Busch Blvd., at North Ednam Place (☎ **813-985-3601;** www.hometown.aol.com\tpabayinfoctr). Owner Jim Boggs worked for the park for 13 years and gives expert advice on how to get the most out of your visit.

Admission options

Busch Gardens has a number of admission schemes, though your options are usually limited to two as a day visitor:

- ✔ **One-day regular park admission** costs $56 adults, $46 for kids 3 to 9, children younger than 3 are admitted free. Prices do not include the 7 percent sales tax.

- ✔ The **FlexTicket** is a multiday, multipark option that may work for you if you plan on visiting Universal Orlando or SeaWorld while in Orlando. The most economical way to see the various "other-than-Disney" parks, you pay one price to visit any of the participating parks during a 14-day period. A five-park pass to **Universal Studios Florida, Islands of Adventure, Wet 'n Wild, SeaWorld,** and **Busch Gardens** is $225 for adults and $190 for kids. You can order the FlexTicket by calling ☎ **888-800-5447** or by going to www.buschgardens.com. For more on the other FlexTicket parks, see Chapters 18 through 21.

Busch Gardens occasionally runs other discount admissions specials and offers a host of other multiday and annual-pass selections (fun cards and the like). If you plan on spending more time in Tampa and want some more details on these options, call ☎ **888-800-5447** or 813-987-5283 or check the Web at www.buschgardens.com.

Seeing the park

Busch Gardens is older than Walt Disney World and, over the years, has managed to age quite well. This park has eight distinctive areas, each of which has its own theme, animals, live entertainment, thrill rides, kiddie attractions, dining, and shopping. A Skyride cable car soars over the park, offering a bird's-eye view of it all. Two things set Busch Gardens apart from its nearest rival (Disney's Animal Kingdom): its vast array of thrill rides (some of best in the country) and the accessibility of its wildlife.

Chasing thrills

Busch Gardens has six — count 'em, *SIX!!* — roller coasters (and that doesn't include the flume and rapids rides) to keep your adrenaline pumping and stomach jumping. New to the collection is *SheiKra,* and she's a doozie. The first of its kind in the Americas (and only the third in the world of its kind, though, of course, this one's higher and faster), this dive coaster hurtles you 90 degrees straight down at speeds reaching 70 mph and 4Gs. If you manage to survive that, its on to a rolling loop, and a second 90 degree drop plummeting you 138 feet through an underground tunnel. Other unexpected thrills await you throughout the three minute adventure. As you may expect, *there is a height restriction of 54 inches to ride this one.*

The *Gwazi* is a wooden wonder named for a fabled African lion with a tiger's head. This $10-million ride slowly climbs to 90 feet, before turning, twisting, diving, and *va-rrroommming* to speeds of 50 mph — enough to give you air time (also known as weightlessness). Fact is, these twin coasters, the *Lion* and the *Tiger,* provide 2 minutes and 20 seconds of thrills and chills, steep-banked curves, and bobsled maneuvers. At six points on the ride, you're certain you're going to slam the other coaster as you hit 3.5Gs.

There's a *48-inch minimum height,* and the 15-inch seat is smaller than an airline seat, so it's a tight squeeze for thin folks and the next best thing to misery for larger models.

Busch's other four roller coasters are made of steel. *Kumba* is a 143-foot-high number that covers 4,000 feet of track at 60 mph. It jerks you with sudden turns and has *a 54-inch height minimum*. *Montu* musses your hair at speeds exceeding 60 mph while the G-force keeps you plastered to your seat *(another 54-inch minimum)*. The *Python* is a tad tamer, running through a double-spiraling corkscrew and a 70-foot plunge *(48-inch minimum)*. The *Scorpion* offers a high-speed 60-foot drop and 360-degree loop *(42-inch minimum)*.

The park's water rides are welcome relief from the summer heat. *Tanganyika Tidal Wave (48-inch height minimum)* is a steep flume, while *Congo River Rapids (42-inch height minimum)* is similar to *Kali River Rapids* in Animal Kingdom (see Chapter 15).

Meeting animals and seeing shows

Busch Gardens has several thousand animals living in very naturalistic environments that continue the park's African theme. Most authentic is the 80-acre *Serengeti Plain,* strongly reminiscent of the real Serengeti of Tanzania and Kenya, upon which zebras, giraffes, and other animals graze. Unlike the animals on the real Serengeti, however, the grazing animals have nothing to fear from lions, hyenas, crocodiles, and other predators, which are confined to enclosures — as are hippos and elephants. Busch's critters have fewer places to hide and, therefore, are much easier to see than those at Animal Kingdom (see Chapter 15).

Twenty-six acres of the Serengeti Plain are devoted to free-roaming white rhinos. *Rhino Rally,* a Land Rover tour through the plains, takes up to 16 passengers on a very bumpy, seven-minute journey where the white rhinos, Asian elephants, cape buffaloes, alligators, antelopes, and other animals roam. There are, of course, a few catches along the way to make the ride a bit more exciting. If you can handle the bumps, it's a pretty good ride, and one of the few that's appropriate for almost all ages.

Nairobi's *Myombe Reserve* is home to gorillas; this area also has a baby-animal nursery, petting zoo, turtle and reptile displays, and an elephant exhibit. **Congo** features rare white Bengal tigers.

In addition to the animals, your kids will love *Land of the Dragons,* which has slides, a tree house, and rides. Kids also like the sandy dig site at *King Tut's Tomb* and the friendly lorikeets of *Lory Landing.* Kids especially love the 22-minute *R.L. Stine's Haunted Lighthouse* film, a family-friendly show that combines sensory effects and 3-D film.

And did I mention the **free beer** if you're 21 or older? This is an Anheuser-Busch park you know. You can sample their products at the *Hospitality House.*

Special tours and options

Although you get close to Busch Garden's predators, hippos, and elephants in their glass-walled enclosures with a regular admission, the only way to mingle with the grazers is on a tour. Here are the best the park offers (note that children must be at least age 5 to participate in any of them):

 ✔ For an extra $30 to $34 (depending on the season) over the admission price, you can go on the 30-minute, guided **Serengeti Safari** tour, which feature an extra close look and a chance to feed giraffes, gazelles, and more (from the back of a flatbed truck). If you're eager for a hands-on wildlife experience, the safari is worth the extra money. You can make reservations for the first tour of the day at the Expedition Africa Gift Shop or by calling ☎ **813-984-4043,** but the midday and afternoon tours are first-come, first-served. Kids must be older than 5 years old to participate.

 ✔ The 5-hour **Guided Adventure** tour gives you the safari, front-of-the-line access to shows and rides, plus lunch, for $90 above park admission. The **Elite Adventure Tours** includes the above plus free parking, free bottled water on the tour, merchandise discounts, VIP seating at shows, and two meals ($180 per person plus park admission). If you want to participate, reserve in advance by calling ☎ **813-984-4043** or online at www.buschgardens.com.

Blasting Off to John F. Kennedy Space Center

Each time a space shuttle blasts into the heavens, someone you know wishes he or she could be an astronaut. Heck — maybe it's you. You can live out your childhood fantasies at the **Kennedy Space Center** located on the so-called "Space Coast" at Cape Canaveral.

Getting there

Though there are shuttles from Orlando to Cape Canaveral, this area really demands a car in order to be seen properly. The Center is an easy hour's drive from Orlando via the BeeLine Expressway (Highway 528, a toll road). Take the S.R. 407 exit going to Kennedy Space Center and Titusville and continue on S.R. 407 until it dead ends into S.R. 405. Turn right (east) onto S.R. 405 and follow the signs for Kennedy Space Center. You will travel approximately 9 miles on S.R. 405. The KSC Visitor Complex will be on your right. Parking is free.

Visitor information

For information before you leave home, call ☎ 321-449-4444 or check out the Center's Web site at www.kennedyspacecenter.com. For general information about the Space Coast, contact the **Florida Space Coast Office of Tourism/Brevard County Tourist Development Council** by calling ☎ 800-872-1969 or 321-868-1126; or by surfing the Web to www.space-coast.com.

The **Visitor Complex** is open from 9 a.m. to 7 p.m. and the **Astronaut Hall of Fame** is open from 10 a.m. to 8 p.m. daily (except Christmas and select launch days). Always call to confirm these hours before you set out for Cape Canaveral.

Admission options

You have two main ticket options:

- ✓ **Standard Admission** includes admission to the Kennedy Space Center, several IMAX films, and access to exhibits and shows. It costs $30 adults and $20 kids 3 to 11.

- ✓ A **Maximum Admission** pass includes admission to the Kennedy Space Center, several IMAX films, access to exhibits and shows, entrance to the Astronaut Hall of Fame, and a chance to ride in an interactive space simulator. It costs $37 for adults and $27 for kids 3 to 11. You can purchase this pass (and others) online at www.kennedyspacecenter.com.

You can also purchase Hall of Fame admission only for $17 adult, $13 children. A 12-month pass runs $46 adult, $30 children. The ATX, or Astronaut Training Experience (see below), costs $225.

Touring the Center

Whether you're a space buff or not, you'll appreciate the sheer grandeur of the facilities and technological achievements displayed at NASA's primary space-launch facility. Highlights of the Center include trips down memory lane and glances into the future of space exploration. You also explore the history of manned flights, beginning with the wild ride of the late Alan Shepard (1961) and Neil Armstrong's 1969 moonwalk. The Center also has dual 5½-story, 3-D IMAX theaters that reverberate with special effects. You'll need at least a full day to see and do everything here.

Begin your visit at the **Kennedy Space Center Visitor Complex,** which has real NASA rockets and the actual Mercury Mission Control Room from the 1960s. You'll find several hands-on activities for kids, including a chance to meet a real astronaut, as well as several dining venues and a shop selling a variety of space memorabilia and souvenirs. Because this privately operated complex has been undergoing an ambitious $130 million renovation and expansion, check to see whether it has changed its tours and exhibits before visiting.

Bus tours of the complex (included with your admission) run continuously. Plan to take the tour early in your visit and be sure to hit the restrooms before boarding the bus — there's only one out on the tour. You can get off at the LC-39 *Observation Gantry,* which has a 360-degree view of shuttle launch pads; the *International Space Station Center,* where scientists and engineers prepare additions to the space station now in orbit; and the *Apollo/Saturn V Center,* which includes artifacts, photos, interactive exhibits, and the 363-foot-tall Saturn V rocket.

Don't miss the **Astronaut Memorial,** a moving black-granite monument that has the names of the U.S. astronauts who have died on missions or while in training. The 60-ton structure rotates on a track that follows the movement of the sun (on clear days, of course), causing the names to stand out above a brilliant reflection of the sky.

The **Astronaut Hall of Fame,** a separate attraction at the Kennedy Space Center Visitor Center, includes displays, exhibits, and tributes to the heroes of the Mercury, Gemini, and Apollo space programs. There's also a collection of spacecraft, including a Mercury 7 capsule, a Gemini training capsule, and an Apollo 14 command module. And in *Simulator Station,* guests can experience the pressure of four times the force of gravity, ride a rover across Mars, and land a space shuttle.

 On launch days, the Center is closed at least part of the day. Although launch days aren't good times to see the Center, they're great occasions to observe history in the making. Schedules for launch tickets entitling you to admission to the Center for the shortened operating hours, plus at least a two-hour excursion to *NASA Parkway* to see the liftoff, are available by calling ☎ **321-449-4444.** You must pick up tickets, available five days prior to the launch, on site.

Special tours and options

The **Kennedy Space Center** offers a number of special programs and tours to visitors. Here are a few that will delight any wannabe-astronauts or avid space buffs:

✔ The ultrapopular **Lunch with an Astronaut** program gives visitors the chance to enjoy an out-of-this-world experience: lunch with an actual astronaut. The opportunity is available at the Center every day during lunch hours. Past participants have included John Glenn, Jim Lovell, and Wally Schirra. Seating is limited, so be sure to reserve well in advance by calling ☎ **321-449-4400** or heading online to www.kennedyspacecenter.com. The program costs $20 for adults and $13 for kids 3 to 11 in addition to the cost of admission to the Center.

✔ The **Cape Canaveral Then and Now** tour includes a visit to the first launch sites, the Air Force Museum, and the Missile Museum. The tour costs $22 adult and $16 kids 3 to 11.

✔ On the 90-minute **NASA Up Close tour,** a space program expert guides you through the intricacies of the space-shuttle program and gives you an up-close look at the space shuttle launch pads. The tour almost always sells out, so reserve in advance of your trip by calling ☎ **321-449-4400** or going online to www.kennedyspace center.com. The tour costs $22 adults and $16 kids 3 to 11 in addition to the cost of admission.

Part VI
Living It Up After Dark: Orlando Nightlife

The 5th Wave   By Rich Tennant

"Actually, they started out as just bickering pianos."

In this part . . .

Orlando's action used to literally rise and set with the sun, but that's hardly the case now. I tip my hat to those of you who still have the pizzazz for a nighttime adventure after a day in the parks. Whether you prefer rocking the night away, slow dancing until dawn, or dining while you watch pirates battle for treasure, you can liven up your evenings in Orlando, and this part of the book shows you how.

Chapter 24

Taking in the Dinner Shows

● ●

In This Chapter

▶ Seeing Orlando's best dinner shows

▶ Getting tickets for everything else

● ●

*I*f a day at the theme parks isn't enough to satisfy your appetite for entertainment, Orlando's dinner theaters serve up a rather diverse menu of amusements to keep you entertained as you dine. In this chapter, I tell you about dinner shows where you can solve a "murder," learn to hula, or cheer on a knight at a medieval joust.

Getting the Inside Scoop on Orlando Dinner Theater

Orlando's busy dinner-show scene is far different than those you find in high-flying cultural centers such as Paris, New York, and London. **Walt Disney World** and Orlando feature family-oriented fun and fanfare rather than critically acclaimed dramatic performances. Most shows focus on entertaining the city's top VIPs: the kids. Expect action, adventure, and corny humor, all generally performed in a very loud stadium setting where the kids can scream to their hearts content.

Did you ever notice that you never see dinner-shows listed in the restaurant section? Ever wonder why? It's not the dinner you're going for. Eating adds its own ingredient of adventure to Orlando's dinner-theater experience. The fare is right off the rubber chicken circuit. The meals usually consist of a choice of two or three generic entrees (often over-cooked) and school-lunch caliber side dishes. This may very well explain why some theaters serve free wine and beer after you've been seated — to dull your palate before dinner is served.

 The prices of the shows that I list in this section include your meal and the aforementioned wine and beer (soda is available, too) but not tax or tips, unless otherwise noted.

You can often find discount coupons to the dinner shows inside the tourist magazines distributed in the tourist information centers, hotel lobbies, gas stations, and sometimes on the listed Web sites. A good place to look for discounted tickets for the dinner theaters is the **Orlando CVB** Web site (www.orlandoinfo.com).

For all dinner shows, advance reservations are strongly recommended.

And when it comes to **Walt Disney World** dinner shows, always, always, *always,* make an Advanced Dining Reservation, ☎ **407-939-3463.** (See Chapter 10 for more about Advanced Dining Reservations.) Disney's shows fill up fast, often months in advance for weekend performances and during peak vacation seasons and holidays. I've actually spent several days trying to make reservations (for the *Hoop-Dee-Doo Musical Review*), calling the very minute the phone lines opened (usually around 7 a.m.) about 1 year in advance and it took four days to finally get a reservation — and I didn't get the day or the time I would have liked.

Arabian Nights
Kissimmee

If you're a horse fan, this show is a winner. It stars many of the most popular breeds, from chiseled Arabians to hard-driving quarter horses to beefcake Belgians. They giddy-up through performances that include trick riding, chariot races, a little slapstick comedy, and bareback daredevils. The premise of the show is the elaborate wedding of the prince and princess — and what wedding would be complete without an uninvited guest? — and so begins the adventure. Locals rate it No. 1 among Orlando dinner shows. On most nights, the performance opens with a ground trainer working one-on-one with a black stallion. The dinner, served during the two-hour show, includes salad, a choice of prime rib, grilled chicken, chicken tenders, chopped steak, or vegetable lasagna, vegetables, garlic mashed potatoes, rolls, and wedding cake for dessert. Unlimited beer, wine, or soda pop comes with the meal.

The Web site usually offers a discount on tickets purchased online.

See map p. 303. 6225 W. Irlo Bronson Memorial Hwy. (U.S. 192, east of I-4 at Exit 25A). ☎ 800-553-6116 or 407-239-9223. www.arabian-nights.com. *Reservations recommended. Shows held daily, times vary. Admission: $47 adults, $29 kids 3–11. AE, DISC, MC, V. Stadium-style seating. Parking: Free.*

Dolly Parton's Dixie Stampede
Lake Buena Vista

What do you get when you combine 32 horses, a slew of talented riders and singers, and Dolly's family-friendly vision of the Civil War? A down-home battle of the North and South featuring corny jokes and plenty of audience interaction. You'll try to resist, but it'll win you over. Come early for entertainment by Gary, the original Electric Cowboy. The all-inclusive price includes unlimited soda, tea, beer, and wine during the meal, as well as a four-course, Southern-style meal (rotisserie chicken and barbecued pork or lasagna, corn on the cob, herb potato, and a turnover for dessert) — the creamed vegetable soup is surprisingly outstanding. Be sure to take a gander at the horse stables after the show.

See map p. 303. 8251 Vineland Ave. (off I-4, next to the Orlando Premium Outlets).
☎ *866-443-4943.* www.dixiestampede.com. *Reservations required. Shows: 6:30 p.m; an 8:30 p.m. show is sometimes added. A holiday version of the show runs during the Christmas holiday season. Admission: $47 adults, $20 kids 4–11. AE, DISC, MC, V. Stadium-style seating. Parking: Free.*

Hoop-Dee-Doo Musical Revue
Walt Disney World

This show at Disney's **Fort Wilderness Resort & Campground** (see Chapter 9 for more on this hotel) is Disney's most popular, so make Advanced Dining Reservations as early as possible. The reward: You feast on a down-home, all-you-can-eat barbecue (fried chicken, smoked ribs, salad, corn on the cob, baked beans, bread, salad, strawberry shortcake, and your choice of coffee, tea, beer, wine, sangria, or soda) all served up family style in tin buckets. While you stuff yourself silly in Pioneer Hall, performers in 1890s garb lead you in a foot-stomping, hand-clapping high-energy show that includes plenty of jokes that you haven't heard since elementary school, but somehow seem just as funny now. The audience is quickly caught up in all the hoopla, and even the most skeptical find themselves having plenty of fun. Although the songs and skits are a bit corny, the talent is absolutely stellar.

If you catch one of the early shows, consider sticking around for the Electrical Water Pageant at 9:45 p.m., viewed from the Fort Wilderness Beach.

Audience participation is heavily encouraged, and the cast is more than happy to help you single out your friends.

Upon arriving at Fort Wilderness, you'll need to park in the guest lot and take the resort's internal bus system to Pioneer Hall where the show is held. Add at least an extra half-hour to your traveling time because of this.

Reservations can be made up to two years in advance. Your travel dates will determine how far in advance to call — during holidays, spring break, and summers you should make reservations as early as possible. The entire bill must be paid when making the reservation, but as long as you call at least 48 hours prior to the day of your reservation, you will be refunded your entire payment if you find you have to cancel.

See map p. 338. 3520 N. Fort Wilderness Trail (at WDW's Fort Wilderness Resort and Campground). ☎ *407-939-3463.* www.disneyworld.com. *Reservations required. Shows: 5, 7:15, and 9:30 p.m. Admission: $50 adults, $25 kids 3–11 including tax and tip. AE, DISC, MC, V. Table seating. Parking: Free.*

Makahiki Luau
SeaWorld

SeaWorld's entry on the Orlando dinner circuit starts with the arrival of the tribal chief via boat, with a ceremonial progression leading the audience into a theater located in the Seafire Inn at the park's Waterfront district (see Chapter 20 for more on the theme park). Throughout the night, you experience the ancient customs, rhythmic music and dance, authentic costumes, and family-style dining on Polynesian-influenced cuisine that includes tropical fruit, mahimahi, sweet-and-sour pork, Hawaiian chicken, island stir-fried vegetables, fried rice, dessert, and beverages, including one free cocktail. My only complaint is that the ventilation in the theater wasn't adequate for all the smoke used during the show. At one point, sitting at one of the front tables, I couldn't see anything, not even my food.

See map p. 291. 7007 SeaWorld Dr. (inside The Waterfront at SeaWorld). ☎ *800-327-2420.* www.seaworld.org. *Reservations required. Park admission not required. Shows: 5:30 and 8:15 p.m. Admission: $43 adults, $28 kids 3–9. AE, DISC, MC, V. Table seating. Parking: Free.*

Medieval Times
Kissimmee

Orlando has one of eight Medieval Times shows in the United States and Canada. Inside, guests gorge themselves on garlic bread, barbecued spare ribs, herb-roasted chicken, vegetable soup, appetizers, herb-roasted potatoes, a pastry dessert, and beverages, including beer. But because this show is set in the 11th century, you eat with your fingers from metal plates while knights mounted on Andalusian horses run around the arena, jousting and clanging to please the fair maidens. Arrive 30 minutes to allow time to tour the Medieval Village, a re-created Middle Ages settlement ($3.50 per person). There are plenty of opportunities to part with your cash, including photos and toys, so set your limits ahead of time or the evening can wind up costing a bundle.

See map p. 303. 4510 W. Irlo Bronson Memorial Hwy. (U.S. Highway 192, 11 miles east of the main Disney entrance, next to Wal-Mart). ☎ *800-229-8300 or 407-396-1518.* www.medievaltimes.com. *Reservations recommended. Shows nightly, times vary. Admission: $49 adults, $33 kids 3–11. AE, DISC, MC, VISA. Stadium-style seating. Parking: Free.*

MurderWatch Mystery Theatre
Lake Buena Vista

Mystery lovers rejoice. The game's afoot every Saturday night at this all-you-can-eat buffet, which offers beef, chicken, fish, and a separate children's buffet while diners try to solve a mystery. The proceedings take place in Baskerville's restaurant, which has 19th-century Edwardian décor and houses a Sherlock Holmes museum. This somewhat sophisticated offering is one of the city's best.

See map p. 303. In the Grosvenor Resort at 1850 Hotel Plaza Blvd. (Turn west off Highway 535 onto Hotel Plaza Boulevard; it's close to Downtown Disney Marketplace.) ☎ *800-624-4109 or 407-827-6534.* www.murderwatch.com. *Reservations recommended. Admission: $40 adults, $11 kids 3–9. AE, DISC, MC, V. Shows: Sat 6 and 9 p.m. Table seating. Parking: Free.*

Pirates Dinner Adventure
International Drive Area

The special-effects show at this theater includes a full-size ship in a 300,000-gallon lagoon, circus-style aerial acts, a lot of music, plenty of swordfights by swashbuckling pirates, and a little drama. Dinner includes an appetizer buffet with the preshow, followed by roast chicken and beef, rice, vegetables, dessert, and coffee. After the show, you're invited to the Buccaneer Bash dance party where you can mingle with cast members. This show gets somewhat mixed reviews; the more favorable come from kids with an affinity for pirates and swordfights (of which there's plenty). The arena is smaller than some of the others in the area, which makes it a slightly friendlier experience overall.

See map p. 303. 6400 Carrier Dr. (from Disney, take I-4 to Sand Lake Road, go east to International Drive, and then north to Carrier). ☎ *800-866-2469 or 407-248-0590.* www. orlandopirates.com. *Reservations recommended. Show times vary. Admission: $53 adults, $32 kids 3–11, tax included. AE, DC, DISC, MC, V. Stadium-style seating. Parking: Free.*

Sleuths Mystery Dinner Theater
International Drive Area

While catering more to an adult crowd (though they do offer two special afternoon versions for kids), the mysteries solved here are absolutely hilarious whodunits. In a smaller, more-intimate theater guests are seated around small tables while enjoying the show. After some of the characters serve hot and cold hors d'oeuvres to guests, the show begins. Dinner is served between acts and includes a choice of Cornish game hen, herb stuffing, baked potato, vegetables, and cranberry sauce; prime rib (for an additional $3) with baked potato and vegetables; or four-cheese lasagna (with or without meatballs), vegetables, and garlic bread, plus dessert and unlimited beer, wine, and soft drinks. Guests are encouraged to discuss the clues to solve the murder. The more the audience participates (which often seems directly related to the amount of alcohol they consume), the more amusing the show can be. Eleven unique mysteries keep guests coming back for more.

Discounts are often available online as well as in many of the tourist publications.

See map p. 303. 7508 Universal Blvd. (take I-4 East to exit 75A, turn right at the light onto Universal Boulevard, go through two lights; Sleuths is on the right in the Republic Square Plaza). ☎ *800-363-1985.* www.sleuths.com. *Reservations recommended. Show times vary with between 1 and 4 shows offered daily. Admission: $47 adults, $24 kids. AE, DISC, MC, V. Table seating. Parking: Free.*

Spirit of Aloha Dinner Show
Walt Disney World

Although not quite as much in demand as the Hoop-Dee-Doo Musical Revue, Disney's Polynesian Resort (see Chapter 9 for more on the hotel) presents a delightful two-hour show, which comes across like a big neighborhood party with an island flair. The luau features Tahitian, Samoan, Hawaiian, and Polynesian singers, drummers, and dancers who entertain you while you feast on a menu that includes tropical appetizers, Lanai-roasted chicken, pork ribs, sliced pineapple, Polynesian wild rice, Polynesian-style bread, South Seas vegetables, dessert, wine, beer, and other beverages. Kids can eat mac 'n' cheese, hot dogs, chicken nuggets, or PB&J if they prefer. The show takes place five nights a week in an open-air theater (dress for nighttime weather) with candlelit tables, red-flame lanterns, and tapa cloth paintings on the walls.

Reservations should be made at least 60 to 90 days in advance (but can be made up to two years in advance), especially during peak periods such as summer and holidays. Payment must be made in full at the time of the reservation, but you can cancel up to 48 hours prior to your scheduled show for a full refund.

See map p. 338. 1600 Seven Seas Dr. (at Disney's Polynesian Resort). ☎ **407-939-3463.** www.disneyworld.com. *Reservations required. Shows: 5:15 and 8 p.m. Tues–Sat. Admission: $50 adults, $26 kids 3–11, including tax and gratuity. AE, DISC, MC, V. Table seating. Parking: Free.*

Getting Information and Tickets

For evening entertainment other than the dinner shows, dozens of rock, rap, jazz, pop, country, blues, and folk stars are in town during any given week in Orlando. You can find schedules in the *Orlando Sentinel's* **Calendar** section, published every Friday and available online at www.orlandosentinel.com. The *Orlando Weekly's* **Calendar** section (www.orlandoweekly.com) is another good source of information for live-music events, including club schedules.

Ticketmaster is the key reservations player for most major events in Orlando, including concerts, shows, and pro-sports events. If you know of an event that's happening while you're in town, check first with your hometown Ticketmaster outlets to see whether they sell tickets for the event. (If you live as close as Miami or Atlanta, they probably do.) Otherwise, call the Ticketmaster outlet in Orlando at ☎ **877-803-7073** or 407-839-3900, or go to its Web site at www.ticketmaster.com.

You can also get additional event information and can often order tickets from the **Orlando/Orange County Convention & Visitors Bureau** (☎ **407-363-5872;** www.orlandoinfo.com).

Chapter 25

Hitting the Clubs and Bars

. . . .

In This Chapter

▶ Rocking the night away at Walt Disney World
▶ Cruising the clubs at CityWalk
▶ Exploring hot spots inside Orlando's hotels
▶ Finding a few more places to party

. . . .

*A*lthough Orlando has a reputation as a daylight destination, its nighttime offerings continue to grow as fun-seekers aren't ready to call it quits after a day at the parks.

Clubs such as *Mannequins* and *House of Blues* at **Pleasure Island** and **Disney's West Side** rock well into the wee hours. **Universal Orlando's CityWalk** entertainment district features nightspots such as *the groove* and *CityJazz*.

Many of the clubs that I list in this chapter are open to anyone 18 or older, but remember: The *minimum drinking age* in Florida is 21, and the clubs will check your ID.

Enjoying the Pleasures of Pleasure Island

This 6-acre entertainment district is the home of several clubs, bars, and restaurants. You can enter the complex for free if you just want to take in the ambience but don't plan to enter any of the clubs. Admission to a single club (you can choose from all but the Comedy Club and the Adventurers Club) is $11, including tax. A single-day pass that allows you to hop from club to club, is $21, plus tax. (If you purchase the Magic Plus Pack, you can choose admission to Pleasure Island's clubs as part of the package — see Chapter 11 for information on Disney's admission passes.) Self-parking is free. For information on **Pleasure Island,** call ☎ **407-939-2648** or check out Disney's Web site at www.disneyworld.com.

The island is designed to look like an abandoned waterfront industrial district with clubs in its lofts and warehouses. But the streets are decorated with brightly colored lights and balloons, giving it a carnivalesque feel. After the clubs open, loud music blasts, a few scantily clad dancers gyrate on outdoor stages, and alcohol is served on the streets. Every evening at Pleasure Island ends with a New Year's Eve celebration at midnight — noisemakers, confetti, lights, countdown, the works. I wouldn't suggest bringing along the kids too late into the evening, as much of the partying is right in the streets — with crowds wandering (sometimes not so steadily) about.

Mannequins Dance Palace is **Pleasure Island**'s main event. It's a high-energy club with a big, rotating dance floor. Just watching the inebriated trying to get on and off the spinning surface can be an evening's worth of entertainment. Being a local favorite makes the club hard to get into, so arrive early, especially on weekends. Three levels of bars and mixing space are adorned with elaborately dressed mannequins. The DJ plays contemporary tunes loudly enough to wake the dead.

You must be 21 to enter, and the staff is *very* serious about that.

The **Adventurers Club** is a multistory building that, according to WDW legend, was designed to be the library and archaeological trophy room for Pleasure Island founder and explorer, Merriweather Adam Pleasure, who was lost at sea in 1941. The club is decorated with early aviation photos, hunting trophies, and a mounted yakoose — a half yak, half moose that speaks, regardless of whether you're drinking. Also on hand are Pleasure's zany band of globetrotting friends and servants, played by skilled actors who interact with guests while staying in character. Improvisational comedy and cabaret shows are performed in the library. You can easily hang out here all night, sipping potent tropical drinks in the library or the bar, where elephant-foot barstools rise and sink mysteriously.

If you're a fan of the BET Cable Network, you'll probably love **BET Soundstage** (☎ 407-934-7666), which offers traditional R&B and the rhyme of hip-hop, with the occasional Latin-music night thrown in here and there. You can dance on an expansive floor or kick back on an out-door terrace. Cover charge for the **Soundstage** is included in the **Pleasure Island** single-day ticket, except for major concerts.

A very talented troupe — the **Who, What and Warehouse Players** — is the main event at the **Comedy Warehouse.** The group performs 45-minute improvisational shows based on audience suggestions. It does five shows a night. Remember that you're in Disney, so the comedy here is pretty much squeaky clean.

Patent leather and polyester rule at **8Trax,** a 1970s-style disco where 50 TV screens air diverse shows and videos over the dance floor. A DJ plays everything from "YMCA" to "The Hustle." Some nights he may even dig into the music of the '80s for a few dance gems.

What was once the **Pleasure Island Jazz Club** has been replaced by **Raglan Road,** an Irish pub featuring traditional Irish music and storytelling.

Downtown Disney

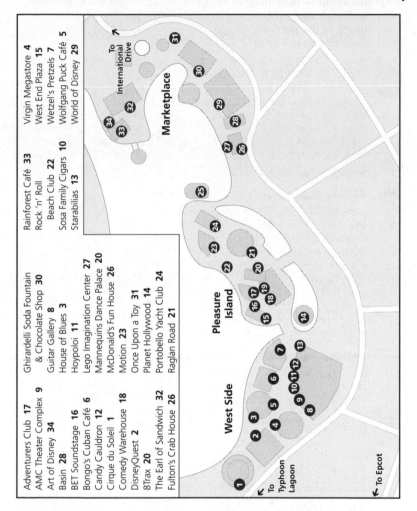

Virgin Megastore **4**
West End Plaza **15**
Wetzel's Pretzels **7**
Wolfgang Puck Café **5**
World of Disney **29**

Rainforest Café **33**
Rock 'n' Roll
Beach Club **22**
Sosa Family Cigars **10**
Starabilias **13**

Ghirardelli Soda Fountain
& Chocolate Shop **30**
Guitar Gallery **8**
House of Blues **3**
Hoypoloi **11**
Lego Imagination Center **27**
Mannequins Dance Palace **20**
McDonald's Fun House **26**
Motion **23**
Once Upon a Toy **31**
Planet Hollywood **14**
Portobello Yacht Club **24**
Raglan Road **21**

Adventurers Club **17**
AMC Theater Complex **9**
Art of Disney **34**
Basin **28**
BET Soundstage **16**
Bongo's Cuban Café **6**
Candy Cauldron **12**
Cirque du Soleil **1**
Comedy Warehouse **18**
DisneyQuest **2**
8Trax **20**
The Earl of Sandwich **32**
Fulton's Crab House **26**

Marketplace

Pleasure
Island

West Side

To
International
Drive

To
Typhoon
Lagoon

To Epcot

If your taste in live music runs more to the Top-40 and rock veins, both the **Rock 'n' Roll Beach Club** and the outdoor **West End Stage** will satisfy your needs.

Pleasure Island's **Motion,** tries hard to be hip and trendy but still features a mix of Top-40 tunes and alternative rock. It's a hyperactive club that appeals to the T-shirt and sneakers theme-park crowd. Moody blue lighting makes you believe you're dancing the night away in deep space, but the effect's more like . . . well, a cool dance floor.

Exploring Downtown Disney's West Side

Immediately adjacent to Pleasure Island, **Disney's West Side** is a district where you'll find clubs, restaurants, and **DisneyQuest** (see Chapter 16).

Singer Gloria Estefan and her husband, Emilio, created **Bongo's Cuban Café** (☎ 407-828-0999; www.bongoscubancafe.com), an eatery/ nightspot where a Desi Arnaz look-alike may show up to croon a few tunes. The upbeat salsa music makes this place noisy, so flee to the patio or upstairs if you want privacy. All in all, this isn't one of Florida's better Cuban restaurants, so you're better off coming for the atmosphere rather than the food (which will run you about $10–$26). The Café is open daily from 11 a.m. to 2 a.m. and doesn't take reservations. You can also find plenty of free self-parking.

Cirque du Soleil isn't your ordinary circus. It doesn't have any lions, tigers, or bears. But you won't feel cheated. This "Circus of the Sun" is nonstop energy. At times, it seems as if all 64 performers are on stage simultaneously, especially during the frenetic trampoline routine. Trapeze artists, high-wire walkers, an airborne gymnast, a posing strongman, mimes, and two clowns cement a show called *La Nouba* into a five-star performance. But if you're on a tight budget, this is gut-check time: Can you blow one or two day's entertainment budget on 90 minutes of fun? If you can, it'll be worth the splurge. The two ticket categories are $87 for adults and $65 for kids 3 to 9 (plus tax) for center of the theater seats, and $75 and $56, respectively, to the right and left of the stage. Don't assume the cheaper seats are the worst — there's barely a bad seat to be had in this well-designed theater. Shows are at 6 and 9 p.m. five nights a week, but times and nights vary, and sometimes a matinee is scheduled, so call ahead (☎ 407-939-7600) or check the show's Web site (www.cirquedusoleil.com) for information and tickets.

Plus-sized guests may find the seating a bit narrow, so request a folding chair upon arrival.

The rafters in the **House of Blues** literally shake with rhythm and blues. The House is decorated with folk art, buttons, and bottle caps, and the patio has a view of the bay. If you like spicy food, offerings such as jambalaya and gumbo ($9–$25) are respectable. Sunday's Gospel Brunch ($30 for adults and $15 for kids 3–12) has foot-stomping music served with decent food (omelets, beef, jalapeño smashed potatoes, cheese grits, and sausage among meats and other items). Brunch is the only time you can make reservations. Guests dining before attending a show that night are often eligible for early admission, which is handy during the general-admission shows. Ask your server for details, call ☎ 407-934-2583, or go to www.hob.com. House of Blues is open daily from 11 a.m. to 2 a.m. and offers free self-parking.

Strolling Along Disney's BoardWalk

Part of the same-named resort (see Chapter 9), the **BoardWalk** is home to several clubs and restaurants and is a great place for strolling and people-watching. Street performers sing, dance, juggle, and make a little magic most evenings. It has something of a midway atmosphere reminiscent of Atlantic City's heyday. Three standout options here include:

✔ **Atlantic Dance** features Top-40 and '80s dance hits Tuesdays through Thursdays and live bands on Friday and Saturday nights. It's open to everyone 21 and older from 9 p.m. to 2 a.m., and admission is free.

✔ The rustic, saloon-style **Jellyrolls** offers dueling pianos. Strictly for the over-21 set, it's open daily from 7 p.m. to 2 a.m. There's a $5 cover.

✔ If you need a game fix, **ESPN Sports** has 90 TV screens (there are a few even inside the bathrooms!), a full-service bar, food, and a small arcade, all without a cover charge. It's *the* sports mecca in town.

You can get information on all of the spots listed here by calling ☎ 407-939-3463 or going to www.disneyworld.com.

Dancing the Night Away at CityWalk

Universal's answer to Pleasure Island is a two-level collection of clubs and restaurants located between its two theme parks. **CityWalk** (☎ 407-363-8000; www.universalorlando.com or www.citywalk.com) is open from 11 a.m. to 2 a.m. daily. Although no admission is charged, several clubs have cover charges after 5 or 6 p.m., sometimes as late as 8 or 9 p.m. CityWalk also offers *party passes*. A pass to all clubs is $10 plus tax; for $13 plus tax, you get a movie at **Universal Cineplex** (☎ 407-354-5998). Universal also offers free club access to those who buy multiday theme-park tickets (see Chapters 18 and 19). Daytime parking in the Universal Orlando garages costs $8, but parking is free after 6 p.m.

Save your parking stub if attending a movie at the **Universal Cineplex** before 6 p.m. The theater will allow you to apply the $8 parking fee toward a concession-stand purchase any time that same day.

Bob Marley — A Tribute to Freedom (☎ 407-224-3663; www.bob marley.com) has architecture said to replicate Marley's home in Kingston, Jamaica. Local and national reggae bands perform frequently. Light Jamaican fare is served under umbrellas. The club is open daily from 4 p.m. to 2 a.m. There's a cover of $5 after 8 p.m.; cover prices increase for concerts on special nights. You must be 21 or older after 10 p.m.

Walt Disney World Nightlife

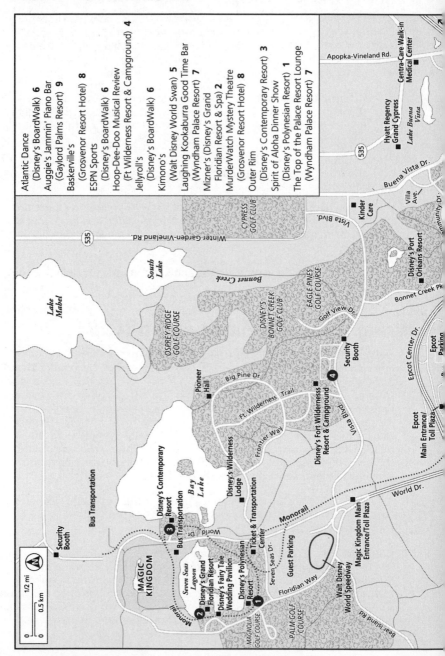

Atlantic Dance
  (Disney's BoardWalk) **6**
Auggie's Jammin' Piano Bar
  (Gaylord Palms Resort) **9**
Baskerville's
  (Grosvenor Resort Hotel) **8**
ESPN Sports
  (Disney's BoardWalk) **6**
Hoop-Dee-Doo Musical Review
  (Ft Wilderness Resort & Campground) **4**
Jellyroll's
  (Disney's BoardWalk) **6**
Kimono's
  (Walt Disney World Swan) **5**
Laughing Kookaburra Good Time Bar
  (Wyndham Palace Resort) **7**
Mizner's (Disney's Grand
  Floridian Resort & Spa) **2**
MurderWatch Mystery Theatre
  (Grosvenor Resort Hotel) **8**
Outer Rim
  (Disney's Contemporary Resort) **3**
Spirit of Aloha Dinner Show
  (Disney's Polynesian Resort) **1**
The Top of the Palace Resort Lounge
  (Wyndham Palace Resort) **7**

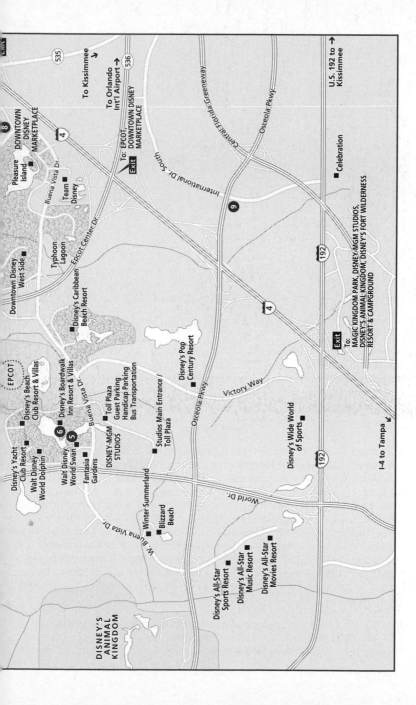

CityWalk

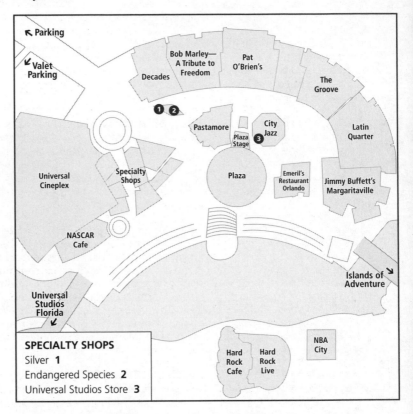

↖ Parking

↙ Valet Parking

Decades

Bob Marley— A Tribute to Freedom

Pat O'Brien's

The Groove

Pastamore

Plaza Stage

City Jazz

Latin Quarter

Universal Cineplex

Specialty Shops

Plaza

Emeril's Restaurant Orlando

Jimmy Buffett's Margaritaville

NASCAR Cafe

Islands of Adventure

Universal Studios Florida ↙

NBA City

Hard Rock Cafe

Hard Rock Live

SPECIALTY SHOPS
Silver **1**
Endangered Species **2**
Universal Studios Store **3**

CityJazz (☎ 407-224-2189) has a cover charge that includes the **Downbeat Jazz Hall of Fame** (with memorabilia from Louis Armstrong, Ella Fitzgerald, and other greats) and the **Thelonious Monk Institute of Jazz,** a performance venue that's also the site of jazz workshops. You can browse through 500 pieces of memorabilia marching through Dixieland, swing, bebop, and modern jazz. Nationally acclaimed acts perform frequently. Thursday through Saturday, the club occasionally hosts national and local comics via special **Bonkers Comedy Club** shows. On the food side, look for tapas, sushi, and lamb chops. It's open Sunday through Thursday from 8 p.m. to 1 a.m. and Friday and Saturday from 7 p.m. to 2 a.m. Cover charge is $5 (more for special events). You must be 18 to enter.

CityWalk's answer to Pleasure Island's Mannequins is **the groove** (☎ 407-363-8000); it's not as crowded here, except on the occasional all-ages teen night, when you'll want to stay as far away from the place as possible. The sound system is loud, and the dance floor is in a room gleaming with chrome. Music-wise, *the groove* features hip-hop, jazz fusion, techno, and alternative. A DJ plays tunes on nights when recording artists aren't booked. Each of the club's three color-themed lounges has a bar and a specialty drink to fit its ambience (the spacey Blue one is the coolest, though the Red is kind of sexy in a bordello sort of way). You must be at least 21 to enter (except for the special teen events), and it will cost you a cover charge of $5. The club is open from 9 p.m. to 2 a.m., sometimes later.

CityWalk's **Hard Rock Cafe** is the largest in the world, and the adjoining **Hard Rock Live** (☎ 407-351-5483; www.hardrock.com) is the first concert hall bearing the name. The cafe also has a free exhibit area, where you can browse through displays of rock memorabilia, including the platform heels and leather jumpsuits of KISS. Concert charges vary by act, and MTV often films concert specials here. The cafe is open daily from 11 a.m. to midnight.

Flip-flops and flowered shirts equal **Jimmy Buffett's Margaritaville** (☎ 407-224-2155). Tunes are piped through the building during the daytime, with a Jimmy sound-alike strumming on the back porch around dusk. Inside, there's nightly live entertainment, though nothing extraordinary. Bar-wise, you have three options. *The Volcano* erupts (I'm not kidding) killer margaritas; the *Land Shark* has fins swimming around the ceiling; and the *12 Volt,* is, well, a little electrifying. The menu screams "Key West!" It includes cheeseburgers in paradise, mahimahi, and Key lime pie. See Chapter 10 for more on the food front. Margaritaville is open from 11:30 a.m. to 2 a.m., and there's a $5 cover after 10 p.m.

The two-level **Latin Quarter** (☎ 407-224-3663) restaurant/club offers you a chance to absorb the salsa-and-samba culture and cuisine of 21 Latin nations. It's filled with the music of the Meringue and the Mambo, with a little Latin rock thrown in for good measure. The sound system is loud enough to blow you into the next county. The club's open Monday through Friday from 5 p.m. until 2 a.m., Saturday and Sunday from noon until 2 a.m. There's a $5 to $10 cover charged after 9 p.m., depending on the evening's entertainment.

An arcade has replaced the live-music stage at the Motown Café, which is now known as **Decades** (☎ 407-224-3663), but you can still refuel on steaks, ribs, and BBQ ($8–$18) surrounded by memorabilia recalling famous people, movies, and music from the past 40 years. It's open daily for dinner at 4 p.m., Saturday and Sunday at 11:30 am for lunch. A DJ plays on Friday and Saturday nights, when there's a cover of $5.

Guessing the focus of a place that has a one-page food menu and a booklet filled with drinks doesn't take a genius. Just like the French Quarter's version, drinking is the highlight at **Pat O'Brien's** (☎ 407-363-8000). You can enjoy dueling pianos and a flame-throwing fountain while you suck down the signature drink — the Hurricane. No one younger than

21 is permitted after 9 p.m. Pat O' Brien's offers a limited menu of sandwiches, snacks, and treats like jambalaya and shrimp Creole, which sets you back $8 to $10. Hours are 4 p.m. to 2 a.m., and a cover of $5 is charged after 9 p.m.

Locating the Best Hotel Lounges

Some of Orlando's best nightlife is located in its hotels. Even the locals head to the resort areas for fun after dark. If you're staying at one of the places listed here, you can do an evening on the town without ever getting behind the wheel. None of the following charges a cover.

Mizner's at Disney's Grand Floridian Resort & Spa has a pianist or band that alternates evenings in a lounge with an elegant library look (☎ 407-824-3000). **Outer Rim** in the Contemporary Resort (☎ 407-824-1000) is trendy and close to the monorail. **Kimono's** in the Walt Disney World Swan transforms into a karaoke bar after 8:30 p.m. (☎ 407-934-4000).

The **Laughing Kookaburra Good Time Bar** in the Wyndham Palace, Lake Buena Vista (☎ 407-827-2727), has dancing and live music or a DJ most nights. **The Top of the Palace Lounge,** also at the Wyndham Palace (☎ 407-827-2727), has a great view of Disney fireworks. **Baskerville's** in the Grosvenor Resort Hotel, Lake Buena Vista (☎ 407-827-6534), features the **MurderWatch Mystery Theater** on Saturday nights (see Chapter 24). And **Auggie's Jammin' Piano Bar** offers dueling pianos at 9 p.m. nightly at the Gaylord Palms Resort (☎ 407-586-0000).

Exploring Orlando's Other Hot Spots

Downtown Orlando is home to a number of clubs and bars, and offers a vibrant nightlife. Here's my list of favorites:

✔ **Club at Firestone,** 578 N. Orange Ave., (☎ 407-426-0005; www.club atfirestone.com), is home to a revolving list of parties that take place each day of the week. It continuously books some of the best DJs in the dance music scene to spin, especially on Saturdays for the popular "gay night" party. The cover ranges from free to $10, depending on the event. It's open daily from 8 p.m. to 2 a.m.

✔ Locals perform at the 200-seat **SAK Comedy Lab,** 380 W. Amelia St. (☎ 407-648-0001; www.sak.com), which offers several performances weekly. Favorite acts include *Duel of Fools,* where two teams face off in improvised scenes based on suggestions from the audience, and *Lab Rats,* where students play in improv formats. Admission costs $5 to $13. Shows usually are Tuesday and Wednesday at 9 p.m. and Thursday through Saturday at 8 and 10 p.m.

✔ The best spot in town for live music, **The Social,** 54 N. Orange Ave. (☎ 407-246-1419; www.orlandosocial.com), offers an eclectic

Downtown Orlando

NIGHTLIFE ◆

Club at Firestone **2**
Sak Comedy Club **3**
The Social **4**
Tabu **1**
Wall Street District Clubs **5**

ACCOMMODATIONS ■

Courtyard at Lake Lucerne **8**
Veranda Bed & Breakfast **7**
Westin Grand Bohemian **6**

mix that changes dramatically from night to night. You're just as likely to hear an urban groove as the next big punk band on the airwaves. A $5 cover is charged for those 21 and older; national act covers vary. It's open daily from 8 p.m. to 2 a.m.

✔ **Tabu,** 46 N. Orange Ave. (☎ **407-648-8363;** www.tabunightclub. com), is one of the city's hottest see-and-be-seen spots. The Art Deco club boasts three dance floors and something of an attitude. DJs spin hip-hop records and live bands provide additional music; the club also hosts theme nights. A private lounge for VIPs means you may see a famous face or two. Leave the denim at home, though — the club's upscale dress code is strictly enforced. Cover is $5 to $10 on most nights. It's open Tuesday through Sunday from 10 p.m. to 2 a.m.

✔ **Metropolis** and **Matrix,** 9101 International Drive (☎ **407-370-3700;** www.metropolismatrix.com), are a pair of sophisticated clubs located close to all the tourist action. The Matrix offers a futuristic atmosphere with a multimillion-dollar light show, and large dance floor with Techno, Eurotrance, Breakout, and Top-40 music. Just next door, the Metropolis features a 13-foot video wall, TV screens surrounding the room, and billiards tables. The Matrix is open Wednesday to Sunday from 9 p.m. to 2 a.m. The Metropolis is open Thursday to Sunday from 9 p.m. to 2 a.m. Cover varies nightly. "Stylish dress" required. Parking (next door at the garage) is $2 to $5. You must be 18 to enter; on Saturday and Sunday nights, guys must be 21.

✔ A handful of Downtown hot spots are clustered in the Wall Street district. **Chillers, Big Belly Brewery,** and **Lattitudes** (☎ 407-939-4270), offer three very different experiences all in a single building. The trio of clubs are all geared to the young adult crowd with an atmosphere that's very casual. **Wall Street Plaza** (www.wallst plaza.net) is home to a wide variety of clubs including **The Globe** (☎ 407-849-9904), a European patio cafe; **Slingapours** (☎ 407-849-9904), a dance club with an indoor and outdoor patio for relaxing; **Waitiki** (☎ 407-849-0471), a retro tiki lounge and restaurant, and **The Monkey Bar** (☎ 407-849-0471), a hip martini lounge and cocktail bar. Hours and cover varies, so call ahead.

Part VII
The Part of Tens

Tell them we work at one of the theme parks, and maybe they won't ask too many questions.

In this part . . .

Ah, tradition. The Part of Tens chapters are to *For Dummies* books what noisemakers and silly hats are to New Year's — an integral part of the experience. In this part of the book, I feed you plenty of useful and fun information that I think is especially handy, such as budget attractions that can stretch your dollars and fun ways to keep active when you're not at the theme parks.

Chapter 26

Top Ten Cheap Alternatives to the Theme Parks

• •

In This Chapter

▶ Spending some time at a museum

▶ Strolling through a real park

▶ Taking a leisurely boat tour

• •

*I*t may shock you to learn that there are things to see and do in this city beyond Mickey, Shamu, and Shrek. I discuss some of the city's smaller but still-popular attractions in Chapter 21, but here are some hidden gems, where you can dodge the enormous crowds, save a few dollars, and still have a great time while others are still waiting in line or emptying their wallets at the big parks.

Central Florida Zoo

The animal collection at the **Central Florida Zoo** includes a number of endangered species including beautiful clouded leopards and cheetahs. In addition to a lovable hippopotamus named Geraldine, you can also meet black howler monkeys, siamangs, American crocodiles, a Gila monster, hyacinth macaws, bald eagles, and dozens of other species. The latest additions to the park include a puma enclosure, a rare king vulture exhibit, and an Australian exhibit featuring kangaroos and emus.

The park is located 20 to 30 minutes from Orlando at 3755 N. U.S. 17/92 in Sanford. (Take I-4 Exit 104, and follow the signs to the zoo.) Call ☎ **407-323-4450** for more information or visit www.centralfloridazoo.org on the Web. Admission is $8.95 for adults, $6.95 for seniors 60 and older, and $4.95 for kids 3 to 12 (children younger than 3 are free). Strollers are available for rent at a cost of $3 or $6, depending on the type. The park is open daily from 9 a.m. to 5 p.m. and closes only on Thanksgiving and Christmas.

Charles Hosmer Morse Museum of American Art

Louis Comfort Tiffany is in the spotlight at **the Charles Hosmer Morse Museum of American Art,** and if you're a fan of the artist, a stop here is a must. This museum, founded in 1942, has 40 vibrantly colored windows and 21 paintings by the master artist. In addition, there are non-Tiffany windows ranging from creations by Frank Lloyd Wright to the works of 15th-century German masters. Also look for leaded lamps by Tiffany and Emile Gallè; paintings by John Singer Sargent and Maxfield Parrish; jewelry designed by Tiffany, Lalique, and Fabergé; and Art Nouveau furnishings.

The museum is at 445 Park Ave. N., in Winter Park. (Take the I-4 Fairbanks Avenue exit east to Park Avenue, go left and through four traffic lights.) Call ☎ 407-645-5311 or 407-645-5324 (a telephone recording) for more details, or check online at www.morsemuseum.org. Admission is $3 for adults, $1 for students 12 to 17, those younger than 12 are free. The museum is open Tuesday through Saturday from 9:30 a.m. to 4:00 p.m. and Sunday from 1 to 4 p.m.

Cornell Fine Arts Museum

This showplace has 6,000 works on display (European and American paintings, sculpture, and decorative art), making it one of Florida's most distinguished and comprehensive art collections. The museum also conducts lectures and gallery-talk walks.

The museum is located at the east end of Holt Avenue on the Rollins College campus in Winter Park. (Take I-4 Exit 45/Fairbanks Avenue east to Park; turn right and then left on Holt.) Call ☎ 407-646-2526 or visit www.rollins.edu/cfam for more information.

Eatonville and the Zora Neale Hurston National Museum of Fine Arts

America's oldest black municipality is located just north of Orlando. Eatonville is the birthplace of Zora Neale Hurston — a too-little heralded, African-American author. The best time to visit is in January during the city's annual festival honoring her and her work. A small gallery on the site displays periodically changing exhibits of art and other work, and you can grab a map for a walking tour of the community, established in 1887.

The museum is at 227 E. Kennedy Blvd., Eatonville. (Take I-4 to Exit 46 and make a quick left onto Lee Road, then left on Wymore, and then right on Kennedy. It's a quarter-mile down the road on the left.) Call

☎ **800-972-3310** or 407-647-3307 or visit www.zoranealehurston.cc for more information. The museum accepts donations as admission and is open Monday through Friday from 9 a.m. to 4 p.m., and Sundays from 2 p.m. to 5 p.m.

Audubon Center for Birds of Prey

This bird sanctuary — one of the biggest rehabilitation centers in the Southeast — has treated more than 8,000 raptors and released more than 3,500 of them back into the wild since opening in 1979. It flies under the radar of most tourists, making it a great place to get to know the winged wonders (eagles, owls, hawks, and other raptors) that earn their keep by entertaining those who do visit. It's a wonderful place for nature lovers and kids who love getting up close with the feathered residents.

The center is at 1101 Audubon Way, Maitland. (Take I-4 to Lee Road/Exit 46 and exit right; turn left at first light/Wymore Road, and turn right at the next light/Kennedy Boulevard. Continue a half-mile to East Avenue, turn left, and go to the stop sign at Audubon Way. Turn left, and the center is on the right.) Call ☎ **407-644-0190** or visit www.audubonof florida.org/conservation/cbop.htm for more information. The center accepts donations: $5 adults, $4 children 3 to 12. Visitor hours are Tuesday through Sunday from 10 a.m. to 4 p.m.

Kissimmee Sports Arena & Rodeo

The **Kissimmee Sports Arena & Rodeo** is a good way to fill a Friday night dance card, and it's only 20 minutes from the major theme parks. The arena stages weekly contests where real-life cowboys compete in several events, including saddle bronc and bull-riding, calf-roping, and barrel-racing.

The arena is located at 958 S. Hoagland Blvd., Kissimmee. (Take I-4 Exit 25A/U.S. 192 east to Hoagland, and then go south 1 mile to the arena.) Call ☎ **407-933-0020** or visit www.ksarodeo.com for more details. Admission is $18 for adults, $9 for children age 12 and younger. The fun begins Friday evenings at 8 p.m. It's closed in December.

Lake Eola Park

This quiet hideaway in Downtown Orlando offers the city's skyline as a backdrop. The 43-acre park has a walking and jogging path, a playground, and swan-shaped paddleboats for rent if you want to take a quiet ride across the 23-acre lake. You can relax and feed the swans, birds, and fish (in certain areas only). There's also a small cafe. A variety of performances happen throughout the year, most of which are free. The **Orlando-UCF Shakespeare Festival** (Apr to early May) costs $10 to

$30 nightly. Call ☎ 407-447-1700 or head online to www.shakespeare fest.org for more information about the festival.

The park is located at Washington Street and Rosalind Avenue, Orlando. (Take I-4 to Anderson Street., exit right, and turn left at the fourth light/ Rosalind. The amphitheater is on the right.) Call ☎ 407-246-2827 or check the Internet at www.ci.orlando.fl.us/cys/recreation/ lake_eola.htm for more information about the park and details on scheduled performances. Admission is free, and the park is open daily during daylight hours, sometimes later.

Lakeridge Winery and Vineyards

The **Lakeridge Winery and Vineyards** produces some of Florida's more noteworthy vintages. Tours include a look behind the scenes at the working vineyard and winery, a video presentation, and, of course, tastings. The winery is at 19239 U.S. 27, Clermont. (Take U.S. 192 west of the **WDW** parks to U.S. 27, turn right and go 25 miles north.) Call ☎ 800-768-9463 or www.lakeridgewinery.com for more information. Tours and tastings are offered from 10 a.m. to 5 p.m. Monday through Saturday, and from 11 a.m. to 5 p.m. on Sunday. Admission is free.

The Peabody Ducks

One of the best shows in town is short, but sweet and free. The posh Peabody Orlando hotel's five mallards march into the lobby each morning, accompanied by John Philip Sousa's "King Cotton March" and their own red-coated duck master. They get to spend the day splashing in a marble fountain. Then, in the afternoon, they march back to the elevator and up to their fourth-floor "penthouse."

The hotel is at 9801 International Drive (between the BeeLine Expressway and Sand Lake Road), Call ☎ 800-732-2639 or 407-352-4000 for more information. Admission is free, and the ducks march daily at 11 a.m. and 5 p.m.

Winter Park Scenic Boat Tour

This peaceful water voyage has been operating since 1938. The narrated, one-hour cruises showcase the area's beautiful lakes and canals, Rollins College, Kraft Azalea Gardens, and a number of historic mansions. Native wildlife, including cranes and alligators, may also make an appearance.

The boat tour launches from 312 E. Morse Blvd., Winter Park. Call ☎ 407-644-4056 or check out www.scenicboattours.com for additional information about the tour. Admission is $8 for adults and $4 for children ages 2 to 11, kids younger than 2 are free. Weather permitting, the tours run daily, except Christmas, every hour from 10 a.m. to 4 p.m.

Chapter 27

Top Ten Fitness Activities in Orlando

● ●

In This Chapter
▶ Enjoying water-related activities
▶ Getting land-based exercise

● ●

*W*ant some exercise other than pounding theme-park pavement? **Walt Disney World** and the surrounding areas offer plenty of recreational jaunts to keep even the most active people busy. The majority of these activities are most convenient for guests of Disney's resorts and official hotels, but many of the area's other resorts offer comprehensive facilities as well. The facilities I describe in this chapter are open to the public, regardless of where you're staying. For further information, call ☎ **407-WDW-PLAY** (939-7529) or visit www.disneyworld.com and click "More Magic," then the "Other Recreation" link.

Biking

Bike rentals (single- and multispeed bikes for adults, tandems, surreys, and children's bikes) are available from the **Bike Barn** (☎ **407-824-2742**) at **Fort Wilderness Resort and Campground.** Fort Wilderness has extensive and well-kept bike trails. Rates run $8 per hour, $22 per day (surrey bikes are $18–$22 per half hour). You can also rent bicycles with training wheels and baby seats. Helmets are available at no additional charge.

Boating

Along with a ton of man-made lakes and lagoons, **WDW** owns a navy of pleasure boats. **Capt. Jack's** at **Downtown Disney** rents Water Sprites and canopy boats ($24–$27 per half-hour). For information, call ☎ **407-828-2204.**

The **Bike Barn** at **Fort Wilderness** (☎ **407-824-2742**) rents canoes and paddleboats ($6.50 per half-hour, $12 per hour); canopy boats ($27 per half hour); Sea Raycers ($24 per half hour); small sailboats ($20–$30 per hour); and pontoon boats ($42 per half hour).

Fishing

Disney offers a variety of fishing excursions (catch and release only) on various Disney lakes, including Bay Lake and Seven Seas Lagoon. The lakes are stocked, so you may catch something, but true anglers probably won't find it much of a challenge. You can arrange special B.A.S.S. fishing excursions 24 hours to 14 days in advance by calling ☎ 407-939-2277 or 407-939-7529. A license isn't required. The fee is $200 to $225 for up to five people for two hours, $395 for four hours ($90 for each additional hour), including refreshments, gear, guide, and tax. Kids can get in on the action as well: General B.A.S.S. tours are available for children ages 6 to 12 at a cost of $28 per child for an hour excursion.

Here's a less expensive alternative: Rent fishing poles at the **Bike Barn** (☎ 407-824-2742; $6 per hour or $10 per day, bait $3.50) to fish in the **Fort Wilderness** canals. A license isn't necessary.

Golf

Walt Disney World operates five 18-hole, par-72 golf courses and one 9-hole, par-36 walking course. All are open to the public and offer pro shops, equipment rentals, and instruction. The rates are $69 to $159 per 18-hole round for resort guests ($10 more if you're not staying at a WDW property). Rates depend on the course, the season, and the time of day you play. Twilight specials (for play after the hours of either 3 or 5 p.m.) are often available. For tee times and information, call ☎ 407-939-4653 up to 60 days in advance (up to 90 days for Disney-resort and official-property guests). Call ☎ 407-934-7639 for information about golf packages.

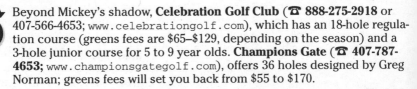

Beyond Mickey's shadow, **Celebration Golf Club** (☎ 888-275-2918 or 407-566-4653; www.celebrationgolf.com), which has an 18-hole regulation course (greens fees are $65–$129, depending on the season) and a 3-hole junior course for 5 to 9 year olds. **Champions Gate** (☎ 407-787-4653; www.championsgategolf.com), offers 36 holes designed by Greg Norman; greens fees will set you back from $55 to $170.

Golf magazine recognized the 45 holes designed by Jack Nicklaus at the **Villas of Grand Cypress** resort as among the best in the nation. Tee times begin at 8 a.m. daily. Special rates are available for children under 18. For information call ☎ 407-239-1909. Greens fees run $120 to $180 for guests, $180 to $250 for non-guests, depending on the season.

Golfpac (☎ 888-848-8941 or 407-260-2288; www.golfpacinc.com) is an organization that packages golf vacations with accommodations and other features and prearranges tee times at more than 40 Orlando-area courses. The earlier you call (months, if possible), the better your options. **Tee Times USA** (☎ 888-465-3356; www.teetimesusa.com) and **Florida Golfing** (☎ 866-833-2663; www.floridagolfing.com) are two other companies that couple course and package information with a reservations service.

Horseback Riding

Disney's Fort Wilderness Resort and Campground offers 45-minute scenic guided-tour trail rides six times a day. The cost is $32 per person. Children must be at least 9 years old, and the maximum weight limit is 250 pounds. For information and reservations up to 30 days in advance, call ☎ 407-824-2832.

The **Villas of Grand Cypress** opens its equestrian center to outsiders. You can go on a 45-minute, walk-trot trail ride (four times daily) for $45. A 30-minute private lesson is $55; a one-hour lesson is $100. Call ☎ 800-835-7377 or 407-239-1938 or surf the Internet to http://grand cypress.com.

Jogging

Many Disney resorts have scenic jogging trails. For example, the **Yacht** and **Beach Club** resorts share a 2-mile trail; the **Caribbean Beach Resort**'s 1.4-mile promenade circles a lake; **Port Orleans** has a 1.7-mile riverfront trail; and **Fort Wilderness**'s tree-shaded 2.3-mile jogging path has exercise stations about every quarter-mile. Pick up a jogging trail map at any Disney property's *Guest Relations* desk.

Surfing

The creative minds at Disney have added a way for you to find out how to catch a wave and "hang ten" at the **Typhoon Lagoon** water park. (See Chapter 16 for the park listing.) Tuesdays, Wednesdays, and Fridays, instructors from **Carroll's Cocoa Beach Surfing School** (☎ 407-939-7529) show up for an early-bird session in the namesake lagoon, which has a wave machine capable of 8 footers. The two and one-half hour session is held before the park opens to the general public. It's limited to 14 people. Minimum age is 8. The $135 cost doesn't include park admission, which you must pay if you want to hang around after the lesson.

If you're staying at WDW and don't have a rental car, note that you can't use the Disney Transportation System to get to the park for the 7:30 a.m. start time of the lessons; the buses don't operate that early.

Ron Jon Surf Park, the worlds first surf park, is scheduled to open in 2006 at Festival Bay (located at the northern-most end of International Drive) where beginners can learn to surf, or the pros can simply ride the waves, and its all indoors. Surf over to www.ronjons.com for the most up to date information.

Swimming

Orlando is home to an amazing number and variety of swimming pools. Whiling away the heat of the afternoon at a pool is a great way to recharge your batteries and cool off after a morning of pounding the pavement at the parks. Keep in mind, however, that you won't be the only one to think that an afternoon retreat is a good idea — there are times the pools can seem as crowded as the parks.

Tennis

Twenty-six lighted tennis courts are scattered throughout the Disney properties (including ten at **Disney's Wide World of Sports**). Most are free and available to resort guests on a first-come, first-served basis. Call ☎ 407-939-7529 to make reservations (they generally cost $8 per hour) or for more information. The **Racquet Club** at the Contemporary Resort has six clay courts (reservations required; $8 an hour), all lighted for evening play, and offers lessons.

Water-skiing and Wakeboarding

You can arrange water-skiing trips (including boats, drivers, equipment, and instruction) Tuesday through Saturday at **Walt Disney World** by calling ☎ 407-824-2621 or 407-939-7529. Make reservations up to 14 days in advance. The cost for skiing is $140 per hour for up to five people. Wakeboarding is $140 per hour for up to four people. You also can wakeboard and ski at the **Sammy Duvall Watersports Centre** at Disney's Contemporary Resort (☎ 407-939-0754; www.sammyduvall. com); it costs $140 for 60 minutes and $100 for every additional hour. Parasailing is available as well; for a single rider the cost is $90, tandem costs $140.

You can snorkel at **Typhoon Lagoon** (see Chapter 16). Scuba-diving is available at Epcot's **Dive Quest** at the Living Seas pavilion (see Chapter 13). Outside Disney, you can get some time behind a boat or at the end of an overhead cable at the **Orlando Watersports Complex,** which has lights for nighttime thrill-seekers. The complex is located close to Orlando International Airport at 8615 Florida Rock Rd. Prices for wakeboarding or water-skiing, including lessons, runs $45 a half-hour, $180 for all you can ride. If you want to ride on the cable, it will cost $21 for an hour and $39 for all day. Basic equipment is included in the rental price, but if you prefer the more advanced stuff, you can rent it separately at the pro shop. For information, call ☎ 407-251-3100 or go to www.orlandowatersports.com. Ask about special rates for later evening hours and for kids.

Quick Concierge

● ●

Fast Facts

AAA

American Automobile Association members can get general information, maps, and optimum driving directions by calling ☎ 800-222-1134 or on the Internet at www.aaa.com.

Area Code

The main area code for Orlando is **407,** although calls to the **321** area code are often considered local as well. *Note:* When calling within Orlando, you must always dial the full 10-digit phone number (including the area code), even if you're trying to get the store right across the street.

ATMs

Machines honoring the Cirrus (☎ 800-424-7787; www.mastercard.com), PLUS (☎ 800-843-7587; www.visa.com), and STAR (www.star.com) ATM networks are common in all Orlando's theme parks. (See Chapters 11–15 and 18–20 for locations.) They're also found in most banks, and at some shopping centers and convenience stores (see Chapter 4 for more details on using an ATM in Orlando).

Baby sitters

Many Orlando hotels, including all Disney's resorts, offer baby-sitting services, usually from an outside service such as Kids Nite Out (☎ 407-828-0920 or 800-696-8105; www.kidsniteout.com), or All About Kids (☎ 407-812-9300 or 800-728-6506; www.all-about-kids.com). Childcare

rates usually run somewhere between $10 and $15 per hour for the first child and $1 to $3 per additional child, per hour, with an additional transportation fee of $7 to $9. Several of Walt Disney World's expensive resorts also have childcare centers that cater to kids ages 4 to 12. If you'd like to take advantage of the kids' programs and enjoy a few hours off, advance reservations are a must; call ☎ 407-939-3463. All three Universal Orlando resorts offer similar services.

Business Hours

Theme-park operating hours vary depending on the time of year, and even on the day of the week. While most open at 8 or 9 a.m. and close at 6 or 7 p.m., you should call or check a park's Web site for its most current schedule before arriving. Other businesses are generally open from 9 a.m. to 5 p.m., Monday through Friday. Bars are usually open until 2 a.m., with some after-hours clubs staying open into the wee hours of the morning (though the alcohol stops flowing at 2 a.m.).

Camera Repair

All Disney's theme parks have a photo shop where you can get minor camera repairs or pick up an extra battery (check for locations in the park guide maps you get upon entering). For more serious repair work, try Southern Photo Technical Service, 606 Virginia Dr. (☎ 407-896-0322; www.spts-orlando.com).

Convention Center

Orlando's Orange County Convention Center (☎ 407-345-9800; www.occc.net) is located at 9800 International Drive.

Credit Cards

Call the following emergency numbers if you lose your card or your wallet is stolen: American Express (☎ 800-221-7282), MasterCard (☎ 800-307-7309 or 636-722-7111), Visa (☎ 800-847-2911 or 410-581-9994). For other credit cards, call the toll-free number directory at ☎ 800-555-1212.

Doctors & Dentists

For minor problems that occur during a theme-park visit (blisters, allergic reactions), visit the park's First Aid Center; these are noted on the park maps you pick up when you enter. Disney offers in-room medical service 24 hours a day by calling ☎ 407-238-2000. Doctors on Call Service (☎ 407-399-3627), makes house and room calls in most of the Orlando area. Centra-Care has several walk-in clinics listed in the Yellow Pages, including ones on Vineland Road near Universal Orlando (☎ 407-351-6682), at Lake Buena Vista near Disney (☎ 407-934-2273), and in Kissimmee near Disney (☎ 407-397-7032). After Hours Pediatrics (☎ 407-827-7113), located in Lake Buena Vista, offers urgent care for children and young adults (up to age 21). There's also a 24-hour, toll-free number for the Poison Control Center (☎ 800-282-3171). To find a dentist, call Dental Referral Service (☎ 800-235-4111; www.dentalreferral.com). Folks there can tell you the nearest dentist who meets your needs. Phones are staffed weekdays from 10 a.m. to 7 p.m. Check the Yellow Pages for 24-hour emergency services.

Emergencies

All Florida uses ☎ 911 as the emergency number for police, fire departments, ambulances, and other critical needs. If you have a cellular phone and need urgent help, dial ☎ *FHP for the Florida Highway Patrol.

For less urgent requests, call ☎ 800-647-9284, a hot line sponsored by the Florida Tourism Industry Marketing Corporation, the state tourism promotion board. With operators speaking more than 100 languages, this service can provide general directions and help with lost travel papers and credit cards, medical emergencies, accidents, money transfers, airline confirmation, and much more.

Hospitals

Sand Lake Hospital, 9400 Turkey Lake Rd. (☎ 407-351-8550), is about 2 miles south of Sand Lake Road. From the WDW area, take I-4 to the Sand Lake Road exit, turn left off the exit ramp onto Sand Lake Road, and make a left on Turkey Lake Road. The hospital is 2 miles on your right. The Florida Hospital, 400 Celebration Place (☎ 407-764-4000), is located near the tourist area of Kissimmee just off of U.S. 192 not far from Disney. Take U.S 192 East and turn right onto Celebration Place, the hospital is about a half-mile up on your left.

Information

To get local telephone information, call ☎ 411.

For local tourism information, see the "Where to Get More Information" section at the end of the Appendix.

Internet Access and Cyber Cafes

Orlando doesn't have too many Cyber cafes (you're supposed to be having fun in the theme parks!), and the ones it does have are generally far from the tourist zones. At Walt Disney World, there is an Internet cafe inside DisneyQuest (see Chapter 16), and you can also send e-mail at *Innoventions* in Epcot (see Chapter 13), though you have to pay the park admission fees to use the Web terminals. Payphones with touch-screen displays offering Internet access have been installed at locations throughout WDW; you can access your e-mail for 25¢ a minute with a 4-minute minimum.

If you're traveling with your laptop, most Orlando hotels offer in-room dataports (ask about access fees when booking your room) with an increasing number offering Wi-Fi in public areas (again, be sure to ask about access fees). Check with your hotel for the most up-to-date information as to what type of service they currently offer and what they charge to use it. Disney offers high-speed and Wi-Fi access to guests at several of its resorts, and all Universal Orlando's resorts offer high-speed Internet access.

Liquor Laws

Florida's liquor laws are pretty straightforward. You must be 21 to buy or consume alcohol. Alcohol is sold in supermarkets and liquor stores daily from 9 a.m. to 2 a.m. It's served at bars and restaurants from 11 a.m. to 2 a.m. Some places that serve liquor allow you to enter if you're younger than 21, but most won't let you sit at the bar.

Note: No liquor is served in Magic Kingdom at Walt Disney World. Alcoholic drinks are available, however, at the other Disney parks and are quite evident at Universal Orlando's parks (even more so at its seasonal celebrations).

Maps

AAA (see "AAA," earlier in this appendix) and other auto clubs generally provide good maps (to members), as do many Orlando rental-car agencies. The Orlando/Orange County Convention and Visitors Bureau, FLAUSA (Florida's official tourist bureau), and the Kissimmee/St. Cloud Visitors Bureau all offer an array of area maps (which can be sent via U.S. mail upon request or picked up locally).

Pharmacies

There are 24-hour Walgreen's at 7650 W. Sand Lake Rd. (☎ 407-345-9497) and 5935 W. Irlo Bronson Memorial Hwy./US192 (☎ 407-396-2002). Many other locations near tourist areas can be found by logging on to www.walgreens.com.

Post Office

The post office most convenient to Disney and Universal is at 10450 Turkey Lake Rd. (☎ 800-275-8777). It's open Monday through Friday from 9 a.m. to 5 p.m., Saturday from 9 a.m. to noon. Additionally, there is a post office located at 12133 Apopka Vineland (☎ 800-275-8777) close to Downtown Disney.

Restrooms

You won't find any public restrooms on the streets in Orlando, but you can usually find one in a bar, restaurant, hotel, museum, department store, convenience store, attraction, fast-food eatery, or service station — and it'll probably be clean. (You may have to purchase something to gain entrance, as many of these places reserve their restrooms for patrons only.) All the major theme parks have an abundance of clean restrooms, many of which also have baby-changing facilities (all are clearly marked on the guide maps you get upon entering the park).

Safety

Don't let the aura of Mickey Mouse allow you to lower your guard. Orlando has a crime rate that's comparable to other major U.S. cities. Stay alert and remain aware of your immediate surroundings.

Keeping your valuables in a safe-deposit box (inquire at your hotel's front desk) is a good idea, although, nowadays, many hotels are equipped with in-room safes. Keep a close eye on your valuables when you're in a public place, such as a restaurant, theater, or airport terminal. Renting a locker is always preferable to leaving your valuables in the trunk of your car, even in the theme-park lots. Be cautious and avoid carrying large amounts of cash, especially if you're carrying a backpack or fanny pack, which thieves can easily access while you're standing in line for a ride or show. If you're renting a car, carefully read the safety instructions that the rental company provides. Never stop in a dark or unpopulated area. Remember that children should never ride in the front seat of a car equipped with air bags and those age 3 and younger must be in a child safety seat while those ages 4 and 5 must either be in a safety seat, booster seat, or a seatbelt.

Smoking

Restaurant space and hotel rooms for smokers are evaporating in Orlando. Disney doesn't sell tobacco, and there are precious few "you can smoke here" areas. And don't expect to light up over dinner. Florida bans smoking in public workplaces, including restaurants and bars that serve food. Stand-alone bars that serve virtually no food and designated smoking rooms in hotels are exempt.

Taxes

Expect to add 11 or 12 percent to room rates and 6.5 to 7 percent (the rate depends on the county you happen to be in) on most everything else — except groceries and health supplies or medical services.

Taxis

Yellow Cab (☎ 407-699-9999) and Ace Metro (☎ 407-855-0564) are among the cab companies serving the area. Rates run as high as $3.25 for the first mile, $1.75 per mile thereafter.

Time Zone

Orlando is on eastern standard time from late fall until midspring, and on eastern daylight time (one hour later) the rest of the year. That means that when both of Mickey's gloved hands are on 12 noon in Orlando, it's 7 a.m. in Honolulu, 8 a.m. in Anchorage, 9 a.m. in Vancouver and Los Angeles, 11 a.m. in Winnipeg and New Orleans, and 5 p.m. in London.

Transit Info

Lynx (☎ 407-841-5969; www.golynx.com) bus stops are marked with a paw print. The buses serve Disney, Universal, and International Drive ($1.25 for adults, 75¢ for kids 8–18 with valid school ID, and seniors), but they're not particularly tourist-friendly. The International Drive area has the I-Ride Trolleys (☎ 407-248-9590; www.iride trolley.com). The Main Line and Green Line stops include most of I-Drive from SeaWorld on the south end and Belz Factory Outlet World on the north. Trolleys run about every 20 minutes with 85 stops along the Main Line and about every 30 minutes with 22 stops along the Green Line. It runs from 8 a.m. to 10:30 p.m. (75¢ for adults, 25¢ for seniors, and kids younger than12 are free with a paying adult; one-day and multi-day passes are also available; exact change is required) and is a good way to avoid I-Drive's dreadfully heavy traffic.

Weather

Call ☎ 321-255-0212 to get forecasts from the National Weather Service. When the phone picks up, punch in 412 from a touch-tone phone, and you'll get the Orlando forecast. Also check with The Weather Channel if you have cable television or go to the Web site, www.weather.com.

Toll-Free Numbers and Web Sites

Airlines

Air Canada
☎ 888-247-2262
www.aircanada.ca

Airtran Airlines
☎ 800-247-8726
www.airtran.com

Alaska Airlines
☎ 800-426-0333
www.alaskaair.com

American Airlines
☎ 800-433-7300
www.aa.com

American Trans Air
☎ 800-225-2995
www.ata.com

America West Airlines
☎ 800-235-9292
www.americawest.com

Continental Airlines
☎ 800-525-0280
www.continental.com

Delta Air Lines
☎ 800-221-1212
www.delta.com

Hawaiian Airlines
☎ 800-367-5320
www.hawaiianair.com

Jet Blue Airlines
☎ 800-538-2583
www.jetblue.com

Northwest Airlines
☎ 800-225-2525
www.nwa.com

Song Airlines
☎ 800-359-7665
www.flysong.com

Southwest Airlines
☎ 800-435-9792
www.iflyswa.com

Spirit Airlines
☎ 800-772-7117
www.spiritair.com

Ted Airlines
☎ 800-225-5833
www.flyted.com

United Airlines
☎ 800-241-6522
www.ual.com

US Airways
☎ 800-428-4322
www.usairways.com

Major car-rental agencies

Alamo
☎ 800-327-9633
www.goalamo.com

Avis
☎ 800-331-1212 in the continental United States
☎ 800-879-3847 in Canada
www.avis.com

Budget
☎ 800-527-0700
www.budgetrentacar.com

Dollar
☎ 800-800-4000
www.dollar.com

Enterprise
☎ 800-325-8007
www.enterprise.com

Hertz
☎ 800-654-3131
www.hertz.com

National
☎ 800-227-7368
www.nationalcar.com

Payless
☎ 800-729-5377
www.paylesscar.com

Thrifty
☎ 800-367-2277
www.thrifty.com

Major hotel and motel chains

AmeriSuites
☎ 800-833-1516
www.amerisuites.com

Baymont Inns & Suites
☎ 800-301-0200
www.baymontinns.com

Best Western International
☎ 800-528-1234
www.bestwestern.com

Clarion Hotels
☎ 800-252-7466
www.choicehotels.com

Comfort Inns
☎ 800-228-5150
www.choicehotels.com

Courtyard by Marriott
☎ 800-321-2211
www.courtyard.com

Days Inn
☎ 800-325-2525
www.daysinn.com

Doubletree Hotels
☎ 800-222-8733
www.doubletreehotels.com

Econo Lodges
☎ 800-553-2666
www.choicehotels.com

Fairfield Inn by Marriott
☎ 800-228-2800
www.fairfieldinn.com

Hampton Inn
☎ 800-426-7866
www.hampton-inn.com

Hilton Hotels
☎ 800-774-1500
www.hilton.com

Holiday Inn
☎ 800-465-4329
www.sixcontinentshotels.com

Howard Johnson
☎ 800-654-2000
www.hojo.com

Hyatt Hotels & Resorts
☎ 800-228-9000
www.hyatt.com

ITT Sheraton
☎ 800-325-3535
www.starwood.com/sheraton

Knights Inn
☎ 800-843-5644
www.knightsinn.com

La Quinta Motor Inns
☎ 800-531-5900
www.laquinta.com

Loews Hotels
☎ 800-235-6397
www.loewshotels.com

Marriott Hotels
☎ 800-228-9290
www.marriott.com

Motel 6
☎ 800-466-8536
www.motel6.com

Quality Inns
☎ 800-228-5151
www.choicehotels.com

Radisson Hotels International
☎ 800-333-3333
www.radisson.com

Ramada Inns
☎ 800-272-6232
www.ramada.com

Red Carpet Inns
☎ 800-251-1962
www.reservahost.com

Red Roof Inns
☎ 800-843-7663
www.redroof.com

Renaissance
☎ 800-228-9290
www.renaissancehotels.com

Residence Inn by Marriott
☎ 800-331-3131
www.residenceinn.com

Rodeway Inns
☎ 800-228-2000
www.choicehotels.com

Sheraton Hotels & Resorts
☎ 800-325-3535
www.sheraton.com

Sleep Inn
☎ 800-753-3746
www.choicehotels.com

Super 8 Motels
☎ 800-800-8000
www.super8.com

Travelodge
☎ 800-255-3050
www.travelodge.com

Westin Hotels & Resorts
☎ 800-937-8461
www.westin.com

Wyndham Hotels and Resorts
☎ 800-822-4200
www.wyndham.com

Where to Get More Information

If you want additional information on attractions, accommodations, or just about anything else that's in Orlando, the city has some excellent sources for tourist information, discounts, maps, and more.

Orlando tourist information offices

The **Orlando/Orange County Convention and Visitors Bureau** can answer your questions regarding area attractions, dining, and accommodations, as well as send you maps and brochures. You should receive the packet in about three weeks, and it includes the *Magicard,* which is good for hundreds of dollars in discounts on accommodations, car rentals, attractions, and more. The Official Visitors Center is located at 8723 International Drive, Suite 101, Orlando, FL 32819. For information, call ☎ **407-363-5872** (voice — you can talk to a real person!), 800-643-9492, or 800-551-0181 (automated). Or log on to the Internet to www.orlandoinfo.com.

Get your info straight from the Mouse's mouth. Contact **Walt Disney World,** Box 10000, Lake Buena Vista, FL 32830-1000 (☎ **407-934-7639;** www.disneyworld.com), to order vacation brochures and get information on all the theme parks, attractions, dining, accommodations, and more.

For information on **Universal Studios Florida** (see Chapter 18), **Islands of Adventure** (see Chapter 19), and **CityWalk** (see Chapter 25), contact

Universal Orlando, 1000 Universal Studios Plaza, Orlando, FL 32819 (☎ **407-363-8000;** www.universalorlando.com). They will also send you vacation brochures, including information on restaurants and accommodations.

SeaWorld offers vacation brochures with information on the park, its restaurants, its hotel partners, and on **Discovery Cove,** where you can swim with dolphins. Write to 7007 SeaWorld Dr., Orlando, FL 32801, or call ☎ **407-351-3600.** Online, surf over to www.seaworld.com. For information on **Discovery Cove,** call ☎ **877-434-7268** or head to www.discoverycove.com.

Get in touch with the **Kissimmee–St. Cloud Convention and Visitors Bureau,** 1925 E. Irlo Bronson Hwy./U.S. 192, Kissimmee, FL 34744 (☎ **800-327-9159** or 407-847-5000; www.floridakiss.com), for maps, brochures, coupon books, and a guide to local accommodations and attractions.

Newspapers and magazines

Check out the Sunday travel section in your hometown paper for the latest bargains, ideas, and tips. After you land in O-Town, pick up a copy of the *Orlando Sentinel* (www.orlandosentinel.com) to find out about current events and deals. **Go2Orlando,** www.go2orlando.com, is the *Sentinel's* online section dedicated to visitors. The paper's **Calendar** and **CityBeat** sections are gold mines for current information on the area's accommodations, restaurants, nightclubs, and attractions, as is the *Orlando Weekly* (www.orlandoweekly.com).

Other sources of information

✔ **Deb's Unofficial Walt Disney World Information Guide (The All Ears Net)** (http://wdwig.com, www.allearsnet.com) is an excellent information source and arguably the best unofficial Disney guide on the Internet. Though Disney doesn't own it, it's run and written by true-blue fans of Mickey, so while it's not entirely objective (and you should take that into consideration when looking at the tips it offers) the information is extremely detailed and up to date. There are also sections aimed at travelers with special needs that include good tips for touring the Disney parks if you're physically challenged, elderly, or with kids in tow.

✔ Visit **www.icflorida.com** for information about dining, clubs, performances, theme parks, sports, and special events.

✔ *Frommer's Walt Disney World & Orlando with Kids* (Wiley Publishing, Inc.) has lots of tips and advice for those traveling with children ages 2 to 16, while *Frommer's Irreverent Walt Disney World* (Wiley Publishing, Inc.) is a fun-filled guide aimed at singles and couples.

Index

• *Y* •

• *Z* •

Accommodations Index

Restaurant Index

SINESS, CAREERS & PERSONAL FINANCE

Also available:
- Accounting For Dummies †
  0-7645-5314-3
- Business Plans Kit For Dummies †
  0-7645-5365-8
- Cover Letters For Dummies
  0-7645-5224-4
- Frugal Living For Dummies
  0-7645-5403-4
- Leadership For Dummies
  0-7645-5176-0
- Managing For Dummies
  0-7645-1771-6

- Marketing For Dummies
  0-7645-5600-2
- Personal Finance For Dummies *
  0-7645-2590-5
- Project Management For Dummies
  0-7645-5283-X
- Resumes For Dummies †
  0-7645-5471-9
- Selling For Dummies
  0-7645-5363-1
- Small Business Kit For Dummies *†
  0-7645-5093-4

-7645-5307-0   0-7645-5331-3 *†

ME & BUSINESS COMPUTER BASICS

Also available:
- ACT! 6 For Dummies
  0-7645-2645-6
- iLife '04 All-in-One Desk Reference For Dummies
  0-7645-7347-0
- iPAQ For Dummies
  0-7645-6769-1
- Mac OS X Panther Timesaving Techniques For Dummies
  0-7645-5812-9
- Macs For Dummies
  0-7645-5656-8
- Microsoft Money 2004 For Dummies
  0-7645-4195-1

- Office 2003 All-in-One Desk Reference For Dummies
  0-7645-3883-7
- Outlook 2003 For Dummies
  0-7645-3759-8
- PCs For Dummies
  0-7645-4074-2
- TiVo For Dummies
  0-7645-6923-6
- Upgrading and Fixing PCs For Dummies
  0-7645-1665-5
- Windows XP Timesaving Techniques For Dummies
  0-7645-3748-2

-7645-4074-2   0-7645-3758-X

OD, HOME, GARDEN, HOBBIES, MUSIC & PETS

Also available:
- Bass Guitar For Dummies
  0-7645-2487-9
- Diabetes Cookbook For Dummies
  0-7645-5230-9
- Gardening For Dummies *
  0-7645-5130-2
- Guitar For Dummies
  0-7645-5106-X
- Holiday Decorating For Dummies
  0-7645-2570-0
- Home Improvement All-in-One For Dummies
  0-7645-5680-0

- Knitting For Dummies
  0-7645-5395-X
- Piano For Dummies
  0-7645-5105-1
- Puppies For Dummies
  0-7645-5255-4
- Scrapbooking For Dummies
  0-7645-7208-3
- Senior Dogs For Dummies
  0-7645-5818-8
- Singing For Dummies
  0-7645-2475-5
- 30-Minute Meals For Dummies
  0-7645-2589-1

-7645-5295-3   0-7645-5232-5

TERNET & DIGITAL MEDIA

Also available:
- 2005 Online Shopping Directory For Dummies
  0-7645-7495-7
- CD & DVD Recording For Dummies
  0-7645-5956-7
- eBay For Dummies
  0-7645-5654-1
- Fighting Spam For Dummies
  0-7645-5965-6
- Genealogy Online For Dummies
  0-7645-5964-8
- Google For Dummies
  0-7645-4420-9

- Home Recording For Musicians For Dummies
  0-7645-1634-5
- The Internet For Dummies
  0-7645-4173-0
- iPod & iTunes For Dummies
  0-7645-7772-7
- Preventing Identity Theft For Dummies
  0-7645-7336-5
- Pro Tools All-in-One Desk Reference For Dummies
  0-7645-5714-9
- Roxio Easy Media Creator For Dummies
  0-7645-7131-1

-7645-1664-7   0-7645-6924-4

*parate Canadian edition also available
*parate U.K. edition also available

lable wherever books are sold. For more information or to order direct: U.S. customers
: www.dummies.com or call 1-877-762-2974.
customers visit www.wileyeurope.com or call 0800 243407. Canadian customers visit
w.wiley.ca or call 1-800-567-4797.

SPORTS, FITNESS, PARENTING, RELIGION & SPIRITUALITY

0-7645-5146-9   0-7645-5418-2

Also available:
- Adoption For Dummies
  0-7645-5488-3
- Basketball For Dummies
  0-7645-5248-1
- The Bible For Dummies
  0-7645-5296-1
- Buddhism For Dummies
  0-7645-5359-3
- Catholicism For Dummies
  0-7645-5391-7
- Hockey For Dummies
  0-7645-5228-7

- Judaism For Dummies
  0-7645-5299-6
- Martial Arts For Dummies
  0-7645-5358-5
- Pilates For Dummies
  0-7645-5397-6
- Religion For Dummies
  0-7645-5264-3
- Teaching Kids to Read
  For Dummies
  0-7645-4043-2
- Weight Training For Dummies
  0-7645-5168-X
- Yoga For Dummies
  0-7645-5117-5

TRAVEL

0-7645-5438-7   0-7645-5453-0

Also available:
- Alaska For Dummies
  0-7645-1761-9
- Arizona For Dummies
  0-7645-6938-4
- Cancún and the Yucatán
  For Dummies
  0-7645-2437-2
- Cruise Vacations For Dummies
  0-7645-6941-4
- Europe For Dummies
  0-7645-5456-5
- Ireland For Dummies
  0-7645-5455-7

- Las Vegas For Dummies
  0-7645-5448-4
- London For Dummies
  0-7645-4277-X
- New York City For Dummies
  0-7645-6945-7
- Paris For Dummies
  0-7645-5494-8
- RV Vacations For Dummies
  0-7645-5443-3
- Walt Disney World & Orlando
  For Dummies
  0-7645-6943-0

GRAPHICS, DESIGN & WEB DEVELOPMENT

0-7645-4345-8   0-7645-5589-8

Also available:
- Adobe Acrobat 6 PDF
  For Dummies
  0-7645-3760-1
- Building a Web Site For Dummies
  0-7645-7144-3
- Dreamweaver MX 2004
  For Dummies
  0-7645-4342-3
- FrontPage 2003 For Dummies
  0-7645-3882-9
- HTML 4 For Dummies
  0-7645-1995-6
- Illustrator cs For Dummies
  0-7645-4084-X

- Macromedia Flash MX 2004
  For Dummies
  0-7645-4358-X
- Photoshop 7 All-in-One Desk
  Reference For Dummies
  0-7645-1667-1
- Photoshop cs Timesaving
  Techniques For Dummies
  0-7645-6782-9
- PHP 5 For Dummies
  0-7645-4166-8
- PowerPoint 2003 For Dummies
  0-7645-3908-6
- QuarkXPress 6 For Dummies
  0-7645-2593-X

NETWORKING, SECURITY, PROGRAMMING & DATABASES

0-7645-6852-3   0-7645-5784-X

Also available:
- A+ Certification For Dummies
  0-7645-4187-0
- Access 2003 All-in-One Desk
  Reference For Dummies
  0-7645-3988-4
- Beginning Programming
  For Dummies
  0-7645-4997-9
- C For Dummies
  0-7645-7068-4
- Firewalls For Dummies
  0-7645-4048-3
- Home Networking For Dummies
  0-7645-42796

- Network Security For Dummie
  0-7645-1679-5
- Networking For Dummies
  0-7645-1677-9
- TCP/IP For Dummies
  0-7645-1760-0
- VBA For Dummies
  0-7645-3989-2
- Wireless All In-One Desk Refer
  For Dummies
  0-7645-7496-5
- Wireless Home Networking
  For Dummies
  0-7645-3910-8

645-6820-5 *†   0-7645-2566-2

Also available:

- Alzheimer's For Dummies
  0-7645-3899-3
- Asthma For Dummies
  0-7645-4233-8
- Controlling Cholesterol For Dummies
  0-7645-5440-9
- Depression For Dummies
  0-7645-3900-0
- Dieting For Dummies
  0-7645-4149-8
- Fertility For Dummies
  0-7645-2549-2

- Fibromyalgia For Dummies
  0-7645-5441-7
- Improving Your Memory For Dummies
  0-7645-5435-2
- Pregnancy For Dummies †
  0-7645-4483-7
- Quitting Smoking For Dummies
  0-7645-2629-4
- Relationships For Dummies
  0-7645-5384-4
- Thyroid For Dummies
  0-7645-5385-2

UCATION, HISTORY, REFERENCE & TEST PREPARATION

7645-5194-9   0-7645-4186-2

Also available:

- Algebra For Dummies
  0-7645-5325-9
- British History For Dummies
  0-7645-7021-8
- Calculus For Dummies
  0-7645-2498-4
- English Grammar For Dummies
  0-7645-5322-4
- Forensics For Dummies
  0-7645-5580-4
- The GMAT For Dummies
  0-7645-5251-1
- Inglés Para Dummies
  0-7645-5427-1

- Italian For Dummies
  0-7645-5196-5
- Latin For Dummies
  0-7645-5431-X
- Lewis & Clark For Dummies
  0-7645-2545-X
- Research Papers For Dummies
  0-7645-5426-3
- The SAT I For Dummies
  0-7645-7193-1
- Science Fair Projects For Dummies
  0-7645-5460-3
- U.S. History For Dummies
  0-7645-5249-X

Get smart @ dummies.com®

- **Find a full list of Dummies titles**
- **Look into loads of FREE on-site articles**
- **Sign up for FREE eTips e-mailed to you weekly**
- **See what other products carry the Dummies name**
- **Shop directly from the Dummies bookstore**
- **Enter to win new prizes every month!**

parate Canadian edition also available
parate U.K. edition also available

able wherever books are sold. For more information or to order direct: U.S. customers
www.dummies.com or call 1-877-762-2974.
ustomers visit www.wileyeurope.com or call 0800 243407. Canadian customers visit
.wiley.ca or call 1-800-567-4797.